9

Steve Pemberton &
Reece Shearsmith

Inside No.9

The Scripts

Series 1–3

HODDERstudio

First published in Great Britain in 2020 by Hodder Studio
An Hachette UK company

3

See page 409 for permissions acknowledgements.

A CIP catalogue record for this title is available from the British Library

Trade Paperback ISBN 9781529349344

Designed and typeset by EM&EN
Printed and bound in Great Britain by Clays Ltd, Elcograf S.p.A.

Hodder & Stoughton policy is to use papers that are natural, renewable and recyclable products and made from wood grown in sustainable forests. The logging and manufacturing processes are expected to conform to the environmental regulations of the country of origin.

Hodder & Stoughton Ltd
Carmelite House
50 Victoria Embankment
London EC4Y 0DZ

www.hodder-studio.com

Contents

SERIES 2

SERIES 3

SERIES
1

Foreword

— Why didn't you just do the lie about the babysitter getting ill?
— Because that needs to be seeded. You need to seed it.

'Sardines'

It was 7 September 2011 and we were sitting in the office of Janice Hadlow, then controller of BBC Two. The meeting, set up by our long-term executive producer Jon Plowman, had been scheduled to consider the fate of our previous show, but with disappointing viewing figures we guessed that the writing was on the wall for *Psychoville* (scrawled in big letters using human excrement).

We hastily discussed what new idea we could pitch in the meeting. Having written a self-contained episode for the first series of *Psychoville*, we idly wondered whether the time was right to resurrect the unfashionable single-play anthology series. *Tales of the Unexpected* and *Play for Today* were mentioned as well as genre shows such as *Thriller* and *Hammer House of Horror*. Using a small cast in a single location, we wanted to tell stories that offered a beginning, middle and end in one sitting, as opposed to the sprawling narrative arcs of the prevailing box-set culture.

We wrote the first pair of episodes early the following year, basing one on a play we had written several years earlier ('Tom & Gerri') and another on the classic family-celebration goes wrong scenario ('Nana's Party'). At this stage there was no overriding theme or connectivity between the episodes, and the series was tentatively titled *Happy Endings*. Luckily everyone at the BBC enjoyed the scripts and they offered to commission two series, one as an anthology and the other as a sitcom based on the 'Nana's Party' characters. We demurred, preferring to focus on the single-play idea, and in the summer of 2012 *Happy Endings* was commissioned.

The first series was written in fits and starts between other filming commitments. 'Silent Assassins' (later to become 'A Quiet

Night In') was written entirely without dialogue; 'Last Gasp' and 'The Harrowing' were largely written separately then rewritten together when time allowed. An idea was introduced to link the episodes by using a common door number: No. 5. Worried that Coco Chanel already had first dibs on that digit, we switched this to the more alliterative No. 9. At the request of the BBC, the 'Inside' was added to help people understand the concept – an idea we resisted, as 'Inside No. 9' sounded like a political docu-series about the chief whip's office. We offered up 'Death's Door' or 'Play Dead', 'No. 9 Nightmare' or 'A Can of Worms' but to no avail.

The scripts were written in an office we had rented from a friend in Muswell Hill. A large wardrobe loomed behind us as we worked, and we wondered whether it might be fun to pack it with a family playing the children's party game Sardines. We made a list of potential characters and started to write, adding a new person every two or three pages. The story ended with the wardrobe full and the realisation that nobody else was looking for them. It was a funny conceit and we were pleased with the idea, but Jon Plowman felt that there was something lacking: a dark heart. The subsequent rewrite, subtly hinting at a devastating secret and ending with a chilling revelation, was possibly the moment when *Inside No. 9* really cemented itself in our minds as a thing rather than a disparate collection of individual plays.

One note: the versions included here are the shooting scripts, the final drafts issued to the cast and crew prior to the first day's filming. There will be bits of extra material that were filmed and subsequently cut in the editing stage as we struggled to make the episodes fit into the 29-minute slot. We hope you enjoy reading them as much as we enjoyed writing them.

Episode 1

SARDINES

CAST LIST

REBECCA – Katherine Parkinson

IAN – Tim Key

LEE – Luke Pasqualino

CARL – Steve Pemberton

STU – Reece Shearsmith

RACHEL – Ophelia Lovibond

GERALDINE – Anne Reid

MARK – Julian Rhind-Tutt

ELIZABETH – Anna Chancellor

JOHN – Marc Wootton

JEREMY – Ben Willbond

ANDREW – Timothy West

EXT. COUNTRY HOUSE. DAY.

A large old house set in rolling English countryside. A number of cars are parked outside. We pull back and see the large wrought-iron gates, which show the number '9'.

TITLE: *'Sardines'.*

INT. BEDROOM. DAY.

A double bedroom in a large house in the country. It is a guest bedroom so devoid of any personal belongings, rather like a hotel room. REBECCA, *a smartly dressed woman in her mid-thirties, runs into the room. She looks around thoughtfully before heading into the en-suite bathroom.*

INT. EN-SUITE. DAY.

REBECCA *draws back the shower curtain but there is nobody there. She stops at the sink, picks up the big block of carbolic soap and smells it. She smiles to herself wistfully.*

INT. BEDROOM. DAY.

REBECCA *re-enters the bedroom and looks under the bed: nothing there apart from a couple of old suitcases.* REBECCA *gets up and looks at the large old wooden wardrobe. She sees herself in the mirrored door, then reaches for the handle and pulls the door open . . .* IAN *is standing in the middle of the wardrobe. He is a socially awkward bespectacled IT consultant in a shirt and tie.*

IAN Oh, hello.

REBECCA Hello!

IAN That was quick.

REBECCA Well, obviously I know the house, so . . .

IAN You have an . . .

IAN/REBECCA . . . unfair advantage.

REBECCA Yes!

REBECCA *gets into the wardrobe with* IAN *and closes the door.*

INT. WARDROBE. DAY.

The wardrobe is fairly empty, save for a couple of boxes of Christmas decorations and some outdoor coats hung up at one end. REBECCA *stands next to* IAN.

IAN We weren't properly introduced – I'm Ian by the way.

REBECCA Hello.

They shake hands.

IAN It's Rachel, isn't it?

REBECCA Rebecca.

IAN That's right. I work with Jeremy.

REBECCA Oh!

IAN Well, I say 'work with', I'm more on the IT side but with Jeremy being the office manager we obviously have overlaps. He's responsible for infrastructure whereas I take more of a lead in programme development . . .

REBECCA Right, right. What did you say your name was again?

IAN Ian.

REBECCA That's right, yes. Jeremy has mentioned you.

INT. BEDROOM. DAY.

LEE, *a good-looking lad in a trendy T-shirt and jeans, enters the room and looks around. He sips from a glass of champagne. He is listening to Ibiza-style club music on his mobile phone and we can hear the beat through the earphones. Occasionally he hums along with the tune, unaware of how loud he's being.* LEE *saunters around the room, pops his head into the bathroom, bounces a couple of times on the bed, then leaves the room again.*

INT. WARDROBE. DAY.

REBECCA *and* IAN *hear* LEE *depart.*

IAN Who was that, I wonder?

REBECCA Don't know!

IAN Could be a long game!

REBECCA Yes!

Silence.

IAN So how does it feel to be engaged, Rachel?

REBECCA Rebecca.

IAN Rebecca, sorry. Have you set a date yet . . .?

REBECCA Ninth of November.

IAN Oh, 9-11. You won't forget that in a hurry, will you?

REBECCA No. I hadn't thought of it that way to be honest . . .

IAN You have to think these things through. My parents christened me Richard Ian Percival, would you believe! Do you get it? R.I.P.

REBECCA R.I.P. Yes, that's . . . morbid.

IAN Hmm. That's why they swapped it to Ian Richard.

REBECCA What about the Percival?

IAN It was quietly dropped.

Suddenly the wardrobe door opens and CARL *is standing in front of them.* CARL *is* REBECCA*'s brother. He wears a smart suit and has a dry sense of humour.*

CARL Boo.

REBECCA Oh Carl, get in quick.

CARL I heard you talking. Why are you hiding in here?

REBECCA I didn't choose it, did I?

IAN Guilty as charged!

REBECCA Have you met Ian?

CARL No, I don't believe I've had that pleasure. Carl – I'm Rebecca's brother.

IAN Ah, so you two'll know all the nooks and crannies of the house then!

CARL Oh yes. I've spent most of my Christmases hiding in various cupboards waiting for my bossy little sister to find me. You never could though, could you?

REBECCA Get in!

CARL *steps into the wardrobe and closes the door.*

INT. WARDROBE. DAY.

CARL *stands next to* REBECCA.

REBECCA Is Daddy playing?

CARL He said he would. He's out showing Mark and Elizabeth the stables.

REBECCA He can do that afterwards; we're meant to be playing the game!

CARL All right, keep your voice down or you'll give us all away.

IAN *(jokily)* Yeah, chill out, bitch!

Silence. REBECCA *and* CARL *are stunned.*

IAN *(cont'd)* Sorry, that was misjudged.

CARL Actually it was quite funny. She is a bit of a bitch, aren't you, Becks?

INT. BEDROOM. DAY.

The bedroom door opens and STU *enters, flamboyantly dressed, camp, forties. He is carrying a glass and a bottle of champagne.*

STU Lollipops, come and get your lollipops! Where are all the children hiding?

STU *looks around the room.*

STU *(cont'd)* Now then . . . if I were to secrete myself in this room, where would I go? Not behind those curtains – they're a migraine waiting to happen. Hanging round the toilet perhaps – it has been known. Or would I enjoy spending time . . . in the closet!

STU *opens the wardrobe door to find* CARL, REBECCA *and* IAN.

STU *(cont'd)* Oh! Not interrupting anything, am I?

REBECCA Come on!

STU *steps in the wardrobe and closes the door.*

INT. WARDROBE. DAY.

STU *joins* CARL, REBECCA *and* IAN.

STU Oh it's like the back room of Cinderella's in Wakefield. Anyone got any poppers or lube?

CARL *(a warning)* Stuart.

IAN You two know each other, do you?

CARL Unfortunately, yes.

REBECCA They're partners.

IAN Oh. In what line?

STU It used to be straight up and down but not any more.

IAN Oh. I'm in IT.

STU Congratulations. I'm in SH-IT cos I got in late last night, didn't I?

CARL Stuart, you can do what you like, it doesn't bother me.

IAN Oh I see, so you're . . . living-together partners?

STU Yes, we're queer, dear, get used to it.

CARL That's it, I can't stay in here . . .

CARL *opens the wardrobe door.*

REBECCA Stuart, behave! This party's not about you, it's about me and Jeremy, so butt out! Carl, please.

CARL *closes the wardrobe door again.* STU *looks at* REBECCA.

STU You're much prettier when you're angry. *(To* CARL*)* So are you. Anyway, changing the subject slightly, I'm not being rude but there's a man downstairs who absolutely stinks.

REBECCA Yes, that's Stinky John.

STU What is it? Is it his clothes, his breath . . .?

REBECCA I don't know. He was at school with us, wasn't he, Carl?

CARL Yes, but that was when he was just John, not Stinky John.

REBECCA Something must have happened to him; he just stopped washing one day. Maybe we should trace it back?

CARL Yes. Maybe we should. 'Who Do You Stink You Are?'

STU And who are all the other people? Who's the really boring one?

REBECCA *coughs and* STU *remembers* IAN *is with them.*

STU *(cont'd)* Oh yes, and what about the old woman that's wandering round?

REBECCA Oh God, that's Geraldine. She's Daddy's cleaner. I asked her to come and serve drinks but she thinks she's a guest.

STU Oh that's hilair. You've got to tell her.

REBECCA I can't now, she's all dressed up.

STU Dressed up? She looks like 'Feed the Birds'.

IAN We have a sandwich guy at work and he wears a – like a yellow T-shirt thing, like a jersey but made from T-shirt material, and the girls all call him Mustard Mike!

Silence.

STU Well, thank God I brought champagne. Who wants a swig?

STU *drinks from his glass of champagne.*

INT. BEDROOM. DAY.

RACHEL*, a pretty but dumb girl in her thirties, runs into the room. She looks around, goes over to the bedside cabinet and looks inside. Unsurprisingly there is nobody hiding there.* RACHEL *looks around the room, then goes over to the wardrobe and flings the door open to reveal* STU, CARL, REBECCA *and* IAN. RACHEL *calls out:*

RACHEL Found them! They're in here!

REBECCA Sssssshhhhh!

RACHEL That's it, isn't it? I've won!

REBECCA No, you've got to hide as well.

RACHEL Oh, OK . . .

RACHEL *hurries over to the window.*

REBECCA No, in here, with us.

RACHEL Oh. There's not much space.

CARL That's why it's fun apparently.

RACHEL But I'm a little bit claustrophobic.

CARL Then it's even more fun.

REBECCA Quick, before someone sees you.

REBECCA *pulls* RACHEL *into the wardrobe and closes the door.*

REBECCA *(V.O.) (cont'd)* Could you just move back a bit, Ian. Have you got space?

IAN *(V.O.)* Er, yes, I've just got a Christmas tree sticking in my bottom.

STU *(V.O.) (sings)* 'Memories . . .'

REBECCA *(V.O.)* Ssshhhh!

INT. WARDROBE. DAY.

RACHEL *is huddled in the wardrobe between* IAN *and* REBECCA. *She whispers:*

RACHEL So what happens now?

REBECCA We wait for the others to find us.

RACHEL So how do you win?

REBECCA Nobody wins, you just wait.

RACHEL Oh. Right. So when does the game start?

REBECCA This is the game, Rachel, we're playing it.

IAN Oh – so *you're* Rachel.

RACHEL Yes, hello!

IAN I've been calling Rebecca 'Rachel', haven't I?

REBECCA Yes.

IAN I think I got you mixed up because Jeremy talks about you all the time.

RACHEL Does he?

REBECCA Does he?

IAN Yes.

REBECCA Who were you talking to?

IAN Erm, which one are you?

REBECCA Rebecca.

IAN Yes.

An awkward silence.

STU I spy with my little eye something beginning with WD.

CARL Wardrobe door?

STU Correct. Oh I haven't seen this much wood since . . .

CARL Don't!

STU *pokes his tongue out at* CARL.

REBECCA *(to* IAN*)* So what does Jeremy say about me?

IAN Sorry?

REBECCA At work. You said he talks about me.

IAN Oh just nice things. The usual boring girlfriend stuff . . .

REBECCA Boring girlfriend?

IAN Not that you're boring but what he said about you was . . .

REBECCA Boring.

IAN Yes.

REBECCA Well, coming from you, Ian, that's quite something. Thank you.

IAN You're welcome.

RACHEL Is anyone else hot in here? Can we just open the door a crack, I need to get some air . . .

CARL Wait 'til Stinky John gets here, you'll need more than a crack.

RACHEL Is Stinky John playing?

REBECCA Everybody's playing, it's Sardines.

RACHEL I might not be able to stay here if he gets in. I do get a bit . . .

RACHEL *fans herself.*

STU Don't worry, dear, me and you'll nip through to Narnia, have a snowball fight and get some Turkish Delight.

RACHEL *opens the door to get some air. She steps out.*

RACHEL I'm sorry, I need to breathe . . .

REBECCA No – you're not allowed!

CARL She's allowed to breathe.

REBECCA I'd rather she didn't . . .

INT. BEDROOM. DAY.

RACHEL *is in the bedroom.*

IAN I wouldn't mind stretching my legs actually. Been here a while . . .

IAN *steps out of the wardrobe.*

REBECCA What? Oh this is ridiculous!

STU Well, I'm going to have a pee break then. All that champagne has gone straight through me.

REBECCA Well, don't flush it!

STU Don't worry, I won't. You know my motto: 'If it's yellow, let it mellow; if it's brown, flush it down.'

STU *gets out and nips across to the en-suite. He opens the door to find* GERALDINE *sitting on the toilet.*

GERALDINE Hang on! Occupied!

STU *slams the door shut.*

STU Sorry! Well, that's something I'll never unsee.

REBECCA Who is it?

STU 'Feed the Birds.'

REBECCA Geraldine?

IAN Shouldn't she be using the staff toilets?

The toilet flushes and we hear the tap running. REBECCA *sees that* CARL *is looking very preoccupied.*

REBECCA Are you OK? What's the matter with you?

CARL *(acidly)* What do you think, Rebecca? Look where we are.

GERALDINE *emerges from the en-suite. She is in her seventies and wears her best dress and hat, also seventies.*

GERALDINE There you go, lovey. It doesn't have a lock, it's an 'on-sweetie'.

STU Well, at least you've warmed the seat for me.

RACHEL Thought it was just a pee break?

STU It is. Ladies sit.

STU *enters the en-suite and shuts the door.*

GERALDINE I heard you all talking in there, but I didn't want to disturb you. *(To* RACHEL*)* Hello, lovey.

RACHEL Hello!

GERALDINE That's a bonny dress.

RACHEL Thank you.

GERALDINE My hip went that colour when I fell up some steps at Legoland.

RACHEL I was just getting some air. I'm a bit claustrophobic.

GERALDINE Oh dear. Is that where you can't bear to touch a snake?

From inside the bathroom, STU *pipes up:*

STU *(V.O.)* You've got that, haven't you, Carl?

CARL I'd hardly call it a snake, Stuart. More of a scaly lizard.

STU *(V.O.)* I heard that!

CARL Good.

IAN Right, shall we, er, assume the position?

IAN *goes to get back into the wardrobe.* REBECCA *turns to* CARL.

REBECCA It's just a game.

CARL *looks away.* RACHEL *gets back in, followed by* GERALDINE. *They close the door.*

INT. WARDROBE. DAY.

IAN, RACHEL, GERALDINE, REBECCA *and* CARL *are now in the wardrobe.*

GERALDINE Room for a little 'un?

IAN Yes, it's like the Time and Relative Dimension In Space! TARDIS . . .

Nobody responds.

GERALDINE So, Rachel, tell me again how you know Jeremy?

There is an awkward pause.

RACHEL Erm . . .

REBECCA Rachel is Jeremy's ex, Geraldine.

GERALDINE That's it. I knew it was something I wasn't supposed to mention.

RACHEL We're just mates now. Text buddies. He BBMs me every now and again at weekends.

GERALDINE Oh lovely.

REBECCA Yes, he BBMs me a lot as well. We're always BBMing.

CARL What it is to be young.

Silence.

GERALDINE It's been ages since I've been in this room. Your dad usually keeps it locked up. You know, after . . .

REBECCA We're not going down that road, Geraldine. It's a party, remember?

GERALDINE Oh yes!

GERALDINE *sings lyrics from the song 'Why Am I Always the Bridesmaid?'.*

During this, RACHEL *smiles at* REBECCA, *who smiles back thinly.* REBECCA *tries to take* CARL*'s hand but he removes it.* STU *opens the wardrobe door and steps back in.*

STU Right I'm coming in, nobody fart.

STU *closes the wardrobe door.* STU *places his fingers under* CARL*'s nose.*

STU *(cont'd)* Smell that. Carbolic. We should get some for our 'on-sweetie'.

GERALDINE Well, this is fun, isn't it?

REBECCA Thank you, Geraldine, yes, it is. Fun.

GERALDINE Do you have a girlfriend, Ian?

IAN Er – no. Young, free and single at the moment. It's fine, you get used to it. I've not been a monk, I've had some experiences . . . but no. Pretty barren at the moment. A pretty arid patch.

GERALDINE We'll have to get you fixed up. Do you like him, Rachel?

RACHEL *(too quickly)* No. I mean, no, I've got a boyfriend. Did you meet Lee downstairs?

GERALDINE Yes, he gave me his jacket and asked me to get him a drink.

REBECCA He's only young.

STU How young? Is he legal?

RACHEL He's 21.

GERALDINE Toy boy!

STU Well, you know what they say. 'If there's grass on the wicket, let play commence!'

CARL Oh for fuck's sake, Stuart, give it a rest!

STU What's got into you?

CARL Can't you just talk like a normal human being for five minutes?

Suddenly they hear a noise in the bedroom. REBECCA *shushes everyone.* REBECCA *peeps through a crack in the wardrobe door to see* ELIZABETH *come into the room and look around.* ELIZABETH *whispers loudly:*

ELIZABETH Mark! In here.

INT. BEDROOM. DAY.

MARK *enters the bedroom to join his wife* ELIZABETH. *Both* ELIZABETH *and* MARK *are tall, elegant, well-dressed snobs.*

ELIZABETH Have you got rid of him?

MARK Yes, he's off looking for the others. God, I loathe playing other people's family games, it's such a bore.

ELIZABETH We've done long enough now. You said we'd be out by three.

MARK Well, why didn't you just do the lie about the babysitter getting ill?

ELIZABETH Because that needs to be seeded. You need to seed it.

MARK You don't need to seed it, you just say it. 'Sorry, we've got to go now, the babysitter's ill.'

ELIZABETH You're so naïve Mark. What awful curtains.

MARK Anyway, the old man might be tedious but he's our way in to Dickie Lawrence so we have to put a shift in.

ELIZABETH I thought you hated Dickie Lawrence.

MARK I do, he's a first-class prick. But I need him to smooth over that merger next year. You know what they say: 'Keep your friends close and your enemies closer.'

ELIZABETH You're such a horrible shit, Mark.

MARK That's why you love me.

MARK *grabs* ELIZABETH *and kisses her. The wardrobe door eases open a crack and we see* REBECCA *peeping out.*

INT. WARDROBE. DAY.

Inside the wardrobe REBECCA *can hear* MARK *and* ELIZABETH *and see bits of them through the crack in the door.*

ELIZABETH *(V.O.)* Mark, stop it . . . no, not here . . .

MARK *(V.O.)* Come on. Just fingers.

ELIZABETH *(V.O.)* No!

RACHEL *(whispers)* Do you think we should say something?

REBECCA We've left it too late now.

RACHEL But what if they start . . . ?

REBECCA I think they've already started.

GERALDINE But anyone could walk in on them.

STU That's the thrill of it, Geraldine. Here, hold my glass, I'm going to film it.

STU *gets out his mobile phone.*

REBECCA No you're not! Somebody make a noise.

IAN *blows a little breath, hardly registering any sound.*

REBECCA *(cont'd)* That was a bit too subtle, Ian.

GERALDINE *cries out:*

GERALDINE Geronimo!

INT. BEDROOM. DAY.

MARK *and* ELIZABETH *break from their embrace.* ELIZABETH *adjusts her clothes.* MARK *smooths his hair and goes to open the wardrobe. Six smiling faces look out at him.*

REBECCA Oh! You found us, well done!

ELIZABETH What the hell . . . ?

MARK *remembers.*

MARK Sardines.

IAN Hi, Mark! Welcome to the wardrobe!

MARK *stares blankly.*

IAN *(cont'd)* Ian. I work for you. In IT.

MARK Of course, hi.

REBECCA We've been hiding here for ages waiting for someone to find us and these doors are so thick, we didn't hear anything, did we?

Assorted mumbles of 'no, no' from the others.

REBECCA *(cont'd)* Do you want to come in then, before Daddy finds us?

MARK Erm . . .

MARK *looks to* ELIZABETH.

ELIZABETH Yes. Though I am a bit worried about the babysitter, she did say she was feeling a bit under the weather . . .

CARL Oh, well seeded.

MARK We'll be all right for a few minutes, won't we?

MARK *raises an eyebrow at* ELIZABETH. *It's an order – we have to do this. She gives him a hard look, then:*

ELIZABETH Yes. Looks like a lot of fun.

ELIZABETH *gingerly moves forward as if she's going to walk into a pig sty. She braces herself and steps into the wardrobe.*

ELIZABETH *(cont'd)* Right. I'm coming in. Please mind the shoes everybody. Maybe I should take them off?

MARK No, just get in, Liz. The sooner we start . . .

MARK *and* ELIZABETH *step into the wardrobe.*

MARK *(cont'd)* Stand there, next to Rachel.

REBECCA Rebecca!

MARK Sorry.

REBECCA It's my engagement party and nobody seems to know my name!

MARK It's just that Jeremy always . . .

REBECCA What?

IAN This one's Rachel!

IAN *points knowingly to* RACHEL.

MARK Ah. Nice to meet you.

RACHEL Nice to meet you too.

LEE *enters the room with an empty glass.*

LEE There you all are! I've already been in here once!

RACHEL Lee! Come in, we're having such a laugh.

LEE Can't believe I didn't check in the fucking wardrobe, what a knob! I thought I heard someone shouting.

GERALDINE That was me, I said 'Geronimo' – don't ask me why.

RACHEL Have you met everyone, Lee? This is Ian, who works with Mark.

IAN *pops his head round the corner.*

MARK *For* Mark actually. I own the company.

LEE Oh right. If you ever need any roofing doing . . .

RACHEL You know Rebecca, obviously. This is Mark's wife, Elizabeth.

ELIZABETH Hello.

LEE You all right, darling? You look like you're crying.

ELIZABETH It's just a bit dusty in here, that's all.

RACHEL This is Rebecca's brother Carl, and Stuart, who's his . . .

CARL Flatmate. Pleased to meet you.

STU Flatmate?

LEE All right.

RACHEL And this is Geraldine.

LEE Yeah, I know. I wouldn't mind a little top-up, if you don't mind.

LEE *proffers his empty champagne glass to* GERALDINE.

GERALDINE Pardon?

LEE A little cheeky champers, there's a good girl.

GERALDINE Why do you keep asking me?

LEE Rebecca said you were serving drinks.

REBECCA No . . .

GERALDINE No, I'm a guest! He's got his wires crossed.

REBECCA Yes, we're all guests here. All equal.

GERALDINE I used to be their Nanny, you know. I've known all three of them since they were so high.

RACHEL Three of them?

REBECCA Yes, we've got a sister, Caroline. She moved away.

GERALDINE Is she not coming, Becky? I'd love to see the boys again. They must be getting big now.

REBECCA No, they can't make it. It's a bit too far to travel.

GERALDINE Aaaahhh . . .

REBECCA *and* CARL *exchange looks.*

LEE I'll go and get my own drink then.

LEE *turns to go.*

STU Here you go, I've got some contraband you can have, Lee . . .

STU *pushes his way out of the wardrobe and approaches* LEE *with his champagne bottle.*

STU *(cont'd)* Let's form a splinter group under the bed.

REBECCA You can't do that.

STU It's all right, I'm sure my flatmate won't mind.

STU *looks back at* CARL, *then starts to drag* LEE *over to the bed.*

LEE All right, but don't try and bum me!

REBECCA I'm sorry, Stuart, but that's against the rules.

STU Homophobic!

GERALDINE Oh you've got that, haven't you, lovey?

RACHEL No, I'm claustrophobic.

ELIZABETH It *is* getting rather crowded in here.

IAN Yes, it's almost like we're a tin of sardines!

MARK Tell you what, Colin, why don't you step out for a bit, make some room.

IAN *climbs out of the wardrobe.*

IAN It's Ian . . .

MARK Sorry, Ian – you can go under the bed with those two.

LEE *and* STU *are climbing under the bed.*

STU No, sorry, private party.

REBECCA Look, you cannot play Sardines unless everyone is hiding in the same place together, that's what makes it fun . . .

MARK *closes the wardrobe door, leaving* IAN *on the outside.* IAN *looks around and heads into the bathroom, closing the door behind him. We stay on the empty room.*

STU *(V.O.)* Oh yes, Lee, that's nice, keep doing that, what big hands you've got, oh yes . . .

RACHEL *(V.O.)* Lee?

LEE *(V.O.)* I'm not doing anything!

CARL *(V.O.)* Leave him alone, Stuart.

STU *(V.O.)* Oh, what's the matter, Carl, are you jealous?

CARL *(V.O.)* Piss off.

REBECCA *(V.O.)* Stop arguing, you two, this is ridiculous!

STU *(V.O.)* It's not my fault that you're afraid of intimacy, Carl!

CARL *(V.O.) (emotionally)* And it's not my fault either! You've got no idea . . .

A moment of silence in the empty room. The door opens and in comes

STINKY JOHN. *He is overweight with long hair and wears an ill-fitting suit. He creeps into the room and looks around.* STINKY JOHN *approaches the wardrobe. He throws the wardrobe door open to reveal* MARK, GERALDINE, RACHEL, REBECCA, ELIZABETH *and* CARL. *They stare at him with looks of horror on their faces.*

STINKY JOHN Ta-dah!

REBECCA John!

REBECCA *instinctively puts her hand over her mouth.*

STINKY JOHN Oh looks like I'm one of the last to join the party. Can I squeeze in?

He makes to step into the wardrobe.

RACHEL/REBECCA/ELIZABETH No!

REBECCA I just think it's a bit too full.

STINKY JOHN No, there's plenty of room . . .

STINKY JOHN *tries to get in. They all bunch up to stop him.*

ELIZABETH I feel sick.

MARK Breathe through your mouth.

CARL Actually, John – some people are hiding under the bed . . .

STU *(V.O.)* Oh no you don't!

RACHEL Yes, we just thought, as I'm claustrophobic . . .

STINKY JOHN But that's not the game, is it? You're all meant to be squashed in together. That's the rules.

REBECCA Yes, but we thought it doesn't really matter about the rules. As long as we're all in the same room it still counts.

STINKY JOHN All right, as you wish.

STINKY JOHN *goes towards the bed and looks under it.* STU*'s face peeps out.*

STU Actually, John, there really isn't room under here. There's suitcases and everything, isn't that right, Lee?

LEE *(V.O.)* Yeah, it's packed mate, sorry.

STINKY JOHN I don't think I'd fit under there anyway to be honest, what with the old 26-pack.

He wobbles his gut.

STU Yeah, you're far better off going with the wardrobe group.

STINKY JOHN All right, pillar to post! I'm back again!

STINKY JOHN *heads back to the wardrobe but the door has been pulled to.* STINKY JOHN *tries to open it but encounters resistance.*

STINKY JOHN *(cont'd)* Hang on. What's going on here? Is it caught or something?

INT. WARDROBE. DAY.

Inside the wardrobe everyone is trying to hold the door closed.

REBECCA It's stuck, John. Maybe try going in the bathroom.

MARK First time for everything.

INT. BEDROOM. DAY.

STINKY JOHN *can see through the crack in the wardrobe door.*

STINKY JOHN I can see what it is. It's fingers, someone's holding it with their fingers.

RACHEL *(V.O.)* No, we're trying to push it.

GERALDINE *(V.O.)* Oh let him in, poor lamb.

ELIZABETH *(V.O.)* You can't! Mark tell them.

MARK *(V.O.)* Maybe try behind the curtains.

STU *(V.O.)* Yeah and open a window while you're there, it's getting a bit close.

STINKY JOHN *shambles over to the window.*

STINKY JOHN All right. Funniest game of Sardines I've ever played.

STINKY JOHN *arranges himself behind a curtain at the window just as* JEREMY *enters the room.* JEREMY *is* REBECCA*'s fiancé, fairly handsome, well turned out, but a bit wet.*

JEREMY Ah, John, have you seen Rebecca anywhere?

STINKY JOHN Argh, caught red-handed! She's hiding in the wardrobe but you can't get in, the door's stuck apparently.

JEREMY Thanks.

STINKY JOHN And there's two under the bed – it's a shambles!

STINKY JOHN *hides behind the curtain as* JEREMY *approaches the wardrobe.*

JEREMY Bex, it's Jeremy.

REBECCA *(V.O.)* Hi!

JEREMY Listen, darling, I'm just going to pop down to the station to pick up a chum who's running late and I can't seem to find my keys. You haven't had them, have you?

REBECCA *(V.O.)* No, they were in your jacket.

JEREMY I looked, they're not there. If I can't find them, I might have to take the Mini, is that OK?

REBECCA *(V.O.)* All right, drive safely though. Love you!

JEREMY Love you too, Rachel!

Instantly JEREMY *knows he's said the wrong thing.*

JEREMY *(cont'd)* Rebecca!

JEREMY *listens for a reaction. Silence.*

JEREMY *(cont'd)* Rebecca? Love you!

Silence. The door opens and in walks ANDREW, CARL *and* REBECCA*'s septuagenarian father. He sniffs the air.*

ANDREW What is that awful smell? That is absolutely vile.

JEREMY Hi, Andrew.

ANDREW Searched this room, have you?

JEREMY Er – yes. I believe there's some people hiding in the wardrobe, some under the bed. And Stinky Jo—John behind the curtains.

ANDREW No, no, no. This is all wrong. Come out from there, boy!

STINKY JOHN *steps out from the curtain, head bowed. He seems cowed by* ANDREW*'s presence.*

ANDREW *(cont'd)* You've all got to be in the same place! This isn't Hide and Go Seek. You know the rules, don't you? Well?

STINKY JOHN Yes, sir.

ANDREW *kicks the bed.*

ANDREW Come on, out! Out, I say!

STU *and* LEE *climb out from under the bed.*

STU It's like *The Diary of Anne Frank*.

LEE I've not seen that one. Is it like *Diary of a Wimpy Kid*?

STU Not really.

ANDREW *opens the wardrobe door.* REBECCA *puts on a brave face.*

REBECCA Hi, Daddy.

ANDREW Here. Five more sardines to go in the tin.

JEREMY Oh, I just need to . . .

ANDREW Come on, chop chop. In we go . . .

JEREMY *gets in next to* REBECCA *but she turns away from him.* STINKY JOHN *squeezes in next to* ELIZABETH, *who blanches and gags.* STINKY JOHN *looks over at* CARL, *who looks down.* LEE *and* STU *climb into the wardrobe, followed by* ANDREW *who closes the door behind him.*

INT. WARDROBE. DAY.

It is now ridiculously packed in the wardrobe, with MARK, GERALDINE, STU, LEE, RACHEL, STINKY JOHN, ELIZABETH, JEREMY, ANDREW, REBECCA *and* CARL *all squashed in two deep.*

ANDREW There we go. That's the name of the game. Sardines.

LEE Fucking hell, this is mental. I've got to Twitpic this. Smile everyone!

LEE *takes a photo on his mobile. The wardrobe lights up briefly with the camera flash.*

JEREMY *(to* REBECCA*)* They both start with an 'R' . . .

GERALDINE Would anybody like a Polo mint? John?

STINKY JOHN No, thank you.

GERALDINE Are you sure? They're very . . . refreshing!

STINKY JOHN They give me diarrhoea.

ELIZABETH Oh dear God.

STU I'll have one. There's something catching in my throat.

GERALDINE Pass them round.

The mints are passed around through the wardrobe.

MARK Oh, Andrew, Elizabeth was just asking after Dickie Lawrence, how is he these days?

ANDREW Dickie Lawrence? Haven't spoken to him for two years. Hateful man.

MARK Oh, I thought . . .

ANDREW Thought you could use me as a stepping stone, did you? Well, tough titty. That bridge was burned a long time ago.

ELIZABETH *looks stricken.*

ELIZABETH *(weakly)* Babysitter . . .?

REBECCA *(to* JEREMY*)* You're still in love with her, aren't you?

JEREMY *falters, but says nothing.* RACHEL *looks away, taking* LEE*'s hand.* STU *and* CARL *are at opposite ends of the wardrobe.*

STU Are you all right, Carl?

Silence

STU *(cont'd)* Sorry if I've embarrassed you in front of your family.

CARL No, you haven't. Quite the reverse.

REBECCA We used to love playing Sardines at parties, didn't we, Daddy?

ANDREW Oh yes. What we call an ice-breaker. Do you remember the 'Sardine Song'?

REBECCA Of course.

As ANDREW *sings,* REBECCA *joins in.*

ANDREW *(sings)* 'A baby sardine saw his first submarine . . .'

CARL Don't you dare sing that.

ANDREW My house, I'll do what I bloody well like!

Silence.

LEE Is it me or is there like a shitty smell in here?

GERALDINE Oh do you remember that year when we had the Cub Scouts jamboree? Chaos, it was, kiddies everywhere . . .

REBECCA That was a long time ago.

GERALDINE We were all having such a laugh and then this one little boy spoiled it, what was his name . . .?

RACHEL Er, I think we should be making a move now . . .

GERALDINE Oh the police were involved and everything, do you remember, John?

STINKY JOHN Philip Harrison.

GERALDINE That was it, Little Pip. Whatever happened to him?

ANDREW The family moved away as I recall. Spain or some such.

GERALDINE Well, good riddance, I say. Accusing you of such horrible things.

CARL He paid them to go away.

ANDREW I was teaching the boy how to wash himself. Basic hygiene.

CARL We weren't all that lucky, were we, John?

STINKY JOHN I can smell carbolic soap . . .

STINKY JOHN *starts to gag.*

ANDREW All right, that's enough!

Silence.

STU Now, before I ring Jeremy Kyle, can I just say there's no one actually looking for us any more? We're all here.

LEE No, we're not. That Ian's not here.

JEREMY Yes, I've got to go and pick him up from the station actually.

MARK He's in the bathroom.

JEREMY What?

MARK The boring chap with glasses on.

JEREMY That's not Ian . . .

INT. BEDROOM. DAY.

A hand is turning the key in the wardrobe door. We hear singing and pull out to see IAN*'s reflection in the wardrobe mirror.*

IAN *(singing)* 'A baby sardine saw his first submarine; he was scared and watched through the peephole . . .'

The wardrobe door rattles.

ANDREW *(V.O.)* Hello? What's going on? Open this door!

IAN *pours lighter fluid on the carpet in front of the wardrobe.*

IAN '"Oh come, come, come," said the sardine's mum, "It's only a tin full of people."'

CARL *(V.O.)* Pip?

IAN *sparks a cigarette lighter into flame . . .*

THE END

Episode 2

A QUIET NIGHT IN

CAST LIST

GERALD – Denis Lawson

KIM – Joyce Veheary

EDDIE – Steve Pemberton

RAY – Reece Shearsmith

SABRINA – Oona Chaplin

PAUL – Kayvan Novak

EXT. GERALD'S HOUSE. NIGHT.

A large, newly built modern house, lots of glazing and white walls. The house sits in its own grounds, with an expensive car in the driveway and a gleaming stainless-steel number '9' by the front door.

TITLE: *'A Quiet Night In'.*

INT. LIVING ROOM. NIGHT.

We are in the large living room of GERALD*'s house – expensively furnished but not conspicuously so. The back of the room is dominated by full-length French windows, which look out into the pitch-black garden at night.*

On the right-hand wall above the fireplace there is a large framed painting suspended from the hanging-rail. The 'painting' appears to be totally white, with a stripe of slightly off-white running down one side. The only mark on the painting is a vague square of yellow in one corner and the artist's signature.

A door at the rear of the room leads to the all-mod-cons kitchen. A door at the front of the room leads to the spacious hallway.

We see GERALD, *a distinguished grey-haired man in his fifties, wearing a silk bath robe and expensive slippers. He walks past the painting, picks up a remote on the way and presses the button. Rachmaninov's Piano Concerto No. 2 begins to play.*

GERALD *wanders over to an impressive dining table, which is set for dinner, and sits down to read the* Financial Times. *He sits with his back towards the French windows.*

INT. KITCHEN. NIGHT.

A small Filipino maid, KIM, *prepares* GERALD*'s dinner. He is having a bowl of tomato soup, which she arranges on a tray, with black pepper and bread on the side. She picks up the tray and leaves the kitchen.*

INT. LIVING ROOM. NIGHT.

KIM *brings the tray of food through to* GERALD. *She places it in front of him at the table.* GERALD *barely acknowledges her over his paper, and she leaves silently.*

GERALD *adds black pepper to his soup and reads the newspaper as the music plays.*

After a few moments the outdoor security lights come on, illuminating the patio outside the French windows.

Two men are revealed in the light, caught sneaking towards the house. RAY *is small and wiry,* EDDIE *large and clumsy. They are dressed in dark clothes and wear tights on their heads.*

EDDIE *and* RAY *look at each other, like rabbits caught in headlights. They look into the house, but* GERALD *has his back to the window and hasn't seen them. The two burglars run to either side of the windows and the security lights go off again.*

GERALD *remains oblivious, eating his soup as the music plays. A moment later the lights snap back on again to reveal* EDDIE *holding a broom aloft, trying to smash a security light.*

RAY *steps in and waves* EDDIE *back to the side and the lights snap off again.*

Another moment later the lights come on again, this time to reveal RAY *spread-eagled on the patio – trying to crawl under the sensors. He gets up wearily and slowly walks away, shaking his head, even pausing to look inside the house. The music plays on;* GERALD *reads and eats.*

The doorbell sounds but is partially drowned out by the music. GERALD *mutes the sound and the doorbell rings again.* GERALD *gets up and leaves the room.*

The garden security lights snap on again to reveal RAY *hurrying towards the French windows. He expertly picks the lock and lets himself in.*

EXT. FRONT DOOR. NIGHT.

GERALD *opens the front door, but there is nobody there. He steps out for a moment and looks around, but all is quiet, so he goes back in again.*

We reveal EDDIE *hiding round the corner of the doorway.*

INT. LIVING ROOM. NIGHT.

RAY *is in the room. He looks over to the painting and is about to go over when he hears* GERALD *close the front door.* RAY *ducks down, hiding behind the breakfast bar that* GERALD *was just sitting at.* GERALD *comes back into the room.* GERALD *sits down on the sofa and puts the music on again with the remote control.*

RAY *takes out a handkerchief and a small bottle of chloroform. He squirts the clear liquid into the cloth. Suddenly he gets a text message and his phone beeps loudly in his pocket.*

RAY *scrabbles in his pocket to fish out his phone, checking that* GERALD *hasn't heard the beeps. He hasn't.* RAY *grabs the phone and reads a text from* EDDIE*: 'Are you in?'*

An exasperated RAY *types in his response: 'Yes.'*

RAY *pockets his phone and crawls towards* GERALD *with the chloroformed handkerchief. His phone beeps again.* RAY *checks his latest message from* EDDIE*: 'Is your phone on silent?'*

RAY *angrily replies: 'No!'*

RAY *sets off again, getting a bit further this time. He is only a few feet from* GERALD*. Then another beep.* RAY *drops down behind the sofa just as a suspicious* GERALD *turns round, narrowly missing him. The latest text reads: 'OK go Settings, click on General and select Sounds.'*

With his back to the sofa, RAY *begins to frantically text his reply.*

EXT. FRONT DOOR. NIGHT.

EDDIE *is waiting by the front door when his phone beeps.* EDDIE *lifts the stocking on his head to read the text from* RAY*: 'STOP TEXTING ME YOU STUPID FAT DUCK.'*

EDDIE *frowns. The door suddenly opens and* RAY *is standing there.* EDDIE *holds up his phone, as if to question 'FAT DUCK'.* RAY *shushes* EDDIE*, grabs the phone from him and throws it in the garden. He beckons* EDDIE *to come in.*

INT. HALLWAY. NIGHT.

RAY *quietly closes the front door behind* EDDIE *and tiptoes into the hallway. The music from the living room can still be heard.* RAY *indicates to* EDDIE *a closed door marked WC.* EDDIE *nods in understanding. Curious, he mimes the question: 'Is he doing a wee or a poo?'*

RAY *doesn't understand.* EDDIE *repeats the mime.* RAY *understands but mimes: 'Why?'*

EDDIE *mimes back that a wee will only be one minute, but a poo will take ten.* RAY *is appalled at the idea of a poo taking ten minutes and explains that his poos take only three.*

EDDIE *is stunned at the idea of a three-minute poo. He holds up three fingers questioningly.* RAY *mimes how quick a process it can be: evacuate, wipe, flush.* EDDIE *has to hand it to* RAY *and mimes applause.*

RAY *beckons* EDDIE *over to the WC and they both listen at the door. After a beat they are rewarded with the sound of a 'plop' and they both agree: it's a number two. They hurry back into the living room.*

INT. LIVING ROOM. NIGHT.

The Rachmaninov concerto is still playing. RAY *and* EDDIE *tiptoe into the living room.*

EDDIE *moves over towards the door and pauses in front of the plain white painting. He looks closely at the painting and then looks to* RAY, *frowning.* RAY *nods.* EDDIE *points at the painting questioningly.* RAY *nods, then rubs his fingers and thumb together, miming that the painting is worth a lot of money.* EDDIE *shakes his head uncomprehendingly.* RAY *shoos* EDDIE *over to the door to keep an eye on the kitchen.*

EDDIE *moves to the door and sees the maid,* KIM, *in the kitchen preparing some food. He gives the thumbs-up to* RAY, *who removes a small bundle of tools from his belt.* RAY *flips over the painting so the back is facing him, selects a small craft knife and starts to cut around the tape holding the back board in place.*

EDDIE *watches* KIM *in the kitchen.*

INT. KITCHEN. NIGHT.

KIM *is chopping vegetables as she waits for the kettle to boil. We see* EDDIE *spying on her from the living room.*

INT. LIVING ROOM. NIGHT.

We see a tiny lapdog appear and pad past RAY *into the room. It stops and starts to bark at* EDDIE. EDDIE *and* RAY *turn to look at it.*

INT. KITCHEN. NIGHT.

KIM *cannot hear the dog over the sound of the warming kettle and the music in the living room.*

INT. LIVING ROOM. NIGHT.

RAY *beckons for* EDDIE *to get rid of the small yapping dog.* EDDIE *shoos it away – but it stands its ground.*

EDDIE *pushes the little dog with his foot, trying to dribble it out like a football. The dog bites his shoe.* RAY *mimes: 'Pick it up!'*

EDDIE *shakes his head, indicating that he is allergic to dogs and if he touches it he will sneeze.* EDDIE *starts to shoo the yapping dog along the length of the room, sliding open the doors at the other end. He grabs* GERALD*'s bread and crumbles a trail of it towards the open door.* EDDIE *beckons for the dog to eat the bread and leave. While he does this, an enormous Irish wolfhound or Great Dane enters through the French doors, eating the bread trail.* RAY *and* EDDIE *are appalled. Now there are two dogs in the room and they run around and bark at each other.*

INT. KITCHEN. NIGHT.

KIM *is shredding vegetables using a food processor.*

INT. LIVING ROOM. NIGHT.

EDDIE *is shooing the large wolfhound out of the French windows. He then turns to find the small dog.* RAY *crosses from cutting the painting to close the French windows so the big dog can't get back in.*

EDDIE *chases and corners the small dog. He grabs it and throws it towards the French windows like a snowball. As* RAY *has already closed the window, the dog splats against the glass and lands on the floor, unconscious.* RAY *rolls his eyes at* EDDIE.

RAY *looks around and grabs an umbrella stand from the corner of the room. He removes an umbrella and walking stick and beckons to* EDDIE *to stuff the dog in.* EDDIE *does so and* RAY *pushes it down the tube with the umbrella and stick. All the time they check to see that* KIM *is still in the kitchen.*

INT. KITCHEN. NIGHT.

KIM *opens the fridge.* KIM *selects a bunch of large red chillies from the fridge. They are marked as being fiery hot and* KIM *handles them carefully, placing them on the chopping board.*

INT. LIVING ROOM. NIGHT.

RAY *motions for* EDDIE *to go and keep an eye on* KIM *in the kitchen and* EDDIE *tiptoes off to resume his spying position.*

RAY *replaces the umbrella stand and is crossing back to the painting when he sees* SABRINA *coming down the stairs. She has just missed spotting* EDDIE *walking past to check on* KIM *in the kitchen.*

SABRINA *is* GERALD*'s wife. She is 15 or 20 years younger than him and wears expensive jeans and a jumper and lots of make-up. She carries a large gin and tonic.*

RAY *immediately spins the painting back round and ducks down behind the sofa.* EDDIE *is oblivious to* SABRINA*'s presence as he is looking into the kitchen.*

SABRINA *walks straight to the sofa and flops down. She looks fed up.*

INT. KITCHEN. NIGHT.

KIM *leaves the kitchen and goes into the utility room. We see* EDDIE *watching from the living room.*

INT. LIVING ROOM. NIGHT.

SABRINA *is oblivious to* RAY, *as she has her back to him.*

RAY *tries to wave to* EDDIE *but he isn't looking.* RAY *throws a small stone from a plant pot at* EDDIE. *It misses and* EDDIE *is oblivious.* EDDIE *looks back to the kitchen.* RAY *throws another small stone.* EDDIE *is annoyed now. He looks round and sees* RAY *crouching on the floor.*

EDDIE *picks up the stone and throws it back at* RAY. RAY *dodges the stone, then points to the sofa where* SABRINA *is looking at a magazine.* EDDIE *is gobsmacked.* RAY *motions for* EDDIE *to hide, and* EDDIE *crouches down behind the sofa with* RAY.

SABRINA *leans over to the CD player and turns down the volume of the music.* SABRINA *presses the TV remote and starts to watch* EastEnders. GERALD *enters.*

GERALD *sees* SABRINA *on the sofa watching TV. He pauses by the door and glares at* SABRINA. *They are clearly in the middle of a big row and are not on speaking terms.* SABRINA *senses* GERALD*'s presence but chooses to ignore him, fixing her eyes on the TV.*

GERALD *calmly walks over to the music remote and turns the volume up louder to drown out the TV.* GERALD *then sits on the other end of the sofa and reads his paper.*

SABRINA *sits for a moment, then takes the TV remote and turns the sound of the television up to compete with the music.*

GERALD *grabs the TV remote from* SABRINA *and turns off the TV.* SABRINA *tries to snatch the TV remote back from* GERALD *but he holds it out of her reach. They scramble around on the sofa, fighting like kids.*

EDDIE *and* RAY, *hiding behind the sofa, listening to the commotion, give each other a look: 'How childish.'*

GERALD *manages to slide the back panel off the TV remote and remove the batteries.* SABRINA *tries to stop him, but he takes the batteries and drops them into* SABRINA*'s gin and tonic.* SABRINA *looks at* GERALD *contemptuously.* GERALD *ignores* SABRINA *and goes back to his paper.*

SABRINA *gets up and storms away to the French windows at the end of the room. She opens them and steps outside onto the patio. The security lights come on.* SABRINA *takes a cigarette from her handbag and lights it.* GERALD *reads his paper.*

EDDIE *and* RAY *stay crouching behind the sofa.*

GERALD *is brooding on the sofa. He can't concentrate on his newspaper. Suddenly he gets up from the sofa and strides to the French windows.* RAY *and* EDDIE *crawl round the sofa so as not to be seen by* GERALD *as he leaves. He steps out onto the patio in front of an outdoor swimming pool to join* SABRINA *and closes the doors.* GERALD *starts to talk to* SABRINA *but she ignores him. He tries again and this time she answers. They start to have a blazing row on the patio, but with the double glazing and the music we can barely hear them.*

EDDIE *crouches down and begins to snake across to the other side of the room, flat on his belly, army-style.* RAY *is shaking his head but* EDDIE *continues.* GERALD *and* SABRINA *are too involved in their argument to notice.*

EDDIE *reaches the other side of the room and slowly and subtly tries to pull a screen slightly further into the room, slightly helping to obscure the view from outside.*

RAY *realises that he can now stand without being seen. He gets up and quickly puts the painting on the floor. He carefully cuts the canvas from the frame and removes it, leaving the wooden backing visible.*

GERALD *suddenly turns away from* SABRINA *and heads for the French windows. He's heard enough.* GERALD *places his hand on the handle and is about to open the door.* RAY, *about to stand with the painting, ducks back down.*

SABRINA *says something that stops* GERALD *in his tracks.* GERALD *stands for a moment with his hand on the handle.* RAY *holds his breath.* EDDIE *watches. Then* GERALD *slowly turns back round to face* SABRINA. EDDIE *breathes a huge sigh of relief.* RAY *carefully moves himself and the painting to the other side of the breakfast bar, so as to be hidden from* GERALD *and* SABRINA.

GERALD *and* SABRINA *continue their conversation, but now it is more measured than the previous shouting.* SABRINA *takes out her phone and offers to make a call.* GERALD *agrees.*

In the living room, RAY *is about to put the back-board back on the painting when he realises that he will need something to hang in the frame as a decoy. He looks around for something large and white.* EDDIE *removes his white handkerchief but it is too small and* RAY *dismisses it.* EDDIE *starts to root through the kitchen drawers.*

RAY *peeps outside and sees* SABRINA *making a call on her mobile. She speaks to someone briefly, then hands the phone to* GERALD. GERALD *speaks to the person on the other end of the line, long enough to confirm what* SABRINA *just told him.*

EDDIE *proffers a roll of plain white kitchen paper and a yellow Post-It note.* RAY *stares at him: is that the best you could do?* EDDIE *tears four squares off and hands them to* RAY, *who starts to place them on the back-board. He then goes to re-hang the picture.*

Outside on the patio GERALD *quits the call. He looks angry and forlorn.* SABRINA *coolly walks past* GERALD *and takes back her phone.* GERALD *grabs* SABRINA*'s wrist and she stares back at him defiantly.* GERALD *releases his grip.* SABRINA *then opens the French windows and re-enters the living room.*

GERALD *sits down on the patio chair, his back to the room. He looks broken.*

SABRINA *enters the living room and pours herself a drink at the breakfast bar.*

SABRINA *puts her hand up to the glass. Just then her phone beeps and* SABRINA *looks down at her message.*

We pan down to find EDDIE *and* RAY *hiding below. They can see* SABRINA*'s feet and she is standing on the expensive canvas painting. They watch with concern as* SABRINA*'s high-heeled shoes are in danger of ruining the painting.* EDDIE *reaches out to take the* *painting but* RAY *slaps his hand back: they have to be patient and wait for her to move.*

SABRINA *steps off the painting and walks towards the door.* RAY *slowly reaches out to grab the painting, but* KIM *the maid re-enters carrying a laundry basket, so* RAY *and* EDDIE *have to crawl to the other end of the bar to remain hidden.*

SABRINA *leaves the room, ignoring* KIM, *who places the basket on the corner of the bar, dropping some items of clothing onto the floor. She has overfilled it. She swipes up the dropped clothes, picking up the canvas on the floor at the same time.*

RAY *and* EDDIE *are distraught.* KIM *carries the laundry through a door into the utility room.* RAY *and* EDDIE *crawl along the breakfast bar. They can see* GERALD *still sitting on the patio.* RAY *sends* EDDIE *through the door to follow* KIM *while he keeps guard.*

INT. KITCHEN. NIGHT.

EDDIE *creeps through the door. He just catches the back of* KIM *leaving the utility room by another door.* EDDIE *creeps in.*

INT. UTILITY ROOM. NIGHT.

EDDIE *sees the washing machine click into action. The white linens inside are slowly being soaked by the rising water and then the washing begins to turn and spin.*

EDDIE *dashes forward and tries to stop the washing machine. He presses all the buttons and tries to force the door open. Just then* KIM *walks back into the utility room, carrying the laundry basket.*

EDDIE *turns to see* KIM *in the doorway. She is about to scream so* EDDIE *clamps his hand over her mouth. They struggle and* KIM *drops the washing basket.* KIM *manages to reach into her pocket and pull out a mace spray. She sprays it in* EDDIE*'s eyes and he cries out in pain, holding his face.* KIM *runs out of the room.*

INT. KITCHEN. NIGHT.

KIM *runs straight into* RAY. *She screams and runs to the front door.* RAY *chases her and manages to place his chloroform handkerchief over* KIM*'s mouth and subdue her.* RAY *can hear* EDDIE *crying out in pain.* RAY *puts the unconscious* KIM *in a cupboard at one side of the front door.* RAY *sees* SABRINA *cross at the top of the stairs. He returns to the utility room and* EDDIE.

INT. UTILITY ROOM. NIGHT.

RAY *shushes* EDDIE, *who is whimpering and nursing his sore eyes.* EDDIE *points to the washing machine.* RAY *looks around and hears a ping. He runs to the end of the utility room and finds the crumpled canvas on top of a pile of clothing, in a small cubby hole.*

RAY *goes to retrieve the painting but the whole basket disappears up a chute, as the cubby hole is actually the entrance shaft of a dumb waiter. It has been activated upstairs and the compartment lifts up out of view.* RAY *leaves* EDDIE *on the floor of the utility room and exits.*

INT. STAIRWAY. NIGHT.

RAY *is creeping up the stairs, following where he thinks the dumb waiter must lead.*

INT. UPSTAIRS LANDING. NIGHT.

RAY *arrives at* SABRINA*'s slightly ajar bedroom door and peeps in. He sees* SABRINA *dumping the basket of clothes into a large suitcase and shoving everything in, including the painting canvas. She locks the case and puts the keys in her jeans pocket.* SABRINA *goes into the bathroom, starting to remove her jumper.*

INT. LIVING ROOM. NIGHT.

GERALD *looks stoically determined. He emerges from the patio, closing the French windows behind him.* GERALD *goes over to a large bureau and slides open a drawer to reveal a small hand gun.*

INT. UTILITY ROOM. NIGHT.

EDDIE *stumbles his way out of the utility room.*

INT. BEDROOM. NIGHT.

RAY *enters the bedroom and tries to open the case but can't. He spots* SABRINA*'s jeans strewn on the floor, half in and half out of the bathroom door. He gets down and creeps towards them. He leans in to get his hand in the jeans pocket, but just as he begins to pull the jeans towards him,* SABRINA*'s blonde hair gets tossed onto the floor also. It is, in fact, a wig. This in turn draws his attention to* SABRINA *herself, standing at the toilet, pissing like a horse, loudly into the bowl.*

SABRINA *is totally naked and, without the wig, completely bald.* RAY *backs out of the bathroom quickly, having not retrieved the keys. The shower is switched on and the door slams shut.*

RAY *can't quite process what he has just seen.*

INT. KITCHEN. NIGHT.

EDDIE *is feeling his way around the kitchen, still blinded by the mace. He opens the fridge door and gropes around in the salad drawer, finding a nice chilled cucumber inside.* EDDIE *places the cucumber on the chopping board and feels for a knife in the kitchen drawer.*

Having selected a sharp knife, EDDIE *goes to cut the cucumber in half, but mistakenly ends up with the large red chilli that* KIM *had been preparing for the food.* EDDIE *chops the red chilli in half and places the pieces on his eyes to cool them, but instead they burn.* EDDIE *opens his mouth to scream . . .*

EXT. PATIO. NIGHT.

We are with a grim-faced GERALD *on the patio. He is solemnly putting bullets into the hand gun. He slides them in slowly, one at a time.*

Inside, through the French windows, and oblivious to everything, a blind EDDIE *staggers and tumbles his way through the living room, causing chaos in his wake. He upturns chairs, falls over, smashes picture frames. He even manages to upturn the umbrella stand, allowing us to complete the story arc of the little dog – showing it is unharmed, as it crawls out and runs off.*

GERALD *misses all this as he finishes loading the gun. He puts the barrel in his mouth and struggles with the decision to pull the trigger. The tension is unbearable. Behind* GERALD, EDDIE *stumbles blindly round the room.*

Finally GERALD *removes the gun from his mouth. He can't go through with it.*

GERALD *gets up and turns to go back inside just as* EDDIE *has made his way out of the other door.*

INT. LIVING ROOM. NIGHT.

GERALD *enters the living room from the patio to see the chaos left by* EDDIE. *He looks around at his precious things, now overturned and broken. He finds a photograph of himself and* SABRINA *smashed in its frame on the floor.*

INT. BEDROOM. NIGHT.

RAY *is trying to pick the lock of the suitcase. Suddenly the bathroom door starts to open and* RAY *quickly hides under the bed. He is staggered to find himself lying next to a fully blown-up sex doll.*

SABRINA *emerges from the bathroom wrapped in a towelling robe. She is replacing her wig as she comes in.*

Under the bed, RAY *can see* SABRINA*'s legs and feet. He looks across at the blow-up doll and is disturbed to find it has a blow-up penis sticking out of the groin area as well as breasts and blonde hair.*

SABRINA *retrieves a fluffy slipper from the side of the bed. She bends down to try to feel for the matching slipper under the bed.*

RAY *has to move backwards, away from* SABRINA*'s hand. He ends up mounting the sex doll, which now stares up at him. The sex doll begins to deflate under* RAY*'s weight, and a gentle hissing sound can be heard as the air escapes from the mouth.*

RAY *puts his hand over the mouth, but now there is a whistling sound as the air escapes through the penis.* RAY *reaches down and grabs the penis with his other hand. There is now a loud farting sound as the air escapes from the back passage.*

SABRINA *thinks she can hear something under the bed as she feels for the slipper.*

INT. DOWNSTAIRS WC. NIGHT.

EDDIE *is splashing cold water on his face and eyes to cool them. He looks up and opens his reddened eyes and sees in the mirror his vision coming back, albeit slightly blurry.*

EDDIE *picks up a pot of cold cream that is on the side and dabs a bit around his puffy eyes. He then examines the other products, sniffing them and looking at the ingredients. He puts a bit of cologne on his cheeks, wrists and behind his ears. Suddenly he hears a song coming from the living room . . .*

INT. BEDROOM. NIGHT.

RAY *is still under the bed with the deflating sex doll. He somehow manages to nudge* SABRINA*'s slipper closer to her reaching hand.*

SABRINA *finds the missing slipper and puts it on. She gets the key out of her jeans pocket and is about to open the case when she becomes aware of the song being played downstairs.*

It is 'Without You' by Harry Nilsson.

SABRINA *stops and listens for a moment. She puts the key in her dressing-gown pocket. A sad smile plays across her lips. She leaves the bedroom.*

RAY *rolls out from under the bed. He jumps up and tries the suitcase, but it is locked. He starts to lift it from the bed, but it is very, very heavy.*

INT. HALLWAY. NIGHT.

EDDIE *emerges from the WC, cautiously looking around. He spots* SABRINA *coming down the stairs and darts quickly back into the toilet and locks the door.*

INT. LIVING ROOM. NIGHT.

GERALD *stands in the living room by the CD player, listening to the loud song. He looks lost.* SABRINA *stands by the door in her dressing gown. She and* GERALD *look at each other for a moment.* SABRINA *goes to speak, but* GERALD *puts his finger to his lips. He holds out his hand.* SABRINA *looks unsure, but* GERALD *looks so broken. She moves towards him.*

INT. BEDROOM. NIGHT.

RAY *drags the suitcase off the bed, where it lands with a thump. He starts to haul it out of the bedroom.*

INT. LIVING ROOM. NIGHT.

GERALD *and* SABRINA *are dancing slowly to the music. He is appreciating one last dance and she doesn't want to begrudge him it.*

INT. STAIRWAY. NIGHT.

RAY *is dragging the heavy suitcase down the stairs. Each step is a massive effort. The door to the WC opens and* EDDIE *emerges. He is confused as to why* RAY *has the suitcase.* RAY *beckons for some help with the heavy case.*

INT. LIVING ROOM. NIGHT.

GERALD *and* SABRINA *are dancing. He lifts her in his arms and lays her down on the sofa.* GERALD *goes to kiss* SABRINA*, but she turns her face away and shakes her head slowly. She is teary-eyed.* GERALD *smiles sadly.*

GERALD *rises, takes a cushion from the sofa and places it over* SABRINA*'s face. With his other hand he reaches for the gun, which he had hidden under the cushion.* GERALD *quickly pushes the barrel into the cushion and shoots* SABRINA *in the face, muffling the sound.*

INT. STAIRWAY. NIGHT.

The suitcase bangs down onto the next step, disguising the sound of the gunshot from the living room.

INT. LIVING ROOM. NIGHT.

GERALD *stands, calmly surveying* SABRINA*'s body. He is wiping his prints from the gun.* GERALD *turns the music off.*

Suddenly the doorbell rings.

INT. STAIRWAY. NIGHT.

RAY *and* EDDIE *freeze when they hear the sound of the doorbell.* RAY *motions that they should take the case back upstairs and* EDDIE *starts to heave it up.*

EXT. FRONT DOOR. NIGHT.

PAUL *stands at the front door. He is a young man who is selling cleaning products, which are stacked in a tray hanging around his neck.*

PAUL *rings the doorbell again.* GERALD *opens the door and regards* PAUL *suspiciously.* PAUL *smiles brightly and hands* GERALD *a card. The card reads: 'Hello, my name is Paul. I am deaf and dumb.'*

GERALD *looks at the card, then at* PAUL. PAUL *smiles and indicates that* GERALD *should turn the card over. The other side reads: 'Do you need any cleaning products today?'*

GERALD *thinks for a moment, turns his head slightly to the living room, then beckons* PAUL *to wait for a moment.*

INT. HALLWAY. NIGHT.

GERALD *goes over to* SABRINA*'s dead body and drags it towards the cupboard next to the door. He opens a cupboard to shove the body inside but is astonished to find* KIM*'s body squashed inside instead. He stands for a moment, looking in disbelief, then closes the cupboard door. He decides to use the cupboard on the other side of the door, and so puts* SABRINA *in there instead.*

EXT. FRONT DOOR. NIGHT.

PAUL *waits patiently, even spotting a bit of dirt, spraying it with polish, and giving it a little clean while he waits.*

INT. LIVING ROOM. NIGHT.

GERALD *hurries back through the living room. He takes his unfinished soup bowl from the dining table and crosses to the sofa, which is soaked with blood. He pours the tomato soup over the blood stain, then hurries back through to the hall.*

INT. HALLWAY. NIGHT.

GERALD *beckons* PAUL *to come in.* PAUL *steps into the house and makes a big show of wiping his feet.*

PAUL *looks around the hallway. He is smiling all the while, happy to be of service.* GERALD *ushers* PAUL *through into the living room.*

INT. LIVING ROOM. NIGHT.

GERALD *shows* PAUL *the soup/blood mess on the sofa and mimes eating soup, then spilling it.* PAUL *mimes his sympathies for the mess, then mimes that he has just the product for him.* PAUL *produces some cleaning products and starts to use them to clean the sofa.*

GERALD *spots some black bin liners in* PAUL*'s tray and picks them out, miming: 'Can I take these?'*

PAUL *smiles and nods that he is pleased for* GERALD *to take the bin liners.* GERALD *exits towards the kitchen with the bin liners.*

PAUL *continues to clean. He bends down to scrub some red marks on the carpet.*

RAY *enters the room. He is looking around for something, then spots a clothes line in* PAUL*'s tray. He reaches to take the clothes line when* PAUL *pops up and smiles at him.* RAY *stares at* PAUL*, caught red-handed stealing from his tray.*

PAUL *hands* RAY *one of his cards, explaining that he is deaf and dumb.* RAY *looks at* PAUL *and indicates that he would like to take the clothes line.* PAUL *holds up seven fingers.* RAY *pulls out his wallet and gives* PAUL *a £10 note.*

PAUL *points to a sign on his try, which states: '2 items for £10'.*

RAY *looks around the tray for a while and selects a small bag of pegs.* PAUL *smiles and bows.* RAY *nods his appreciation and hurries out of the room.* PAUL *continues to clean the sofa.*

PAUL *moves the cushion to clean underneath it. He notices that the cushion has a small hole in the middle of it. He shoves his finger through the hole, before placing the cushion to one side and carrying on with his cleaning.*

As PAUL *scrubs the sofa, we see the outside lights snap on again. The heavy suitcase is being lowered from the upstairs window, down in front of the glass windows at the end of the room. The clothes line is tied to the suitcase. It is lowered down in small increments.*

PAUL *stops the cleaning and watches the suitcase being lowered. It sways slightly from side to side.* PAUL *stands to watch it, smiling.*

GERALD *re-enters from the kitchen. He walks over to* PAUL *without looking back at the window. The suitcase is tugged back up and out of sight.*

PAUL *smiles and points to* GERALD. GERALD *is confused.* PAUL *points outside and tries to mime what he has seen.* GERALD *turns around, but the suitcase is no longer visible.*

GERALD *walks over to the French windows. He walks outside and closes the door behind him.* GERALD *looks around outside, suspiciously. He then slowly looks up . . .*

Suddenly the suitcase falls from above and smashes down on GERALD*'s head.* GERALD *falls to the ground and remains immobile. The suitcase has broken open and its contents have fallen out onto the patio.*

PAUL *watches, open-mouthed. He is rooted to the spot, unsure what to do.*

RAY *and* EDDIE *run into the room. They run past* PAUL, *who points to the scene outside.*

RAY *and* EDDIE *arrive at the French windows in time to see the canvas – now ruined – floating in the jacuzzi end of the pool. To add insult to injury, one of the dogs jumps in and starts tearing it to bits.*

EXT. PATIO. NIGHT.

We see RAY *and* EDDIE*'s reactions. They are screaming 'No!' but we cannot hear them through the glass as they look on helplessly.*

Suddenly two splats of red hit the inside of the glass windows as RAY *and* EDDIE *are both shot in the head. We see them look stunned for a moment and each fall to the ground.*

Once they have fallen we reveal PAUL *standing behind them, holding a gun.*

INT. LIVING ROOM. NIGHT.

PAUL *stands with his gun pointing towards the windows. The dead bodies of* RAY *and* EDDIE *lie on the ground.*

PAUL *places his gun back in a secret compartment in his tray. He walks over to the painting above the fireplace.*

He takes out his mobile phone and dials.

PAUL Hi, it's me. Yeah, it's done. I've got it right here. Yes, it was fine. Not a peep out of anyone.

PAUL *carries the painting out of the room.*

THE END

Episode 3

TOM & GERRI

CAST LIST

Tom – Reece Shearsmith

Gerri – Gemma Arterton

Migg – Steve Pemberton

Stevie – Conleth Hill

EXT. HIGH STREET. DAY 1.

A busy high street in North London. Cars and pedestrians rush by.

Establisher of a flat above a shop. A lone figure stands at the window, looking out onto the road. This is TOM, *a teacher in his late thirties, who wears a shirt and tie.*

We move in on the front door to the flat, next to the shop entrance. Sellotaped next to the buzzer is written in biro 'nine'.

TITLE: *'Tom & Gerri'.*

INT. BEDROOM. DAY.

TOM *stands by the desk in his bedroom, staring out of the window. A pile of children's exercise books sits on his desk waiting to be marked.*

TOM*'s girlfriend,* GERRI, *scurries into the room. She is quirkily dressed and is in her late twenties. She holds up two skirts.*

GERRI Which one of these is the frumpiest?

TOM *sits at his desk.*

TOM Hmmm?

GERRI I'm trying to choose my outfit for this audition. She's meant to be a frumpy spinster.

TOM What you're wearing now is good.

GERRI I haven't changed yet! I meant out of these two.

TOM Oh, the blue one.

GERRI Really? Not this one?

TOM Whichever. What are you auditioning for?

GERRI *D-Day Doris.*

TOM Ha!

GERRI What?

TOM I thought you said *D-Day Doris.*

GERRI I did say *D-Day Doris*. It's a play about land girls.

TOM And would you be Doris?

GERRI Well, you play everyone! You're the husband, the sister, the voice on the radio . . .

TOM Sounds like the kind of shit they tour round old people's homes.

GERRI It is. I haven't worked in five months, Tom. Beggars can't be choosers.

TOM Yeah. Speaking of which, have you seen that tramp down there?

TOM *points out of the window and* **GERRI** *glances out.*

GERRI Where?

TOM There, between the cars down there, look. He's been there ages.

GERRI I can't see anything.

TOM Exactly! What kind of a place is that to be begging if no one can see him?

GERRI He might not be begging. He might be waiting for someone.

TOM Course he's begging, he's got a polystyrene cup in front of him.

GERRI He could be a pavement artist.

TOM Piss artist, more like.

GERRI Yes, well – there but for the grace of God.

TOM What, are you saying I could be a tramp?

GERRI Don't use that word, Tom.

TOM What, tramp?

GERRI Yes, it's insulting! It's like 'gypsy' or 'half-caste'. You can't say it.

TOM Whatever it is – I don't like it. It's weird. Do you want me to walk you to the Tube?

GERRI No, I'll be fine. He's hardly going to attack a spinster called Doris, is he?

GERRI *sits in* **TOM***'s lap.*

GERRI *(cont'd)* How are you getting on with your marking?

TOM Oh fine. I'm giving them all a 'Wow' stamp and every fifth one gets a 'Brilliant'.

TOM *rubber-stamps one of the books.*

GERRI I think you should be really truthful. It matters what you write. I remember teachers' comments.

TOM If I read all these and marked them properly I'd be here all night.

GERRI And what would you rather be doing? Staring out of the window at your little . . .

TOM What?

GERRI Indigent.

TOM You see, you don't know what to call him either, do you? A tramp's a tramp.

GERRI I've got to go.

TOM All right, good luck.

GERRI I won't get it – I haven't learnt it.

TOM Just be confident. That's what I tell my kids at assemblies.

GERRI They're six.

TOM Oh, and do a wee before you go in. I'll walk you to the Tube.

GERRI You don't have to.

TOM I am.

GERRI Ah. I love you, Tom.

She kisses him. He grabs his coat.

TOM I need some milk anyway.

They walk out of the room. We see the doodle he's been doing in his jotter of a sinister-looking bearded man sitting next to a polystyrene cup.

INT. LIVING ROOM. NIGHT.

TOM *is watching TV with the sound down while speaking on his phone.*

TOM Yeah . . . Yeah . . . Oh well, that sounds positive. Like you say, little things lead to big things – as I can demonstrate to you if you come round later . . . OK, not to worry.

The buzzer sounds by the front door and TOM *goes to answer it.*

TOM *(cont'd)* Got to go, I think my pizza's arrived. OK, love you, speak later, bye.

TOM *hangs up and answers the door entry-phone.*

TOM *(cont'd)* Hello?

MIGG *(V.O.)* I've got your wallet.

TOM Pardon?

MIGG *(V.O.)* I think I've got your wallet. I found it outside.

TOM Just a sec.

TOM *checks his pockets and his coat, which is by the door.*

TOM *(cont'd)* OK, come up.

TOM *buzzes the downstairs door open, then opens his flat door. Suddenly fearful, he grabs an umbrella, but it seems a bit lightweight. He quickly puts it down and picks up a* Yellow Pages, *which he tries to roll into a weapon, but it's too thick to roll.*

MIGG *appears in the doorway. He is a tramp, dressed in filthy old clothes, with long, matted, straggly hair and beard. He is of indeterminate age and quite timid and deferential. He hovers in the doorway holding* TOM*'s wallet.*

MIGG Sorry, I just found it.

TOM Where was it?

MIGG By the shops.

MIGG *hands over the wallet to* TOM. TOM *checks inside.*

TOM Oh . . . I didn't even know I'd lost it.

MIGG It's all there, I didn't take anything.

TOM No, I was just . . . I have some dry cleaning in and . . . You know what it's like if you can't find your ticket.

TOM *smiles at* MIGG.

MIGG I don't do much dry cleaning.

TOM *laughs.*

TOM No.

An awkward silence.

TOM *(cont'd)* Well, look, thank you very much and I'd like to give you something . . .

TOM *opens his wallet.*

MIGG You don't have to . . .

TOM No, I'd like to . . . Oh, I've only got twenties . . . Erm – you haven't got any change, have you?

MIGG I've got a bit in my cup.

MIGG *holds up his polystyrene cup with a few coppers in it.* TOM *peers inside.*

TOM No, that won't be enough. Erm . . . Here you go, look. I'm going to give you two twenties . . .

TOM *hands over two £20 notes.*

MIGG No, no, that's too much.

TOM Yeah, it is. Ideally, I'd have given you 30 but . . . You have saved me a lot of hassle, you know, cancelling cards and – well, you know. So thanks.

MIGG Migg.

TOM Sorry?

MIGG My name is Migg.

TOM Mick?

MIGG No, Migg.

TOM Ah, Migg. Like pig.

MIGG Two 'g's.

TOM Steady on, I've already given you two twenties!

MIGG Do you want it back?

TOM No, it was a joke about 'g's being like grands. Anyway, I need to shut this door because . . . it's freezing outside.

MIGG Yeah, I know.

TOM Of course you do. Well. Thanks.

TOM *slowly closes the door in* MIGG*'s face. He puts his wallet in his pocket, then looks back at the door.* TOM *can see* MIGG*'s shadow in the crack under the door.* TOM *carefully puts the chain on the door, trying not to make a noise.*

TOM *looks under the door again and the shadow moves away.*

INT. LIVING ROOM. NIGHT.

TOM *sits on the sofa later that night, still trying to mark the homework. There is a knock at the door.* TOM *frowns, then looks at his watch. He goes over to the door and looks through the spyhole. There he sees* MIGG, *looking sinister in the fisheye lens.*

TOM Hello?

MIGG *(V.O.)* Hi, Tom, it's Migg.

TOM Sorry? Who is it?

MIGG *(V.O.)* Migg. I found your wallet.

TOM What, again?

MIGG *(V.O.)* No, before. Can I come in?

TOM Oh, erm . . . I've just come out of the shower.

MIGG *(V.O.)* I brought you a present.

TOM Oh – just a minute!

TOM *runs to the bathroom and wets his hair. Grabbing a towel on the way out, he puts it round his neck. He kicks off his shoes and opens the door to find* MIGG *holding a cheap bottle of whisky.*

TOM *(cont'd)* How did you get in?

MIGG The door was open . . . Here, I used the money you gave me.

MIGG *offers up the bottle.* TOM *sees that it's only three-quarters full.*

MIGG *(cont'd)* I did have a little nip, sorry. It's bitter out there tonight.

TOM Is it?

MIGG Well, I just wanted to say thanks.

TOM What for? I haven't done anything.

MIGG It's just nice to talk to a fellow human. Makes me feel like I exist. See you, then . . .

MIGG *looks down and slowly starts to turn.*

TOM Do you want to come in and have a quick drink?

MIGG Sorry?

TOM I get the impression you'd like a drink. One for the road! One.

MIGG Erm . . . I suppose so.

MIGG *steps into the flat.*

MIGG *(cont'd)* Should I take my shoes off?

TOM *looks down at* MIGG*'s dirty, broken-down boots.*

TOM If you don't mind . . .

MIGG It's been a while.

MIGG *pulls off one boot to reveal a foot wrapped in even dirtier bandages, covered in dried pus and blood, with black toenails protruding from the end.*

TOM Actually . . . fuck it. Keep them on. It's fine.

MIGG *replaces the boot and* TOM *moves inside.*

TOM *(cont'd)* Right, I'll get some glasses, shall I?

TOM *goes into the kitchen and pours two glasses of whisky, cursing himself for getting into this situation. He looks at the whisky and sniffs it suspiciously.*

TOM *(cont'd)* I'm afraid I haven't got any ice!

MIGG *(V.O.)* It's all right, I'm cold enough.

TOM *(to himself)* Yes, so you keep saying.

TOM *brings the whiskies back into the living area.* MIGG *is sitting on the sofa.* MIGG *sees* TOM *wince.*

MIGG Sorry, should I not sit in this chair? Shall I move to that one?

MIGG *makes to get up and change chairs.*

TOM No, no. You've done it now. Best to just . . . contain it.

TOM *hands the whisky over to* MIGG.

TOM *(cont'd)* There you go. Cheers.

MIGG Cheers.

They sip their whisky. MIGG *picks up one of the exercise books* TOM *was marking.*

MIGG *(cont'd)* Are you doing your homework?

TOM Yes – marking. Ancient Egypt's come round again.

MIGG How old are the kids?

TOM Year 2. Spoilt little brats already, most of them. We've got an assembly tomorrow, so I can't stay up too long . . .

MIGG No. Must be a rewarding job.

TOM It's all right. It's not really what I want to do.

MIGG What do you want to do?

TOM I'm writing a novel actually.

MIGG Really? What about?

TOM Oh, it's a bit like an English Charles Bukowski – you won't have heard of him.

MIGG I know Charles.

TOM Oh, which one have you read?

MIGG No, I mean I knew him. I met him, in New York.

TOM No! Really? He was a . . . one of you, for a while.

MIGG I know. He took a bit of a shine to me. I spent a couple of weeks with him while he was writing his last book . . .

TOM *Pulp*!

MIGG That's the one. I've never actually read it.

TOM I've got a copy of it here.

TOM *races to his bookshelf to grab a copy of Pulp.*

TOM *(cont'd)* Wow. So what was he like?

MIGG C.B.? Oh, he was an amazing man. He told me such stories . . .

MIGG *leans forward and fills their glasses.*

MIGG *(cont'd)* Such stories . . .

INT. LIVING ROOM. DAY.

TOM *is fast asleep, slumped on the sofa, still dressed. On the coffee table is the now-empty whisky bottle, and several other empty bottles and cans. A makeshift ashtray has been made from a tea saucer. Full of butts. The front door slams, waking* TOM *with a start.*

GERRI *(V.O.)* Tom?

GERRI *comes into the living room and surveys the scene.*

GERRI *(cont'd)* What are you doing here? Shouldn't you be at work?

TOM What time is it?

TOM *reaches out to look at his phone.*

GERRI Twenty past ten. I thought you had an assembly?

TOM Oh shit – 12 missed calls.

GERRI What have you been doing?

TOM It was Migg.

GERRI Who?

TOM The guy across the road.

GERRI What, the tramp?

TOM Don't call him that. He met Charles Bukowski.

GERRI He's been in the flat?

TOM He's still here, I think. Migg?

GERRI Don't! I can't believe this. You invite a tramp in off the street and get pissed with him?

TOM It wasn't like that. He found my wallet. He was being kind. It's good, anyway, he's given me loads of ideas for the novel. You wait 'til you meet him.

GERRI I don't want to meet him. Get rid of him. And you better ring the school and make your apologies. You need that job – you're not a writer yet.

TOM At least I've got a job, D-J Doris.

GERRI Thank you very much. Anyway, I just came round to tell you that I've been offered the job, so piss off, Tom. And it's 'D-DAY' Doris actually.

GERRI *storms out.*

TOM Gerri!

The front door slams. MIGG *appears from the bathroom. He has* TOM*'s dressing gown on and is towelling his hair dry.*

MIGG Morning, Tom. I hope you don't mind – I had a bath.

TOM Er, no, that's fine.

MIGG I left the water in if you want to . . .

TOM *peers into the bathroom and sees that the bath water is chocolate brown, like a swamp with bits floating in it.*

TOM Thanks, but . . . I'm late for work. I'd better get going . . .

TOM *gathers his keys and wallet from the table.*

MIGG I'm not being funny, Tom, but is that wise? It's one thing to miss your assembly, but I think you'll make it worse, turning up stinking of booze. I'd phone in sick if I were you.

TOM *hesitates.*

TOM Yeah. I'll tell them I'll go in for the afternoon.

MIGG Who's Gerry? Is he your flatmate?

TOM It's my girlfriend. Gerri with an 'i'.

MIGG Ah – 'the mad actress'.

TOM Eh?

MIGG That's what you were calling her last night.

TOM Oh God. I don't remember.

MIGG Let me make you some breakfast. I need four eggs and some liver.

MIGG *goes off to the kitchen.* TOM *slumps back down on the sofa.*

TOM Listen, Migg, I think maybe you should be making a move. I've got a lot of marking to do and Gerri's coming back later, so . . .

MIGG *emerges from the kitchen.*

MIGG That's fine, Tom, but – I haven't got any clothes.

TOM What?

MIGG You put them all in a bin bag last night and threw them out.

TOM Did I?

MIGG Yeah. You said you'd give me some of your clothes so I didn't look like such an incident.

TOM I meant 'indigent'. I'll sort some stuff out for you . . .

MIGG No rush. Sit down. I'll do that breakfast, shall I?

TOM Yes. Sorry. Thanks.

MIGG *smiles and goes back into the kitchen and starts whistling.* TOM *puts his head in his hands.*

INT. LIVING ROOM. NIGHT.

TOM *and* MIGG *are playing the board game Risk. The box and rules are strewn across the floor.* MIGG *is wearing some of* TOM*'s old clothes – all slightly too small for him. He seems bright and alert.* TOM *wears yesterday's clothes and looks exhausted. Lager cans, a half-empty wine bottle and a mound of cigarette butts fill the rest of the table.*

MIGG Right. Three on Kamchatka.

TOM What? Where the hell's Kamchatka?

MIGG There. I can move my infantry over from Alaska.

TOM How?

MIGG There's a sea-lane across the Pacific.

TOM Oh Jesus Christ. We've been playing this for six hours and I still don't know the rules.

TOM *throws his dice.*

MIGG Unlucky. Well, that means I control Asia, so I get seven bonus armies, plus five for North America, two for South America and three for Africa.

TOM So what do I own now?

MIGG Erm . . . New Guinea and Iceland.

TOM OK, you know what? You win.

MIGG Don't you want to see it through to the end?

TOM It doesn't end! It never ends!

MIGG Do you want to play Monopoly?

TOM No! I'm sorry, I just want to have a bath, have some food and get ready for school tomorrow.

MIGG It's Saturday tomorrow.

TOM Oh piss off. You even win the days!

They laugh. MIGG *pours* TOM *some more wine.* TOM *picks up his mobile phone and checks it.*

TOM *(cont'd)* I wish Gerri would phone.

TOM *presses the button on the landline answerphone.*

ANSAPHONE You have no messages.

MIGG I'd like to meet this Gerri.

TOM Yeah. You'd like her.

MIGG Tom and Gerri.

TOM *(laughs)* Yeah. And her last boyfriend was called Ben.

MIGG I don't get it.

TOM Ice cream. Never mind. I might go and get some actually, I'm a bit peckish. Do you want anything?

MIGG Couple of bottles of red wouldn't go amiss. Oh, and we're running out of cigarettes . . .

TOM OK, see you in a minute.

MIGG Thanks, Tom. I really appreciate it.

TOM *smiles and leaves.* MIGG *lights up a cigarette and walks around the flat. The phone rings and goes to answerphone. As the message kicks in,* MIGG *walks over to the bureau by the front door. Tries on a pair of* TOM*'s shoes. He looks at himself in the mirror, then searches through the drawers for anything of interest. He picks out some keys and pockets them. All the while the following is heard on the answerphone . . .*

TOM *(V.O.)* Hi, this is Tom, can't get to the phone, please leave a message.

STEVIE *(V.O.)* Hi, Tom, it's Stevie. Just checking to see you're OK. Jaqui said you'd phoned in sick. Shame you missed the assembly; they did you proud, except instead of saying 'Tutankhamun', Dylan said 'Tooting Common', which got a good laugh, and little Mandy Smith had to run out for a wee during 'Walking on Sunshine'. Everyone sends their love. I hope you're OK. I know it's not been easy. Call me, will you? Hope to see you Monday. Take care, bye.

MIGG *presses the button on the answerphone.*

ANSAPHONE Play message.

STEVIE *(V.O.)* Hi, Tom . . .

MIGG *presses another button.*

ANSAPHONE Message deleted. You have no messages.

MIGG *sits down on the sofa and picks up* TOM*'s mobile phone. He pushes it deep down into the crack of the sofa.*

MIGG *then takes up a photo of* TOM *and* GERRI. TOM *is wearing the same clothes in the photo that* MIGG *now wears.* MIGG *smiles.*

INT. BEDROOM. DAY.

One week later. TOM *sits in bed reading a Bukowski poetry book. He has not shaved for a week. He looks tired and bleary-eyed. A half-drunk bottle of wine by his bed. The bedroom door opens and* GERRI *comes in. She looks at* TOM *with concern and puzzlement.* TOM *stares, then goes back to his book.*

TOM Well, look who it is. D-Day Doris finally emerges from the bomb shelter.

GERRI It's not called that any more actually, Tom. Ollie's changed the title.

TOM To what?

GERRI *Lucy Land Girl.*

TOM Oh, that's much stronger. Close the door, please, it's freezing.

GERRI *closes the door.*

GERRI Is it true?

TOM What?

GERRI Stevie said you've resigned from your job.

TOM Yes, it was a waste of time. I just found it childish.

GERRI You're a primary school teacher.

TOM Was. I'm a writer now. I create things.

GERRI Can I please open a window? It stinks of pumps.

TOM Shoe pumps or bottom pumps.

GERRI Both.

GERRI *goes to open the bedroom window.*

TOM Look, you can't just turn up here after a week and start running my life for me.

GERRI I told you, I've been rehearsing in Portsmouth all week.

TOM No, you didn't.

GERRI Tom, I left half a dozen messages.

TOM I lost my phone.

GERRI That's not my fault, is it! Look, I've spoken to Stevie and he says if you go in and speak to Mr Patterson . . .

TOM I don't want to speak to Mr Patterson. I don't want to work, OK? Migg's gone down to the dole office to get the signing-on forms and . . .

GERRI Migg? You mean the tramp?

TOM He's not a tramp.

GERRI He isn't now, he's got himself a nice little flat now. He's using you, Tom!

TOM Oh, are you jealous 'cos someone's nicked your idea?

GERRI What's that supposed to mean?

TOM 'Oh, I'm doing pub theatre, oh, I'm doing *Lucy Land Girl*, I haven't got much money this week, can I stay over at yours? Can I borrow 50 quid . . .?'

GERRI*'s eyes fill with tears.*

GERRI Nice.

GERRI *leaves the room.* **TOM** *sighs. He punches the pillow.*

INT. LIVING ROOM. DAY.

Another week later. **MIGG** *sits at the coffee table laying out a Scrabble board.* **TOM** *emerges from his room looking rougher than ever. He has matted hair and a two-week beard. He crosses to the answerphone and presses the button.*

ANSAPHONE You have no messages.

TOM Sorry, what was that?

ANSAPHONE You have no messages.

TOM No post either. Are they on strike, do you think?

ANSAPHONE You have no messages.

TOM I'm waiting for my giro to come in, I'm running out of money. Oh, have I any messages?

ANSAPHONE You have no messages.

TOM I thought not.

MIGG *shakes the Scrabble bag without even looking up and* **TOM** *gravitates towards the sofa like Pavlov's dog. He sits and pulls out some letters and they start to play.*

TOM *(cont'd)* It's my birthday today.

MIGG Happy birthday.

TOM Didn't get a single card. Even my family forgot. I can't believe it. My grandma normally sends one recorded delivery three weeks in advance! Could have done with that tenner.

MIGG Maybe it's in the second post.

TOM Everyone's forgotten about me. I've dropped out of society. Pot, five.

TOM *takes more tiles.*

MIGG Have a beer.

TOM I don't want one.

MIGG *lays down his word.*

MIGG Why don't you do the washing-up?

TOM I beg your pardon?

MIGG If you're so bored. It's been sitting there for two or three days.

TOM Whose flat is this?

MIGG I'm only saying . . .

TOM Well, don't say! 'Do the washing-up!'

MIGG Twenty-nine.

TOM I do it anyway.

MIGG With respect, Tom, you don't. Putting it in some warm water and leaving it does not constitute 'doing the washing-up'.

TOM It has to soak.

MIGG Not for a fortnight. At some stage you should really take the things out of the mucky, teabag-stained water and put them on the draining board. That way – and there's no such word as that – that way you don't have to start using your collection of Easter-egg mugs from years back simply because there are no clean cups left.

TOM Well, why don't you do it then? Or are you still using your little polystyrene tramp cup?

MIGG There's no need for that.

TOM There's every need. You stank when you first came in here! You stank like a dirty bag of wet washing. How much washing-up did you do then, Nanette fucking Newman?

MIGG Don't judge me, Tom. You have no right to judge me.

MIGG *stares at* TOM. *A long pause.* TOM *looks at the board.*

TOM 'La'? What's 'la'?

MIGG A note to follow 'so'.

TOM Fuck this.

TOM *tips the Scrabble board over and goes back to his room.*

MIGG *reaches under the sofa cushion and produces some opened birthday cards. He takes the cash from the top one and heads for the door.*

INT. LIVING ROOM. DAY.

Ten days later. TOM *sits on the sofa wrapped in a duvet, watching TV. The theme tune to* This Morning *blares out. He can barely keep his eyes open. The flat is a total mess now, with plates, takeaway packages and bottles dotted around. The buzzer sounds.* TOM *turns off the TV and shuffles over to the entry-phone, still in the sleeping bag.*

TOM Hello?

STEVIE *(V.O.)* Avon calling! Can you buzz me in?

TOM *buzzes* STEVIE *in and opens the door.* STEVIE *enters, a middle-aged, slightly camp man, also a teacher. He is visibly shocked by* TOM*'s appearance, but quickly covers it up.*

STEVIE *(cont'd)* Tom? What's that – designer stubble?

TOM What do you want, Stevie? It's not a good time.

STEVIE I know it's not. I know it's not. That's why I come bearing Krispy Kremes, and you and I is gonna have a chat. Any clean plates?

TOM Dunno, have a look.

STEVIE *picks his way gingerly through the mess to find plates.*

STEVIE Ooh, *Life of Grime* – here we are.

STEVIE *plates up the doughnuts.*

STEVIE *(cont'd)* So how are you, Tom? Haven't seen you for weeks. Are you bearing up?

TOM I'm all right. Just taking a bit of time for myself. Get off that treadmill.

STEVIE Oh, don't talk about treadmills. I've just renewed my gym membership and I've still never been. Now I'm not being nosey – brackets 'am' – but how are you getting on for money? Because I thought you were still paying off your student debt?

TOM I'm trying not to think about it.

STEVIE Well, a few of us at the school had a whip-round. Not everyone took part – naming no names, Linda Price. And it was up to me to get you something. So I thought, what would he rather have, cash . . . or Body Shop vouchers? So, I got you . . .

STEVIE *pulls out an envelope.*

TOM Cash?

STEVIE No. Body Shop vouchers. I'll just leave them there. Don't lose it among the . . . debris.

TOM Oh.

STEVIE I'm getting the feeling now you'd rather have had the cash.

TOM No, it's all right. I'll be fine once my benefits start coming through. In fact, Migg says I'll probably be better off.

STEVIE Migg? Who's 'Migg'?

TOM Oh, he's just a friend.

STEVIE Oh, I've never heard of him. 'Mystic Migg'. What are your plans for tonight?

TOM Nothing.

STEVIE In that case, why don't you jump in the shower and I'll take us to Wagamama's. We'll get chicken katsu curry and fuck the diet. Me, not you. What do you say?

TOM I can't really, Stevie.

STEVIE It's my treat.

TOM No, I . . . I just don't want to.

TOM *gets up and walks over to the front door and opens it.*

STEVIE Well – I can see you're busy.

STEVIE *gets up and goes to the door and stops.*

STEVIE *(cont'd)* Promise me you'll phone if you want to chat and that.

TOM OK. Bye.

STEVIE Don't forget about those Body Shop vouchers. They might come in handy.

STEVIE *leaves and* TOM *returns to the sofa. As he slumps back down we see* MIGG *has appeared and is now also sitting on the sofa. He cracks open a can of lager, and hands it over to* TOM.

INT. BATHROOM. NIGHT.

Three weeks later. A hand reaches over to the bath taps and starts to fill the bath. The hand wipes the condensation from the mirror. It is TOM, *looking more haggard than ever, almost full beard and greasy, unkempt hair. He hears a muffled voice from the other room over the sound of the taps and shuffles into the living room.*

INT. LIVING ROOM. NIGHT.

TOM *enters the living room, but there is nobody there.*

TOM Migg? Gerri?

He looks around and sees the red answerphone light is blinking. He presses the button.

ANSAPHONE You have one message.

TOM *recoils slightly. He can't believe it. He presses the button again.*

ANSAPHONE *(cont'd)* You have one message.

TOM *plays the message.*

MALE VOICE Hello, Mr Farish, this is Brian from Eastway Electricity. Just to remind you that as your bill for £126.15 is still outstanding and as you haven't replied to any of our messages, we will have to terminate your supply at 1800 hours toda–

The flat is suddenly plunged into darkness and the machine stops playing. The only light comes from the streetlights outside. **TOM** *sinks to the ground and puts his head in his hands. The front door opens. It is* **MIGG**. *He is now shaved and well dressed in* **TOM**'s *best clothes. He tries the light switch but nothing happens.*

MIGG Shit, what's going on here? Have we blown a fuse?

TOM We've been cut off.

MIGG Oh, come on, Tom! Have you not paid the bill or something?

MIGG *goes over to the coffee table and lights the candles there and on the mantelpiece with his cigarette lighter. He lights up a cigarette and gives it to* **TOM**.

TOM Where's my money, Migg? You said my giro would come . . .

MIGG It will come, it just takes a while to process. Maybe . . . maybe I should take over the rent or the lease or something. Just 'til your housing benefit comes through.

TOM How . . .?

MIGG I started a new job today. A new beginning.

TOM What are you doing?

MIGG Working with kids on an outreach programme. It's going to be so rewarding. Here, take this . . .

MIGG *takes out his wallet and offers* **TOM** *a £20 note.*

TOM It's too much . . .

MIGG I'd like you to have it. You've done so much for me.

TOM *takes the money.*

MIGG *(cont'd)* Ah, are you running me a bath. That's very thoughtful. Thanks, Tom.

MIGG *closes the bathroom door. At the same moment, the front door opens and* **GERRI** *comes in.*

GERRI Tom? What are you doing sitting in the dark?

GERRI *tries to turn on the lights. Nothing happens.*

TOM We've been cut off. I'm sorry, Gerri. I miss you so much – everything is going wrong.

GERRI You can't carry on like this, Tom.

TOM I know. Please don't leave me.

GERRI I'm not going anywhere. You need to sort your head out. You're just in a slump.

TOM I know – Migg says I'll be all right once my benefits come through. Then I can get on with my writing.

GERRI Tom . . .

TOM Maybe I can write a play for you to be in. Migg says . . .

GERRI Tom! There is no Migg.

TOM What?

GERRI Look around you. There's nobody else here. Where are his things?

TOM I threw them away.

GERRI Tom, Migg doesn't exist. It's just you. You've invented him to cope with what's been happening.

TOM No, I haven't.

GERRI Where is he, then? Show him to me.

TOM He's here – in the bathroom.

TOM *heads for the bathroom.*

INT. BATHROOM. NIGHT.

TOM *opens the door, but there is no one there.* GERRI *appears behind him.*

GERRI See? Look, Tom, you've been depressed for a long, long time. You just wanted to give yourself an excuse to leave your job, start drinking, drop out of this life you hated.

TOM I don't . . .

GERRI You're not Charles Bukowski. You're just a primary school teacher who had a nervous breakdown.

TOM *takes this in. It becomes clear –* GERRI *is right.* TOM *sits on the edge of the bath.*

GERRI *(cont'd)* I've got to go, I've got to put my hair in a bun for *D-Day Doris*.

TOM I thought it was *Lucy Land Girl*?

GERRI No, we changed it back. We'll get through this, Tom. You just have to be strong.

TOM But Migg . . .

GERRI No. Get this Migg out of your head – once and for all. Love you.

GERRI *kisses* TOM, *then leaves the bathroom. When she closes the door we see* MIGG *standing there. He looks down at* TOM.

MIGG Everything all right, Tom?

TOM *looks up at* MIGG *with a steely look in his eye.*

INT. LIVING ROOM. DAY.

Two days later. TOM*'s flat appears much brighter and is now very tidy.* GERRI *is in the kitchen area making two coffees, but we don't see who she's talking to.*

GERRI And instead of saying, 'Bombs, barrage balloons and blackouts,' I came out with, 'Bombs, blackout balloons and barrages.' I don't know where it came from. Tim looked at me and I could tell he was going to go. Luckily most of the audience were asleep or deaf, so they didn't clock it.

She walks over with the coffees to the sitting area.

GERRI *(cont'd)* Well, this is a transformation, isn't it? You look like a new man.

She places the coffee down in front of TOM, *who is now smartly dressed once more and clean shaven but still looks a little subdued.*

TOM Well, I've got you to thank for that. I don't know what I'd do without you.

GERRI *kisses him on the forehead and* TOM *smiles. The buzzer sounds.*

GERRI Who's that?

TOM *slowly moves to the door and picks up the entry-phone.*

TOM Hello?

STEVIE *(V.O.)* Hi, it's Stevie!

TOM Come up!

TOM *turns and smiles at* GERRI.

TOM *(cont'd)* It's Stevie.

GERRI I'll put the kettle on.

GERRI *heads towards the kitchen as* TOM *opens the door and* STEVIE *enters.*

STEVIE Hello, stranger! I was just doing a Costa run for my builders and thought I'd skooch by. You're looking well!

TOM I'm feeling a lot better, thanks.

STEVIE That Worzel Gummidge look was doing you no favours! Well, we're all missing you still. They've had that awful supply teacher in – you know, the one who can't say her 's's.

TOM 'Thit up thwaight!'

STEVIE That's the one. We're hoping that you might reconsider. I'm sure Patterson'd take you.

TOM I just need a bit more time . . .

STEVIE I know you've been through a lot and it hasn't been easy, but it might do you some good to get back to work!

TOM That's what Gerri's been telling me.

STEVIE Aww.

TOM Come in, anyway. I'll tell her you're here – Gerri?

TOM *moves into the room.* STEVIE *looks concerned.*

TOM *(cont'd)* Gerri? Where's she gone? Stevie's here!

STEVIE Tom.

TOM She was just here a second ago.

STEVIE Gerri died, Tom. Remember? In the car accident?

TOM *looks bewildered.*

TOM But I was only talking to her a second ago.

STEVIE We all said you'd come back to work too soon. We know how much you loved her. But it's time to let her go now.

TOM But she saved me. She saved me from Migg.

STEVIE I'll get you a tablet.

STEVIE *goes into the bathroom. Slowly he retreats back out in horror.*

STEVIE *(cont'd)* Tom . . . oh my God – what have you done?

TOM *joins* STEVIE *by the bathroom door and peers inside. We see* MIGG*'s body floating under the cloudy bathwater – dead.* TOM *smiles.*

TOM Oh, that's just Migg. He's not real. Come and have a coffee. Gerri's just putting the kettle on . . .

THE END

Episode 4

LAST GASP

CAST LIST

GRAHAM – Steve Pemberton

JAN – Sophie Thompson

TAMSIN – Lucy Hutchinson

FRANKIE J. PARSONS – David Bedella

SALLY – Tamsin Greig

SI – Adam Deacon

EXT. CUL-DE-SAC. DAY.

A quiet suburban cul-de-sac in Middle England.

Establisher of the Vickers' house, a nicely presented semi in the middle of the cul-de-sac. We push in on the door, which has a 'Happy Birthday' banner across the top.

A ceramic tile by the door shows the number '9'.

TITLE: *'Last Gasp'.*

INT. LIVING ROOM. DAY.

Camcorder footage. JAN *doesn't know the camcorder is on, so we see lots of floor, feet and furniture. Occasional flashes of* JAN*'s husband,* GRAHAM, *who is attempting to blow up a balloon.*

The house is neat and tidy, with modest but tasteful furnishings. There are sliding doors, which open onto a dining room, which has been converted into a downstairs bedroom for JAN *and* GRAHAM*'s nine-year-old daughter* TAMSIN, *who is seriously ill with an unspecified disease.*

JAN *(V.O.)* How do you put it on?

GRAHAM It is on.

JAN *(V.O.)* No, I mean how do you record?

GRAHAM Just press the button.

JAN *(V.O.)* This one?

GRAHAM Yeah.

JAN *(V.O.)* Why's the light on?

GRAHAM It's in standby.

JAN *(V.O.)* All right. Tam . . .

INT. TAMSIN'S ROOM. DAY.

JAN *carries the camcorder into* TAMSIN*'s room.* TAMSIN *is sitting up in bed, an oxygen pipe attached to her nose. A heart-shaped helium balloon is tied to her bed.*

JAN *(V.O.)* Tamsin, when I say 'go' I want you to explain what day it is and who's coming, OK, love?

TAMSIN Why?

JAN *(V.O.)* So we have a record of it. You don't want to forget it, do you? Hang on, let me find the button . . . Ready? And . . . go!

The camcorder is switched off.

INT. TAMSIN'S ROOM. DAY.

The camcorder is switched back on again.

JAN *(V.O.)* Well done. Do you want to watch it back?

TAMSIN No thanks.

JAN All right, we'll watch it later. He'll be here in a minute.

JAN *places the camcorder on a table.*

INT. LIVING ROOM. DAY.

GRAHAM *is trying to blow up a balloon as* JAN *comes in and tidies up.*

GRAHAM I can't bloody do it. Where's the pumper?

JAN What do you mean, you can't do it?

GRAHAM It's these stupid long ones . . .

JAN Stretch them.

GRAHAM Just get me the pumper.

JAN I told you to do them last night.

The doorbell sounds.

JAN *(cont'd)* He's here! Oh my God, Graham . . .

GRAHAM Calm down, he's only flesh and blood.

JAN I know, but in our house! Oh my God . . .

GRAHAM His turds are brown, aren't they?

JAN Graham!

GRAHAM Well . . .

GRAHAM *heads down the hall.* JAN *dashes into* TAMSIN*'s room.*

JAN He's here, Tam. Ooooohhhhh!

JAN *checks her hair in the mirror. Down the corridor we see* GRAHAM *admitting the guests and coming back into the living room.*

GRAHAM Come in, come in. She's in here.

GRAHAM *shows* FRANKIE *into the living room.* FRANKIE J. PARSONS *is a handsome popstar in his forties. Expensively dressed but not ostentatiously so, he has an easy charm and effortless charisma.*

FRANKIE *is accompanied by his driver/assistant* SI *and charity worker* SALLY.

GRAHAM *(cont'd)* You found us all right, then?

FRANKIE Yeah, no problem. Well, I say no problem, I was asleep for most of it . . .

Everyone laughs sycophantically.

GRAHAM This is my wife Jan.

FRANKIE *shakes hands with* JAN.

FRANKIE Hi, Frankie Parsons.

JAN Yes, I know!

GRAHAM She's a big fan of yours.

JAN Graham!

FRANKIE Lovely to meet you. You've got beautiful eyes.

JAN Oh . . . !

JAN *shakes her head and blushes.*

FRANKIE You know Sally from the Wishmaker charity, don't you?

SALLY Yes, we've spoken on the phone, hi! Gosh, what a lovely house!

JAN Thanks. It's not much, compared to what you must be used to, but . . .

FRANKIE And this is Jasmine through here, is it?

SALLY Tamsin.

FRANKIE Tamsin, that's it . . .

FRANKIE *heads into* TAMSIN*'s room.*

INT. TAMSIN'S ROOM. DAY.

FRANKIE *enters and smiles at* TAMSIN. JAN *hurries in after him.*

FRANKIE Hello, Tamsin! Happy birthday! You're nine today, are you?

JAN Oh, one second, I just want to video this, do you mind?

JAN *picks up the camcorder and we cut to camcorder footage once more:*

FRANKIE No, not at all. I'd like to get a copy myself actually. I'm excited to meet this brave little girl who I've heard so much about. Do you want me to step out and come back in again?

JAN Ooh yes.

FRANKIE *steps out of the room, then reappears.*

FRANKIE Ready? Hey . . . !

The camcorder is turned off.

INT. TAMSIN'S ROOM. DAY.

The camcorder is turned back on again. We can now see FRANKIE *sitting on* TAMSIN*'s bed. He is trying to blow up a purple balloon. He looks red-faced, like he's been blowing too hard.*

JAN *(V.O.)* . . . No need for you to do that. I'll go and get you the pumper.

JAN *hurries out.*

FRANKIE It's OK, I've got it . . . *(to* TAMSIN*)* Too many cigarettes!

FRANKIE *winks at* TAMSIN.

TAMSIN Are you OK?

FRANKIE *nods as he continues to blow, putting more and more effort into it. We can hear the conversation in the living room.*

GRAHAM *(V.O.)* So would we be able to get parking passes as well?

SALLY *(V.O.)* Er, not sure about that actually, let me . . .

GRAHAM *(V.O.)* 'Cause it's an absolute bugger to park round there and with Tamsin's chair . . .

SALLY *(V.O.)* Yes, absolutely . . .

JAN *(V.O.)* Where's that pumper, Graham?

GRAHAM *(V.O.)* I dunno, I couldn't find it.

JAN *(V.O.)* I told him to do them last night.

FRANKIE *has blown the balloon almost to its full size. He doesn't look well.*

FRANKIE Nearly done. One more push . . .

FRANKIE *blows one last breath into the balloon, but the effort is too much and he slumps forward.* TAMSIN *takes the balloon from* FRANKIE*'s hand.*

TAMSIN Daddy!

FRANKIE *falls from the bed onto the floor, landing with a heavy thump.* GRAHAM *and* SALLY *run in, followed by* SI *and* JAN.

GRAHAM What happened?

TAMSIN He fell!

SI Mr Parsons! Mr Parsons!

SALLY Should we get a cold compress?

GRAHAM Let Jan look at him, she's a nurse.

JAN What did he do?

SI He's not breathing. Mr Parsons!

SALLY Oh Christ, erm . . .

JAN I'll try CPR.

JAN *bends down with* SI. TAMSIN *is left with the balloon.*

SI Give her some space! Give her some space!

GRAHAM *and* SALLY *move back, knocking the camera over and off.*

INT. LIVING ROOM. DAY.

We are no longer in camcorder mode. JAN *and* SALLY *sit on the sofa.* JAN *is weepy;* SALLY *rubs her back.* GRAHAM *brings in a tray of teas.*

TAMSIN *is now in a wheelchair at the back of the room, still on oxygen, still holding the inflated purple balloon.*

GRAHAM Here. Do you have sugar, Sally?

SALLY No. Yes, actually! Do you have sweeteners?

GRAHAM Jan, do we have sweeteners?

JAN In the drawer.

GRAHAM Which . . .?

JAN The one with the hoover bags.

GRAHAM Sorry, I still don't . . .

JAN I'll get them!

JAN *storms out.*

GRAHAM She's upset. She wanted him to sign her CDs.

SALLY We have some autographs on file, we can arrange to have one sent.

GRAHAM Thanks. Be worth a few bob now, I should think.

SALLY *smiles.* SI *enters the room.*

SI Mr Fourboys is on his way. He says not to touch anything until he gets here.

SALLY Right. *(To* GRAHAM*)* Mr Fourboys is Frankie's manager. Was Frankie's manager . . .

JAN *returns with the sweeteners.*

JAN Here. They're packet ones, I'm afraid.

GRAHAM She nicked them off a train.

JAN Graham!

GRAHAM Well, it hardly matters now, does it? We've got a world-famous dead popstar in our Tamsin's bedroom, no one's going to mind about a few stolen Canderels!

Silence. TAMSIN *sobs quietly.* JAN *goes to comfort her.* SALLY *turns to* SI, *who is standing outside the bedroom door.*

SALLY Are you sure we shouldn't call 999?

SI Mr Fourboys said to wait. He said the place will be crawling with pigs if we do that.

SALLY Oh, yes, I suppose so. You mean, police?

SI Nah, the press, man. They find out Mr Parsons died, and in this way? They'll be like vultures.

GRAHAM Must be awful, doing that job. You're either a pig or a vulture, aren't you? You're never . . . a horse or a creature with dignity.

JAN It's horrible.

SALLY I suppose they'll all want to get the first picture.

GRAHAM Just another job to them, isn't it? Look what they did to Diana.

JAN And Kate!

GRAHAM Yes. Her boobs are out there now. She can't take them back.

SI We've got to protect Frankie's legacy.

SALLY Absolutely.

JAN Are you all right, Tam?

TAMSIN *nods.*

JAN *(cont'd) (pointing to the balloon)* Do you want me to take that off you?

TAMSIN *shakes her head.* GRAHAM *has a thought. He looks at the balloon.* SI *sees him looking and stares at him suspiciously.*

SI Could I take that balloon, please, Miss?

GRAHAM Aw, let her keep it.

SI *holds out his hand.* TAMSIN *isn't sure what to do.*

SI The balloon?

JAN What do you want it for?

SI I believe you are in infringement of Mr Parson's Intellectual Property Rights.

JAN What?

GRAHAM It's a comfort to her.

SALLY It's only a balloon, for goodness' sake.

SI One that contains Mr Parsons' breath. His actual dying breath.

SALLY Oh, good Lord. Oh, that's made me go all funny.

JAN Just give it to him, Tamsin.

TAMSIN *hands the balloon over to* SI. *A little bit of air farts out during the handover.*

GRAHAM Careful!

SI *grips the balloon tightly and carefully.*

GRAHAM *(cont'd)* Tie a knot in it.

SI *carefully tries to tie a knot in the balloon but is ham-fisted and a bit more air farts out of it.*

GRAHAM *(cont'd)* Whoa!

SI I can't do it!

GRAHAM Use two fingers . . . Wrap it . . . Here, let me . . .

GRAHAM *approaches and offers to take the balloon from* SI. SI *reluctantly hands it over.* GRAHAM*'s forehead beads with sweat. It's like they are handling an unexploded bomb.* JAN *hasn't grasped the magnitude of the situation.*

JAN If you'd only used the pumper, none of this would have happened.

GRAHAM Jan, please!

GRAHAM *carefully ties a knot in the balloon.*

GRAHAM *(cont'd)* There.

SI Thank you.

SI *goes to take the balloon back.*

GRAHAM Whoa, whoa, whoa! Let's just take a breath, shall we?

GRAHAM *holds the balloon out of* SI*'s reach.*

GRAHAM *(cont'd)* Jan, go and get Tamsin's laptop from her room, please.

JAN But Frankie's in there . . .

GRAHAM Just get it, please. We need to find out what we're dealing with here.

JAN *goes into the bedroom to fetch the laptop. As she opens the door we catch a glimpse of* FRANKIE*'s body lying on the floor. He has been covered with* TAMSIN*'s girly duvet and only his legs protrude.* JAN *closes the door behind her and edges into the room.*

SALLY*'s phone rings. She fishes it out and checks the caller ID.*

SALLY *(to* SI *and* GRAHAM*)* My boss. Should I answer it?

SI Yes.

GRAHAM No!

SALLY *answers the phone.*

SALLY *(cont'd)* Hi, Nigel! Oh gosh, yes, I'm so sorry, I completely forgot . . . *(To* SI *and* GRAHAM*)* I've got a little boy with cerebral palsy who wants to play chess with Noel Edmonds. *(Into phone)* Nigel, could you get Sandy to cover for me, at all? I'm just dealing with a situation here . . . No, no, it's all going well, you don't have to come . . .

GRAHAM *shakes his head.*

SALLY *(cont'd)* It's just Mr Parsons wants to stay and . . .

GRAHAM *mimes singing into a microphone.*

SALLY *(cont'd)* . . . suck off . . .

GRAHAM *shakes his head and mimes karaoke.*

SALLY *(cont'd)* Erm, sing off with Tamsin on the karaoke. Yes, they're having a ball, they're doing 'La Bamba' as I speak . . .

GRAHAM *sings a few variations on 'La Bamba' and beckons* TAMSIN *to join in.* TAMSIN *just stares.* SI *joins in with 'La Bamba' as* SALLY *heads out to the hallway to finish the call.*

SALLY *(cont'd)* Yes, she's such a lucky girl, isn't she! What memories! So I don't really want to break up the party . . .

JAN *emerges from the bedroom with a child's pink laptop.*

JAN What's all that about? Frankie's lying dead next door and you're singing Billy Joel?

GRAHAM Billy Joel? That wasn't Billy Joel.

SI Who's Billy Joel?

GRAHAM Are you serious? – 'Who's Billy Joel?' I've heard it all now.

JAN Well, whoever it was, I don't think it's appropriate.

SALLY *re-enters the room, having finished the phone call.*

SALLY Right, disaster averted. We don't really want anybody else coming round, do we?

SI Not 'til Mr Fourboys gets here.

GRAHAM *holds the balloon out to* SALLY.

GRAHAM I'm giving this to you as a neutral, OK?

SALLY Yes, fine. Oh, just let me take my ring off, it's a bit spiky.

SALLY *takes off her ring and takes the balloon as if it were a new-born baby.* GRAHAM *takes the laptop.*

SALLY *(cont'd)* There. That's better, isn't it?

JAN Is this some sort of party game?

SI Step away from the balloon, Miss.

JAN But what's going on . . .?

SI Miss, I need you to step away.

JAN Oh, you've all lost your heads.

JAN *goes to sit with* TAMSIN. GRAHAM *has been tapping away on the laptop.*

GRAHAM Right, look at this. Justin Bieber's fringe, 40 thousand dollars.

SALLY Gosh!

GRAHAM Elvis's hair, 120 thousand. Michael Jackson's glove, 400 thousand!

JAN What's this got to do with anything?

GRAHAM Jan, we've got a balloon here containing Frankie Parsons' final breath. His actual dying breath, captured and preserved for eternity, we've even got the video to prove it!

JAN That's sick.

GRAHAM The world's sick, Jan – someone paid five and a half grand for Scarlett Johansson's used tissue. It's like Billy said, 'We Didn't Start the Fire'.

JAN You're going to sell Frankie's last breath?

GRAHAM We don't know what we're dealing with here, do we? Could be 50 quid or 50 thousand.

SALLY Or more. At Wishmaker UK we get to see how much value people attach to celebrities and, really – it's quite staggering, I tell you. This could make a lot of children's wishes come true.

GRAHAM Yeah, but this is Tamsin's wish. Isn't it, Tam-Tam? That wish belongs to us.

Close on TAMSIN*'s face. She turns to look at her bedroom and through the crack in the door she can see* FRANKIE *lying dead on the floor.*

INT. LIVING ROOM. DAY.

The balloon now sits on a cushion on the coffee table in the centre of the room. SI *stands in front of the door.* SALLY *sits on the sofa and* TAMSIN *is still in her wheelchair.* JAN *kneels by the CD player going through some CDs by Frankie J. Parsons.*

JAN What about 'Bermuda Love Triangle'?

SALLY It's a little bit . . . rocky. Given the circumstances.

JAN Yes, I suppose we want something more sombre, don't we? But not maudlin, he was never maudlin.

SALLY How about 'Feel You Up, Feel You Down'?

SI Is that the one where he tried to rap?

SALLY Yes.

JAN I don't like it, Sally. He uses language.

SALLY Yes, shit, I'd forgotten. Sorry.

She remembers TAMSIN *is behind her.*

SALLY *(cont'd)* Sorry!

JAN Frankie was best when he was just classic, do you know what I mean?

SALLY *(agreeing)* Mmmm.

JAN Timeless.

SI My favourite was 'More Than Anyone'.

JAN *and* SALLY *both 'ah' together: the perfect choice.*

SALLY Yep.

JAN That's the one. 'More Than Anyone'.

She finds the CD and takes it from the box. SALLY *turns to* SI.

SALLY Were you actually a fan of his before you started to work for him?

SI Not really. I prefer hip-hop, gangsta rap, that sort of thing.

SALLY Oh. I once met Jazzy J in a lift.

Silence. SALLY *looks at the balloon on the pillow.*

JAN *puts the CD on and a gentle gospel number begins. We drift around seeing the reactions to the song. Everyone looks very moved.* GRAHAM *enters and abruptly turns the CD off.*

GRAHAM Right, I've got some numbers for you. I spoke to a man at Christie's and got a ballpark figure for the last breath of Nelson Mandela and Robbie Williams – I reckon Frankie was somewhere in-between.

SALLY These are hypothetical last breaths?

GRAHAM Yeah, hypothetical ones obviously.

TAMSIN *starts to power her wheelchair out of the room.*

GRAHAM *(cont'd)* Ah, you need a wee-wee, Tam? Go with her, Jan.

TAMSIN I don't need a wee.

JAN Come on, your dad wants to talk some business.

JAN *takes* TAMSIN *out into the garden.*

GRAHAM So I said, 'Suppose you were at Nelson Mandela's deathbed with a jam jar . . .'

SALLY A jam jar?

GRAHAM I was improvising, wasn't I . . . ?

EXT. GARDEN. DAY.

JAN *sits with* TAMSIN *in the garden. Behind them we can see through the French windows as* GRAHAM *talks to* SALLY *and* SI.

JAN Well, this is one birthday you won't forget in a hurry, isn't it?

TAMSIN How many birthdays do I have left?

JAN We don't know, darling. Lots and lots, we hope.

TAMSIN I liked Frankie. He was nice.

JAN Was he? I never really got the chance to talk to him properly.

TAMSIN Can I hear some of his music?

JAN Course you can, sweetheart. I've got all his CDs, you know that. I went with your Auntie Irene to see him at Wembley, do you remember? Frankie J. Parsons in our house. That was going to be my moment. Now it's gone.

Behind them in the living room SALLY *shrieks with joy and claps her hands.* GRAHAM *is nodding and smiling.* SI *punches the air.*

TAMSIN Is it my fault?

JAN No, darling, no! Why would it be your fault?

TAMSIN I wanted him to blow up the balloon.

JAN Well . . . you weren't to know.

TAMSIN Will his soul go to heaven?

JAN Yes. Yes, it will.

JAN *looks at* TAMSIN *teary-eyed and takes her hand.*

INT. LIVING ROOM. DAY.

GRAHAM, SALLY *and* SI *are gathered around the coffee table. The balloon still sits on a cushion between them.*

SI Right, so how are we going to do this?

SALLY Well, as a neutral, I would say the only fair way is equal shares.

GRAHAM *(to* SI*)* Absolutely.

SALLY A third for you, a third for me and a third for the family.

SI That sounds about right.

GRAHAM Hang on a minute, what do you mean, 'a third for the family'?

SALLY That's a lot of money.

GRAHAM Yes, but there's three of us.

SI So what are you saying?

GRAHAM We should split it in fifths. Me, Jan, Tamsin, you and Sally.

SI A fifth? I worked for him all those years on shitty wages and all I get is a fifth?

GRAHAM Well, that's equal shares, isn't it? Five people!

SALLY What about we compromise and say quarters?

GRAHAM Quarters?

SALLY Yes, 25 per cent each.

GRAHAM So who loses out?

SALLY Nobody. You and your wife get half and we split the other half between us.

GRAHAM What about Tamsin?

SI She's underage.

GRAHAM So?

SI She's just a kid, she shouldn't get that much money.

GRAHAM She's earned it.

SI What, by making him blow into a balloon and giving him an aneurysm!

SALLY *(to* GRAHAM*)* Mr Vickers, with respect, if we give Tamsin an equal fifth, well, that's going to revert back to you pretty quickly, isn't it?

GRAHAM What?

SALLY I mean, without being emotional, when the inevitable happens, you and your wife are going to be sitting on three-fifths between the two of you and Simon and I don't think that's particularly fair, do we?

GRAHAM *grabs the balloon and stands up.*

GRAHAM Now just a minute . . .

SALLY *and* SI *stand up.* SI *reaches for the balloon.*

SI Put it down! Put it down!

GRAHAM This balloon actually belongs to us; we paid for it – Jan'll have the receipt somewhere – so you two can just fuck off.

SALLY I beg your pardon?

GRAHAM You heard me, fuck off! This is my house, my party and my balloon.

SALLY You invited us here, Mr Vickers. Mr Parsons gave up time from his busy schedule . . .

GRAHAM I don't give a shit! He's dead now and I want him, and you, out of my house.

SI We'll go just as soon as you give us what's rightfully ours.

GRAHAM It's rightfully ours, pack of 12, £1.99.

SI But what's inside it isn't yours, is it? You own the skin, but you don't own the air.

SALLY That's right, nobody owns the air.

GRAHAM All right then . . . All right, if you want the air you can have it!

GRAHAM *steps onto the sofa, grabs a pair of scissors from a side table and holds them up to the balloon.*

GRAHAM *(cont'd)* Is this what you want? Is it? Is this what you want?

SI/SALLY No, no, no . . .

JAN STOP IT!!!!

GRAHAM, SALLY *and* SI *turn to see* JAN *and* TAMSIN *in the doorway.*

JAN *(cont'd)* Get down off the sofa, Graham.

GRAHAM *carefully climbs down from the sofa.*

JAN *(cont'd)* Give the balloon to Tamsin. It's her birthday, it belongs to her.

GRAHAM *looks to* SI. SI *nods.*

SI She's neutral.

SALLY I thought I was neutral?

GRAHAM Not any more you're not. You went from Switzerland to Nazi Germany in one fell goose-step. Here . . .

GRAHAM *carefully hands the balloon back to* TAMSIN.

GRAHAM *(cont'd)* Be very careful with it, Tam-Tam. You know you wanted to go to Disney? The proper one, not the Froggy one? Well, imagine that's your ticket in. Your golden ticket.

JAN Don't make promises you can't keep, Graham, she's been through enough.

GRAHAM Trust me. Now let's sit down, and talk about this like adults, OK?

INT. KITCHEN. DAY.

JAN *and* SALLY *are making sandwiches in the kitchen.*

JAN It must be very rewarding, your job.

SALLY Yes, yes, I suppose it is. When you see a little boy's face light up because John Terry's brought him a signed England shirt, well . . . you can't put a price on that.

JAN But you can put a price on a popstar's last ever breath.

SALLY It's just a guestimate, something to put in the budget, you know?

JAN What's the best dream you've ever made come true?

SALLY Hmm, I often get asked that. I'd have to say, and it sounds silly really . . . there was a little girl with, I think, Hodgkin's disease – I don't get involved with the illness side – and her dream was to be a postman. That's all. Not give a letter to the Queen or meet Postman Pat, just be a postman. Nigel shunted it my way – zero press interest there, of course, but when we gave her that letter and told her to put it through the letter box . . . the little giggle after it landed . . . as if it meant the whole world to her.

JAN *smiles.*

SALLY *(cont'd)* Then she dropped down dead, right there on the doorstep. Press went mad for it. So up yours, Nigel! That was my favourite one.

INT. TAMSIN'S ROOM. DAY.

GRAHAM *is taking a photo of the dead* FRANKIE *on his mobile phone.* SI *enters.*

SI Mr Fourboys says he'll be here in 20 minutes with the coroner and an ambulance crew. They'll be incognito so as not to raise any alarm. He wants to do this with dignity.

GRAHAM Absolutely.

GRAHAM *takes another photo.*

GRAHAM *(cont'd)* You didn't tell him about the . . .?

SI No. I'll claim ignorance.

GRAHAM Probably best.

GRAHAM *looks down at* FRANKIE.

GRAHAM *(cont'd)* Was he a good boss?

SI Mr Parsons? Bit of a dick, if I'm honest.

GRAHAM Yeah?

SI Yeah. He knew how to work it, but I don't think he was a happy man. You should have heard him bitching about having to come here.

GRAHAM No!

SI For real. 'I shouldn't have to mix with these sick kids, they make me depressed . . .'

GRAHAM Aw, how disappointing! Don't say anything to Jan, will you? She'll be mortified.

SI I won't.

GRAHAM You see, that's the trouble with being famous, isn't it? Your life's not your own any more.

SI True dat.

There is a loud bang from next door. SI *and* GRAHAM *look to each other and race into the living room.*

INT. LIVING ROOM. DAY.

SI *and* GRAHAM *race in, then* SALLY *and* JAN. TAMSIN *sits holding the balloon.*

GRAHAM Oh, thank God!

SALLY It was just a car backfiring.

SI Look, I'm not being funny but I think we should put the item upstairs out of the way somewhere. This place is going to be crawling with quacks in a few minutes and anything could happen.

SALLY Yes. And are the quacks linked to the pigs, or . . .?

GRAHAM We'll put it in the spare room.

SI As long as it's safe, yeah?

GRAHAM It will be. Come on, Tam-Tam, give it to Daddy . . . Come on . . .

GRAHAM *has to pull the balloon from* TAMSIN*'s hand. She doesn't want to let it go. The balloon stretches at the knot end.* SALLY *and* SI *look tense. Then the balloon pulls out of* TAMSIN*'s hand and* GRAHAM *has it safely. He carries it upstairs.* SALLY *nods towards* SI.

SI I'll come with you.

SI *follows* GRAHAM *upstairs.* JAN *goes to put on a CD.*

JAN Let's put some music on, Tam. Cheer you up a bit.

A soulful pop song by Frankie J. Parsons plays. JAN *dances a little in front of* TAMSIN. SALLY *smiles.*

INT. SPARE ROOM. DAY.

GRAHAM *and* SI *enter the room.* GRAHAM *carries the balloon with two hands, like a baby with a full nappy.* SI *pulls back the duvet and feels the mattress with his hands to make sure they are clean and smooth, then* GRAHAM *lays the balloon on the bed.* SI *gently pulls the duvet over the balloon, the top sticking out like a sleeping child.*

INT. LIVING ROOM. DAY.

Music plays as GRAHAM, JAN, SALLY *and* SI *sit in the living room, waiting.* TAMSIN *sits in her chair.* SI *checks his watch.*

SI Be about seven or eight minutes.

GRAHAM Cool. Thanks, man.

Silence. They wait. JAN *looks over at* TAMSIN.

JAN You all right, Tam-Tam?

TAMSIN *looks forlorn.*

JAN *(cont'd)* Do her another balloon, Graham. She misses it.

GRAHAM How can she miss it? It's only a . . .

GRAHAM *sighs and reaches for the packet of balloons.*

GRAHAM *(cont'd)* What colour do you want? There's blue, yellow, purple . . .

GRAHAM *holds up the purple balloon and has an idea.* SALLY *is ahead of him.*

SALLY How many more purple ones?

GRAHAM Two.

SALLY You know, if we could sell the first one to a private bidder . . . no public auction, confidentiality clause . . .

GRAHAM We've got the video evidence!

SALLY Just add a bit of Frankie's DNA . . .

SI Do it.

GRAHAM *starts to inflate a purple balloon.* SALLY *grabs the other one and starts to blow.*

JAN Isn't that cheating?

SI Doesn't matter. A thing is only worth what someone's willing to pay for it.

GRAHAM *and* SALLY *are red-faced with the effort of blowing up the long purple balloons.*

JAN Careful, Graham, you'll do yourself an injury!

GRAHAM Go and get the bloody pumper then!

JAN We don't know where it is!

JAN *hurries into the kitchen.*

SI Here, give that to me . . .

SI *takes* SALLY*'s balloon.*

SALLY Oh God, I've gone all light-headed.

GRAHAM Stretch it first.

SALLY I'm seeing stars.

SALLY *gets unsteadily to her feet as* SI *and* GRAHAM *strain and blow in the purple balloons.* JAN *runs in with the pumper.*

JAN Found it! It was in the – aarghhh!!

JAN *screams.* GRAHAM, SI *and* SALLY *look to the sliding doors into* TAMSIN*'s room and are stunned to see* FRANKIE*'s twitching arm sticking through the crack of the doors. The hand is clawing the carpet.*

SI *gulps down all the air he's just blown into the balloon.* GRAHAM*'s balloon flies out of his hands and swoops around the room, expelling air.* SALLY *falls backwards onto the stereo system, making the CD jump.*

FRANKIE'S VOICE 'And I live for today – live for today – live for today – live for today . . .'

GRAHAM *rushes to the stereo and pulls the plug. Silence. All eyes are on* FRANKIE*'s arm.*

TAMSIN Is Frankie better now?

GRAHAM Jan, take Tamsin to the toilet, please.

TAMSIN I don't want to go.

GRAHAM Just do it!

JAN *crosses over to* TAMSIN.

JAN Come on, sweetheart.

TAMSIN No!

JAN Mummy'll change your bag for you . . .

TAMSIN NO!! I don't want to!!

JAN *pushes* TAMSIN *out of the room.* SI *goes to feel* FRANKIE*'s pulse.*

SALLY Is he . . .?

SI He's alive.

GRAHAM Good. Well, that's fantastic, isn't it?

SALLY Yes.

SI It's a very faint pulse.

GRAHAM Well, we just have to cross our fingers and hope for the best.

SALLY Right.

SALLY *crosses her fingers.*

SALLY *(cont'd)* What is the best?

GRAHAM How long until the ambulance crew get here?

SI Five minutes.

GRAHAM OK.

GRAHAM *paces the room.* SI *stands up.*

GRAHAM *(cont'd)* I mean, it's still worth something.

SI *fishes in his pocket for a coin.*

GRAHAM *(cont'd)* Someone bought Justin Timberlake's toast crumbs for, like, three grand. I mean, it's not like it's been a total waste of time . . .

SI *presents* GRAHAM *with two fists.*

SI Pick a hand.

GRAHAM What? No . . .

SI Pick a hand. We've got to do this quickly.

GRAHAM Do what? What are we talking about here?

SALLY Just pick one, for fuck's sake!

GRAHAM *taps the left hand and* SI *opens it. There is a coin.*

SI It's your job, man.

GRAHAM What, my job? I won! I found the coin!

SI Coin loses.

GRAHAM Says who?

SALLY Just flip it. Heads or tails.

GRAHAM Hang on a minute, how is this just a two-man thing?

SI You want that money or not?

GRAHAM Yes, but . . .

SI Well, call it then. She knocked herself out blowing up a balloon, never mind that.

SALLY To be fair, so did he.

SALLY *points to* FRANKIE.

SI Call it.

GRAHAM No, I'm not prepared to . . .

SI Call it!

GRAHAM . . . to play God in this way. I mean, look, the man's a huge star, he brings pleasure to millions of people . . .

SALLY Not like that he doesn't.

GRAHAM How do we know?

SALLY He had a brain aneurysm, he's a vegetable! He'll spend the rest of his life bedbound, eating through a straw and shitting into a bucket – what kind of life is that? No offence.

GRAHAM No offence? That's one of the most offensive things I've ever heard!

SALLY Look, I spend my whole life making other people's dreams come true, standing by and smiling while they fly off in a helicopter with a candy floss in one hand and a D-lister in the other – why can't it be my turn? What about my needs, my wishes?

GRAHAM The man's alive!

SALLY Not for much longer, now call it!

GRAHAM I can't . . .

SI Call it!!

GRAHAM Heads!!

SI *flips and shows everyone the results.*

SI Heads, you win. Fuck!! Get me a cushion.

SALLY *hands* SI *a cushion.* SI *steels himself to go into the room.*

GRAHAM I can't be here for this. I can't witness this . . .

SI *enters* TAMSIN*'s room. He pulls* FRANKIE *back by the ankles.*

GRAHAM *(cont'd)* Oh God.

SALLY *gathers up the other two balloons and hands them to* SI.

SALLY Here, get his DNA on these. We might be able to do something with them at a later date.

SALLY *slides the door closed.*

SALLY *(cont'd)* Right, I'll go and have a little chat with Tam-Tam. Tell her the bad news.

SALLY *heads for the exit, leaving* GRAHAM *alone in the room. He can see* SI *through the frosted glass doors to* TAMSIN*'s room.* SI *is standing over the body with the cushion in his hands.*

SI *bends down.* GRAHAM *closes his eyes.*

EXT. CUL-DE-SAC. DAY.

A body bag on a gurney is pushed quickly out of the house and into the back of an unmarked ambulance. SI *is talking with* MR FOURBOYS. *He comes over to* SALLY, GRAHAM *and* JAN, *who are gathered on the pavement.*

SI Right, I'm going with Mr Fourboys. The pigs are going to be onto this within the hour so be ready, yeah? Sit tight. I'll be in touch.

SI *shakes hands with* GRAHAM.

SI *(cont'd) (to* JAN*)* Nice to meet you.

SI *goes to get into a car with* MR FOURBOYS.

SALLY Wow. The press are going to have a field day with this. *(To* GRAHAM*)* We should have a look at that camcorder footage actually. If we cut it into 30-second segments, we might be able to sell a chunk to each of the networks . . .

GRAHAM I wouldn't bet on it, Jan did most of the filming . . .

GRAHAM *opens the camcorder and views the footage with* SALLY. *An elderly neighbour,* MAGGIE, *approaches* JAN *as she tearfully watches the ambulance drive off.*

MAGGIE What's going on, Jan?

JAN I can't tell you, Maggie. You'll hear about it soon enough.

MAGGIE It's not the child, is it?

JAN Oh God, no.

JAN *has a thought.*

JAN *(cont'd)* Tamsin . . .

JAN *realises they've left* TAMSIN *inside. She rushes into the house.*

INT. HALLWAY. DAY.

TAMSIN*'s empty chair sits in the hallway.*

JAN Tam-Tam?

INT. TAMSIN'S ROOM. DAY.

JAN *runs into the bedroom, but* TAMSIN *isn't there either.*

JAN Where are you, darling?

The helium heart balloon is missing . . .

INT. SPARE ROOM. DAY.

TAMSIN *is crawling into the spare room. She is holding the helium balloon. She pulls herself up onto the bed with great difficulty, then pulls back the duvet and takes the purple balloon.*

EXT. CUL-DE-SAC. DAY.

JAN *runs out of the house.*

JAN Graham, where's Tamsin? I can't find her.

SALLY *looks up at the spare room just in time to see* TAMSIN *opening the window.*

SALLY She's there, look.

JAN Tamsin!

TAMSIN *opens the window. She launches the purple balloon out of the house. It is tied to the heart-shaped helium balloon and it starts to float up and away.*

GRAHAM No! Tamsin, what . . . ! What are you doing?

TAMSIN *smiles as she watches the balloon fly up and up, tied to the heart.*

JAN *smiles, teary-eyed.*

SALLY Shit – film it, film it – it's all we've got!

Camcorder footage of the purple balloon as it floats away up into the clouds.

THE END

Episode 5

THE UNDERSTUDY

CAST LIST

KIRSTIE – Rosie Cavaliero

TONY – Steve Pemberton

JIM – Reece Shearsmith

BILL – Roger Sloman

JEAN – Di Botcher

LAURA – Lyndsey Marshal

FELICITY – Julia Davis

NICK – Richard Cordery

MALCOLM – Bruce Mackinnon

MACDUFF – Jo Stone-Fewings

EXT. THEATRE. NIGHT.

Establisher of a large West End theatre. The hoardings outside advertise a production of 'MACBETH *by William Shakespeare. Starring Anthony Warner.'*

MALCOLM *(V.O.)* '. . . this, and what needful else / That calls upon us, by the grace of Grace . . .'

INT. BACKSTAGE CORRIDOR. NIGHT.

We move down the corridor following KIRSTIE, *a black-clad young dresser. She is carrying a tall glass full of green wheatgrass juice and a towel. The final speech from the play can be heard over the tannoy system.*

MALCOLM *(V.O.)* 'We will perform in measure, time and place: / So, thanks to all at once and to each one, / Whom we invite to see us crown'd at Scone.'

KIRSTIE *arrives at dressing room number 9 and enters. The door closes. There is a star around the number '9'.*

TITLE: *'The Understudy'.*

CAPTION: *'Act I'*

INT. DRESSING ROOM. NIGHT.

The dressing room is quite large, with a sofa, a fridge with a kettle on top and a chair in front of a large mirror. The mirror is surrounded by bulbs and 'Good Luck' cards Blu-Tacked around the edge.

There are hanging rails for costumes, a sink and a curtained-off shower area. KIRSTIE *places the glass and the towel on the dressing table and fetches down a wig-block from a shelf.*

We hear audience applause through the tannoy speaker, as the door opens and in walks TONY, *who plays Macbeth.* TONY *is in his late forties and is handsome but self-obsessed. He is dressed in a traditional 16th-century costume, which is covered with blood. He wears a long-haired wig.*

He calls down the corridor:

TONY Yeah, I'll see you down there! I'll bring that book in for you . . .

The door closes and TONY *drops the bonhomie. He removes his tunic and drops it on the floor.*

TONY *(cont'd)* Arsehole. That bloody speech gets longer and longer every night. I'm lying there with that belt buckle sticking in me . . .

TONY *sits down and* KIRSTIE *goes to help him with his boots.*

TONY *(cont'd)* And he's just droning on. I mean, I'm dead, the play's over, isn't it? Who gives a toss about Malcolm? Ow!

KIRSTIE Sorry. I'll take them up to Wardrobe and get them stretched out for you.

TONY That would be good because I did ask for that three weeks ago, didn't I?

KIRSTIE Sorry, Tony.

TONY *looks at his watch as* KIRSTIE *removes his trousers.*

TONY You see, that's four minutes added to the second half, just because the casting director of the Donmar's in. Good acting does not mean slowing down. People have got to get trains!

TONY *drinks his juice as* KIRSTIE *picks up the trousers and tunic. A message comes over the tannoy.*

STAGE DOOR *(V.O.)* Visitors at stage door for Mr Warner, thank you.

TONY Oh shit! I'd totally forgotten I've got friends in. They want to come round. What are people like? I've just done three hours of Shakespeare, now I've got to give another performance in here!

KIRSTIE Do you want me to get them?

TONY *sprays his armpits with deodorant;* KIRSTIE *gets caught in the indiscriminate spraying.*

TONY I suppose so. But after five minutes remind me I've got something on tomorrow morning.

KIRSTIE What?

TONY I don't know, a voiceover or something – use your imagination! I just don't want to get stuck with them.

KIRSTIE OK.

KIRSTIE *heads out of the door with the Macbeth costume. She is shocked to find* JIM *loitering in the corridor.*

JIM *is* TONY*'s understudy, younger and greener than* TONY *and not as jaded. He holds the door for* KIRSTIE*, then edges into the room.* TONY *is getting dressed and removing his make-up.*

JIM Hi, Kirstie. Hey, Tony!

TONY *(wearily)* Hi, Jim.

JIM Well done for tonight. Good audience, I thought.

TONY Were they? There was a lot of reading of programmes from what I could see. 'Oh look, Malcolm was in *Doc Martin*' – so what! Look up, people, this is theatre, it's happening now in front of you!

JIM They seemed to really enjoy it.

TONY It's a tragedy, they're not meant to enjoy it. How are you getting on with the lines?

JIM Good, it's really useful watching you every night, helps it all sink in. We've got an understudy run on Friday if you wanted to come . . .

TONY Oh, I'd love to, but I'm pretty sure I've got a voiceover on Friday . . . what time is it?

JIM Two o'clock.

TONY Yep. That's when it is. Exactly then. Damn!

JIM Not to worry. So who have you got coming round? Is it the woman from the Donmar?

TONY No. They won't see me for the Donmar. I'm not their type of actor apparently. No, this is my neighbours, Bill and Jean. I can't believe they've come to be honest. I've got absolutely nothing to say to either one of them.

A knock at the door and KIRSTIE *enters followed by* BILL *and* JEAN, *a homely couple in their late middle age,* BILL *carrying a programme of the show.*

TONY *(cont'd)* Bill! Jean! How lovely to see you! Thanks so much for coming!

There is an awkward exchange as BILL *tries to shake* TONY*'s hand, and* TONY *goes to embrace them both.*

BILL No, we enjoyed it, didn't we, Jean?

JEAN Oh yes. 'When shall we three meet again!'

BILL I still don't know how you learn all those lines.

TONY Well, it's just my job. I probably couldn't do what you do. What do you do?

BILL Hospital porter.

TONY There you go, you see?

JEAN There was a porter in this, wasn't there? I said to Bill, that should be you.

TONY Ha, good. So you enjoyed it then?

JEAN Yes, the sets and the lighting make it, don't they? Give it the atmosphere.

TONY Yes, nothing to do with the boring old actors, is it?

JEAN No, I'm not saying that. We liked Malcolm, didn't we? And you'd seen him in that programme, what was it . . .?

TONY/BILL *Doc Martin.*

JEAN That's it. He likes it for the Cornwall.

BILL He played a fisherman in that and you'd never believe it was the same person, would you?

TONY No, he's a very clever chap.

JEAN And he has lovely diction, doesn't he? I could have listened to him for hours.

TONY Yes, well, I do. Every night! So, Kirstie, is there . . .?

TONY *gives a discreet nod to* KIRSTIE.

KIRSTIE Oh sorry, yes, would you like a drink?

TONY No, no! She forgets I'm four years on the wagon!

JEAN Really?

TONY Yes, haven't touched a drop and I feel a lot better for it. No, I was just wondering if there was anything . . .?

KIRSTIE Oh yes, sorry! Remember, you've got a voiceover tomorrow morning.

TONY Oh, have I?

KIRSTIE I think so. Yes. For tampons.

TONY Tampons? Oh well, in that case I'd better . . .

TONY *looks at his watch.*

JIM No, you said that was Friday.

TONY Did I . . .? Yes, I'm not sure now.

JEAN Well, we are taking you out for dinner.

TONY No, you're not.

BILL Yes, we are. We've booked a table at Papa Dell's. Come on, grab his coat, Jean.

TONY *is furious. Mock-protesting but meaning it.*

TONY No! I don't want to go!

They bundle him out of the door. KIRSTIE *grabs* TONY*'s phone from the dressing table.*

KIRSTIE Tony, your phone . . .

JIM *is left alone in the dressing room. He smiles. He crosses to the dressing table and picks up* TONY*'s half-drunk glass of wheatgrass juice. He sniffs it, takes a sip and pulls a face.*

JIM *sees the Macbeth crown on the floor. He picks it up, puts it on his head and turns to look at himself in the mirror. The bulbs flash off and on, and for a moment* JIM *sees himself reflected back in the full Macbeth costume.*

CAPTION: *'ACT II'*

INT. DRESSING ROOM. DAY.

JIM *lies on the sofa rattling through his lines at breakneck speed. His girlfriend* LAURA *is testing him with the play-script.* LAURA *is understudying Lady Macbeth and is pretty but with an inner steel.* JIM *and* LAURA *sip from Starbucks-type coffees.*

JIM And pity, like a naked new-born babe, / Striding the blast, or heaven's cherubim, horsed / Upon the sightless couriers of the air, / Shall blow the horrible deed . . .

LAURA No.

JIM Terrible deed?

LAURA No.

JIM Awful?

LAURA No.

JIM Dreadful?

LAURA No.

JIM Evil?

LAURA No.

JIM Nasty, crap, shitty . . .?

LAURA No, it's 'horrid'.

JIM I said 'horrid'!

LAURA No, you said 'horrible'.

JIM Oh come on, that's close enough!

LAURA Yeah, it's close enough if you want to be an understudy all your life.

JIM Don't start . . .

LAURA Sitting in your dressing room and doing sudokus while Tony gets all the glory.

JIM That's just the job! There's nothing I can do about it, is there?

LAURA Yes, there is! We're about to do a run-through in front of the director – make an impression!

JIM Sorry, I don't do impressions!

LAURA *sighs and shakes her head at* JIM*'s feeble joke.*

LAURA Come on, 'shall blow the horrid deed . . .'

JIM '. . . blow the horrid deed in every eye, / That tears shall drown the wind. / I have no spur / To prick the sides of my intent . . .'

The company manager FELICITY *enters. She is a black-clad butch Australian lesbian.*

JIM *(cont'd)* '. . . but only / Vaulting ambition, which o'erleaps itself / And falls on the other . . .'

FELICITY Er, excuse me – what the fudge are you doing in Tony's dressing room? That is a sackable offence.

JIM Oh hi, Fliss, Kirstie said it would be OK . . .

FELICITY Oh, and you take your orders from the dresser now, do you, not the company manager?

LAURA We don't take 'orders' from anyone, we're not in the SS.

FELICITY Speak for yourself, sweetheart. I'll allow it this time, as it's good for you to get used to the routine, should you ever need to go on for Tony, which you won't.

FELICITY *hands out payslips to* JIM *and* LAURA *and places* TONY*'s on his desk.*

FELICITY *(cont'd)* Your understudy run starts in T-minus 50 minutes. We're doing it all 'as is', except no blood, no swords and no fog.

JIM No swords?

FELICITY No, the fight director's been hospitalised – apparently Derek Jacobi caught him in the goolies with a nunchuck. Don't remember that in *The Merry Wives of Windsor*, but there you go . . .

JIM We're not using the walking sticks, are we?

FELICITY It's just an understudy call, Jim, it really doesn't matter.

FELICITY *notes the coffee cups.*

FELICITY *(cont'd)* Are those shop-bought lattes?

JIM Yeah. Sorry, I would have got you one, but . . .

FELICITY Did you sign yourself out and sign yourself back in again?

JIM No, I was only gone for two minutes.

FELICITY Go and do so, please, stage door.

LAURA You can't be serious?

FELICITY *Fire* is serious, Laura, that's why we have procedures. Jim?

JIM It's OK.

JIM *exits.* FELICITY *crosses to the mirrors and switches on the mirror lights: she's checking all the bulbs are working. When she finds one that isn't, she makes a note of it.*

FELICITY *sneaks a look at* LAURA *in the mirror.*

FELICITY Your Lady Macbeth frock is being pressed, but it would be good if you could just pop your jeans and blouse off now.

LAURA What? Why?

FELICITY It'll save time.

LAURA No, I'm not doing that!

FELICITY Oh well, you can't blame a girl for trying.

LAURA You're not supposed to say that anyway.

FELICITY For goodness' sake, Laura, it was a joke.

LAURA I mean the 'M' word. You're not supposed to say it in the dressing room.

FELICITY What, 'Macbeth'?

LAURA Yes. It brings bad luck.

FELICITY To who?

LAURA I don't know. The production.

FELICITY Actors, you make me laugh. Macbeth. Macbeth, Macbeth. See, I'm still here.

LAURA Exactly.

JIM *re-enters.*

JIM There. I'm officially back.

FELICITY Thank you, Jim. Warm-up in five, then we'll aim to start the run at half past. Oh, and try to talk quickly if you don't mind – some of us have got to do it for real tonight.

FELICITY *leaves and* LAURA *starts to tear open her payslip.*

LAURA I can't fucking stand her. Why is it all company managers hate actors?

JIM It's in the job description.

LAURA 'Wanted: sneery, wine-guzzling lesbian to work backstage. Must have own black sweatshirt and no sense of humour.'

JIM She's only doing her job.

LAURA You know your problem, Jim? You're too *nice.*

LAURA *looks at her payslip.*

LAURA *(cont'd)* Oh God, I could do a sandwich round and get paid more.

JIM We don't do it for the money, do we? We do it 'cause we love it.

LAURA We *do* do it for the money – we're getting married in six months.

LAURA *indicates the engagement ring on her finger.*

JIM I know, it's expensive, isn't it? Shall we just not bother?

LAURA Jim!

JIM I'm joking, I'm joking!

JIM *kisses* LAURA. KIRSTIE *enters the room with the Macbeth costume. She looks embarrassed.*

KIRSTIE Sorry, I just need to hang this up.

LAURA *looks at* TONY*'s payslip on the table.*

LAURA Kirstie, do you know how much Tony gets paid?

JIM You can't ask that!

KIRSTIE I don't know. He never opens his payslips.

LAURA Really?

KIRSTIE Yeah, he just throws them in the bin.

LAURA Oh well, in that case . . .

LAURA *takes* TONY*'s payslip from the table and opens it.*

JIM What are you doing?

LAURA I want to know.

JIM Laura!

LAURA *has opened the payslip.*

LAURA Jesus!

She shows JIM *the payslip.*

JIM Well, he's the lead, isn't he? I'll get there.

LAURA How much more do you get if you go on for him?

JIM Not that. But at least double what I'm on now. He won't go off, though. He's never been off, has he, Kirst?

KIRSTIE No.

LAURA Maybe you should just leave the soap on the floor near the shower. That would do it.

JIM Don't be mean.

LAURA *picks up the Macbeth costume.*

LAURA But don't you for once want to go on as the real thing in front of a real audience . . .? Ouch!

JIM What is it?

LAURA There's a pin in this, Kirstie! Shit!

KIRSTIE Sorry, it just needed stitching . . . I'll get you a plaster.

KIRSTIE *leaves.*

LAURA Clumsy bitch – that could have hurt someone.

JIM Let's have a look.

LAURA *shows* JIM *her thumb, which is beading with blood.*

JIM *(cont'd)* Oh dear. 'By the pricking of my thumbs . . .'

JIM/LAURA '. . . Something wicked this way comes.'

They laugh. JIM *starts to suck* LAURA*'s thumb.*

LAURA Stop it! Vampire . . . 'Make thick my blood, / Stop up the access and passage to remorse, / That no compunctious visitings of nature / Shake my fell purpose . . .'

LAURA *holds* JIM*'s eye.*

FELICITY *(V.O.)* Ladies and gentlemen of the *Macbeth* company can you make your way to the stage, please, for the warm-up. This afternoon's understudy run of *Macbeth* will begin in 45 minutes. Thank you.

LAURA She's doing that to wind me up.

JIM Just ignore her. Good luck.

LAURA You're not supposed to say that either.

JIM Good luck playing Lady Macbeth in *Macbeth*.

LAURA Stop it! You don't want to tempt fate, do you?

JIM What do you want me to do, turn around three times and spit over my left shoulder?

LAURA Only if Felicity's standing behind you. Come on. They've started already . . .

LAURA *leaves the room. We can hear a humming sound coming from the tannoy, the sound of a small company of actors starting their vocal warm-up. The humming opens up into a discordant ahhhing as* JIM *spots a single drop of* LAURA*'s blood, which is soaking into the carpet under the dressing table.*

As JIM *stares at it, the blood seems to spread into a large pool.* JIM*'s eyes widen as the pool gets bigger and bigger, then starts to bubble.*

LAURA *(V.O.) (cont'd)* Jim!

JIM *turns back down the corridor, and when he looks back into the room the spot of blood is simply a spot once more. He shakes the vision from his head and leaves the room.*

CAPTION: *'ACT III'*

INT. DRESSING ROOM. NIGHT.

The tannoy in dressing room 9 is relaying Act Four, Scene Three between MACDUFF *and* MALCOLM. *We hear* MALCOLM *droning on.*

The dressing room is empty, but we can hear TONY *approaching down the corridor. He is very drunk and leery.*

TONY *(V.O.)* Boring! Why don't you fuck off back to Cornwall and do some more *Doc Martins*, you hateful little prick? Honestly, I have never in my life witnessed – is this me?

TONY *has appeared in the doorway of the dressing room.* KIRSTIE *is guiding and supporting him.*

KIRSTIE Yes.

TONY I have never in my life witnessed such a selfish performance on a stage, and do you know the most annoying thing? It works! This tedious little queen – give me my juice . . .

KIRSTIE *passes* TONY *his drinking bottle, then gallantly tries to change* TONY*'s costume as he rants.*

TONY *(cont'd)* . . . has just been offered Uncle Vanya at the Donmar Warehouse. Vanya! That's my part! I was born to be Vanya and they give it to him! Fucking. Arse. Holes. Which, by the way, Kirstie, is how he got the part in the first place.

KIRSTIE *is removing* TONY*'s boots.* TONY *looks at her.*

TONY *(cont'd)* Is your name Kirstie?

KIRSTIE Yes.

TONY Have I always known that?

KIRSTIE Yes.

TONY Amazing.

TONY *drinks from his water bottle.* FELICITY *hurries into the room.*

FELICITY What in God's name is going on?

KIRSTIE I don't know.

FELICITY I've just had to issue eight refunds because Macbeth vomited on stage and said, 'Is this a dildo I see before me?'

KIRSTIE He's not well.

FELICITY He's pissed! Give me that bottle, Tony . . .

TONY Juice!

FELICITY Give it to me!

FELICITY *snatches the water bottle and takes a sip.*

FELICITY *(cont'd)* Jesus Christ, that's two-thirds vodka!

TONY So what?

FELICITY No wonder when Banquo came on you said, 'Fuck me, there's a ghost.' I thought he was on the wagon?

TONY Get the director down here, Flissty, I want to make some changes.

FELICITY Oh, we'll be making some changes all right . . . *(To* KIRSTIE*)* Go and get Jim.

KIRSTIE I'm sure he'll sober up . . .

FELICITY Tell him to think through Act Five – he might be going on.

KIRSTIE *leaves.*

FELICITY *(cont'd)* Right, Tony, how many fingers have I got up?

FELICITY *holds up three fingers.*

TONY Don't talk to me like that, I'm not your girlfriend.

FELICITY I'm serious!

TONY Three.

FELICITY What's your first line in Act Five?

TONY 'Bring me no more reports! Let them fly all! / Till Birnam Wood remove to Dunsinane, / I cannot taint with fear.'

FELICITY Right, we're just going to pop you in the shower, Tony, OK . . .?

FELICITY *hauls* TONY *up onto his feet and into the shower.*

TONY Saucy . . . are you coming in?

FELICITY No, I'm not.

TONY I bet you've got a nice little pair of titties under that big black top, haven't you?

FELICITY You've got five minutes.

FELICITY *puts on the shower and draws the curtain shut.*

TONY *(V.O.)* I could cure you, you know!

FELICITY *unscrews the water bottle and pours the liquid down the sink.*

FELICITY Actors. Nothing but trouble.

KIRSTIE *appears with* JIM.

JIM What's going on, Fliss?

FELICITY Do you know the lines?

JIM I think so . . .

FELICITY Are you sure? You dried in the understudy run last week.

JIM That was just nerves. There were some people watching from *The Lion King* and I didn't expect to see Pumbaa in full make-up . . .

FELICITY Look, I don't like doing this, but if he doesn't sober up in the next four minutes I'm going to have to send you on to finish the show. You can be on book if you have to.

JIM Shit . . .

FELICITY I need to know if you're ready.

JIM I . . .

FELICITY Well?

LAURA *has appeared in the doorway.*

LAURA He's ready. Get the costume on, Jim, and we'll go through the lines. You can do this; it's what we've been waiting for.

FELICITY I'll make that call, thank you, Laura.

A look between LAURA *and* FELICITY.

FELICITY *(cont'd) (to* KIRSTIE*)* Get Tony out of the shower. I'll be back in two minutes and I'll make a decision.

FELICITY *leaves.* KIRSTIE *hovers by the shower with* TONY*'s tunic.*

JIM Oh God – I can't do it.

LAURA Course you can.

JIM It's all the fights – we weren't allowed to practice them, were we?

LAURA The other actors will help you; you'll get through on adrenaline. This is your chance, it's on a plate for you. All you have to do is take it. Here . . .

LAURA *holds out the prop dagger.* JIM *hesitates. He stares at the dagger. He suddenly sees a flash of the dagger and* LAURA*'s hand dripping with blood.* JIM *blinks the vision away. He reaches for the dagger and is about to take it when the shower curtain swishes open and a dripping-wet* TONY *appears.*

TONY Right! I'm ready – let's do this.

TONY *takes the dagger from* LAURA.

KIRSTIE Are you sure you're all right?

TONY Course I'm all right. Get me my juice . . .

LAURA Look, you don't have to do this, Tony. Actors are allowed to be ill. David Suchet missed the last act of *Cat on a Hot Tin Roof* with chronic diarrhoea.

TONY Yes, but he still made the curtain call! Shame he was in a white suit, though . . .

JIM If he's feeling better then he should do it. It'll make more sense for the audience.

TONY Exactly.

KIRSTIE *starts to dress* TONY *in his tunic.*

TONY *(cont'd)* 'Before my body / I throw my warlike shield. Lay on, Macduff, / And damn'd be him that first cries, "Hold, enough!"'

TONY *exits, followed by* KIRSTIE, *leaving* LAURA *and* JIM *alone.*

LAURA Oh Jim. That was it. That was your chance.

JIM It's not my fault, he says he's all right . . .

LAURA He's drunk a full bottle of vodka.

JIM How do you know?

LAURA Well, look at the state of him! I try to help you, Jim, but you just don't want it enough.

JIM I'm only the understudy. I'm there if they want me.

LAURA What, stuck in the corner of the room like a television on standby?

JIM Yes! I'm sorry, Laura, I can't change who I am.

JIM *leaves the room.*

LAURA *is pensive and upset. She starts to twist off her engagement ring. We hear the show continue onstage.*

TONY *(V.O.)* 'Out, out, brief candle! / Life's but a walking shadow, a poor player / That struts and frets his hour upon the stage / And then is heard no more . . .'

LAURA *places the engagement ring on the dressing table. In the mirror* **LAURA** *sees the shower curtain billowing slightly: could there be someone inside? She approaches slowly.*

TONY *(V.O.)* 'It is a tale / Told by an idiot, full of sound and fury, / Signifying nothing . . .'

LAURA *pulls back the shower curtain but the cubicle is empty. Suddenly there is the sound of an almighty tumble and crash, followed by gasps and cries from the audience.* **LAURA** *looks up at the tannoy.*

STAGE MANAGER *(V.O.)* Medic to the stage, please, medic to the stage, urgently!

We hear rising panic onstage. **FELICITY** *runs on and asks* **TONY** *if he is all right, but he doesn't respond.*

LAURA *crosses back to the dressing table and places the ring back on her finger, giving the tiniest flicker of a smile.*

CAPTION: *'ACT IV'*

INT. DRESSING ROOM. NIGHT.

KIRSTIE *is placing a crown onto* **JIM**'*s head, as he sits in front of the mirror. He is dressed in Macbeth's 'King' costume.*

KIRSTIE That's fine, isn't it?

JIM I think so.

KIRSTIE It's not slipping?

JIM No, it's perfect – thanks, Kirst.

KIRSTIE Great. Do you need anything else?

JIM No, I'm all right, I think.

KIRSTIE *makes to leave.* **JIM** *applies his make-up.*

KIRSTIE Oh, nearly forgot, I got you this.

KIRSTIE *presents* **JIM** *with a card and some chocolates.*

JIM Oh Kirstie!

KIRSTIE It's nothing – just some chocolates, card. I'm sure you're going to be brilliant.

JIM Oh, that's really kind – you shouldn't have.

JIM *gives* KIRSTIE *a kiss on the cheek.* LAURA *knocks on the door and comes in.* KIRSTIE *is embarrassed and hurries to leave.*

LAURA Knock, knock.

KIRSTIE Right, I'll leave you to it.

JIM Thanks. Oh actually, Kirstie – can you get me one of those juice drinks you used to do for Tony? And I can't find my boots, are they . . .?

KIRSTIE Oh sorry, I'll get them.

JIM *smiles and* KIRSTIE *leaves.*

LAURA So how are you doing? I feel like I haven't seen you.

JIM Well, I've been rehearsing, haven't I? Finally got to go through the fights. With a sword this time, not a roll of wrapping paper.

LAURA Are you nervous?

JIM No. No, I'm all right.

LAURA Well, I just popped down to say break a leg.

JIM That's a bit near the bone under the circumstances.

LAURA I know – how is he?

JIM He's still in hospital. They're still doing tests on his spine.

LAURA He's going to be all right, though, isn't he?

JIM It's too early to tell.

LAURA Poor Tony. Still, that's what happens if you get pissed on the battlements.

JIM It could have been worse, but he fell on a gargoyle.

LAURA Felicity wasn't onstage, was she?

JIM It's not funny, Laura.

LAURA *reads some of* JIM*'s 'Good Luck' cards as he continues with his make-up.*

LAURA It's weird – now she's gone I quite miss her.

JIM I thought you hated her?

LAURA Yes, but I do feel sorry for her. She just made the wrong call, that's all. She should have sent you on.

JIM You shouldn't have said she was sexually harassing you, though.

LAURA I never said that! I don't know where that's come from.

JIM Well, that's why she was sacked.

An awkward silence.

JIM *(cont'd)* Where's Kirstie with that drink?

LAURA Anyway, I've booked a table at Papa Dell's for after the show. My sister's in and we can . . .

JIM Ah – I'd love to, but I'm already going out with the cast. They're taking me to Joe Allen's. I couldn't say no, could I?

LAURA We'll come with you.

JIM Your sister?

LAURA Yeah.

JIM At Joe Allen's?

LAURA Why not?

JIM It's always very awkward mixing actors and civilians. You know what they're like, they're even funny about including the understudies.

LAURA I'm an understudy.

JIM I know you are.

An announcement on the tannoy breaks the awkward silence.

STAGE MANAGER *(V.O.)* Ladies and gentlemen of the *Macbeth* company, this is your half-hour call. Thirty minutes, please.

JIM Look, just let me get through this and we can sort it out after, OK?

LAURA You'll be fantastic.

JIM I won't if I don't concentrate. Sorry, Laura, I just need to get my head together.

LAURA Are you asking me to go?

JIM I am really, yes. I need to . . . prepare. Sorry.

LAURA *is put out but tries to hide it.*

LAURA All right. I'll see you later then.

JIM Laura?

LAURA Yes?

JIM Thanks.

LAURA What for?

JIM *indicates the dressing room around him.*

JIM This.

LAURA *leaves.* JIM *looks at himself in the mirror – it is the same image he saw reflected at the end of Act One.*

Over the tannoy we hear a distorted witch-like voice.

WITCH VOICE *(V.O.)* All hail, Macbeth, that shalt be king hereafter . . .

The mirror drips with blood. The tannoy sounds a loud blast of feedback that sounds like a woman's scream.

CAPTION: *'ACT V'*

INT. DRESSING ROOM. DAY.

Dressing room number 9 has been refurbished: new sofa, different-coloured wallpaper and a whole new set of 'Good Luck' cards around the mirror.

JIM *is on the phone to his agent. He seems more confident and mature. The new company manager,* NICK, *stands by his side, sliding away poster after poster as* JIM *casually signs them. The poster is for* 'Richard III *starring JIM BAILEY.'*

JIM And do we know who's playing the girl? OK, well, if it was an offer it might be different, but I don't want to do it for that kind of money, so I'll pass. Oh, by the way, did I tell you I got my old dressing room back for 'Dick the Shit'? . . . Yeah, it's all been done out. Is that anything to do with me? . . . Come on, I bet it was . . . All right, well, we'll speak soon. Bye.

NICK *has been waiting for* JIM *to finish.*

JIM *(cont'd)* Sorry about that.

NICK *is very posh and very polite.*

NICK Not at all. Now, do you remember the conversation we had about a meet-and-greet with some lovely disabled people?

JIM Oh, that's not now, is it? Why can't we do it after the show? You know I don't like people in during the half.

NICK They won't have time after the show, but that's not a problem. I can tell them you are unavailable and that's just the way it is . . .

JIM No, it's all right, Nick. Send them in. Five minutes, though, yeah? Then say I've got to do something.

NICK You are a gentleman, sir. And thank you very much for signing the posters. The understudies will be delighted.

NICK *rolls up the posters and leaves.* JIM *puts his boots on over his tights and sips from a wheatgrass juice. He clears his throat and does a bit of voice work.*

JIM 'Now . . . now . . . now is the winter . . . is the winter of our discontent . . .'

TONY *(V.O.)* '. . . Made glorious summer by this son of York.' Played him in Stratford '82. Michele Dotrice was my Lady Anne.

JIM *turns around to see* TONY *in his wheelchair.* TONY *is paralysed from his accident, but can manipulate his chair with some hand movement.*

TONY How are you, Jim?

JIM Tony!

TONY Good to see you, mate.

JIM What are you doing here?

TONY I've come to see you, haven't I? Crip trip. We get free tickets, you know?

JIM God, it's so nice to see you. How long has it been?

TONY It's been nineteen months and three weeks. How's things with you? I've heard nothing but raves.

JIM Well, I learned it all from the master, didn't I? Look, I've even got my juice drink!

JIM *realises this is rather a sensitive area.*

TONY Ah yes. I, er . . . I don't drink that stuff any more.

JIM No.

TONY Still, every cloud has a silver lining. You've been busy.

JIM Yes, it's been non-stop. Obviously we took Maccers to Broadway and then I was straight to Ireland for *Game of Thrones* . . . What about you? I heard you're doing talking books?

TONY Yes, I'm giving Jarvis a run for his money. Keeps me out of trouble anyway.

JIM Good.

There is an awkward silence.

TONY They've done this room out nice.

JIM Yes, it was my agent, I think. Embarrassing, really.

TONY Well, my agent gave me this blanket. Small checks. Haha.

JIM Good. So good to see you.

Pause.

TONY How's that lovely girlfriend of yours? Have you done the decent thing yet?

JIM You mean Suzie?

TONY No – the blonde piece. Understudied Lady M? You were engaged, weren't you?

JIM Laura? Oh no, we're not together any more. Don't know what she's up to these days.

TONY Shame, she was a sweet girl.

JIM Hmm. Anyway, listen, I don't want to chuck you out, but I've got to get my calipers on and, er . . .

TONY Of course – looking forward to it. Well, you're doing something right anyway. Keep at it. You're having the career for both of us now.

JIM Thanks.

TONY *wheels away towards the corridor.*

TONY OK, wagons roll!

KIRSTIE *comes in and goes to take* TONY *out. She is styled similarly to how Laura dressed.*

KIRSTIE All done? Thank you very much.

KIRSTIE *wheels* TONY *out of the door.*

JIM Kirstie?

NICK *is in the doorway with* TONY *as* KIRSTIE *turns back to* JIM.

NICK I'll get the lift for you, if you'd like to walk this way, so to speak.

NICK *leads* TONY *away.* KIRSTIE *remains in the room.*

KIRSTIE Hello, Jim.

JIM It *is* you!

KIRSTIE I'm surprised you remember me.

JIM Course I remember you. So, what, you're looking after Tony now?

KIRSTIE Yes. I'm his full-time carer. He's calmed down a bit since . . .

JIM Yes, obviously. Well, it's lovely to see you. I hope you enjoy the show . . .

KIRSTIE Oh, I've already seen it.

JIM Really?

KIRSTIE Yeah, I've seen everything you've done since we worked together. Sometimes I come three or four times a week, just to see the little changes in your performance.

JIM Gosh . . .

KIRSTIE I always knew you'd go far. You just needed a little push. 'Some people are born great, some achieve greatness and some have greatness thrust upon them.'

JIM Sorry, what do you mean?

KIRSTIE This room looks better now. More fitting for a star like you. She made a real mess of it.

JIM Who did?

KIRSTIE Laura. When she killed herself.

JIM What!?

KIRSTIE Sorry, didn't you know? She slit her wrists in the shower. Blood everywhere apparently. Right through to the floorboards.

JIM Laura's . . . died?

KIRSTIE Hmm. I'm surprised you didn't know, but then why would you? You've been away.

JIM Yes, I was . . . recurring character in *Game of Thrones* . . . Shit . . .

KIRSTIE Which you are brilliant in, by the way.

JIM Thank you, thank you.

NICK *makes a tannoy announcement.*

NICK *(V.O.)* Ladies and gentlemen, this is your Act One beginners call, Act One beginners to the stage, please, thank you.

JIM Erm . . .

JIM *is stunned and looks towards his calipers.* KIRSTIE *takes them from him and kneels in front of him.*

KIRSTIE I'll do that for you. Just like old times.

KIRSTIE *fastens the calipers onto* JIM*'s legs.*

KIRSTIE *(cont'd)* Sorry, I shouldn't have said anything – they obviously didn't want you to know. I hope it doesn't affect your performance.

JIM No, it's fine, it's just a shock. I think I know why she did it actually.

KIRSTIE Why?

JIM She was responsible for Tony's accident. She obviously couldn't live with the guilt.

KIRSTIE That wasn't Laura. It was me. I spiked Tony's drink that day. It was pure alcohol – I took it from the Wig Store.

JIM What?

KIRSTIE And I got rid of Felicity for you. She never would have put you on – she couldn't see what I could see. I said she'd cupped my breast in the Wendy house backstage. Instant dismissal.

KIRSTIE *takes* JIM*'s leather costume coat and helps him on with it.*

JIM But . . . why would you do that?

KIRSTIE For you, Jim, for your career. I've seen it happen too many times: genuine talent not being recognised. Looking after Tony is the price I pay for what I did. Just as Laura's death is the price you pay.

JIM But that's nothing to do with me.

KIRSTIE I know it's not. Your career had to come first. You told her that.

KIRSTIE *kisses* JIM *on the cheek and starts to leave.*

KIRSTIE *(cont'd)* Oh look, Jim . . .

KIRSTIE *shows* JIM *that she is wearing* LAURA*'s engagement ring.*

KIRSTIE *(cont'd)* I took it from Laura. I think she wanted me to have it. I'm waiting in the wings, like an understudy. Have a good show.

KIRSTIE *leaves, stopping at the doorway.*

KIRSTIE *(cont'd)* I'll be watching.

JIM *looks devastated. He closes his eyes.*

INT. DRESSING ROOM. NIGHT. (FLASHBACK)

JIM *sees the flash of* LAURA*'s hand holding the bloody dagger, only this time we pull out to see* LAURA *holding the dagger having slit her wrists. Blood on the carpet. Blood on the mirror.*

NICK *(V.O.)* Knock, knock.

INT. DRESSING ROOM. DAY.

A knock on the door. JIM *opens his eyes as* NICK *pops his head into the room.*

NICK All set to smile and smile and be a villain?

JIM Yes, sorry.

NICK *helps* JIM *to limp out of the room. Blackout.*

THE END

Episode 6

THE HARROWING

CAST LIST

KATY – Aimeé-Ffion Edwards

TABITHA – Helen McCrory

HECTOR – Reece Shearsmith

SHELL – Poppy Rush

ANDRAS – Sean Buckley

EXT. MOLOCH HOUSE. EVENING.

A large, imposing house set back from the rest of the street. The Moloch house is a scary-looking Gothic building with a small overgrown front garden. All the curtains of the latticed windows are closed. The front door is dark and heavy-looking with ivy and brambles growing around it. A stained-glass panel in the door shows the number '9' . . .

TITLE: *'The Harrowing'.*

INT. KITCHEN. EVENING.

A pair of female hands is preparing some milk from baby powder. Three big scoops are spooned out of a tin and put into a baby's bottle, which is taken over to a kettle and filled with warm water. One hand shakes the bottle to mix it as the other brings some rusks out from a cupboard.

The bottle and a rusk are placed on a tray. Finally, our mysterious hands go to a drawer and take out an ugly-looking pair of pliers, which they also place neatly on the tray before picking it up and leaving the room.

EXT. STREET. EVENING.

KATY HEPWORTH, *a neat, well-behaved student in a brace and glasses, walks along the pavement of a grand-looking row of Victorian houses. She carries a bag and is on her phone.*

KATY I can't while I'm talking to you, can I? I'm using locations. I'm going to be there all night – £11 an hour . . . I'm not! I swear. And it's 'til two! Yeah, £88 for the night! I'll text you the address, shall I . . .? Shell? Hello?

KATY *has lost her phone signal. Holding her phone out, she tries to track her progress on her GPS map. She stops, looking puzzled at a particular house. The Moloch house.*

Resorting to more old-fashioned methods, she gets out a piece of paper, checks it and approaches.

EXT. MOLOCH HOUSE. EVENING.

KATY *walks up the path of the spooky house. She arrives at the door and rings the bell.*

TABITHA MOLOCH, *a formidable woman in her fifties, answers the door. She towers in the doorway, tall, thin and with long white hair. She is dressed for what looks like a very special black-tie occasion. She speaks very softly, almost serenely.*

TABITHA Miss Hepworth?

KATY That's right. Katy. Mrs Moloch?

TABITHA Miss. Come in, please. We're so pleased you could do this . . .

KATY *goes inside.* TABITHA *looks around, then gently closes the door.*

INT. PORCH. EVENING.

KATY *and* TABITHA *are in the porch. There are large fur coats and overcoats hanging up.*

TABITHA Did you bring an extra coat as I advised?

KATY Yes, it's in here.

TABITHA You might want to put it on now, please.

KATY *gets another coat out of her bag and puts it on.* TABITHA *opens the inner door.*

INT. LOBBY. EVENING.

Inside the house is not what you would expect from its Victorian exterior. It is very stark, marble floors, columns. But mainly it is FREEZING. Even with her extra layers on, KATY *is cold. As they breathe, we can see their breath condensing in the air.* KATY *shivers.*

KATY Oh, you weren't joking.

TABITHA The house is maintained at three below freezing at all times. My eldest brother has a medical condition and the air humidity is critical . . . Anyway, it's a small price to pay.

Dark paintings cover the walls. These depict religious scenes and iconography and many show demons and hell, as well as the crucifixion of Christ. There's something of the hotel lobby about it, with a bit of the Uffizi mixed in. KATY *looks at the paintings.*

KATY Wow.

TABITHA Ah!

KATY These are . . . old.

TABITHA You're studying art, aren't you?

KATY Yes. Well, Art and Design Technology.

TABITHA A broad church indeed.

KATY Are these originals?

TABITHA What would be the point otherwise? I've never understood the notion of 'prints'. Puts me in mind of wax fruit.

KATY Well, I suppose some people can't afford the real thing.

TABITHA I disagree. Bananas are very cheap if you buy them ripe. I'm joking, of course.

KATY *looks at some of the details in the paintings. Demons leering at Christ, pitchforks, flames and the tortured, contorted bodies of souls in Damnation.*

KATY Are they all . . . religious?

TABITHA Most depict the Harrowing of Hell, all of which is non-canonical to the Bible.

KATY 'The Harrowing of Hell'?

TABITHA Jesus is said to have descended into Hell and released its captives. He set free Adam and Eve, all the Old Testament saints – you can read it in the Gospel of Nicodemus.

TABITHA *points to an ancient medieval painting.*

TABITHA *(cont'd)* This is a lesser-known Andrea da Firenze from the 14th century. You recognise it?

KATY Not really. We do more collages and stuff.

TABITHA What are you working on at the moment?

KATY I'm doing a still life of a pair of trainers and a jack-in-a-box.

TABITHA Sounds . . . charming.

KATY Our teacher says the Renaissance was the biggest dead end in art.

TABITHA You don't like them?

KATY They're not what I would choose, but . . .

TABITHA And what would you choose? A topless man holding a baby? A kitten in a champagne glass? A 'Keep Calm and Carry On' poster?

KATY Well . . .

TABITHA I'm teasing. You find them frightening, it's understandable. You're still too full of life to find solace in them.

KATY I don't agree with my teacher.

TABITHA Good.

KATY *gazes up the staircase. It has been fitted with a rail that would carry a wheelchair up and down it.* TABITHA *sees* KATY *looking at it.*

KATY Is that for your brother?

TABITHA For my other brother, Hector.

KATY Oh right. Is he . . .?

TABITHA Disabled? No. Just lazy. One day in 1998 he complained his knees hurt on the stairs and within three days he installed this.

KATY Oh. Wow.

TABITHA He's impulsive in all the wrong ways. We now have zinc roofs because he tired of galvanised steel. The blinds were torn down in favour of blackout curtains. I have a waste-disposal unit in the sink, but he won't take me to Florence.

KATY Maybe one day he'll surprise you.

TABITHA He doesn't know the meaning of the word. We live like clockwork mice. Nothing is ever different. But he'll be down in a moment – you can draw your own conclusions. Come through.

TABITHA *takes* KATY *through a door into the kitchen.*

INT. KITCHEN. EVENING.

The kitchen is more blandly modern. Nothing particularly odd about this, except perhaps quite a few tins of powdered baby milk lining one shelf. And far too many packs of rusks.

KATY You've got a lovely house.

TABITHA 'We have put her living within the tomb.' Madeline Usher and I have a great deal in common. Do you know Poe?

KATY From the *Teletubbies*?

TABITHA Who are they?

KATY It's a children's programme. There's four of them. The smallest one is called Po.

TABITHA That's not who I meant. You come highly recommended by Gracie Proud, a friend of mine who attends the church.

KATY Yes. She said she'd spoken to you about me. I look after Gabriel and Ethan.

TABITHA I know you do. They speak fondly of the day you dressed them as – what was it? – Jedward?

KATY We did do that, yes.

TABITHA Yellow wool for hair or something?

KATY That's right, yeah.

TABITHA Well, I'm very pleased to have found someone like you.

KATY Like me?

TABITHA Someone I can be confident in. Championed. It's impossibly rare, you know?

A chugging, clanging noise begins from outside. KATY *looks puzzled.*

KATY What's that?

TABITHA Hector. He's on his way down. That's the noise of the stairlift, ironically enough on its last legs. But to business. As *people*, Hector and I never leave the house. We have an event tonight that surfaces so rarely, it would be considered rude not to attend.

KATY Mrs Proud said your older brother . . .

TABITHA Andras. He, unlike Hector, IS disabled. Terribly so. Born 'inside out' as my mother used to say. He will be of no concern to you, however. He is confined to his room at the top of the house and will sleep for most of the night. He is the reason we live in the ice like this.

KATY Right.

TABITHA Your stay here this evening is more to look after the house than to babysit Andras.

HECTOR *(V.O.)* He's nearly 55, Tabs, he's hardly a baby.

KATY *looks around to see* HECTOR MOLOCH *coming into the kitchen. In his tuxedo, he is also tall, grey-haired and very imposing, despite being slightly waspish. His bow tie is undone and he has a stick, which he grips with hands that bear unusually groomed fingernails. Too long to go unnoticed.*

TABITHA Miss Hepworth – this is my brother Hector.

HECTOR How do you do?

He holds out a hand, showing off those long nails. KATY *can't help but falter slightly.*

HECTOR *(cont'd)* I play guitar, Miss Hepworth. I'm not a vampire, if that's what you're thinking.

KATY Oh no! I wasn't. And Katy – my name's Katy. Hello.

TABITHA We thought we heard you chugging down the stairs on your little throne. You have to fix it, Hector. It shouldn't make that horrible noise.

HECTOR That's no way to speak about our poor brother.

TABITHA Don't.

HECTOR I'll call that man Tyler back. He was good with the sink, wasn't he?

TABITHA *rolls her eyes at* KATY.

HECTOR *(cont'd)* Can you tie a bow tie, Katy?

KATY No, I don't know how to, sorry.

HECTOR It'll have to be you then, Tabs.

TABITHA *ties* HECTOR*'s bow tie for him.*

HECTOR *(cont'd)* Has Tabitha gone through the phone numbers?

KATY Not really, no. She was just talking about . . . Adrian, was it?

TABITHA Andras.

HECTOR Well, he's not going anywhere, he can wait. Mobiles in this street are useless. It's a dead zone.

KATY Yes, my signal went.

HECTOR I think it's due to foliage or some such, and since rounding the corner your phone will have been in a state of outage.

TABITHA We were offered something called 'broadbands', weren't we?

HECTOR Yes, but the man was sootified so I closed the door. Therefore the landline is of vital importance to us here. Follow me.

HECTOR *leads* KATY *out of the kitchen.*

INT. HALLWAY. EVE.

HECTOR *shows* KATY *a cupboard under the stairs that has an old-fashioned phone tucked away inside it.*

HECTOR This evening, if the need arises, it is from *this* phone that you can call us. You won't need to ring it. You just won't. Nothing will happen. *Nothing* ever happens. And we are back by 2 a.m. at the very latest. But. But, but, but . . . *should* an emergency occur, this is the number to ring. We do share a party line here, so try and avoid eavesdropping if it's engaged.

KATY Party line?

HECTOR Yes, we share our telephone line with a second subscriber. It is a 20th-century arrangement that we've never readdressed. Annoying as it is, we do often know what they're having for tea.

KATY *looks up the stairs.*

KATY Right. Do I need to check on Andras? Is that something you need me to do?

HECTOR You have no need to go up there. He is fine in his room. He has everything he needs. He knows you're here this evening – we told him all about you.

TABITHA He won't disturb you.

At this, HECTOR *laughs in spite of himself.*

TABITHA *(cont'd)* TV and everything is through there – we have all three channels, you just need to give it five minutes to warm up. Let me quickly show you where the food is.

TABITHA *returns to the kitchen.* KATY *follows.* HECTOR *goes to get his coat and scarf.*

INT. KITCHEN. EVENING.

TABITHA *opens some of the kitchen cupboards.*

TABITHA There's food in here – obviously we have no need of a refrigerator.

KATY Obviously.

TABITHA I don't suppose we have the kinds of thing you like. I presume from your skin you eat pizza?

KATY Sometimes.

TABITHA We don't have those. But don't go hungry. Please take what you like.

KATY *comments on the baby powder.*

KATY Plenty of milk.

TABITHA That's Andras. Milk and rusks. That's all he can have. He doesn't eat properly, you see.

KATY The disability?

TABITHA That. And the fact he doesn't have a mouth.

KATY *takes this in.* HECTOR *comes into the kitchen.*

HECTOR Car's here, Tabs, better get moving. Got everything?

TABITHA I just need my bag. One last thing, Katy – just so you know, Andras has a bell by his bed. He has never rung it. He won't ring it. But I'm telling you – just in case. Right, *you* have keys?

HECTOR *nods.*

TABITHA *(cont'd)* Then we'll be off. Goodnight, Katy.

KATY Night!

HECTOR Be good.

TABITHA *and* HECTOR *leave. After some hubbub, the door finally shuts. They have gone. The first thing* KATY *does is check her phone again. She tries getting a signal by moving about the kitchen. Nothing. She looks in the bread bin. Pulls out a loaf, snaps off a slice. The bread is frozen. Giving up on food, she takes her bag and goes out into the hall.*

INT. HALLWAY. EVENING.

KATY *opens the cupboard that contains the phone. She picks up the receiver and listens to the dial tone. She puts it back. Freezing, she puts on a hat and scarf from her bag. She makes her way into the living room.*

INT. LIVING ROOM. EVENING.

The living room is different again. Gloomy, with the feel of a grandmother's parlour. You could easily hold a seance in here and not feel out of place. The television set is old, wooden and clearly doesn't have Sky.

KATY *sees a copy of the* Radio Times *from 1973 and picks it up. She flicks through and sees in the listings 'New series –* Last of the Summer Wine*'. It has been ringed in red pen.*

KATY *spots a black cat lying asleep on the sofa. She goes over to stroke it.*

KATY Hello. Hello, you.

It doesn't take long for KATY *to realise the cat is stuffed. She picks it up – stiff as a board. The absurdity of her having stroked it makes* KATY *laugh.*

On the side table is a framed photograph from the early 1960s of HECTOR, TABITHA *and* ANDRAS *when they were children. They are posing with their pet black cat.* ANDRAS *is nine years old,* TABITHA *is four and* HECTOR *is two.* KATY *looks at* ANDRAS*'s smiling face.*

KATY *(cont'd)* He doesn't look disabled . . .

The doorbell suddenly rings. KATY *jumps up and leaves the room.*

INT. MOLOCH PORCH. NIGHT.

KATY *opens the door to her friend* SHELL, *a plump girl, dressed in all black. She is a goth and wears a large crucifix around her neck. Looking part geisha, part Tim Burton, she looks vaguely ridiculous.*

SHELL God – who lives here, the Munsters?

KATY I can't believe you found it. I never gave you the address, did I?

SHELL I've been ringing you . . .

KATY I know, there's no signal. Come in.

INT. HALLWAY. NIGHT.

SHELL *notices the cold immediately.*

SHELL Oh my God, it's freezing. What is this? Is there no heating?

KATY No, there's someone upstairs . . . they need it cold.

SHELL What is he, a snowman? I can't stay here, Katy, it's unbearable.

SHELL *has spotted the paintings. She looks at them.*

SHELL *(cont'd)* Urgh. These are vile. I love them.

KATY I knew you would. It's all religious stuff.

SHELL Who'd have these up in their house, except me?

KATY I don't know. They're all demons.

SHELL This lot looks like One Direction.

KATY Do you think things like that actually exist?

SHELL One Direction? Sadly, yes, they do.

KATY I meant the demons.

SHELL I know you did. I was being ironical. Yes, I do think demons exist – we have one teaching us maths.

KATY Funny. Hell definitely exists.

SHELL How do you know?

KATY No smoke without fire.

SHELL Not funny.

KATY It's all just made up to scare people.

SHELL What's wrong with that? I like scaring people.

KATY It comes so easily to you, doesn't it?

SHELL I think I'd have definitely been burnt as a witch if I lived in them days.

KATY You would dressed like that. Speaking of witches, come and see the cat. It's so cute.

SHELL Have you found out where they keep the drink?

KATY They haven't got any. All they've got is milk and rusks.

SHELL I love rusks! This house is amazing. I could so live here. Look at this.

SHELL *has got in the stairlift and presses the button to set it going. It clangs into action, sounding louder and closer to breaking than before.*

SHELL *(cont'd)* Chessington!

SHELL *glides up the stairs. Halfway up, she presses the button and the chair changes direction and comes down. She chops and changes the chair. Up. Down. Up. Down.*

KATY Don't, Shell, you'll break it.

SHELL It's like Rattlesnake!

KATY Get off it. You're too big.

SHELL Oh thanks, bitch. I'm here two minutes and I'm getting called fat.

KATY It's not that. They said it's going to break.

The phone rings. It is loud, even over the chugging of the stairlift.

KATY *(cont'd)* Turn it off!

SHELL But the ride hasn't finished.

KATY Quick, I've got to answer it.

SHELL All right, all right.

SHELL *stops the chair in the dark near the top of the stairs, and* **KATY** *answers the phone.* **SHELL** *comes down and all through the conversation annoyingly mimes a version of* **KATY** *speaking on the phone.*

KATY Hello? Oh hello, Mr Moloch. The what is it? OK. Whereabouts? In the cupboard itself. OK. No, no, I've just got the TV on. OK then. No problem. I will. Bye.

KATY *hangs up.*

KATY *(cont'd)* What are you trying to do? I nearly laughed in his face then! I think he heard you!

SHELL What did he want anyway?

KATY I've got to check the heating.

SHELL But there isn't any.

KATY Exactly. I have to make sure it stays this cold.

KATY *makes her way back to the kitchen.* **SHELL** *follows.*

SHELL This is just weird, Katy. Even for me. It's just as well we're being paid shitloads.

KATY 'We'??

INT. KITCHEN. NIGHT.

KATY *comes into the kitchen, calling back through to* **SHELL**. **KATY** *opens the kitchen cupboards.*

KATY You're not having any of it. I'm the one that's been 'championed'.

KATY *finds the thermostat. She checks the heating, steady at minus three.*

KATY *(cont'd)* It's fine. Still freezing.

KATY *wonders where* **SHELL** *has got to.*

KATY *(cont'd)* Shell?

SHELL *enters the kitchen.*

SHELL What?

KATY What are you doing? Look at this.

KATY *has spotted that the cupboard containing the thermostat is packed full of tins of cat food.*

SHELL So what? You said they had a cat.

KATY Yes, but . . .

The cat wanders into the room. And purrs round **SHELL***'s legs.*

KATY *(cont'd)* Argh!

SHELL Katy! What's the matter?

KATY No, Shell – that cat was stuffed!

SHELL What?

KATY It was dead on the sofa. I stroked it. It was rock hard.

SHELL She was probably cold – weren't you, little one?

SHELL *picks up the cat and strokes it.*

SHELL *(cont'd)* Shall we feed it?

KATY No. Get it away from me.

SHELL Don't be mean.

KATY It was dead.

KATY *runs out of the kitchen.*

INT. LIVING ROOM. NIGHT.

KATY *enters the living room and looks for the stuffed cat. It isn't there anymore.* SHELL *enters holding the cat.*

SHELL Oh, this is great. *Antiques Roadshow*!

KATY It was on there. It was stuffed. Look, it's in the pictures with them.

KATY *shows* SHELL *the family photograph, then starts to punch in a number on her mobile phone.*

SHELL What are you doing?

KATY I'm ringing my dad. I want to go home.

SHELL Not on that, you're not.

KATY *remembers that there's no signal here.*

KATY Shit. Doesn't matter. I'll use theirs.

KATY *leaves the room*

INT. HALLWAY. NIGHT.

KATY *runs to the phone under the stairs. She picks up the receiver and is about to dial when she hears voices.*

KATY Brilliant.

SHELL What's wrong?

KATY It's the party line.

SHELL What?

KATY Excuse me . . . excuse me. I need to use the phone . . . Do you think . . . I . . . It's an emergency.

KATY *puts the phone down.*

SHELL What did they say?

KATY Try again in 15 minutes. They're having bolognese apparently. That's it – I'm off.

SHELL You can't just leave, Katy. What about . . . Frosty the Snowman upstairs? He might melt.

KATY He's not going anywhere – he's an invalid.

Suddenly the stairlift starts up. The girls look up the stairs into the blackness. Transfixed, they stare up, waiting for the chair to emerge. The clanking grows louder and louder as it makes its way down the staircase. Out of the darkness the chair emerges – empty. It chugs its way down to the bottom and stops.

SHELL Well, you said it was faulty.

KATY Come on – let's go.

SHELL Are you really going to leave?

KATY Yes, I am.

SHELL What about the money?

KATY Forget it. This is just too weird.

KATY *goes to the door.*

KATY *(cont'd)* Are you coming or what? You're not even meant to be here . . .

SHELL All right. See you, puss puss.

SHELL *puts the cat down and it runs up the stairs. The girls are about to leave when . . . Ring! Ring! Ring! Ring! A bell from upstairs starts to ring frantically. Both girls stop dead in their tracks.*

KATY Oh no.

SHELL What is it?

KATY It's him.

SHELL Who?

KATY Him! The snowman. The brother. Oh fuck.

The bell keeps ringing. Horribly insistent.

SHELL What shall we do?

KATY I don't know. Oh God. They said this wouldn't happen. He said NOTHING ever happens.

SHELL We'll have to go up.

KATY I can't.

SHELL We have to. He might be ill or something.

KATY He IS ill.

SHELL Well, come on then. Come on, Katy. We can't just leave him.

KATY *thinks for a moment. The ringing stops.*

KATY It's stopped now. Maybe he's all right.

SHELL Yeah. It's either that. Or he died.

KATY Don't say that!

SHELL We have to check, come on.

KATY I'll call them – tell them he's ringing the bell.

SHELL You can't, can you? The Dolmio family are on the other line.

KATY Oh . . . GOD!

KATY *thinks for a second.*

KATY *(cont'd)* Come on then. Stay with me.

KATY *and* SHELL *begin to climb the stairs. A long, slow walk.* KATY *tries to ignore the paintings, now all the more horrible and lurid.* SHELL *is bolder, catching sight of a particularly ghastly one of a spindly demon attacking a woman, tearing at her flesh with long talons.*

SHELL Look at this! If she had glasses and a brace she'd look like you!

KATY Don't, Shell!

SHELL What? You could be a reincarnation. Me and Carl Crawford did a Ouija board once and a ghost from the future came through.

KATY How did you know he was from the future?

SHELL Because he told us he wasn't even dead yet.

KATY *tries to compute this but gives up.*

KATY I can't even . . . come on.

KATY *and* SHELL *reach the top of the stairs. It is very dark, lit only by moonlight through the odd window.*

INT. LANDING. NIGHT.

They stand in the dark. Several doors are before them. They speak in scared whispers.

SHELL Which one is it?

KATY I don't know.

SHELL What? Why?

KATY They never said. 'He won't ring the bell. He never rings the bell.'

SHELL *suddenly calls out.*

SHELL Hello?

KATY Don't!

SHELL We have to! Hello? Are you OK?

KATY He can't answer.

SHELL Why not?

KATY He . . . just can't, all right? Come on.

KATY *walks down the landing and slowly tries the first door. It opens with a creak.*

INT. HECTOR'S BEDROOM. NIGHT

KATY *goes into a dark bedroom. She snaps on a light and is relieved that* ANDRAS *isn't there.*

SHELL *(V.O.)* He's not here.

KATY *jumps.*

KATY Don't do that! Shit. Come on.

SHELL Cool. Look at this.

SHELL *has picked up* HECTOR*'s guitar and starts strumming it.*

KATY Put that down.

SHELL I always wanted a guitar. Fucking cello. No one plays the cello.

KATY Leave it, please.

SHELL *puts the guitar back on the bed and spots that the bed is surrounded by a thin trail of salt.*

SHELL Urgh – look at this.

KATY What is it?

SHELL Salt.

KATY Why's he got salt round his bed?

SHELL Dunno. Maybe they've got slugs.

KATY Come on . . .

SHELL *follows* KATY *out.*

INT. LANDING. NIGHT.

They walk along to the next door.

KATY I'll try this one. Just so you're aware, I know that cat is going to jump out at some point and I'm still going to scream, OK?

SHELL OK.

KATY *opens the door slowly. Screech! The cat does jump out and runs away.* KATY *screams like she said she would, as does* SHELL. *They recover and begin to laugh.*

SHELL *(cont'd)* Thought I'd join you.

KATY This isn't worth £88!

SHELL I told you it was like Chessington! At least we haven't had to queue.

Their laughter is interrupted by the bell ringing again. It is close. The next door in fact. They walk up and stop outside it.

KATY OK. You ready?

SHELL Yep.

KATY *opens the door slowly and goes inside.*

INT. ANDRAS'S BEDROOM. NIGHT.

KATY *enters the bedroom. It is lit only by a small light in the corner. The four-poster bed in the middle of the room is veiled, so we are unable to see who or what lies beneath. A drip stands by the bed. The red light of a heart-monitor machine flashes quietly on and off.*

SHELL Stinks.

KATY Mr Moloch?

SHELL *comes close behind* KATY.

SHELL 'Moloch' as in 'bollock'?

KATY Shh.

SHELL Creepy bed.

KATY Andras? Just checking you're OK. My name's Katy Hepworth, I'm . . . looking after the house while your brother and sister are out. I think they told you about me.

Nothing. KATY *approaches the side of the bed. It is extremely cold. The girls shiver.*

KATY *slowly pulls back the thin curtain. Lying on the bed is the sad figure of* ANDRAS MOLOCH. *He is very thin, with wispy white hair cobwebbing across his dirty pillow. His eyes are white with cataracts and his mouth is bound tight shut with dirty bandages.*

ANDRAS *has been tied up but has managed to free one arm to grab the bell. His wrist is bloody and sore from working it free; his nails are like yellow, overgrown talons, some roughly cut. The end of the drip trails from* ANDRAS*'s skeletal arm.*

KATY *(cont'd)* Oh my God.

SHELL Shit.

SHELL *stares in disbelief at what she is seeing.*

KATY Shell – help me. Shell!

KATY *makes to untie* ANDRAS.

SHELL Wait!

KATY *stops and looks at* SHELL.

SHELL *(cont'd)* Don't release him. Not yet.

KATY What are you talking about? Come on.

SHELL *pulls back the thin bedsheet to see his legs, which are tied tight with electrical cable.*

SHELL Katy, look.

KATY *sees that* ANDRAS*'s feet are deformed. The toes merged together. You might almost say cloven.* KATY *freezes, then gathers herself.*

KATY What have they done to you?

KATY *slowly takes off the bandages from around* ANDRAS*'s mouth. He gasps air through his mouth, as if for the first time in many years. His teeth are sharp and rotten, tongue black; his mouth a raw, gaping maw.*

KATY *(cont'd)* All right. You're all right now.

ANDRAS *tries to speak – but it is a hoarse, cracked whisper.*

SHELL He's trying to say something.

KATY All right. All right . . . slowly. Slowly.

ANDRAS Free . . . free . . .

KATY Yes, yes. We'll get you out.

ANDRAS Mischief . . .

SHELL What did he say?

KATY I don't know – come on.

KATY *begins to loosen the cords around* ANDRAS*'s wrist.*

From outside on the landing the girls hear the guitar start playing. It is 'Frosty the Snowman'. In the doorway steps the imposing figure of HECTOR MOLOCH. *He sings as he plays.*

HECTOR 'Frosty the Snowman was a jolly happy soul . . .'

Behind him, carrying her cat, steps TABITHA MOLOCH.

TABITHA 'A jolly happy soul'. Oh dear. Is that right, Andras? Are you a happy soul?

KATY I don't know what you've been doing but we're calling the police.

HECTOR Really? What with? Your phone is in a state of outage.

HECTOR *puts his guitar by the end of the bed.*

SHELL You keep forgetting that.

TABITHA 'Were he as fair once, as he now is foul, / And lifted up his brow against his Maker, / Well may proceed from him all tribulation.'

SHELL Dante's *Inferno.*

TABITHA Well done.

HECTOR Dante's Hell was ice. And just as Lucifer was kept in ice, so our brother the demon is kept in ice.

KATY What are you talking about? Your brother's not a demon!

HECTOR Technically you are right. Andras was possessed when he was ten years old.

KATY Possessed?

SHELL Like *The Exorcist*?

TABITHA His name is Castiel – demon of Mischief.

ANDRAS Mischief . . .

HECTOR Begat by the seed of He Who Walks Backwards.

SHELL Michael Jackson?

HECTOR No, not Michael Jackson. The Goat of Mendes. The Devil himself.

TABITHA Castiel was loosed upon the world during the Harrowing. Accidentally set free during that infamous raid on Hell.

SHELL Ask them how they did the cat.

KATY Shut up! Have you been here all along?

HECTOR Yes. You see, despite what my sister says, I am capable of some surprises.

KATY So you've . . . just been hiding?

TABITHA I told you we never leave the house.

KATY You said you had a function?

TABITHA 'Event', I said 'event' – and this is it. *You* are it.

SHELL Ask them how they did the cat.

HECTOR For almost half a century we have kept the demon from roaming the earth by confining Andras to this room. Alas, the host body is only mortal and when our brother passes, Castiel will be free.

TABITHA And that's where you come in, Katy. You have the strength and faith to tame the beast. You will house the demon for another 50 years.

KATY Fuck off!

SHELL Ask them how they did the cat.

TABITHA I think you should have that pleasure, Michelle.

KATY Wait . . . How do you . . .?

TABITHA Michelle comes to our church, Miss Hepworth. She is one of us.

SHELL We're just keeping order, Katy. Without us, it really would be Hell on earth. And I did the cat if you must know.

KATY What?

SHELL I hid the stuffed one when you went to the kitchen.

KATY Why?

SHELL To scare you! I like scaring people. I told you.

KATY Well, I'm sorry but you're all mad. This is just abuse. Your brother's not possessed, he's just a frightened old man who's been tied to a bed for 50 years. You're worse than the Fritzls!

KATY *starts to untie* **ANDRAS***'s hand.* **HECTOR** *has pulled something from a bureau in the room. It is a taser gun. He points it at* **KATY**.

HECTOR Stop that, please.

KATY What is that?

HECTOR It's a taser gun. This was only ever to be used in case of an emergency, but I'm afraid to say this is one.

KATY How can you have not heard of 'broadband' but you own a taser gun?

TABITHA Be still, Miss Hepworth. I just need you to lie down on the bed and relax. Michelle? Prepare the epidural, please . . .

SHELL *goes to prepare a hypodermic syringe and rubber tubing.*

KATY Look, if your brother's a demon, where's the proof?

HECTOR As you can see, his feet are cloven.

KATY I'm not going by the feet – my mum's got feet like that, it's just hard skin.

SHELL *brings over the medical equipment on a small trolley.*

SHELL It's ready.

HECTOR Turn around, please, Miss Hepworth, and remove your top. We'll try and make this as painless as possible . . .

KATY *starts to undo her blouse but then grabs the guitar, which is near the bed, and swings it at* HECTOR*'s head.* HECTOR *accidentally fires the taser, which lands on* TABITHA*'s chest.*

TABITHA *spasms and judders and* KATY *runs out of the room.*

INT. LANDING. NIGHT.

KATY *rushes down the landing and bolts down the stairs.*

INT. HALLWAY. NIGHT.

KATY *runs to the front door but it is locked.*

KATY Shit!

SHELL *(V.O.)* There's no point running, Katy, there's no way out.

KATY *rushes off to the living room.*

INT. ANDRAS'S BEDROOM. NIGHT.

HECTOR *is holding his head, which is bleeding. He removes the taser wires from* TABITHA*'s chest.* ANDRAS *is pulling at his bonds and screeching.*

HECTOR Quiet, Andras! Sorry about that, Tabs. You always said they were like two fried eggs.

TABITHA*'s speech is slurred and her hair is frizzled.*

TABITHA Thass no' funny, Hector. Where's the girl?

ANDRAS Mischief!

INT. LIVING ROOM. NIGHT.

SHELL *enters the living room with the hypodermic needle. There's no sign of* KATY *so* SHELL *searches the room.*

SHELL Come on, Katy. This is an honour. Your sacrifice keeps Misrule from the whole world, and for that you'll be rewarded in Paradise. Plus you'll still get your babysitting money, so it's not all been for nothing.

KATY *steps out from behind the curtain.*

KATY I thought you were my friend.

SHELL I am. I wouldn't be doing this otherwise.

KATY Why don't you let the demon go into you?

SHELL I wanted to, but they said I was too weak-willed. I think it's because I'm fat. You were chosen.

KATY Why?

SHELL *thinks.*

SHELL I can't remember now.

SHELL *quickly plunges the hypo needle into* **KATY***'s neck.*

INT. HALLWAY. NIGHT.

HECTOR *is on the telephone in the hallway.*

HECTOR That's right. No, she didn't turn up. We booked her for 7.30 p.m. Yes, well – just thought you ought to know.

INT. KITCHEN. NIGHT.

We continue to hear **HECTOR** *speaking over* **SHELL** *preparing powdered milk and rusks in the kitchen.*

HECTOR *(V.O.)* Yes, I understand, but you must see it from our point of view – we had an evening planned. Well, when she does turn up please tell her we were most upset. You shan't be hearing from us again. Goodbye.

TABITHA *watches on as* **SHELL** *prepares a bottle and a rusk.* **SHELL** *spoons the powdered milk but also adds a scoop of rat poison from another box.*

She looks to **TABITHA***, who smiles her approval.*

TABITHA Perfect. You're a godsend, Michelle.

SHELL *smiles and takes the milk and rusks out on the tray.*

INT. ANDRAS'S BEDROOM. NIGHT.

The room is as before. **ANDRAS** *lies in the bed, hungrily suckling from the baby bottle that* **SHELL** *is feeding him.* **TABITHA** *and* **HECTOR** *are untying* **ANDRAS***'s feet and hands.*

SHELL That's it . . . won't be long now.

HECTOR This is Andras's Last Supper, Katy.

We see KATY *is tied to a chair opposite the bed, wearing only her bra and pants. Her mouth is bandaged and she is groggy from an epidural, which we can see running into the base of her spine.*

TABITHA Castiel will soon be leaving this withered old husk, and he will find a new home inside you. We'll leave you to get acquainted.

HECTOR You're going to be spending a long time together.

TABITHA, HECTOR *and* SHELL *start to leave the room.* SHELL *smiles at* KATY.

SHELL I'm so jealous.

They leave and KATY *turns to hear the door being locked behind them. She turns back round to look at the bed.*

ANDRAS *slowly starts to raise himself from the bed. Free of his bonds for the first time in years, he is weak and disoriented, like a new-born calf.*

KATY *tries to move back in her chair as* ANDRAS *approaches from the shadows, slowly, menacingly.* KATY *is terrified as* ANDRAS *gets closer and closer. Then he stops.*

ANDRAS Mischief...

He smiles and KATY *can see his rotten teeth and milky cataract eyes.*

THE END

SERIES 2

Foreword

— Oh. I think I know what this is now.

'The 12 Days of Christine'

Embarking on the second series, we already had a feel for the scope of invention that the premise of *Inside No. 9* afforded us. It became evident that staying playful and surprising with *how* we tell our stories was just as important an ingredient as the storylines themselves.

Quite quickly it became exciting to break any rules we might have had about the time period or geographical setting of a *No. 9*, and that led us to an exploration of the arcane language and frightening absurdity of a 17th-century witch trial. Meanwhile, the French sleeper carriage of 'La Couchette' had shades of 'A Quiet Night In' as we watch a fastidious man trying to sleep and being interrupted by a series of unwelcome fellow passengers. The eventual discovery of a dead body in the carriage and the collective decision to simply 'do nothing' was in part reminiscent of Raymond Carver's short story *So Much Water So Close to Home.*

Other more experimental ideas came to us for inclusion in this second series. A gripping three-hour FBI interview with a Canadian murder suspect that we discovered on YouTube became the inspiration for the structure of 'Cold Comfort', told using four fixed CCTV cameras. We took the challenge further by deciding to direct this episode ourselves, as well as the 'Nana's Party' story, which we reworked from Series 1.

We ended Series 2 with another Gothic horror story but this time framed in the world of a reality TV show, once again giving ourselves permission to explore the pomposity of actors and television-makers, hopefully without alienating the audience with a story that was too 'in'.

But it would seem – from the endless lists and rankings of every episode of *Inside No. 9* that have emerged over the course of the programme's lifespan – that Series 2 is conspicuous for having within it the episode that seems to be most people's favourite ever: 'The 12 Days of Christine' (also known as 'The Sheridan Smith One'.)

Our story recounts the fragmented existence of Christine Clarke, whose life begins to unravel as she tries to make sense of everything around her becoming increasingly jumbled up. The combination of two ideas – charting a relationship over 12 years by jumping forward a year and a month each time, and a story that takes place within the last few seconds of someone's dying brain – gave us an episode that was mysterious and moving. Everything we had learned from the previous series – the seeding of clues to an inevitable climax, the experimentation with form and structure, the willingness to allow drama to shade out comedy – were brought to bear on this particular story. It came together swiftly and organically, the final episode of the series to be written, and it became clear during the filming that we had something very special on our hands. But still we were blown away by the visceral reaction that people had to this very ordinary young woman's journey through life.

'The 12 Days of Christine' packs a proper emotional punch because we invest so much in such a short space of time with Christine. No one expected to cry watching *Inside No. 9*, but you do with 'Christine', and that's due in no small part to Sheridan Smith, who gave a remarkably heartfelt performance, and to the direction by Guillem Morales, who gave the episode an emotional drive that takes your breath away. But before all those things came our words – and here they are for you to enjoy again now. And it's fine if you find you have something in your eye by the end. We won't tell anyone.

Episode 1

LA COUCHETTE

CAST LIST

MAXWELL – Reece Shearsmith

JORG – Steve Pemberton

KATH – Julie Hesmondhalgh

LES – Mark Benton

SHONA – Jessica Gunning

HUGO – Jack Whitehall

YVES – George Glaves

EXT. FRENCH TRAIN STATION. NIGHT.

A French SNCF train is pulling out of a busy station.

INT. TRAIN CORRIDOR. NIGHT.

The train GUARD *walks along the corridor as an announcement in French tells us the train is heading for Bourg St Maurice and is expected to arrive at 07:40.*

We see a train sleeper compartment – a couchette – with a number '9' on the door.

TITLE: *'La Couchette'.*

INT. COUCHETTE. NIGHT.

A small railway compartment, which has six beds, three stacked on the left wall and three on the right. A single ladder is attached at the window end for people to access the top bunks.

The beds are narrow, with a pillow and blanket folded up at one end, a toiletries pack and a night light. The window blind is down and the carriage is dimly lit.

The train is pulling out of the station and there is the constant sound and steady motion of a moving train.

An elderly Frenchman, YVES, *lies on the middle-left bunk, fast asleep.*

A small professorial man, MAXWELL, *is preparing to go to bed. He is sleeping on the middle-right bunk and has already laid out his bed. He is wearing silk pyjamas and dressing gown and has an eye-mask ready on his forehead.* MAXWELL *removes his wristwatch, checks the time and places it in the net compartment for personal belongings.*

MAXWELL *removes his dressing gown, folds it up and places it at the foot of his bed, then climbs up into the bunk, takes one last look at the sleeping* YVES, *then closes his eyes.*

After a moment of peace, the door opens noisily. JORG, *a large, sweaty German businessman in a shabby suit, enters with a small holdall bag. He totters into the room.*

JORG Sheisse!

JORG *surveys the small carriage and plumps for the top bunk. He swings his holdall onto the upper-right bed, then sits on the lower-left one to remove his shoes and socks. As he is doing this, he lets out an enormous fart, then groans. He is clearly unwell.*

JORG *(cont'd) (muttering)* 'Schuldigung.

MAXWELL *rolls over on his side.*

JORG *throws his shoes and socks up to the top bunk, bringing his sweaty armpits level with* MAXWELL*'s face.*

JORG *removes his trousers and jacket. As he does this he noisily coughs and hawks up some phlegm. He ends up with a mouthful and looks around, not knowing what to do with it. He pulls up the blind and opens the window. Cold air billows into the carriage, blowing the net curtains.*

JORG *hoicks his phlegm out of the open window, but it blows back into his face.*

JORG *(cont'd)* Ach, verdammt noch mal!

JORG *wipes his face.* MAXWELL *has had enough.*

MAXWELL Could you close the window, please?

JORG Ha?

MAXWELL Schliessen Sie das Fenster, bitte.

JORG *closes the window and the blind.* JORG *shoves his jacket and trousers under the bottom-right bed, then heaves himself up the ladder and into the top-right bunk.*

We see MAXWELL *staring up at the squeaking and groaning upper bunk. After a lot of shifting,* JORG *settles.*

A beat. Then in the silence we hear the buzzing of a phone on vibrate. JORG *has a text alert.*

JORG Ach, Gott . . .

JORG *hauls himself back out of bed and down the ladder, much to* MAXWELL*'s annoyance.*

JORG *finds his phone in his trouser pocket and checks his text, his phone lighting up the dark carriage. He then switches off his phone and climbs back up the ladder to bed, farting as he goes. After a moment* MAXWELL *sighs and closes his eyes. Silence. Then the sound of* JORG *snoring heavily above.*

MAXWELL *retrieves the earplugs from the net compartment and furiously shoves them in.*

Outside in the corridor we hear the voices of working-class Yorkshire couple LES *and* KATH.

KATH *(V.O.)* It's here, look.

LES *(V.O.)* Where?

KATH *(V.O.)* Here! Number nine.

The door opens and LES *and* KATH *enter from the corridor.*

KATH *(cont'd) (whispering)* Oh God, there's people in here already.

LES So?

KATH They're asleep!

LES Yeah, it's a sleeper train. What do you expect them to be doing, playing ping-pong?

KATH Keep your voice down! *(To the coach)* Sorry.

LES I'll put these cases away.

KATH What about these? We don't want them all creased up for the wedding.

KATH *has two suit-carriers.*

LES Hang them up. And check the tickets, see which are ours.

LES *carries two large cases away as* KATH *closes the door.* KATH *tiptoes to the ladder and hangs up the suit-carriers.*

KATH *zips one of the pockets in the suit-carrier. She is aware that the zip is loud in the quiet carriage.*

MAXWELL *pulls out one of his earplugs to listen.* KATH *goes even more slowly with the zip, exacerbating the noise.* MAXWELL *can bear it no longer.*

MAXWELL Just get on with it, would you? I'm trying to sleep.

KATH Yeah, sorry.

KATH *unzips the suit bag and reaches in for the tickets, just as* LES *returns.*

LES They've got sinks for brushing your teeth but the water's brown, I don't trust it. Where are we then?

KATH *is looking at the tickets.*

KATH I can't see.

LES Well, put big light on.

LES *turns on the main light.*

KATH Les!

LES *switches it off again.*

KATH *(cont'd)* I think it's these top two but someone's in that one.

She indicates the lightly snoring JORG.

LES Oh, you're joking!

KATH It's all right, we'll take these two.

KATH *points to the bottom bunks.*

LES No, I want to go on top!

KATH Les, you're not six!

LES It was the only thing I was looking forward to.

KATH What, more than your daughter's wedding?

LES Let's just wake him up.

KATH No! I've already disturbed this gentleman. We'll both go in this one if you're so fussed. It'll be an adventure.

KATH *starts to climb the ladder.*

LES It's not *The Crystal Maze*! Why did she want to get married in France anyway? We could have had that back room at the Cheese for free.

KATH Because she wanted to wake up in the French mountains, Les, not in a pub garden in Hull!

LES They'd have put on a good spread. They'd have had an artist on for the night do . . .

LES *follows* KATH *up the ladder.*

KATH They'll do a good spread here, you're in France. The cuisine capital of the world!

LES Yeah, well. I'm not eating frog's legs.

KATH Oh shut up about that. You have crab's dicks.

LES What?

KATH You eat crab's dicks, in the pub.

LES That's crab *sticks*, you idiot! What's a crab's dick?

KATH I don't know, I thought they were big.

MAXWELL *addresses them from his bunk.*

MAXWELL Would you be quiet, please?

KATH Sorry, love, we're just sorting ourselves out.

KATH *and* LES *are now both in the top bunk, stooped as their heads hit the ceiling, trying to lay out the blanket.*

SHONA *enters with a large rucksack. She is dressed like a traveller with a dirty T-shirt, cut-off jeans and a bandana. She talks quietly on her mobile phone.*

SHONA Yeah . . . aw, me too, babe . . . I absolutely stink, I haven't had a shower since Prague. Oh fuck knows, I'll ask someone . . . *(To the room)* Excuse me, does anyone know what country we're in?

KATH You're in France, love.

SHONA Oh my God, we're in France apparently! What happened to Austria! Yeah, right . . .

SHONA *dumps her rucksack on the bottom-left bunk.*

SHONA *(cont'd)* One sec, hon, I'm going to go in the corridor 'cos I'm in the couchette . . . No, it's a room – it's like a hostel on wheels, it's so fucked!

SHONA *exits, leaving the door open. The light from the corridor fills the room, irritating* **MAXWELL**.

MAXWELL Would you close the door, please? Excuse me. Excuse me!

An enraged **MAXWELL** *flings back his covers and climbs down to slam the door closed, then stomps back into his bunk. He looks again at his watch and sighs.*

MAXWELL *(cont'd)* Ridiculous . . .

On the top-left bunk **KATH** *and* **LES** *look at each other and raise their eyebrows, laughing.* **KATH** *mouths:*

KATH Come on, let's get undressed.

LES *and* **KATH** *try to undress, both squashed into the one tiny bunk.* **KATH** *tries to remove her jumper but is bent double as her arms scrape on the ceiling.* **LES** *tries to remove his jeans but hasn't got space. They fumble and wrestle like this for some time before getting completely tangled in their own clothes.*

LES Kath, we can't do this, we're going to have to wake him up.

KATH No!

LES There's no room!

LES *leans over and shakes* **JORG**.

LES *(cont'd)* Excuse me! Excuse me, bud!

JORG *wakes with a start.*

JORG Ah! Was . . .? Was willst . . .

LES Sorry, mate, you are in our bed.

JORG Ha?

LES That is my wife's bed

LES *points to* **JORG**, *then to* **KATH**, *then mimes sleeping.*

JORG Ja?

LES Ja. Is that OK?

JORG Ja, warum nicht? Komm . . .

JORG *indicates for* **KATH** *to join him.*

KATH No, not with you. You have to go down!

KATH *points down.*

JORG Ja, das klingt gut.

LES Don't give him ideas.

LES *brandishes the tickets.*

LES *(cont'd)* You're in the wrong bed, look – 9D . . . 9D . . .

MAXWELL *intervenes.*

MAXWELL Sie sind in der falschen Bett, Sie müssen bewegen!

JORG Was hat das mit Ihnen zu tun, ha?

MAXWELL Sie haben die Fahrkarte.

JORG Was für einen Unterschied macht es? Ich bin schon in Bett!

MAXWELL Weil ich nicht schlafen kann!!

KATH *and* LES *look to each other as* JORG *starts to climb down the ladder.*

KATH We've started World War Three here.

LES Watch those suits, pal.

JORG *harrumphs as he climbs down the ladder, knocking* LES *and* KATH*'s suits as he goes.*

JORG Das ist lächerlich. . . verdammt lächerlich . . .

LES The suits! Ignorant.

KATH Les!

LES Well, look at him. Barbapapa.

JORG *climbs into the bunk below* MAXWELL, *banging and bumping* MAXWELL*'s bunk above.*

KATH *(to* MAXWELL*)* Thank you, sir. We didn't mean to cause a fuss, but better to get it sorted now, isn't it?

MAXWELL *is looking at his watch.*

MAXWELL Look, I have a very important interview tomorrow. We have eight hours and 42 minutes before we arrive in Bourg St Maurice. I would like to spend the majority of that time sleeping.

KATH Yeah, so would we. Sorry. Les, go on, shift yourself.

LES Why am I going in it? All sweaty and horrible.

KATH The gentleman's just told you he's trying to get to sleep.

LES I'm getting those suits hung up first.

LES *climbs down and picks up the suit bags. He shakes them in front of* JORG.

LES *(cont'd)* These are for our daughter's wedding!

JORG Verpissen sich.

JORG *farts loudly.*

LES Ah, you pig!

MAXWELL PLEASE!

LES *re-hangs the suits and goes back up to the top-right bunk.*

LES Sorry. I'll be quiet now.

LES *settles himself down. He looks across to* KATH, *who mouths 'Goodnight'.* LES *smiles back.*

MAXWELL *puts on his eye-mask and settles down.*

JORG *hawks up some more phlegm and swallows it down.*

Finally, all is quiet, save for the noise of the train tracks.

After a moment of silence, a watch alarm starts to sound. The beeping is coming from one of the suit bags and is getting increasingly louder.

KATH Les!

LES I know, it's my watch.

KATH Turn it off.

LES It's only 30 seconds, it'll be off soon.

MAXWELL *clenches his jaw as the sound gets louder.*

LES *(cont'd)* Not long now.

They all listen to the rising sound of the beeping.

KATH Les!

The beeping stops.

LES Told you.

MAXWELL *settles down to sleep.* JORG *farts and groans once more.*

INT. COUCHETTE. NIGHT.

The carriage is silent. Everyone is asleep. After a beat, the doors open and SHONA *returns with* HUGO*, a rather posh young man. They whisper to each other.*

SHONA I'm just down here.

HUGO Excellent. This is actually nicer than first class.

SHONA Seriously?

HUGO Yeah, it's more real, if you know what I mean.

SHONA Here.

SHONA *has pulled two tins of beer out of her rucksack. She hands one to* HUGO *as they both crouch on the bottom bunk.*

They open the cans quietly.

SHONA *(cont'd)* It reminds me of a hostel I stayed in out in Phuket. The toilets were disgusting.

HUGO I love all that shit. Have you done India?

SHONA Yeah, it was awesome. I got hepatitis.

HUGO Really? A or B?

SHONA Only A.

HUGO Still . . . My friend Callum got typhoid in Mumbai. His parents had to order an air ambulance to get him out, it was like *The Killing Fields*.

SHONA Shit. Was he OK?

HUGO Yeah – he lost three stone, he was really pleased. He was a bit of a blob.

They drink from their cans.

HUGO *(cont'd)* So, what are your impressions of Europe so far?

SHONA I just love all the buildings and history and stuff.

HUGO What have you seen?

SHONA Er . . . what's the one in Belgium of the little boy with his dick out?

HUGO *Le Manneken Pis* in Brussels. Designed by Hieronymus Duquesnoy in 1618, I think.

SHONA Yeah, I climbed over the railings and got a picture of it pissing in my mouth.

HUGO *(laughing)* Wow, you're vile – I love you.

SHONA Well, if someone lends me their toilet paper, I'm anybody's.

HUGO No worries. There's plenty more where that came from.

They chuckle. JORG *groans.*

SHONA Fuck, I keep forgetting there's other people in here. Shall we go to your carriage?

HUGO No, I prefer it here actually. It's a right giggle.

SHONA It is now you're here.

SHONA *kisses* HUGO.

HUGO Mmmm, barbecue sauce. So, how have you found the men from country to country? Not that I'm implying you're a slag or anything. Or maybe you are, I don't know.

SHONA No, I am. You could say I've . . . covered a lot of ground.

SHONA *starts to undo* HUGO*'s belt.*

HUGO Gosh. And who comes out on top?

SHONA That depends if we're in the marshy wetlands or in the arid desert.

HUGO Right. I can't actually think of a desert in Europe, apart for the Tabernas in Spain.

SHONA No, I meant up the shitter.

HUGO Ah, right. Got you.

SHONA Are you much of an explorer?

HUGO I can be quite adventurous. Potholing in Derbyshire was properly intense.

SHONA So you're used to going in pretty deep . . .?

SHONA *hands* HUGO *a condom. He smiles and tears it open, holding the unrolled condom in his hand.*

HUGO Yes, as long as it's not too cavernous . . .

Suddenly there is a jolt from the train that rocks SHONA *and* HUGO *violently back and forth on the bed. They laugh.*

HUGO *(cont'd)* Fasten your seatbelts, it's going to be a bumpy . . .

SHONA *screams.*

HUGO *(cont'd)* What? What's the matter?

SHONA *has seen that* YVES, *the French man in the bunk above them, is now dangling half out of his bed, lolling upside down. Dead. His blank eyes stare out.*

HUGO *turns and sees it, panics and shoves the body away.* YVES *falls fully out of the bed and lands with a thump on the floor.* SHONA *and* HUGO *wake up the rest of the carriage with their screams.*

LES What's going on?

SHONA He's dead! He's dead!

KATH Les – put big light on!

LES *switches the main light on. We see the body on the floor.* MAXWELL *wakes up.*

MAXWELL What's happened? Who are you?

HUGO I was just having a little night cap with – I'm sorry, I don't know your name . . .

SHONA Shona.

HUGO . . . when this chap just fell out of the sky.

MAXWELL Get out of the way. I'm a doctor.

MAXWELL *inspects the body.* JORG *rolls over and looks down.*

JORG Was passiert? Haben wir ankommen?

MAXWELL Dieser Mann ist zusammengebrochen.

KATH I thought he was very quiet.

LES Is he all right, bud?

MAXWELL He's dead.

HUGO Shittington.

MAXWELL *turns* YVES*'s face and sees the condom stuck to his cheek.*

MAXWELL He appears to have some sort of lesion or blister on his face. Could be an erysipelas . . .

HUGO Oh sorry, that's mine actually . . .

HUGO *peels the condom from the man's face.*

HUGO *(cont'd)* Might just keep it for later. Fingers crossed.

HUGO *smiles at* SHONA, *who scowls back.*

KATH What do we do?

MAXWELL I'll go and find a guard. Everyone stay here. Don't let anybody in or out.

MAXWELL *leaves the carriage.* JORG *groans.*

JORG Ich fühle mich schreklich . . .

LES What's he say?

KATH Something about Shrek.

LES He does look a bit green.

SHONA It was awful. He was just staring at me with these horrible glazed eyes.

HUGO I'm sorry, that's just my sex face.

KATH Do you want to come up here, love, out of the way of it?

SHONA Yes, thank you.

SHONA *climbs up the ladder to join* KATH *in her bunk.*

HUGO Well, I think I had better be heading back to first class . . .

HUGO *makes to leave.*

LES Hang on. The fella said we should all wait here for a guard to come.

HUGO Oh, I just don't want to get – what was your name again, Shirley?

SHONA Shona.

HUGO Shona – I don't want to get you into any trouble. Late-night romps, etcetera.

KATH Is that what you were doing, in a room full of people?

HUGO I'm sure you would have slept through it.

LES You know about that, don't you, Kath?

LES *laughs,* KATH *frowns.*

JORG *gets up and starts rifling through the dead man's pockets.*

LES *(cont'd)* What's he doing? Hey, hey, what's the idea, pal?

JORG Ich suche ein Reisepass . . .

LES Get your fingers out of him!

JORG *pulls out a photograph of* YVES *surrounded by a family: his daughter, son-in-law and grandchildren.*

JORG Er muss ein Grossvater sein.

JORG *shows the photo to* KATH *and* SHONA *in the top bunk.*

KATH Aah, he had grandkids, look.

SHONA His poor family. They don't even know yet.

HUGO Cool. It's like we're the kids in *Stand By Me*. Bags I'm River Phoenix!

The others stare at HUGO.

HUGO *(cont'd)* Good film.

MAXWELL *comes back into the carriage.*

LES Well?

MAXWELL I couldn't find anybody. All the carriages are closed.

KATH They're never around when you need them, are they?

LES There's got to be someone! It's not *Runaway Train.*

JORG *indicates the emergency stop button behind glass.*

JORG Warum nicht drucken dass?

MAXWELL Vielleicht das ist nicht geboten.

JORG Wass meinst du 'geboten' – der Mann ist tot!

LES What are you saying? Speak English.

MAXWELL He's suggesting we use the emergency stop.

JORG Ja.

LES Can I do it? I've always wanted to smash one of them.

LES *bangs the emergency glass box with his hand.*

KATH Don't cut yourself . . .

LES *unzips the suit bag to retrieve a shoebox.*

LES I'll have to use one of your shoes, Kath.

KATH Eh, I got them from Next!

LES *is about to smash the glass box when* HUGO *blurts out:*

HUGO I haven't got a ticket!

LES What?

HUGO Please, you can't stop the train, I haven't got a ticket. I'm sort of a stowaway.

JORG Was passiert?

MAXWELL Er hat kein Fahrkarte.

JORG Tun was Sie wollen, ich brauche mein Bett.

JORG *sits back down on his bunk, clutching his stomach.*

SHONA You told me you were in first class!

HUGO I lied, sorry. I'm completely broke.

SHONA You bastard! So you just hang around the toilet waiting for some Australian slapper to offer you a bed, is that it?

HUGO Pretty much, yes.

LES I'm sorry, pal, I'm pressing it – we've got a dead body here.

MAXWELL Well, I have to declare an interest. I have an interview tomorrow morning with the World Health Organization in Geneva.

LES What do you want, a round of applause?

MAXWELL If we stop the train, there will be a major delay and I will miss my appointment – an appointment that it's taken me 18 months to arrange.

SHONA So what are you saying here?

MAXWELL This man has been dead for at least four hours; another three or four will not make any difference.

KATH What – you want to just leave him there?

MAXWELL I propose we put him back to bed, continue our journey without delay, and have the guards find the poor gentleman first thing tomorrow morning.

KATH Oh, that doesn't sound right. Don't they have to examine the body like a Quincy?

LES Exactly. They have to find out the cause of death.

HUGO Apparently when you hang yourself you get an erection.

They all look at HUGO.

HUGO *(cont'd)* Sorry, irrelevant.

MAXWELL From what I can see it looks like a myocardial infarction. Heart attack. There's nothing we can do for him. It really would mean the world to me if we could just finish this journey without interruption.

SHONA Am I going mad here? Are you suggesting we all bunk-up with a rotting corpse in the room just so you can get to your job interview?

KATH Yeah, it's ridiculous. Smash the glass, Les.

LES *hesitates.*

LES We have got our Leanne's wedding tomorrow. What if he's right and we end up late for it?

KATH The day-do's at 12, we'll easily make that.

LES Will we, though? What if they don't let anyone off?

KATH He just rolled out of bed dead, it's not *Murder on the Orient Express.*

HUGO Another good film.

MAXWELL I'm fairly sure that if we do alert the authorities, we both will miss our respective engagements.

LES Exactly. It's just a few more hours and they'll find him anyway. We'll all be gone and that's that.

HUGO I have to say I agree.

MAXWELL Good. I'll just explain the situation to our German friend so we're all on the same page.

MAXWELL *sits with* JORG.

We move to the top bunk where LES *is facing* KATH *and* SHONA.

LES Come on, Kath, we've come all this way. We don't want to let our Leanne down, do we?

KATH *doesn't respond. She and* SHONA *stare at him accusingly.*

LES *(cont'd) (to* SHONA*)* Can you give us a minute, please, love?

SHONA Sure.

SHONA *climbs down the ladder.* HUGO *helps her down.*

HUGO Let me give you a hand.

SHONA Are you still here? Why don't you go back to first class?

HUGO Well, there's a spare bunk going now, isn't there, so I thought I might . . . get my head down for a couple of hours.

SHONA What?

HUGO Or would you rather we carried on from where we left off?

HUGO *pulls out the condom.*

SHONA That's been on a dead man's face! Have some respect.

HUGO Sure. It's too soon. You haven't got any more beer, have you?

LES *and* KATH *are on the top bunk together.*

KATH I can't believe what I'm hearing, Les. Who are you? I don't know who you are?

LES I'm a man who wants to walk his daughter down the aisle on her wedding day.

KATH Yeah, having slept with a dead body the night before.

LES I've been doing that for 25 years. Joke! Come on, Kath. If that Aussie bird hadn't screamed, we'd have slept through this and been none the wiser. We don't know who this man is. He makes no difference to us.

KATH Imagine if that was you? Slung in a corner and ignored because it's more convenient for everybody else. Shame on you, Les Cook.

LES Do you not think you're overreacting?

KATH No. I think I've just woken up.

On the bottom bunk JORG *is groaning as* MAXWELL *stands up and screws the cap on a medicine bottle.*

JORG Danke schön.

MAXWELL Ich hoffe Sie fühlen sich besser.

HUGO Is he all right?

MAXWELL Yes, he's just a little bit compacted, that's all. Too much beer and bratwurst probably! That should get him moving again.

Now, I do think we ought to put the cadaver back where we found it.

SHONA 'Cadaver'? He was a human being, you know?

MAXWELL Sorry?

SHONA *brandishes the family photo of* YVES.

SHONA He had a family – he's not a piece of meat.

MAXWELL Of course. Er . . . would anyone like to say a few words?

SHONA Yeah, I would.

SHONA *gets up and hands her can of lager to* HUGO. *She's a little tipsy by now. She looks at the photograph.*

SHONA *(cont'd)* This man . . . was a good husband, father and grandfather. He always had a smile for everyone . . . and a wicked sense of humour.

HUGO Well . . . we don't actually know that.

SHONA *(indignant)* I'm going by the picture. He loved sitting in his green chair, his family all around him . . . yes, he liked a drink, who doesn't? But the main thing is . . . he was a man. And that's it.

SHONA *sits back down to a smattering of applause.*

MAXWELL Thank you. Right, shall we?

HUGO *and* MAXWELL *lift* YVES *back to the middle-left bunk.*

HUGO Not my first time handling a stiff!

KATH *tuts and gives him a sharp look.*

HUGO *(cont'd)* Boarding school.

MAXWELL There. And that leaves us . . .

MAXWELL *checks his watch.*

MAXWELL *(cont'd)* Three hours and 52 minutes. Could you get the light, please, Mr . . .?

LES Cook.

MAXWELL Thank you.

LES *turns off the big light.* MAXWELL *climbs back into his bunk.*

MAXWELL *(cont'd)* Goodnight.

HUGO *is left as the only person without a bed.* HUGO *bends down to* SHONA*'s bunk.*

HUGO Right. Erm, Shirley, did we decide . . .?

SHONA Fuck off!

HUGO Sure. Well . . .

HUGO *climbs up to share with* YVES.

HUGO *(cont'd)* You don't mind if I top and tail, do you?

HUGO tops and tails with the dead man.

LES addresses KATH, who still has her small night light on.

LES Night night, Kath. Kath? You all right?

No reply. LES lies down and closes his eyes. We move down to see MAXWELL below him, placing his earplugs in. Then down to JORG, who is moaning and sweating in his bunk.

We move across to find SHONA sipping from her can of lager and looking up to the bunk above. Then we move up to see HUGO lying next to YVES's body.

Finally we move up to find KATH, her face staring into the darkness. After a beat she turns out her night light.

INT. COUCHETTE. EARLY MORNING.

All is quiet save for the rhythmical sway of the train and the clackety-clack of the wheels. A weak early-morning light leaks through the blind.

JORG groans and farts. HUGO is half out of the bunk he shares with the dead YVES. On the top bunk LES is practising his speech, muttering to himself.

LES . . . but it's been a very moving service – even the cake was in tiers . . . Leanne has known Phil for 14 years now, which is funny 'cos I don't remember her breaking two mirrors . . .

MAXWELL Ssshh!

LES Soz. I'm just going through my speech. Getting a bit nervous now.

MAXWELL I'm sure you'll do just fine.

LES Eh, we've both got big days tomorrow, haven't we? What's your interview for anyway?

MAXWELL Pharmaceutical development.

LES Oh right.

MAXWELL The WHO are offering a sizeable grant for new research into the degenerative effects of angina. If my bid is chosen it could be . . . life-changing.

LES Yep, it's exactly like me and my decorating. When I do a quote for a back bedroom, say, I've got to think 'what's the other fella coming in at, and can I undercut him without looking like a twat?' you know what I mean?

MAXWELL Yes, it's . . . similar.

Pause.

LES Well, good luck to you, pal, I hope you get it.

MAXWELL I'm optimistic.

LES My Auntie Gladys had acute angina. Her tits weren't bad either. Do you remember that one, Kath?

LES *looks across to* KATH*'s bunk, but it is empty.*

LES *(cont'd)* Kath? Where's she gone?

Suddenly the train screeches to a shuddering halt, as if someone has pulled the emergency cord.

HUGO *tumbles out of the middle bunk and onto the floor. The body of* YVES *lands on top of him.*

HUGO Ah!

JORG Scheisse!

SHONA Are you OK?

LES Has anyone seen Kath?

MAXWELL *goes to check the emergency stop button.*

LES *(cont'd)* She's just disappeared!

HUGO Get him off me . . .

SHONA *rolls* YVES *off* HUGO.

JORG Ach, ich muss scheisse . . .

JORG *is clutching his stomach.*

LES *(calling down to* SHONA*)* Excuse me, love, have you seen my wife?

SHONA No . . . what's happened?

SHONA *goes to look out of the window.*

MAXWELL If she's stopped this train . . .

LES She wouldn't do that.

JORG *is struggling out of his bunk and fiddling with his belt.*

HUGO Whoa, whoa, what are you doing?

JORG Ich muss scheisse!

HUGO You want to go to the toilet?

SHONA Get him some paper!

JORG *pulls down his trousers.*

JORG Nein, nein!

HUGO Hold on!

SHONA I can see something on the track . . .

HUGO *reaches up for* KATH*'s shoebox.*

LES Hey, that's our Kath's shoebox.

MAXWELL *(to* SHONA*)* What is it?

SHONA I can't . . . looks like a body . . .

LES What? Who . . . ?

MAXWELL If she's jumped, we'll be here for fucking hours!

JORG Argh!

HUGO Oh God, no . . .

HUGO *holds the shoebox under the crouching* JORG.

LES It's not her, is it?

SHONA I can't see . . .

MAXWELL Of course it's her! The stupid cow's cost me my job!

LES You shut your mouth, this is all your fault . . .

LES *throws a pillow across to* MAXWELL. JORG *groans.* HUGO *holds the shoebox and looks away as ungodly noises emerge from* JORG*'s back passage.*

HUGO Try and keep still . . . oh God, here it comes . . .

LES *is swinging on the ladder, trying to get* MAXWELL.

LES We should have just told them in the first place, you selfish prick.

MAXWELL Stay away from me!

SHONA I can see, they're bringing it out . . .

JORG Aaaaarghhhh.

HUGO Try and aim it away from the dead man's face!

SHONA I can see blood . . .

LES Bastard!

MAXWELL Leave me alone!

HUGO We're going to need a bigger box.

SHONA It's . . . it's a deer.

Just at that moment the carriage door opens and KATH *stands in the doorway with a coffee.*

She sees JORG *and* HUGO *on the floor,* MAXWELL *cowering on the top bunk and* LES *hanging on the ladder.*

KATH Les, what're you doing? And what is that smell?

KATH *covers her nose with her hand.* HUGO *looks down into the box.*

HUGO *(to* KATH*)* You might need to get some new shoes.

INT. COUCHETTE. DAY.

SHONA *is on the bottom-left bunk packing her rucksack.* LES *and* KATH *are sorting their things out on the top bunk.*

MAXWELL *is now dressed and putting on his wristwatch.*

An announcement in French declares that the train will shortly be arriving in Bourg St Maurice and apologises for the delay.

MAXWELL Well, that was only a 32-minute delay. Not too bad at all.

SHONA Try telling that to all the little fawns that have just lost their mother.

MAXWELL I'm sorry, I don't speak deer. I'm not Dr Dolittle.

SHONA *(sarcastically)* Well, you are to me.

HUGO *enters from the corridor. He is now wearing a pink T-shirt reading 'I heart Aussie Boys'.*

SHONA *(cont'd)* Is he OK?

HUGO Yes, he's just hosing himself down. That was pretty traumatic.

SHONA He must be mortified.

HUGO No, I mean for me! I felt like Augustus Gloop. Thanks for the T-shirt by the way.

SHONA No worries.

HUGO I don't know how I'm going to . . . get it back to you.

SHONA Well, where are you heading to next . . .?

On the top bunk LES *and* KATH *have packed and are enjoying a quiet moment.*

LES Thought I'd lost you there.

KATH Don't be daft. I'm not going to kill myself on the day of my daughter's wedding, am I?

LES But you're feeling better about it now?

KATH We've robbed that man of dignity in his final moments, and for that I'll never forgive myself.

LES But you're not going to say anything, are you?

KATH No. But after the wedding, I want you to find out who that man was, where his family live, and we're going to go to his funeral. That's what I want.

LES Right. *(Pause)* And who's paying for that?

SHONA *and* HUGO *get up.* MAXWELL *is still packing his things.*

SHONA We're off then. Enjoy your wedding.

KATH Thanks, love. It's at the Pavillion Hotel in Vallandry if you wanted to pop in for a drink.

SHONA Ah, no, I think we're just going to do some exploring, aren't we?

She smiles knowingly at HUGO.

HUGO Yeah, can't wait to see those valleys. Is someone going to . . .?

HUGO *points at the body of* YVES.

MAXWELL Yes, I'll alert the guard, don't worry. Nice to meet you.

HUGO *and* SHONA *leave as* KATH *and* LES *climb down.* KATH *goes to* YVES. *She sees the family photograph on the floor and places it in* YVES*'s jacket pocket.*

LES Right, well, good luck with your interview, I hope you get it. And remember, if you ever need any decorating doing . . .

MAXWELL Yes, I have your card, thank you.

MAXWELL*'s phone rings.*

MAXWELL *(cont'd)* Excuse me.

MAXWELL *answers the phone.*

KATH Come on, Les.

KATH *and* LES *leave with their suits. We hear* MAXWELL*'s French-accented* DRIVER *on the other end of the line.*

MAXWELL Hello?

DRIVER *(V.O.)* This is Dr Maxwell?

MAXWELL Speaking.

DRIVER *(V.O.)* I am your driver, I'm at the car park.

MAXWELL Yes, we're just pulling in now, sorry about the delay.

DRIVER *(V.O.)* We are also waiting for the other candidate, Dr Meyer – I believe he is also on the same train.

MAXWELL *crosses to look at the dead* YVES.

MAXWELL Is he? Well, I'll keep my eye open for him. See you shortly.

MAXWELL *hangs up. He surveys the body of* YVES.

MAXWELL *(cont'd)* I'm terribly sorry about all this, but there really could only ever be one candidate for this grant. Goodbye, Dr Meyer.

JORG *(V.O.)* Ja?

MAXWELL *turns to see* JORG *in the doorway, now in his clean suit.*

MAXWELL Bitte?

JORG Ich bin Dr Meyer.

MAXWELL *looks puzzled.*

MAXWELL Nein, er ist Dr Meyer.

JORG Nein, das ist mich.

MAXWELL No, no, that's not right. Dr Meyer was in 9B . . . neun B . . . I checked.

JORG *shrugs.*

JORG Ach, ich kann überall schlafen. Vielen dank für die Hilfe, ich fühle mich jetzt viel besser.

MAXWELL Gut, I . . .

JORG Ich habe eine wichtige Interview heute.

MAXWELL Yes, so have I . . .

JORG Ah, Dr Maxwell! Sehr gut!

JORG *shakes* MAXWELL*'s hand.*

JORG *(cont'd)* Unsere Auto ist hier, ja!

JORG *chuckles.*

JORG *(cont'd)* Wie sagt man auf Englisch? 'May ze best man win!'

JORG *goes with his bag, leaving* MAXWELL *alone with* YVES.

THE END

Episode 2

THE 12 DAYS OF CHRISTINE

CAST LIST

CHRISTINE – Sheridan Smith

ADAM – Tom Riley

FUNG – Stacy Liu

MARION – Michele Dotrice

STRANGER – Reece Shearsmith

BOBBY – Steve Pemberton

ERNIE – Paul Copley

ZARA – Jessica Ellerby

JACK – Joel Little and Dexter Little

EXT. BLOCK OF FLATS. NIGHT.

A high-rise block of flats in a city centre.

INT. HALLWAY. NIGHT.

We are inside a compact flat up on a high floor of the block. The lights inside are dim. We hear laughter and voices on the other side of the door.

CHRISTINE *(V.O.) (laughing)* Put it in!

ADAM *(V.O.)* I can't.

CHRISTINE *(V.O.)* Don't . . . you're dropping me . . . arghh!

The door flies open and ADAM *carries* CHRISTINE *inside. We linger on the number on the front of the door: '9'.*

TITLE: *'The 12 Days of Christine'.*

INT. LIVING ROOM. NIGHT.

A studenty flat with cheap furniture, beanbags, posters on the wall, etc. There is an artificial Christmas tree in the corner with flashing blue lights.

ADAM *is a handsome young man in his mid-twenties. He is dressed as a fireman (fancy-dress costume) and he is carrying* CHRISTINE, *a bubbly girl who is a bit pissed.* CHRISTINE *is dressed as a naughty nun, with a wimple and fishnets.*

CHRISTINE Is this a proper fireman's lift?

ADAM I dunno, I'm not a proper fireman. Have you got anything to drink?

CHRISTINE Probably, have a look in the fridge.

ADAM *goes to look in the kitchen.*

CHRISTINE *(cont'd)* Don't touch anything with 'Fung' on it.

ADAM *(V.O.)* What?

CHRISTINE She's my flatmate. She's labelled everything.

ADAM *(V.O.)* Fung? What's that, Chinese?

CHRISTINE Yeah. Don't say her name, she'll appear.

ADAM What is she, a genie?

ADAM *comes through with two cans of lager.*

CHRISTINE Shh, she's only through there. She'll have been in bed since nine o'clock.

ADAM Well, they have a different New Year, don't they?

CHRISTINE Yeah, she won't come out 'til February.

ADAM Is that when it is?

CHRISTINE Yeah. I'm a Dog apparently.

ADAM Oh, I've seen worse.

She hits him playfully and they laugh.

ADAM *(cont'd)* Ow! I thought you were going home with John Lennon anyway.

CHRISTINE He wasn't John Lennon, he was Harry Potter.

ADAM Was he?

CHRISTINE I think so. To be honest it was only a pair of round glasses.

ADAM Did he show you his wand?

CHRISTINE *laughs.*

CHRISTINE No. Anyway, I told him I'd rather see the fireman's pole.

They kiss on the sofa.

ADAM My name's Adam by the way, if you're interested.

CHRISTINE Oh, I'm Eve!

ADAM Really?

CHRISTINE No, I just said it. I'm Chrissie. Happy New Year.

They shake hands.

ADAM Happy New Year. Where's your toilet?

CHRISTINE It's just down there.

ADAM I just need to . . . unravel my hosepipe.

CHRISTINE Urgh, don't have it on sprinkle!

ADAM *smiles and departs for the toilet.* CHRISTINE *lies back and takes a glug of her lager, the blue Christmas lights flashing behind her.*

The landline phone rings. CHRISTINE *slowly gets up and goes over to answer it. We stay close on the phone.*

CHRISTINE *(cont'd)* Hello?

INT. LIVING ROOM. DAY.

We now see that the flat is in daylight and CHRISTINE *is dressed in her normal work clothes (skirt, jacket with name-badge and blouse). We hear* ADAM*'s voice.*

ADAM *(V.O.)* Hi, sexy. Did you get my Valentine's card?

CHRISTINE No, I didn't, but the post hasn't been yet. Did you get mine?

ADAM *(V.O.)* Yes, it's probably among the pile somewhere.

CHRISTINE Ha ha. So what time are you picking me up?

ADAM *(V.O.)* Seven-ish? Do you want sex then meal or meal then sex?

CHRISTINE What about sex meal sex?

ADAM *(V.O.)* That depends – is 'The Grudge' going to be in?

We see **FUNG**, *a long-haired Chinese girl, sitting at the breakfast table eating toast.*

CHRISTINE I'm not sure, I'll get back to you with that information.

ADAM *(V.O.)* Is she there?

CHRISTINE Yes.

ADAM *(V.O.)* I'll call you later then, bye.

CHRISTINE *hangs up and approaches the dining table.*

CHRISTINE Hi, Fung.

FUNG Good morning.

CHRISTINE What have you got on today?

FUNG I have a seminar this morning and another seminar this afternoon.

CHRISTINE More maths?

FUNG Continuous quantity, yes.

The morning post arrives and **CHRISTINE** *goes to collect it.*

CHRISTINE Sounds complicated.

FUNG Not necessarily, it depends on your approach to measurable magnitudes.

CHRISTINE Right.

CHRISTINE *is opening a Valentine's card.*

FUNG Like you have been going out with Adam for 13 months, which is one year and one month. This is referred to as a portable vector, because the month is quantitively divisible by the year . . .

CHRISTINE Oh my God! How weird.

FUNG Not really, it's number theory.

CHRISTINE I've got a Valentine's card from my ex-boyfriend.

FUNG Maybe he still likes you.

CHRISTINE I haven't seen him since I was 12, I can barely remember him.

CHRISTINE *shows the card to* **FUNG** *and she reads the poem.*

FUNG 'Roses are red / Violets are blue / What is that smell? / I need a poo.'

CHRISTINE His sense of humour hasn't changed much. I wonder how he got my address?

FUNG Right, I've got to go to my seminar. I won't be back 'til 7.30 if you want to have sex with Adam.

CHRISTINE Oh, thanks . . .

FUNG *goes off to her room.* CHRISTINE *considers the card, then tears it up and throws it in the bin.*

We see the torn-up card at the bottom of the bin.

MARION *(V.O.)* Oh Christine, I've still got that teddy, you know!

INT. LIVING ROOM. DAY.

CHRISTINE*'s mum,* MARION*, sits on the sofa with* ADAM*. She is a jolly lady in a nice floral dress. She is showing* ADAM *a series of loose photos.*

CHRISTINE *enters from the kitchen with a tea tray.*

CHRISTINE You haven't!

MARION I have. It was bigger than you! Oh, she had a lovely peachy bottom, Adam. Look at that . . .

MARION *shows* ADAM *a photo of* CHRISTINE *as a baby.*

ADAM Aahh . . .

CHRISTINE Mum, you're embarrassing Adam!

MARION No, dear, I'm embarrassing you.

CHRISTINE *places the tray on the coffee table and* MARION *starts to pour the tea.*

MARION *(cont'd)* Right, shall I be mother?

CHRISTINE Yeah, go on, it is Mother's Day.

MARION *sees* ADAM *looking at the photos.*

ADAM Who's that?

MARION Oh, that was Christine's first boyfriend. Such a shame. He died when he was 16.

CHRISTINE Did he?

MARION Yes! He got . . .

MARION *mouths the word 'leukaemia'.*

MARION *(cont'd) (to* ADAM*)* She's got a memory like a sieve. But she's done well with you, Adam. You're smashing, though you could do with getting a haircut.

CHRISTINE Mum!

MARION When are you going to marry her anyway?

ADAM Er . . .

CHRISTINE Oh for God's sake.

MARION Well, you've been courting for two years. I was married with a daughter by then.

CHRISTINE Well, that was you. I've got my career to think about.

MARION Career! Measuring feet in Clarks is hardly a career, Christine.

CHRISTINE Thank you very much.

MARION I'm just saying. Your father would like to walk you down the aisle while he still can.

Awkward silence. ADAM *senses the tense atmosphere.*

ADAM Does anybody want a biscuit?

MARION Yes please.

CHRISTINE No thanks.

ADAM *(cont'd)* OK.

ADAM *gets up and goes to the kitchen.*

CHRISTINE *(whispering)* Just stop it, all right!

MARION There's nothing wrong with getting married, you know. Your generation thinks it's old-fashioned – it's not, it's a commitment.

CHRISTINE We don't even live together . . .

MARION Exactly. That would be a start.

CHRISTINE Well, we're not doing it, Mum, so you can stop going on about it. I'm not even sure if Adam's really . . .

ADAM *(V.O.)* Chrissie?

INT. LIVING ROOM. NIGHT.

ADAM *comes back in carrying a heavy cardboard box.*

ADAM Where shall I put my CDs?

CHRISTINE There. God, you've got so much stuff.

ADAM I told you. You're not regretting it, are you?

CHRISTINE No, of course not. Now Fung's moved out someone has to pay the rent, so . . .

ADAM So . . .

ADAM *kisses* CHRISTINE.

ADAM *(cont'd)* Right, I've got to take the van back before it closes.

CHRISTINE Here.

CHRISTINE *hands* ADAM *a keyring with keys.*

ADAM What's this?

CHRISTINE Your new house keys.

ADAM Aw – thank you. What's that? A pair of seagulls?

CHRISTINE It's two doves. Me and you.

ADAM Oh right. Weird.

CHRISTINE It's romantic! Don't be long – I've got a surprise for you when you get back.

ADAM Oh, OK.

ADAM *leaves.* CHRISTINE *opens the box of CDs; she has a quick look through, picks one out and puts it in the player. The song is 'Time to Say Goodbye' by Andrea Bocelli.*

As the song plays CHRISTINE *takes out a bag of chocolate Easter eggs and starts hiding them around the flat. She hides the first one in the fold of a Happy Easter card on the mantelpiece. Then she puts one in the grate of the fireplace; another under the TV. She leaves for the bedroom.*

INT. MASTER BEDROOM. NIGHT.

CHRISTINE *comes into the bedroom and sees lots of* ADAM*'s clothes on hangers in a big pile on the bed. She lifts them off and puts them in the wardrobe, creating a side for his clothes.*

CHRISTINE *returns to the bed and lifts up the pillow to place a chocolate egg under it. As she bends down a real egg is thrown at the wall behind her and smashes. She is shocked.*

CHRISTINE Shit! Adam?

She looks scared and confused, then hears another egg splat in the hallway. She cautiously leaves the bedroom to investigate.

INT. HALLWAY. NIGHT.

CHRISTINE *sees another broken egg on the floor in the hallway.*

CHRISTINE This isn't funny, Adam.

INT. KITCHEN. NIGHT.

CHRISTINE *walks into the kitchen. She is confronted by ten eggs on the floor. All smashed. She sees the door to the pantry move slightly and walks towards it.* CHRISTINE *slowly pushes open the pantry door. There is nobody there. From behind she hears a voice:*

STRANGER *(V.O.)* I'm sorry.

CHRISTINE *swings round and sees a* STRANGER *standing in the middle of the smashed eggs. He's a small man in glasses and a raincoat. He reaches out to her.*

INT. MASTER BEDROOM. MORNING.

CHRISTINE *wakes up with a start. The alarm is going off.* ADAM *is sleeping in bed next to her.*

CHRISTINE God . . .

ADAM What?

CHRISTINE Horrible dream.

ADAM Oh. Get the alarm, would you?

CHRISTINE *presses the alarm – it stops beeping. By the alarm we see a framed photo of* ADAM *and* CHRISTINE*'s wedding.*

CHRISTINE You're going to be late for work.

ADAM It's a bank holiday, isn't it?

CHRISTINE Oh yeah.

ADAM But I'll have a cup of tea now you're up.

CHRISTINE *gets out of bed and we see she is heavily pregnant.*

CHRISTINE What shall we do today?

INT. LIVING ROOM. DAY.

The floor is covered in pieces of unassembled cot. CHRISTINE *sits perched on the edge of the sofa. She holds the instructions.* ADAM *is kneeling on the floor trying to work out how the cot fits together.*

CHRISTINE 'Align sliding panel AB alongside bar EF.'

ADAM Yeah. Done that.

CHRISTINE Are you sure that's EF? It looks like CD to me.

ADAM Just carry on.

CHRISTINE All right. 'Insert groove dowel pins into B1 and B2.'

ADAM I don't know what they are.

CHRISTINE They look like that, like maggots.

ADAM *inserts the groove dowel pins.*

ADAM OK – then what?

CHRISTINE 'Align sliding panel AB alongside bar EF.'

ADAM We've already done that!

CHRISTINE 'Insert rod into top hole until base connects.'

ADAM Isn't that how we got into this mess in the first place?

CHRISTINE *bursts into tears.*

ADAM *(cont'd)* Don't cry, it was only a joke. Hey . . .

ADAM *tries to hug* CHRISTINE.

ADAM *(cont'd)* What are you worried about?

CHRISTINE I don't know. I just . . . I don't want the baby to spoil everything.

ADAM Course it won't. How's it going to do that, eh?

INT. MASTER BEDROOM. NIGHT.

CHRISTINE *and* ADAM *lie in the dark of their bedroom, wide awake. A baby monitor flashes as they listen to a mournful cry.*

BABY JACK *(V.O.)* Dada!! Dada!!

ADAM What shall I do?

CHRISTINE I don't know. We're meant to be leaving him.

ADAM I can't bear it.

ADAM *sits up like he is going to go.*

CHRISTINE Don't.

ADAM OK.

ADAM *lies back down. The baby continues to cry.*

ADAM *(cont'd)* Can I give him more Calpol?

CHRISTINE Not for another half an hour.

ADAM That's close enough, isn't it?

CHRISTINE No, you can't just drug him!

ADAM *gets up and leaves.* CHRISTINE *lies in the bed listening to* ADAM *settle* BABY JACK *over the monitor.* ADAM *sings a line or two of 'Time to Say Goodbye'.* CHRISTINE *takes out a Father's Day card from her bedside drawer and writes it: 'To Daddy, Sorry for keeping you up all night – that should be Mummy's job! Love, Jack xxx.'*

The baby monitor has gone quiet. CHRISTINE *seals the card and puts it on* ADAM*'s pillow. Over the monitor we suddenly hear a scream from* JACK*, followed by the* STRANGER*'s voice.*

STRANGER *(V.O.)* Come on, little man, let's get you out of there . . .

CHRISTINE *jumps up and runs out of the room.*

INT. JACK'S BEDROOM. NIGHT.

CHRISTINE *runs into the baby's bedroom and turns the light on.* JACK*'s cot is empty.*

CHRISTINE Jack? Adam! Adam! Someone's taken Jack!

ADAM *appears behind* CHRISTINE. *He is carrying a sleeping* JACK.

ADAM What are you doing?

CHRISTINE I heard somebody talking.

ADAM Yeah, it was me trying to get him to sleep.

CHRISTINE It wasn't you!

ADAM Calm down, you'll set him off again.

ADAM *puts* JACK *back in his cot.*

ADAM *(cont'd)* You're just over-tired. Come back to bed.

ADAM *leaves.* CHRISTINE *takes one last look at the sleeping* JACK*, then switches off the light.*

In the darkness we hear MARION*'s voice.*

MARION *(V.O.)* That's it . . . keep them closed . . . a few more steps.

INT. LIVING ROOM. DAY.

CHRISTINE *has her hands in front of her face.*

MARION *(V.O.)* And . . . open your eyes!

CHRISTINE *removes her hands from her eyes. She's another year older and her hairstyle has changed slightly. She looks more mumsy. The flat is more maturely decorated, but there are toys and toddler paraphernalia around.*

CHRISTINE *sees that the table has been laid with some gifts and a birthday cake. There is a 'Happy Birthday' helium balloon.*

MARION *is by* CHRISTINE*'s side.* CHRISTINE*'s dad,* ERNIE*, is there but looks glazed and distant.* CHRISTINE*'s friend* BOBBY *is there.*

ALL Surprise!

The guests cheer and pop party-poppers.

CHRISTINE Oh my God! Hi, Dad!

CHRISTINE *goes to hug* ERNIE*, but he doesn't appear to recognise her. He's not all there.*

MARION He's been so excited all week, haven't you, Ernie?

ERNIE *looks bemused.*

MARION *(cont'd) (quietly to* CHRISTINE*)* He did know he was coming, but I think it's gone again. I shouldn't have brought him.

CHRISTINE No, I'm glad he came.

MARION He wouldn't want you to remember him like this.

CHRISTINE *kisses* ERNIE*'s cheek.* BOBBY *hands over a present.*

BOBBY Here you go, dear, happy birthday. I bet you can't guess what these are.

The present is shoebox-sized.

CHRISTINE But they didn't have them in my size.

BOBBY Well, someone rang Ipswich and got them DHL'd.

CHRISTINE Oh Bobby, you shouldn't have! Thank you.

CHRISTINE *hugs* BOBBY.

BOBBY Two words: 'staff' 'discount'. Where's Adam?

CHRISTINE I don't know actually. Mum, where's Adam?

MARION I'm not sure, he said he'd be here . . .

The door opens and ADAM *enters with* ZARA*, an attractive girl.*

ADAM Hi, darling, happy birthday!

ADAM *pecks* CHRISTINE *on the cheek.*

CHRISTINE Thanks. Hi, Zara.

ZARA Happy birthday, Chrissie. You look fab.

CHRISTINE Oh, I don't, but thanks anyway.

ZARA No, I'm sure you've lost a bit, turn round.

CHRISTINE *self-consciously turns round.*

ZARA *(cont'd)* Yeah, you definitely have.

MARION It's just baby fat, it'll be gone soon enough.

ADAM He's not a baby, he's two now. Where is he?

CHRISTINE Having a nap. How was your work do?

ADAM Yeah, we popped our heads in, didn't we? Schmoozed a few clients. Hiya, Bobby.

BOBBY Hi, Adam.

ADAM This is Zara, she's just started under me.

BOBBY Has she?

CHRISTINE *looks away.*

CHRISTINE My dad's here, look. Go and say hello to him.

ADAM All right, I'll just get us a drink first.

MARION Come on then, Chrissie, it's that time.

CHRISTINE No, Mum.

MARION *takes off her scarf.*

MARION It's tradition! Every birthday since she was six we've played Blind Man's Buff . . .

CHRISTINE Not every birthday!

MARION Yes, we have! Though last year I think it was Blind Drunk Buff.

BOBBY Excuse me, I wasn't there!

ADAM She said 'buff' not 'puff'.

MARION *starts to tie the scarf around* CHRISTINE*'s eyes.*

MARION She's always enjoyed party games, haven't you, love? First person you catch can give you your main present.

ZARA Where should I put my coat?

ADAM Oh yeah, it's just through here . . .

ADAM *and* ZARA *disappear down the corridor.* CHRISTINE *is blinded and strains to hear them go.*

MARION Right, you spin her, Bobby.

BOBBY My pleasure.

BOBBY *spins a confused* CHRISTINE *round three times.*

BOBBY *(cont'd)* One, two, three . . . and off you go.

We see **CHRISTINE** *start to play the game, and see from her POV opaque images through a scarf.*

CHRISTINE *moves around the room, but people edge away from her as she approaches. She approaches one figure and grabs him, but he cries out, afraid. It is* **ERNIE**.

CHRISTINE Sorry, Dad, sorry.

CHRISTINE *moves towards the hallway, her arms outstretched.*

INT. HALLWAY. DAY.

CHRISTINE *stumbles into the corridor and makes her way towards the bedroom, feeling the walls as she goes. She becomes aware of the sound of a squeaking bed.*

CHRISTINE Adam?

CHRISTINE*'s POV as she moves towards the closed door at the end of the corridor. She feels for the door handle as the squeaking sound gets louder and faster.*

CHRISTINE *removes the blindfold and sees the door. She reaches for the handle and throws open the door.*

INT. MASTER BEDROOM. DAY.

It is another year on. **ADAM** *is pushing on a large suitcase on the bed, trying to make it shut.*

ADAM I can't close this case, you'll have to take something out.

CHRISTINE *is now dressed in summery clothes.*

CHRISTINE You always pack the cases.

ADAM *removes a pair of nude peep-toe shoes.*

ADAM You don't need these shoes, do you?

CHRISTINE They were my birthday shoes from last year, I've barely worn them.

ADAM Well, we can't take all these toys.

ADAM *takes out various children's toys.*

CHRISTINE He won't sleep without that.

ADAM Well, make him choose one thing. You're too soft on him.

CHRISTINE It's his holiday too.

ADAM It wasn't meant to be, was it?

CHRISTINE Don't start.

ADAM This was supposed to be just me and you, get away from this miserable flat for a while.

CHRISTINE Well, I'm very sorry my dad died. I couldn't expect Mum to take him now, could I?

ADAM I'm not saying that.

CHRISTINE Well, what are you saying then?

ADAM I wanted it to be fun, like it used to be.

CHRISTINE Well, that's just life, Adam! We're doing what everybody else does, we're going on holiday as a family.

ADAM Yeah, and I can't fucking wait. Bring the passports.

ADAM *storms out of the room.* CHRISTINE *opens the drawer of* ADAM*'s bedside table. She goes through the drawer, finding the old keyring with two doves that she gave to* ADAM *four years ago. It is now grubby and worn.*

CHRISTINE *gets out the passports. She looks at the picture in her passport showing a younger, happier* CHRISTINE.

CHRISTINE *stares at herself for a sad moment. She looks at the younger* ADAM, *then at* JACK*'s passport. There she sees a photograph of* JACK *as a small baby.*

INT. LIVING ROOM. DAY.

We see JACK, *now aged four and a half, dressed in a school uniform and holding a small book bag. We see him through the viewfinder of a camera, which is videoing him.*

CHRISTINE *(V.O.)* That's it, give me a big smile! What day is it, Jack?

JACK September the first.

CHRISTINE *(V.O.)* And what's happening today?

JACK I got school.

CHRISTINE *(V.O.)* Yes, that's right, you're a big boy now. Show us your bag.

JACK *holds up his school bag.*

We cut out of viewfinder mode to see CHRISTINE *holding the camera.* MARION *moves towards* JACK.

MARION Right, come on, Grandma's going to walk you down.

JACK *(to* CHRISTINE*)* I want you to take me.

CHRISTINE Mummy's got to go to work, darling, but I'll be there to pick you up, OK? You have a brilliant day, I'm so proud of you.

CHRISTINE *hugs* JACK. MARION *looks on sadly.*

MARION Come on then. Let's not be late on our first day. See you later, love.

CHRISTINE Thanks, Mum.

MARION Are you going to show me the way?

MARION *and* JACK *leave.* CHRISTINE *is bereft. She sobs, then rallies herself and goes over to the CD player.*

There are a few boxes of possessions and a case in the corner of the room. CHRISTINE *picks up a few CDs from a pile and places them into the box. She sees the CD she remembers putting on when* ADAM *first moved in, and this sets her off crying again.*

CHRISTINE*'s dad,* ERNIE, *appears behind her. He's now much fitter and healthier.* CHRISTINE *carries on packing the box.*

ERNIE Come on, Chrissie, don't upset yourself.

CHRISTINE I just didn't think it would turn out like this.

ERNIE Well, I never thought I'd end up walking naked into the garden centre and peeing on the hydrangeas, but there you go.

CHRISTINE But you weren't well, it wasn't your fault.

ERNIE And this isn't yours, girly.

CHRISTINE Isn't it? Adam's left me, Jack's left me . . .

ERNIE Only 'til three o'clock.

CHRISTINE I know, but 35, divorced and working in a shoe shop with my gay best friend. It's hardly the Cinderella story, is it?

ERNIE Now come on, enough of that nonsense. It's Jack's first day at school, this is meant to be a happy memory.

CHRISTINE Well, I'm sorry, Dad, but it doesn't feel like it.

The door buzzer sounds. CHRISTINE *looks round and* ERNIE *has disappeared. The buzzer sounds again, followed by the sound of the key in the lock, and the front door opens.*

ZARA *appears. She looks shocked to see* CHRISTINE.

ZARA Oh sorry, Chrissie, I thought you'd be at work . . .

CHRISTINE I'm just leaving.

ZARA I'll wait outside.

CHRISTINE No, it's all right, you're here now. Has he got you collecting his things?

ZARA Yeah. Something came up at work . . .

CHRISTINE Huh, I bet it did.

CHRISTINE *gets her bag ready for work.*

CHRISTINE *(cont'd)* Well, it's all in that corner, help yourself. If he wants his Anusol tell him I chucked it, it's out of date.

ZARA OK.

CHRISTINE *puts on her coat.*

ZARA *(cont'd)* Isn't it Jack's first day at school today?

CHRISTINE Oh, he remembered, did he? Well, a phone call would have been nice.

ZARA Chrissie, can I just say . . . I hope that at some point in the future we can just sit down, open a big bottle of wine, stick on a rom-com and have a proper girly chat, like a couple of mates. What do you think?

CHRISTINE I think you should fuck off.

CHRISTINE *goes to the front door.*

ZARA Sorry?

CHRISTINE I don't do rom-coms.

CHRISTINE *closes the door. The buzzer sounds.*

INT. LIVING ROOM. NIGHT.

The flat is decorated for Halloween, with a pumpkin on the table, bats hanging from the ceiling and cobwebs round the picture frames.

The flat is empty. The buzzer sounds again.

CHRISTINE *(V.O.)* Will you get that, Bobby?

BOBBY *(V.O.)* I can't, I'm putting my contacts in.

CHRISTINE *emerges into the living room. She is dressed as a witch, with a green face, long nose, black cloak and pointed black hat. She goes to the entry-phone.*

CHRISTINE Yes?

ADAM *(V.O.)* It's me, can you buzz me in?

CHRISTINE You're late.

CHRISTINE *presses the buzzer and hangs up, then opens the front door. She then crosses back down the hallway and into the bathroom.*

INT. BATHROOM. NIGHT.

BOBBY *is in front of the mirror dressed as a vampire. White face, drawn-on widow's peak and a drip of blood down his chin. He is struggling to put a contact lens in.* CHRISTINE *comes in.*

CHRISTINE Adam's here now – are you ready?

BOBBY *turns to* CHRISTINE.

BOBBY What do you think?

CHRISTINE Are they the contacts or just your eyes?

BOBBY Contacts!

CHRISTINE It's good. Are you a zombie waiter?

BOBBY Oh piss off, Chrissie – I'm meant to be a vampire.

CHRISTINE Right.

BOBBY I'm changing it to a werewolf.

He starts drawing lots of black lines on his face.

BOBBY *(cont'd)* I've got teeth somewhere. So is your new fella going to be there?

CHRISTINE He's not my new fella, be quiet.

BOBBY You want him to be though, don't you?

CHRISTINE I've only seen a picture of him on a website.

BOBBY It's fancy dress – how will you know it's him?

CHRISTINE He's going to have an alien bursting out of his chest.

BOBBY And did you just say you were going as yourself?

CHRISTINE Ha ha.

The front door slams shut. CHRISTINE *calls out to* ADAM*:*

CHRISTINE *(cont'd)* Jack's in his room.

The figure of a MAN *flashes past the bathroom.*

CHRISTINE *(cont'd) (to* ADAM*)* You've got some explaining to do.

BOBBY Do I look hairy enough?

CHRISTINE You look like Tony the Tiger. Here . . .

CHRISTINE *takes the eye-liner pencil and draws on his face.*

CHRISTINE *(cont'd)* I'll turn it into a cobweb. Remember ten years ago when I first moved in here and I was living with – what was her name? – Fung.

BOBBY Oh my God, 'The Grudge', that would have been a good one.

CHRISTINE We said if neither of us were with someone in ten years' time, we'd get married to each other, do you remember?

BOBBY Aw, you're not that desperate, are you, babe?

CHRISTINE I was just thinking, it's funny how things turn out, isn't it?

There is a knock on the flat door.

BOBBY Trick or treaters. Go and scare 'em.

CHRISTINE *leaves the bathroom.*

INT. HALLWAY. NIGHT.

CHRISTINE *answers the door.* ADAM *is standing there dressed as a devil. He's exhausted.*

ADAM You didn't tell me the lift was broken. I'm knackered.

CHRISTINE *looks down the corridor and races towards* JACK*'s room.*

CHRISTINE Jack?

INT. JACK'S BEDROOM. NIGHT.

CHRISTINE *pushes open the door and finds the* STRANGER *– last seen in her kitchen – standing over* JACK*'s bed, holding the child in his arms.*

STRANGER It's all right. I've got him.

INT. HALLWAY. NIGHT.

The front door bursts open and CHRISTINE *runs in carrying a crying* JACK*. She is on her phone.*

CHRISTINE It's all right, I've got him. Just get back here, quick as you can.

CHRISTINE *puts down her phone and takes* JACK *to the bathroom.*

INT. BATHROOM. NIGHT.

CHRISTINE *runs into the bathroom and turns on the cold tap. She quickly pulls* JACK*'s hand under the tap.*

CHRISTINE Keep it under the tap – it might sting, but don't move it, all right? I'm just going to ring Daddy.

JACK *cries and whimpers.* CHRISTINE *races into the corridor.*

INT. LIVING ROOM. NIGHT.

CHRISTINE *runs to the phone and dials a number.*

Outside we can hear sporadic fireworks going off, and maybe see some in the darkness through the window.

ADAM *(V.O.)* Hello?

CHRISTINE Adam, Jack's had an accident.

ADAM *(V.O.)* What . . . ?

CHRISTINE He's all right, he just burned his hand on a sparkler.

ADAM *(V.O.)* OK, erm, well, you need to get a wet tea towel . . .

CHRISTINE That's chip-pan fires.

ADAM *(V.O.)* Is it? Well, just run it under a tap then. Are you at home?

CHRISTINE Yes. Can you come round? I need you.

ADAM *(V.O.)* OK, I'm on my way.

CHRISTINE Thanks. He's probably fine, I'm just over-reacting. I've seen too many public information films.

ADAM *(V.O.)* 'I am the spirit of dark and lonely water . . .'

CHRISTINE It's not funny, Adam.

MARION *enters and approaches* CHRISTINE.

MARION Christine?

CHRISTINE *(to* MARION*)* He's in the bathroom.

MARION *hurries off towards the bathroom.*

CHRISTINE *(cont'd)* My mum's here now, so . . .

ADAM *(V.O.)* I'll be there in five minutes, OK?

CHRISTINE OK . . .

ADAM *(V.O.)* Hang on. I love you.

ADAM *hangs up.* CHRISTINE *replaces the receiver. She's thoughtful: does* ADAM *still love her? A firework explodes outside.* CHRISTINE *snaps out of her musing.*

CHRISTINE Is he all right, Mum?

MARION *enters with* JACK.

MARION Yes, he's fine. There's not a mark on him, look . . .

MARION *holds out* JACK*'s hands. They are perfectly normal and not marked.*

CHRISTINE But . . . he was crying . . .

MARION You frightened him!

MARION *ushers* JACK *out.*

MARION *(cont'd)* Go and watch the fireworks, Jack, you can see them out of your window.

CHRISTINE *is confused. She slumps down in a chair.*

CHRISTINE He picked up a sparkler and burnt his hand. I saw it . . .

MARION He can't have done, there's nothing wrong with him. You did, when you were his age. Burnt right through your mittens, do you remember?

CHRISTINE *looks at her hand. There is an old burn scar from when she was a little girl. She stares at it.*

MARION *(V.O.) (cont'd)* Maybe you were thinking of that. Let me make you a cup of tea.

CHRISTINE I don't know what's wrong with me, Mum. I'm getting everything jumbled up . . .

As we move round, the Christmas tree with the flashing blue lights has appeared behind CHRISTINE.

MARION *(V.O.)* Well, put your hat on then.

CHRISTINE What?

INT. LIVING ROOM. DAY.

CHRISTINE *is sitting at the dining table in the middle of the room. It is Christmas Day, and the table is decked out with crackers and a turkey dinner.*

MARION, BOBBY, FUNG *and* ERNIE *sit at the table wearing Christmas hats.* CHRISTINE *is momentarily confused.*

MARION Put your hat on!

MARION *places a red paper hat on* CHRISTINE*'s head.*

MARION *(cont'd)* That's better.

BOBBY Right . . . *(Reading)* 'Why are Christmas trees so bad at sewing? They always drop their needles.'

ERNIE Terrible.

BOBBY Fung?

FUNG *(reading)* 'What does Santa suffer from if he gets stuck in the chimney? Claustrophobia.' I don't get it.

ERNIE Neither do I, dear.

MARION You never had a sense of humour, did you, Ernie?

ERNIE Oh I don't know, I married you, didn't I?

Everyone laughs apart from CHRISTINE, *who is feeling a sense of disconnectedness.*

CHRISTINE Are you all right, Dad?

ERNIE Yes, I'm tickety-boo. I had to be here for this, didn't I? Wouldn't have missed it for the world.

ADAM *comes in and sits next to* CHRISTINE.

ADAM You all right, love? Well done on this, it looks gorgeous. Just like you.

ADAM *kisses* CHRISTINE *on the cheek.*

MARION I did the sprouts!

BOBBY And we'll be hearing from them later!

Laughter.

CHRISTINE Where's Jack?

ADAM He's just getting his outfit on for the Nativity.

MARION Aw, bless him.

CHRISTINE *(to* ADAM*)* Are we . . . back together, Adam?

ADAM Yeah, course we are. You remember Bonfire Night, last year . . . ?

FUNG I think it's time for the present now.

CHRISTINE I don't want the present.

BOBBY Yes, go on.

ADAM *goes to get the present, which is under the tree.*

ERNIE This is from all of us, dear, we all contributed. I hope you like it.

ADAM *hands* CHRISTINE *a wrapped-up book.* CHRISTINE *opens the present to reveal a printed photo album. On the front is a photo of*

CHRISTINE *as a baby next to one of her as an adult. The title is 'Christine Clarke: A Life in Pictures'.*

CHRISTINE Oh no! Is that me?

MARION Yes!

CHRISTINE *flicks through the book. She sees photos of herself as a child, in her younger days with* FUNG *and with* BOBBY. *A photo with* ERNIE *and* MARION. BABY JACK *and* ADAM . . .

CHRISTINE Remember that cot? We couldn't put it up, could we?

ADAM Took us three days.

CHRISTINE Ha, look!

CHRISTINE *shows* BOBBY *a picture from Halloween.*

BOBBY Tony Tiger.

CHRISTINE *leafs through the book and we see a variety of pictures. She smiles, wrapped up in her comforting memories.*

CHRISTINE Oh my God, you've got everything! It's almost like my whole life flashing . . .

CHRISTINE *stops. An awful realisation has hit her.*

CHRISTINE *(cont'd)* Oh. I think I know what this is now.

The sound of police radio static.

EXT. BLOCK OF FLATS. DAY.

Close on CHRISTINE*'s bloodied face at the wheel of her crashed car. Her eyes flicker as she clings onto life. The windscreen is smashed and steam rises from the engine. There are eggs smashed on the windscreen and passenger seat. The car has crashed into a bollard at the side of the road.*

The fire brigade are in attendance, as are police and paramedics. A FIREMAN *is prising open the car door. The car stereo is playing 'Time to Say Goodbye'.*

The STRANGER *from* CHRISTINE*'s nightmares is nearby talking to a* POLICEMAN. *A* WPC *holds onto a shocked* JACK.

STRANGER It's my fault, I just stepped out onto the road, I wasn't looking . . .

A FIREMAN *is carefully lifting* CHRISTINE *from the wrecked car. Her eyes flicker.*

INT. LIVING ROOM. NIGHT.

CHRISTINE *remembers being carried by* ADAM *dressed as a fireman.*

CHRISTINE *(V.O.)* I don't know what's happening to me, I'm getting everything jumbled up . . .

EXT. BLOCK OF FLATS. DAY.

CHRISTINE *is laid onto the* PARAMEDIC*'s gurney. The blue light of an ambulance illuminates* CHRISTINE*'s face.*

INT. LIVING ROOM. NIGHT.

CHRISTINE *lies on the sofa, the blue Christmas tree lights in the background.*

MARION *(V.O.)* She's got a memory like a sieve . . .

EXT. BLOCK OF FLATS. DAY.

The PARAMEDICS *swarm around trying to save* CHRISTINE.

PARAMEDIC We're losing her . . . BP's dropping rapidly.

INT. LIVING ROOM. DAY.

CHRISTINE *is motionless in her chair.*

ADAM Jack, Mummy's going now!

CHRISTINE No . . . I don't want to . . .

JACK *appears. He is dressed for his Nativity as an angel, with a halo made from a coat hanger and tinsel.*

EXT. BLOCK OF FLATS. DAY.

The STRANGER *looks on as the* PARAMEDICS *fit a neck brace onto* CHRISTINE. JACK *is still with the* WPC. *He stares at his mum.*

STRANGER I managed to get the kid out, but I couldn't get to her. I'm sorry . . .

CHRISTINE*'s eyes flicker as the* PARAMEDICS *fit an oxygen mask.*

MARION *(V.O.)* He wouldn't want you to remember him like this.

CHRISTINE *(V.O.)* That's just life, Adam!

ERNIE *(V.O.)* This is supposed to be a happy memory.

They shine a light in her eyes.

INT. LIVING ROOM. DAY.

CHRISTINE *is faced by her family and friends.*

MARION It's time, Christine.

JACK *runs up to* CHRISTINE *and hugs her.* CHRISTINE *smiles and gets up from the table with her book.*

CHRISTINE Bye, everyone. Love you.

THE END

Episode 3

THE TRIAL OF ELIZABETH GADGE

CAST LIST

MR WARREN – Reece Shearsmith

MR CLARKE – Steve Pemberton

SIR ANDREW PIKE – David Warner

SARAH NUTTER – Sinéad Matthews

THOMAS NUTTER – Jim Howick

GEORGE WATERHOUSE – Trevor Cooper

RICHARD TWO-SHOES – Paul Kaye

ELIZABETH GADGE – Ruth Sheen

EXT. ELIZABETHAN BARN. NIGHT.

1649. The sign for the small English hamlet of 'Little Happens' swings and creaks in the wind.

Rain lashes the muddy street as three black-cloaked figures with lanterns hurry towards a large wooden barn. As they enter we settle on a rusted '9' nailed onto a gatepost.

TITLE: *'The Trial of Elizabeth Gadge'.*

INT. BARN. NIGHT.

The three men burst through the large doors into the barn.

There is a long wooden refectory table and three upholstered chairs, with wooden benches and bales of hay arranged around them. The men set their lanterns on the table and remove their wet cloaks and hats.

MR WARREN *is serious and severe, with quite an extravagant wig.* MR CLARKE *is officious, putting up with* MR WARREN *thinking he is slightly more in charge. It becomes apparent* MR WARREN *is much more fervent than* MR CLARKE, *who is growing tired of the charade.* MR CLARKE *carries all the luggage.*

The Justice of the Peace, SIR ANDREW PIKE, *is much older and stately. He shakes his hat of the rain and pours himself a glass of wine. They gather round the table.*

SIR ANDREW PIKE Our hamlet is not the first to have heard such strange stories, but I will not cry 'witch' without proper council.

MR WARREN Which is why we have come, Justice Pike.

SIR ANDREW PIKE You must be weary. 'Tis a great distance you have travelled.

MR WARREN I never tire of God's work. I feel not the miles we cross.

MR CLARKE Because 'tis I that take the reins of the steed whilst you slumber behind, Mr Warren.

MR WARREN *ignores this.*

MR WARREN But what spurs you to send for us so urgent, Justice Pike?

SIR ANDREW PIKE 'Tis not for nothing we are called 'Little Happens'. The last event of import here (as I recall) was a cow did loose from 'neath a gate and walk along . . .

WARREN *and* **CLARKE** *wait for more. There is none.*

MR WARREN We will hear you out nonetheless. Witchcraft is rife and our work . . . plentiful. Is that not so, Mr Clarke?

MR CLARKE *does not like being made to agree with* **MR WARREN**. *His reply is perhaps a little sarcastic.*

MR CLARKE Indeed. Devils walk the countryside and hedgerows as close as the next shire.

SIR ANDREW PIKE What is their shape? Should I meet one in the lane.

MR CLARKE They are cunning, Justice Pike, and will be transformed into something of the field. A fox, perhaps, or a stoat.

SIR ANDREW PIKE A tree?

MR WARREN A tree?

SIR ANDREW PIKE Yes, a tree perhaps? I did once spy a tree with a face in the bark. I thought it wicked and felt it mocked me.

MR WARREN 'Tis unusual, but could be so.

SIR ANDREW PIKE What about a step?

MR CLARKE A step . . .

SIR ANDREW PIKE Two weeks since I did trip and fall on a step on the edge of the green. Could it not be a devil all hunched down? I did hurt my hand as I fell and little stones did stick in my palm.

MR WARREN 'Tis possible, but we have yet to hear of it.

SIR ANDREW PIKE Well, we thank God you are at hand, Mr Warren, and you also Mr Clarke. There is, here in the village, a young couple who claim their mother, Elizabeth Gadge, is a sorceress and much talk of her devilry do they recount.

MR WARREN We shall be the judges of what is or is not 'devilry', sir.

MR CLARKE Indeed. We have just ridden from Southampton, where an iron founder hath reported a black imp hopping side to side in a chimney stack and taunting him that his hair was fair like a maiden.

SIR ANDREW PIKE Oh, monstrous!

MR CLARKE In truth, the imp was nothing but a carrion crow caught by the leg in a griddle.

SIR ANDREW PIKE Indeed, things are not always as they first seem.

MR WARREN 'Tis true. The crow may not have been an imp, but it was in fact a familiar, and did tell us, when questioned, the iron founder was himself bedevilled.

MR CLARKE The crow did not tell *me* that, Mr Warren. *I heard it say nothing.*

SIR ANDREW PIKE What action was served?

MR CLARKE We were paid by the Mayor, quite handsomely, and the iron founder was set to trial in accordance with our methods.

SIR ANDREW PIKE Was he found guilty?

MR CLARKE After many hours his tongue was made loose . . .

SIR ANDREW PIKE By what persuasion?

MR WARREN It was cut from his head with tailor's scissors, to which he died.

MR CLARKE The Devil did throttle him, so he would not reveal his accomplices.

SIR ANDREW PIKE Your reputations precede you, gentlemen. News of our witch has spread. The inns are thriving with new trade. Not since the escaped cow has there been such excitement here.

MR WARREN Then let there be investigation and arraignment of this old woman, and in the morning we will consider how far Satan prevails amongst you in respect of witchcraft.

MR CLARKE Heaven save us.

A distant rumble of thunder can be heard.

INT. BARN. DAY.

It is the next morning. Daylight now streams into the barn through the roof, but it is still dim inside. The barn is set for the trial and a couple of VILLAGERS *are taking their places on the benches, namely* THOMAS *and* SARAH NUTTER *and landowner* MR WATERHOUSE.

SIR ANDREW PIKE *approaches* MR WARREN *and* MR CLARKE *at the trestle table. The town cobbler* RICHARD TWO-SHOES *stands by, acting as a guard.*

SIR ANDREW PIKE Have you enough light, Mr Clarke?

MR CLARKE It will suffice.

MR WARREN I have a list of fees and expenses thus far, Justice Pike.

SIR ANDREW PIKE Of course, you will be paid forthwith.

MR WARREN *opens his bag and produces a list.*

MR WARREN Linen and sundries; pomade and foot powder; various inns and dwelling houses in and of our three-day ride and to maintain the company of our horse: 20 shillings.

SIR ANDREW PIKE Twenty shillings! I suppose there are yet two of you . . .

MR WARREN This was for *my* services alone. Mr Clarke has his own bill for presentment.

SIR ANDREW PIKE Ah – I see.

MR CLARKE Which can be visited after a verdict is settled, Justice Pike. Lest she is innocent and her accusers proved wrong.

MR WARREN 'Tis unlikely from the little I have heard.

MR CLARKE Which is nothing. Let us at least hear the testimony of the poor old crone before we reward ourselves with gold for burning her to death.

A look between WARREN *and* CLARKE. SIR ANDREW PIKE *intervenes.*

SIR ANDREW PIKE Before we begin, Mr Warren, would you permit me to set down your likeness in my book, that I may remember this time of our meeting?

MR WARREN Of course.

SIR ANDREW PIKE Thank you. I shall have it framed and hang it in your honour.

SIR ANDREW *begins to sketch* MR WARREN. *The guard* RICHARD *steps in.*

RICHARD Sir Andrew, would you like me to take a likeness of the both of you?

SIR ANDREW PIKE Oh, well, if it is no imposition?

MR WARREN Very well.

SIR ANDREW *crosses to stand by* MR WARREN *and leans in to him as* RICHARD *sketches the pair of them together.*

SIR ANDREW PIKE This is our cobbler, Richard Two-Shoes. He will serve to guard the old woman during the course of our trial.

RICHARD God bless you, gentlemen. 'Tis a great honour for me to aid you in the trial of this witch.

SIR ANDREW PIKE Indeed, Richard. But use not the word 'witch' until she hath confessed. *(To* CLARKE*)* We must give the hag a fair hearing.

MR CLARKE *looks doubtful. From outside there are cries of 'Witch!', 'Burn the witch!'*

RICHARD *proffers the sketch to* SIR ANDREW PIKE *and heads to the door.*

RICHARD She must be here. Shall I let them in, your honour?

SIR ANDREW PIKE Very well.

SIR ANDREW PIKE *looks at the sketch of himself and* MR WARREN.

It is extremely rudimentary and childlike. SIR ANDREW PIKE *is disappointed.*

SIR ANDREW PIKE *(cont'd)* Perhaps we can do another one later.

The crowd of VILLAGERS *stream in and take their places on the benches and hay bales.*

SIR ANDREW PIKE *rises to address the crowd. He bangs the table and brings the room to order.*

SIR ANDREW PIKE *(cont'd)* Order, order. Welcome, one and all, to the Little Happens witch trial. Many of you are strangers to our parish and we welcome your company here today. Whilst visiting Little Happens, may I recommend that you explore our village green, where there is a pond, with a duck!

From the crowd a large older man, WATERHOUSE, *calls out proudly:*

WATERHOUSE And a bench!

SIR ANDREW PIKE Yes, let us not forget the bench. And should that not be excitement enough, we now welcome two of our country's leading Witchfinders – Mr Warren and Mr Clarke.

The two MAGISTRATES *step forward to much applause.*

MR WARREN We are but here to serve our Lord in his quest to rid England of these damnable practices.

SIR ANDREW PIKE And now bring forth the witch . . . er . . . the accused woman.

The crowd jeer and cry out as ELIZABETH GADGE *is brought in by* RICHARD. *She is ancient but feisty.*

ELIZABETH GADGE What is happening here?

ELIZABETH GADGE *spots her daughter* SARAH *and son-in-law* THOMAS.

ELIZABETH GADGE *(cont'd)* Sarah? What is this? I was a-bed – I had hot milk.

MR WARREN *launches straight in.*

MR WARREN Or was it cold milk from a devil's tit, Elizabeth Gadge?

ELIZABETH GADGE Eh? Who are you that asks with such authority?

SIR ANDREW PIKE Elizabeth Anne Gadge, you are hereby accused of the practice of witchcraft and sorcery.

ELIZABETH GADGE What?

SIR ANDREW PIKE There are those here that think you an enchantress. You are to be tested.

ELIZABETH GADGE Who? Who here calls me 'witch'?

From the crowd, THOMAS GADGE *stands.*

THOMAS I do.

THOMAS *motions for* SARAH *to also stand. She seems less certain.*

SARAH And I.

ELIZABETH GADGE What? Oh, devils. This is for their attic room returned. They have want rid of me since my husband took sick and died. He and four cows in one morning. A week did it take to dig a hole big enough.

SIR ANDREW PIKE If after trial by council being of any of the said offences duly and lawfully convicted, ye shall suffer pains of death and shall lose the privilege of clergy and sanctuary.

SARAH *(to* THOMAS, *quietly)* What means he by that?

THOMAS *(to* SARAH, *quietly)* Sshh, quiet, Sarah, all will be well.

ELIZABETH GADGE Oh, my daughter! You need only have asked for the space – I was moving out within one month . . . I'd found a little cottage in the next village.

SIR ANDREW PIKE *(to* WARREN*)* Much Happens, an exceedingly dull place . . . *(To* ELIZABETH GADGE*)* You will have time anon to confront your accusers. Let us hear what has led you to this point. Come forward, Thomas and Goodwife Nutter.

THOMAS *and* SARAH NUTTER *approach and take the stand together.*

SIR ANDREW PIKE *(cont'd)* Warren, Clarke, you may proceed.

MR WARREN So tell us now of all ye spied, Thomas Nutter, and Mr Clarke here will take heed of it and writ as evidence your cursed testimony.

MR CLARKE *carefully places his spectacles on his nose.*

MR CLARKE That we may better remember the facts of this matter.

THOMAS My name is Thomas Nutter, this here be my wife Sarah Nutter. We did yesternight and for many nights afore spy Elizabeth Gadge, mother of my wife, creep abroad and meet with a fiend covered, as we saw, in brown fur and suck upon a black teat until sunrise.

ELIZABETH GADGE What?

MR WARREN Swear you to these sights, Goody Nutter?

SARAH Indeed 'tis true, sir. I have followed her myself whilst Thomas has been sleeping or at shit, and sometimes seen a white dog appear and dance a jig.

ELIZABETH GADGE Yes, it lives next door. 'Tis a spaniel called Rorie!

SIR ANDREW PIKE Silence!

MR WARREN How oft has Old Gadge, creeping, met and suckled at the black teat?

ELIZABETH GADGE *cries out again.*

ELIZABETH GADGE Never! I've suckled on a few things in my three score and ten but never a black teat.

SIR ANDREW PIKE *stands.*

SIR ANDREW PIKE By the authority of this court, I demand silence!

RICHARD *leans in to whisper to* ELIZABETH GADGE.

RICHARD You shut your hole, Elizabeth Gadge. May I strike the witch, sir?

SIR ANDREW PIKE Not just yet, Richard Two-Shoes.

MR WARREN Perhaps we should introduce Mistress Gadge to the Witch's Stitch, your honour?

SIR ANDREW PIKE Is this one of your fabled witch-finding devices?

MR CLARKE No, 'tis but a needle and thread, your honour. Mr Warren will sew up the crone's mouth, that she may be more encouraged to listen than talk.

ELIZABETH GADGE *pulls her lips tight.*

ELIZABETH GADGE I'm listening.

THOMAS Sarah – relate also the sighting of the imp that met in your mother's company.

SIR ANDREW PIKE *swigs some wine and leans in.*

SIR ANDREW PIKE Now we get to it.

SARAH I did see my mother converse with an imp in the shape of a small mouse, which she keeps hid in a wicker bottle.

MR WARREN I see.

MR CLARKE *looks up from his note-taking.*

MR CLARKE Could the imp in fact *be* a small mouse in a wicker bottle?

SARAH Er

THOMAS I had thought so too, but Sarah did hear it speak in a strange language and Elizabeth Gadge did reply.

MR WARREN Had the creature a name?

SARAH She called it Snowflake and did whisper to it and laugh.

MR CLARKE Was this 'language' like that of a mouse squeaking?

SARAH You know it!?

SIR ANDREW PIKE These are learned men, Goody Nutter, and have witnessed much that is strange.

MR WARREN So you concede, Elizabeth Gadge, that you gave this creature a title?

ELIZABETH GADGE Yes, he was as white as the snow, so I named him Snowflake.

MR WARREN You . . . named him?

ELIZABETH GADGE Aye. What manner of crime is that?

MR WARREN And what is 'named' backwards?

A pause while the assembled villagers work it out. MR CLARKE *rolls his eyes.*

SIR ANDREW PIKE Fetch me ink and paper!

In the crowd, WATERHOUSE *has worked it out.*

WATERHOUSE Demon!

THOMAS Demon!

The VILLAGERS *gasp and whisper 'demon'.* SIR ANDREW PIKE *shushes them and writes with his pen and paper.* MR WARREN *smiles. After a beat,* SIR ANDREW PIKE *has finally worked it out.*

SIR ANDREW PIKE 'Demon'!

MR WARREN Precisely.

ELIZABETH GADGE Well, no, it's 'deman', isn't it?

SIR ANDREW PIKE 'Tis close enough.

MR WARREN Make a note, Mr Clarke, that Elizabeth Gadge confesses to having discourse with the demon known as Snowflake.

MR CLARKE Such an imputation is somewhat lacking in evidence, would you not agree, Mr Warren?

SIR ANDREW PIKE Then add the creature to our list of witnesses, Mr Clarke. We will hear before God what this Snowflake has to say.

MR CLARKE *shakes his head.*

MR CLARKE Squeak, squeak, squeak.

INT. BARN. DAY.

WATERHOUSE *stands before the bench.* THOMAS *and* SARAH *are on the benches, watching, along with the* VILLAGERS. RICHARD *stands by.*

MR WARREN What is your name?

WATERHOUSE George Waterhouse.

MR WARREN And you have witnessed events which may be of interest to this hearing?

WATERHOUSE Well, only this. I did see Elizabeth Gadge fly out of the window on a shovel, whereat she rode to the Sabbat and did kiss the Devil's arse and eat a baby's face off.

There is a silence in the court as this is taken in.

MR WARREN When . . .

MR CLARKE *has to stop* MR WARREN *so he can finish writing this.*

MR CLARKE Just a moment . . . 'and eat a baby's face off'. Continue.

MR WARREN When was this?

WATERHOUSE Last Tuesday night. About five past – ten past eleven.

SIR ANDREW PIKE Tell us more of this arse-kissing. How close did thou spy it? Was it right on the hole or just the cheeks?

Before WATERHOUSE *can answer,* MR CLARKE *questions him.*

MR CLARKE Mr Waterhouse, I take it you are known to Elizabeth Gadge, are you not?

WATERHOUSE I suppose.

MR CLARKE In what capacity?

WATERHOUSE We have had some dealings in livestock. She did sell me a cow of late.

MR CLARKE And after a short time, I surmise this cow did die, did it not?

WATERHOUSE Yes, it bloody well did, and I paid good money to her husband and he too did die owing me 10 shillings.

MR CLARKE You may sit down, Mr Waterhouse. Your unbiased testimony is noted.

MR WARREN Please, your worship, we move the proceedings to the questioning of Elizabeth Gadge.

SIR ANDREW PIKE Very well. But we must hear more of the Sabbat and all its rites. For example, is it only the Devil that has his arse kissed, or can anyone be forced to endure it?

ELIZABETH GADGE *is roughly pushed forward by* RICHARD.

MR WARREN Elizabeth Gadge, what manner of fiend is it that you creep to nightly and suckle on?

ELIZABETH GADGE *is horrified.*

ELIZABETH GADGE I know not of what you speak. I am but a frail old woman who is a-bed by evensong. My tormentors know this to be true.

ELIZABETH GADGE *looks to her daughter and son-in-law. They say nothing.*

MR WARREN So you deny any knowledge of a brown thing of fur?

ELIZABETH GADGE A brown thing of fur?

SIR ANDREW PIKE Think carefully before you answer, Old Mistress Gadge.

ELIZABETH GADGE *considers.*

ELIZABETH GADGE I have a brown hat of such a description – it is for winter and the cold.

MR WARREN And does this hat walk upright on two legs and have hang from it a black teat?

ELIZABETH GADGE 'Tis plain as I remember. And, being a hat, has no legs or titties to speak of.

This provokes laughter among the VILLAGERS, *which annoys* MR WARREN.

MR WARREN Something amuses you, Mr Waterhouse?

WATERHOUSE A hat with titties!

More laughter.

MR WARREN It would be unfortunate that our discovery of this sorceress should uncover diverse others in this court. Not since summer last have Mr Clarke and myself unearthed a *coven* of witches!

SIR ANDREW PIKE I read of it! 'Twas in Leeds.

ELIZABETH GADGE And what was the cause? Did they find a tree with three teats and a cunny? Or did they spy the Devil's bush upon your chin?

ELIZABETH GADGE *points at* WARREN*'s beard.*

More laughter. SIR ANDREW PIKE *snorts with laughter, immediately suppressing it. Even* THOMAS *and* SARAH *share a giggle.* MR WARREN *seethes at the impertinence.* MR CLARKE *senses where this is heading.*

MR CLARKE Silence! If you value your lives, silence!

MR WARREN Laughter contorts the face and makes monkeys of men. Only the Devil would turn such sport. The next person here to laugh will immediately die as a witch . . . starting from . . . now.

Everyone shuts up. From nowhere, it is now a massive game of 'first one to laugh'. MR WARREN *walks round staring at the faces, looking closely for a glimmer of a smile.* WARREN *looks to* WATERHOUSE, *who is struggling to keep a straight face, then to* THOMAS *and* SARAH.

As this is happening, ELIZABETH GADGE *realises the power she now has and starts pulling faces and trying to make the others laugh.*

ELIZABETH GADGE *mimes that* WARREN*'s chin is a vagina and pokes out her tongue, miming devil horns.* WATERHOUSE *laughs.*

MR WARREN *(cont'd)* Who was that? Which of you was that?

ELIZABETH GADGE Aye – confess it! Which is the witch!

ELIZABETH GADGE *laughs her head off.*

RICHARD It was Old Waterhouse, Mr Warren.

WATERHOUSE Shut up, you rat, or she won't be the only one to have kissed the Devil's arse.

The court is in chaos, with some VILLAGERS *still laughing,* ELIZABETH GADGE *prancing around,* RICHARD *and* WATERHOUSE *arguing.*

MR CLARKE Enough! You undermine the solemn purpose of this undertaking. Let us stay focused on Old Mistress Gadge.

SIR ANDREW PIKE Indeed. I move that we continue this trial in private.

MR WARREN I agree. Perhaps it is just as well, for the testing of the accused is not for the faint-hearted.

MR WARREN *uncovers a table, which is lined with horrible-looking torture instruments.*

MR WARREN *(cont'd)* Court dismissed.

Groans of disappointment from the VILLAGERS *on the benches. They start to troop out.*

SIR ANDREW PIKE Well, you've spoilt it for yourselves.

INT. BARN. DAY.

The barn has been cleared of the crowd. Only THOMAS *and* SARAH NUTTER *remain.*

SIR ANDREW PIKE, MR CLARKE *and* MR WARREN *examine the instruments of torture that have been laid out on the table.* SIR ANDREW PIKE *is examining a thumbscrew.*

SIR ANDREW PIKE And these can be used on thumbs or toes?

MR CLARKE That is correct, your honour.

SIR ANDREW PIKE Oh, most versatile. And this?

SIR ANDREW PIKE *picks up a long pear-shaped metal instrument.*

MR CLARKE 'The Pear'. It can be inserted into any orifice and expanded to the point of . . .

SIR ANDREW PIKE Ecstasy.

MR CLARKE Agony.

SIR ANDREW PIKE Agony, yes.

MR WARREN But my preferred method . . . is pricking.

MR WARREN *holds up a long, thin spike.*

MR WARREN *(cont'd)* Lay bare her back. Cut the cloth if need be and hold her still.

RICHARD *has tied* ELIZABETH*'s arms to a broom handle and she is seated on a stool. He approaches her with a knife.*

ELIZABETH GADGE Please! Have mercy – this top was a present. Let me but take it off carefully, there is no need to ruin it . . .

RICHARD *cuts and rips the blouse, exposing her back.*

MR WARREN The Devil may have laid his mark upon you. It is for us to discover it.

MR WARREN *stands over the bare back of* ELIZABETH GADGE, *brandishing his long needle.*

SIR ANDREW PIKE So, just to be clear, if she bleeds, she is a witch?

MR WARREN No, quite the opposite.

SIR ANDREW PIKE If she bleeds, she is not a witch!

MR WARREN Not necessarily. The Devil's mark may be well hidden.

SIR ANDREW PIKE So we must keep pricking her 'til she do stop bleeding, at which time we will know that she is or is not a witch. Possibly.

MR WARREN Correct.

SIR ANDREW PIKE All is clear. Proceed.

MR WARREN *pricks the first of* ELIZABETH GADGE*'s 'marks' (i.e. any blemish on her body). She cries out and she bleeds.*

ELIZABETH GADGE Oh Sarah! Am I not still your mother? Have mercy on me!

SARAH *is appalled at what is happening to her mother.*

SARAH Thomas . . . please . . .

THOMAS We know what we saw.

SARAH It was dark, it could have been anyone.

THOMAS Or any*thing*! Besides, the attic would be of good use, Sarah. Where else are we to dry the sheets?

Another scream from ELIZABETH. SARAH *can't bear it.*

SARAH Please, stop!

MR CLARKE What is it, Sarah Nutter? Did you not expect horrors such as these to unfold?

SARAH We may have been mistook. Perhaps it was a shadow, a trick of the twilight . . .

MR WARREN You lie, Goody Nutter!

SARAH No! Truth is, we don't know what we saw.

THOMAS Sarah!

MR WARREN *threatens* ELIZABETH GADGE *with the needle once more.*

MR WARREN Who is this night-time fiend you so visit? An incubus? Beelzebub? What is his name?

ELIZABETH GADGE *is pricked again.*

ELIZABETH GADGE Ahhh! It was him, Richard Two-Shoes!

ELIZABETH GADGE *points to the guard* RICHARD.

ELIZABETH GADGE *(cont'd)* Richard Two-Shoes, the cobbler.

RICHARD She lies! She lies, your worship, prick her again!

ELIZABETH GADGE I did meet sometimes with him after dark. He would pay me a shilling a suck, and I would do it!

SIR ANDREW PIKE Is this true, Richard?

RICHARD No, sir, I swear it. I do not stir out after dark, my wife will vouch for it.

SIR ANDREW PIKE Very well, we must get to the bottom of this. Call forth Goody Two-Shoes!

INT. BARN. DAY.

RICHARD *is being questioned.* ELIZABETH GADGE *sits beside him on her stool.*

MR WARREN Richard Two-Shoes, have you spent night after night with this vile hag?

RICHARD Yes, your worship.

We move across to reveal GOODY TWO-SHOES, *a large lady with bad teeth.*

RICHARD *(cont'd)* But she is my wife and 'tis the law, is it not?

MR CLARKE We are referring to Old Mistress Gadge. Is it true you have had several night-time meetings with her?

A severe look from GOODY TWO-SHOES *to her husband.*

RICHARD No, sir. On the eyes of my children, I swear it.

ELIZABETH GADGE 'Twas not for love, Goody Two-Shoes. 'Twas done only to pay my son-in-law rent. He would always cry your name when he did climax and throw out his curdle.

SIR ANDREW PIKE For the court records, is that of any comfort, Goody Two-Shoes?

GOODY TWO-SHOES *shakes her head.*

ELIZABETH GADGE He spoke fondly of my mouth. He liked not your teeth and said they were like a box of nails, should he put in his rod.

RICHARD I never said that! My wife can suck like a leech. Show them, Rachel, show Sir Andrew what miracles your mouth can work!

GOODY TWO-SHOES *looks at* SIR ANDREW PIKE *with her big brown teeth. He's terrified.*

SIR ANDREW PIKE That will not be necessary.

MR CLARKE Come, come, Mr Two-Shoes. The old woman's life hangs in the balance if you do not confess it.

ELIZABETH GADGE Richard . . . please. They will burn me else. Did I not bring you pleasure?

RICHARD Never. I had no such meetings!

MR WARREN Justice Pike, I move to adjourn the court and continue afresh tomorrow.

MR WARREN *approaches* ELIZABETH GADGE.

MR WARREN *(cont'd)* We will apply hot oil and other methods overnight to freshen the old woman's recollection of events.

SIR ANDREW PIKE Very well. Until 8 a.m. tomorrow. I will to my chambers.

SIR ANDREW PIKE *moves away and a metallic thud sounds.* SIR ANDREW PIKE *looks down and 'the Pear' has dropped from his robes.*

SIR ANDREW PIKE *(cont'd)* Oh! Just put that back . . .

He reluctantly places the Pear back on the table.

INT. BARN. DAY.

The next morning MR WARREN *and* MR CLARKE *debate the next step over a hearty breakfast.*

MR CLARKE Yet more imps and devils in the fireplace, Mr Warren. We can do this no more.

MR WARREN Evil can be found peeping from anywhere, Mr Clarke. As you well know.

MR CLARKE But care you not for this old woman, Warren? 'Tis as plain as day the Nutters want rid of her from under their roof and have cried witch as a solution!

MR WARREN Whatever the reason, the trial will uncover it.

MR CLARKE By the continuation of her torture.

MR WARREN Yes, as is our usual practice she has been subjected overnight to the five steps: preparatory torture, ordinary torture, extra-ordinary torture, additional and occasional torture and finally, final torture. What possible reason have you to question the fairness of our work, Clarke?

MR CLARKE Witchcraft is punishable by death and perhaps the burden of pointing the finger has made me weary.

MR WARREN Burden? You live handsomely and are commended by God and the law alike.

MR CLARKE We began as seekers of truth.

MR WARREN We are still.

MR CLARKE But what of this dear old mistress, presently dragged here to convince us of her purity? Having done no more than keep a mouse in a bottle and suck to completion a man in a brown coat? If we consign her innocent body to the flames, do we not do the Devil's work ourselves?

MR WARREN Tread cautiously, Mr Clarke, lest you find yourself accused. Whatever the cost, the Lord's work will be done.

MR CLARKE I agree. And I will pray to Him for guidance.

SIR ANDREW PIKE *approaches.*

SIR ANDREW PIKE Good morning, gentlemen! I trust you slept well?

MR CLARKE Not really.

SIR ANDREW PIKE Thank Heaven we had no rain and the pyre has remained dry for tonight – should we have a confession of guilt, of course.

MR WARREN Of course.

SIR ANDREW PIKE We have heard tell of visitors from all three shires and a travelling fair has alighted on the green, if you can countenance it! Pin the Tail on the Devil, Witch-Bobbing, that sort of thing. The innkeepers are saying it could be bigger than Pendle!

MR CLARKE You will need change the name of your town, Justice Pike.

SIR ANDREW PIKE Indeed. They will be most envious in Much Happens.

ELIZABETH GADGE *is led in by* RICHARD. *She is a mess, barely conscious, she has to be held up to speak.* SIR ANDREW PIKE *is shocked at the terrible sight.*

SIR ANDREW PIKE *(cont'd)* Is that the same woman as yesterday?

RICHARD It is, Justice Pike.

SIR ANDREW PIKE She seems taller than before.

MR WARREN She has been stretched, your honour, in pursuit of the truth. *(To* RICHARD*)* Bring in her accusers.

RICHARD *heads back to the door.* SIR ANDREW PIKE *takes his place and* MR WARREN *leans in to talk to* ELIZABETH GADGE.

MR WARREN *(cont'd)* Are you ready to confess, Elizabeth Gadge?

ELIZABETH *groans and shakes her head.*

MR WARREN *(cont'd)* You are weak. Perhaps some food might revive you.

MR WARREN *sneaks some cheese from the breakfast plate and crumbles it around* ELIZABETH GADGE, *placing it under her skirt as she lies on the ground.*

SIR ANDREW PIKE Call the court to order!

WARREN *wipes his hands and takes his seat with* PIKE *and* CLARKE. SARAH, THOMAS, WATERHOUSE, RICHARD *and* GOODY TWO-SHOES *are taking their seats.*

SIR ANDREW PIKE *(cont'd)* Mr Warren, Mr Clarke, you may proceed.

MR WARREN *stands.*

MR WARREN Elizabeth Gadge is yet to confess to her sorcery. I propose one final test that will seal her fate in your eyes and in the eyes of God. Mr Clarke?

MR CLARKE The court calls the demon known as Snowflake.

A flurry of panic amongst those watching. RICHARD *goes to fetch the mouse.*

SIR ANDREW PIKE Please, please, remain calm, there is nothing to fear . . .

RICHARD *enters, holding a large wicker bottle. He approaches the table.*

SIR ANDREW PIKE *(cont'd)* Oh Christ in Heaven! It has transformed itself into the shape of a bottle!

MR WARREN *whispers to* SIR ANDREW PIKE.

SIR ANDREW PIKE *(cont'd)* Ah. The bottle is indeed a bottle and the familiar hides inside. Richard, release the imp. But look you, be careful lest it bite.

RICHARD *shakes the bottle to free the mouse.*

SNOWFLAKE, *a little white mouse, falls from the bottle and scurries into the room.* SARAH *cries out.* GOODY TWO-SHOES *stands on a chair.*

MR WARREN Now, let us observe the demon as it seeks out its mistress, the witch.

SNOWFLAKE *scurries around towards the benches, then approaches the table. It sniffs around* SIR ANDREW PIKE*'s boots.*

SIR ANDREW PIKE Argh!

MR WARREN Be calm, Justice Pike. The truth will out.

SNOWFLAKE *scurries along to* ELIZABETH GADGE *and starts to nibble at the cheese.* ELIZABETH *picks him up; she is weak from torture.*

ELIZABETH GADGE Snowflake! Hello, my lovely.

The crowd gasp. MR CLARKE *bows his head.* THOMAS *points.*

THOMAS She is a witch! *(To* SARAH*)* See, 'tis proved!

SARAH *(sadly)* It's only a mouse.

MR WARREN Elizabeth Gadge, do you now acknowledge your

crimes? Did you meet and have relations with a fiend, dance with a white dog and keep council with this monstrous familiar?

ELIZABETH GADGE No, sir . . .

SIR ANDREW PIKE And did you by transvection fly to the Sabbat on a shovel, and lick and caress the Devil's arse with your hot probing tongue?

ELIZABETH GADGE Never!

MR WARREN But your familiar has proven otherwise. Prepare the witch for execution.

RICHARD *crosses and places a large white smock over* ELIZABETH GADGE *and ties her hands before her.*

SIR ANDREW PIKE Elizabeth Anne Gadge, you have been found guilty of witchcraft and will be taken to a place of execution where you will be burned at the stake until you are dead. Tickets are now on sale at the Green Man Inn, family tokens include a free potato to bake in the fire, and may the Lord have mercy on your soul.

RICHARD *places a sackcloth bag on* ELIZABETH GADGE*'s head.*

MR CLARKE *storms out of the court, passing* WATERHOUSE, *who looks troubled.*

MR CLARKE Art thou content?

MR CLARKE *leaves.* WATERHOUSE *looks across to the hooded and robed figure of* ELIZABETH GADGE *slumped on the hay bale. He crosses himself.*

INT. BARN. NIGHT.

ELIZABETH GADGE *is bound and hooded and sits on a hay bale in the barn. Outside we can hear preparations for the execution, and it sounds like there is quite a lively crowd.*

The barn door opens and THOMAS *and* SARAH *appear. They approach the slumped figure of* ELIZABETH GADGE.

SARAH Mother, 'tis I, Sarah. Thomas is here too. We've come to say goodbye.

THOMAS Don't know why, witch.

SARAH Thomas! Justice Pike has let us have two seats on the front row, so that's nice.

THOMAS As is only fair. And we've put all your belongings on the fire, two birds with one stone and all that!

SARAH We have moved the babes up to your . . . the attic room.

THOMAS Aye, we have yet so much space. Goody Garden next door is green with envy.

SARAH She says she's going to accuse her mother.

THOMAS She better not, else they'll all be doing it.

MR CLARKE *comes in.*

MR CLARKE I'm sorry but you must leave now. It is my duty to administer the last rites to your mother before she burns.

THOMAS Righto. Let's get our seats. Kiss the Devil's arse for me!

SARAH Goodbye, Mother. I'm sorry . . .

THOMAS *and* SARAH *leave.* MR CLARKE *watches them go, then crosses to* ELIZABETH GADGE.

MR CLARKE I am sorry. I can scarce believe it has come to this.

MR CLARKE *lifts the sack from her head to reveal . . . it is in fact* MR WARREN, *gagged and groggy from being knocked out.*

MR CLARKE *pats* MR WARREN*'s cheeks to wake him up a bit.* WARREN *looks confused, then manages to focus on* CLARKE.

MR CLARKE *(cont'd)* We were partners, you and I, Matthew. Against evil. But you have become infected. Evil has grown within you. Your zealotry has turned to bigotry and worse. You said we must do God's work, whatever the cost. May He have mercy on your wretched soul.

The door opens and MR CLARKE *quickly returns the sack over* MR WARREN*'s head.* SIR ANDREW PIKE *arrives with a witch's pointy hat on his head and a toffee apple. Two* GUARDS *approach with him.*

SIR ANDREW PIKE They are selling these hats at the fair! Most amusing, I thought. Did you want a toffee apple?

MR CLARKE I thank ye, no. The witch is prepared.

SIR ANDREW PIKE Excellent, well. Guards, take her outside and bind her to the stake.

The GUARDS *march* MR WARREN *outside. He puts up a struggle and moans weakly through his gag but is swept along by the* GUARDS.

SIR ANDREW PIKE *(cont'd)* I haven't yet seen Mr Warren, I have monies here to present him.

MR CLARKE I shall see that he gets it. Let us hope there are no more witch trials in Little Happens.

SIR ANDREW PIKE For myself, I am glad of it. It has been a most rewarding endeavour. I shall rather miss all the excitement! You don't think the daughter may have been involved . . .?

MR CLARKE I think not.

SIR ANDREW PIKE No, no, just a thought. Oh well, I must attend outside. They have insisted that I be the one to light the fire.

He shakes MR CLARKE*'s hand.*

SIR ANDREW PIKE *(cont'd)* You are ridding us of a great evil, Mr Clarke.

MR CLARKE Yes – I do believe I am.

SIR ANDREW PIKE *leaves.* MR CLARKE *runs over to some bales of hay and looks behind them.*

MR CLARKE *(cont'd)* All is clear. You may show yourself.

ELIZABETH GADGE *emerges from behind the hay bales.*

ELIZABETH GADGE Thanking you kindly, sir. How can I ever repay you?

MR CLARKE Your continued life is my reward, Elizabeth. Take this.

MR CLARKE *hands the bag of money to* ELIZABETH GADGE.

MR CLARKE *(cont'd)* You must away from this village lest our stratagem be discovered.

ELIZABETH GADGE Let me first but suck you a little sir. To show my gratitude.

MR CLARKE There is no need, Mistress Gadge.

ELIZABETH GADGE But you murdered your friend, Mr Clarke!

ELIZABETH GADGE *holds* CLARKE*'s face tenderly in her hands.*

MR CLARKE What I did, I did for the Lord.

ELIZABETH GADGE And the Devil thanks you kindly.

SNAP! ELIZABETH GADGE *twists* MR CLARKE*'s head sharply 180 degrees and his neck is broken.* MR CLARKE *falls to the floor, dead.*

Outside we hear the roar of the bonfire taking light. The crowd cheer and cry 'Burn the witch', 'Rot in Hell', etc.

Strangulated screams from MR WARREN.

ELIZABETH GADGE *looks up to the top window. The fire burns brightly, casting a red glow into the barn. Smoke also creeps into the barn. She smiles.*

ELIZABETH GADGE *(cont'd)* Come, Snowflake, our work here is done. Let us to the Sabbat and tell our master these happy tidings.

ELIZABETH GADGE *reaches down and we see* SNOWFLAKE *scurrying around* CLARKE*'s body.* ELIZABETH GADGE *picks him up.*

We remain on the body of MR CLARKE *and see the feet of* ELIZABETH GADGE *float up off the ground and disappear. Smoke envelops the room.*

THE END

Episode 4

COLD COMFORT

CAST LIST

ANDY – Steve Pemberton

LIZ – Jane Horrocks

GEORGE – Reece Shearsmith

JOANNE – Nikki Amuka-Bird

MICHAEL – Tony Way

CALLERS

Edward Easton

Vilma Hollingbery

Kath Hughes

James Meehan

Vicky Hall

EXT. CSL OFFICE. DAY.

CCTV image of a municipal building in a high street. A slightly closer image shows the first-floor offices of CSL – Comfort Support Line.

TITLE: *'Cold Comfort'.*

INT. CSL OFFICE. DAY.

We are in the office of Comfort Support Line, a small charity organisation manned by volunteers. There are two banks of partitioned booths, each with a telephone.

The main action is filmed on a CCTV camera (CAM 1), which is stationed above one of the booths. There is an empty desk and chair, with a phone, notepad and pen. This gives a close view of people sitting at booth number 9, as well as a view of LIZ, *who sits in the booth opposite. In the bottom corner of the screen is the date and the caption '09'.*

To the right-hand side of the screen we see three inset CCTV images.

CAM 2 is a wide shot of GEORGE*'s office, which is just off the main room.*

CAM 3 is a wide-angle shot of the whole room.

CAM 4 is a shot of the stairwell leading up (or down) to the CSL office.

After a moment, the phone starts to ring. A red light shows that it is the phone on the desk. It rings for a long time, six or seven rings, before LIZ *wheels across on her chair and picks up the call.*

LIZ *is a gossipy woman in her late forties.*

LIZ Hello, Comfort Support Line?

Too late. She hangs up.

LIZ *(cont'd)* George, remind me, are we allowed to do 1471?

GEORGE *is emerging from his office (CAM 2) with* ANDY.

GEORGE No.

LIZ Well, we need to get somebody on nine.

GEORGE I'm aware of that, thank you.

GEORGE *approaches with* ANDY. GEORGE *is an earnest jobsworth in a patterned jumper.* ANDY *looks like an office worker in a suit.*

LIZ *tries the pen on the paper, sees that it works and takes it with her as she wheels herself away.*

GEORGE *(cont'd)* So I'm going to pop you in here, opposite Liz – have you met?

ANDY I don't think so. Hi, I'm Andy.

LIZ Oh, he's giving you prime location there.

ANDY Really?

GEORGE Yes, this was Victoria's booth – she was one of our longest-standing volunteers, but she's had to take a bit of gardening leave. She had three dead dads in two days and it tipped her over the edge.

LIZ That was probably her phoning just then.

GEORGE Yes, and if it was, we'd have respected her confidentiality, wouldn't we, Liz?

LIZ Of course we would, George.

GEORGE Right, let's get you sat in, shall we?

ANDY *sits in the chair and we see him for the first time.*

GEORGE *(cont'd)* As you can see, it's compact and bijou, with a south-facing terrace and en-suite facilities.

LIZ Don't worry, Andy, I didn't laugh either.

GEORGE Obviously you've done your induction, but when the call comes through we like to pick up within three rings and begin every dialogue with 'Hello, Comfort Support Line.'

ANDY OK.

GEORGE I don't mind people using the abbreviation CSL because Comfort Support Line does sound a bit like bras.

LIZ You've got one for your moobs, haven't you, George!

GEORGE Ignore her. Now, whatever the caller wants to talk about, we offer active listening, though I'd say one in every five calls will just be silent.

ANDY Right, because they're plucking up the courage.

GEORGE Yes. You just have to make sure they're not plucking something else.

ANDY Oh, you mean masturbating?

GEORGE It has become a bit of an epidemic.

ANDY How will I be able to tell?

LIZ *makes a strange slapping sound from her booth.*

GEORGE Liz! Your ear soon becomes attuned. Now you might find you have a dead hour or so when no one rings. I don't mind you bringing in a novel or a newspaper, a word search is fine, but I do frown on people watching box sets of *The Walking Dead* on their mobile phone.

LIZ It was the season finale, leave me alone.

GEORGE The point is, you have to be focused and ready to go at the drop of a hat.

The phone rings.

GEORGE *(cont'd)* There you go, do you want to plunge straight in . . .?

ANDY OK.

GEORGE *nods to the phone as he puts on headphones to listen in.* ANDY *takes a deep breath and answers the phone.*

ANDY *(cont'd)* Hello, Comfort . . . CSL line. How can I help you?

AUTOMATED VOICE Hi, this is an important message regarding your Payment Protection Insurance Policy. In order to process your refund . . .

GEORGE Hang up.

ANDY I thought I wasn't allowed to terminate the dialogue.

GEORGE Well, that's not a dialogue, is it? We'll have to get something done about this, there's more PPIs than wankers . . .

INT. CSL OFFICE. DAY.

Four hours later. ANDY *sits at the booth. He looks a little bored. He is looking at the puzzles page in his newspaper.*

On CAM 2 we see GEORGE *in his office.*

On CAM 4 we see an attractive business-like woman, JOANNE, *walk down the stairs towards the office.*

ANDY Liz, do you have a spare pen there?

LIZ No, sorry.

JOANNE *enters the office (CAM 3) and walks to her booth.* ANDY *cranes his neck to see her.*

LIZ *(cont'd)* Don't even go there.

ANDY What? No, I'm just trying to work out who everyone is.

LIZ *wheels across to* ANDY.

LIZ Joanne Chillingham, which is appropriate 'cos she's colder than a witch's tit.

ANDY Really?

LIZ Oh yeah. You'd get more compassion from an answerphone. Two words: 'a-void'.

ANDY Right. So have you been volunteering long?

LIZ Me? I was going to do it for two weeks five years ago. I just got addicted to it, I love it. What about you?

ANDY Oh, I just thought it was a really good thing to do. You know, when my sister died I really wished I could have . . .

LIZ*'s phone rings and she answers it.*

LIZ Hello, Comfort Support Line, how can I help you?

ANDY *pulls out his wallet and pulls out a photograph. When he turns it round we see a photo of* ANDY *with his sister.*

ANDY *pins the photo to the partition wall.*

The phone rings. ANDY *looks round to* GEORGE*'s office.*

ANDY George! I've got . . .

GEORGE *comes over from his office. He is wearing a small Bluetooth headset, over which he puts on the headphones.*

GEORGE OK, remember: no leading, no counselling. Just active listening.

ANDY *picks up the phone.*

ANDY Hello, CSL?

Silence. ANDY *hears breathing.* ANDY *wonders to* GEORGE *whether this might be masturbatory, but* GEORGE *shakes his head.*

ANDY *(cont'd)* Do you want to talk to someone?

VERA Oh God. Well, a couple of years ago . . . there was an incident.

ANDY Right.

VERA After the incident I was pretty depressed, obviously, but I did manage to get back on track even though it was quite a serious incident.

ANDY I see.

VERA And as Steve said at the clinic, with that kind of incident you're not going to bounce back overnight, are you? It takes its toll. But I can't sleep now for thinking about the incident. I'm having nightmares about it. And all I can think when I wake up is, 'God! The incident, the incident.'

ANDY What was the incident?

VERA I'd rather not talk about it.

ANDY OK . . . so without revealing to me the nature of the incident . . .

GEORGE It's not a magic trick!

ANDY Sorry.

VERA It was an abortion if you must know.

ANDY Right, good. Well, that was your choice . . .

VERA I know it was.

ANDY No, I mean, that was your choice to tell me. I didn't force it out of you.

VERA *hangs up.* GEORGE *takes off his headphones.*

ANDY *(cont'd)* That went well.

GEORGE Don't beat yourself up, that was good. I'm just glad you didn't say anything about terminating the call.

INT. CSL OFFICE. DAY.

ANDY *sits sipping a Frappuccino. He can hear* LIZ *in the booth behind him.*

LIZ Yeah . . . yeah . . . oh my God, did he? Yeah, well, I would say if it's brown, take it straight back . . .

ANDY *looks across, baffled by the conversation.*

INT. CSL OFFICE. DAY.

ANDY *answers the phone.*

ANDY Hello, Comfort Support Line. Can I help you?

GRUFF VOICE Fuck off, you queer prick.

The GRUFF VOICE *hangs up.* ANDY *hangs up resignedly.*

INT. CSL OFFICE. DAY.

ANDY *is on the phone to* IAIN, *a depressed-sounding man.* LIZ *isn't in.*

IAIN . . . and it wasn't even like we'd had a bad holiday, it was good. We went out for some nice meals and the hotel was nice, and I'd got a good deal – I'd got one of those deals you get where you cut and paste the numbers . . .

ANDY *looks at his watch. He crosses his legs anxiously.*

ANDY Uh-huh.

IAIN . . . and she seemed happy with it at the time, but I think the weather was quite bad so there was a lot of sitting in cafés, so that doesn't help.

ANDY *writes a note on his pad and holds it up to the camera: 'I need a wee!!!' But* GEORGE *isn't in his office.*

ANDY No . . .

ANDY *pours a bit of ice from his Frappuccino into the empty sandwich container.*

IAIN And it kind of makes you realise you've got nothing to say to each other. But I'm talking like it came from me; it didn't.

ANDY *places the empty cup under the desk, checks no one is watching and surreptitiously relieves himself into it as* IAIN *drones on.*

IAIN *(cont'd)* I mean, I tried to start conversations, but she'd . . . they'd just be one-word answers, like 'Yes' or 'Dunno'. I felt like she wasn't really interested in what I had to say, do you know what I mean?

ANDY Hmmm.

IAIN Anyway, I'm going to go now because I've just heard her come back in, but thanks very much, you've really helped me.

ANDY Oh good, well . . . that's why we're here. Nice talking to you.

IAIN Bye. Mother, is that you . . . ?

ANDY *hangs up, relieved. He lifts the Frappuccino cup, which is now almost full of amber urine.*

JOANNE *passes by* ANDY*'s booth.*

JOANNE I bet that's a relief.

ANDY Yeah – what?

JOANNE That call, seemed like a long one.

ANDY Yeah, it was. I was dying . . . for him to finish. Not that I didn't want to hear what he had to say, just that I was relieved when he said it. I'm Andy.

JOANNE Joanne. Hi.

ANDY Just get rid of this . . .

ANDY *shoves the wee-cup into a corner of the desk.*

JOANNE Do you mind if I sit down for a second?

ANDY No, not at all.

JOANNE *pulls up a chair and sits by* ANDY.

JOANNE I know you're quite new, and please don't think I'm being patronising. 'Patronise' means to talk down to someone.

ANDY Right . . .

JOANNE That was a joke by the way.

ANDY Yes, good.

JOANNE It's just, I've been a volunteer here for three years and I always say the same thing to all the new recruits: don't get involved.

ANDY Oh right, no. I wasn't going to – I'm not even looking.

JOANNE I don't mean with me, I mean with the callers.

ANDY Right, yeah. George has said. It's not a good idea.

JOANNE No, it's not. These people are not your friends, in spite of what Liz might say.

ANDY Yes, she seems quite chatty.

JOANNE She's probably been bitching about me already, has she? Has she?

ANDY Not that I know of.

JOANNE Let her. I don't care. I don't want any part of that clique.

ANDY I don't.

JOANNE Just keep your guard up, and your shutters down. Anyway, I'll let you finish your drink.

ANDY Yeah . . .

JOANNE Good luck, Andy.

ANDY *picks up his cup and makes to take a sip as* JOANNE *leaves. He holds it to his lips until she leaves, then puts it back down, spitting.*

INT. CSL OFFICE. NIGHT 3.

GEORGE *is in his office on his laptop (CAM 2).* ANDY *is at his desk when the phone rings.*

ANDY Hello, Comfort Support Line?

Silence.

ANDY *(cont'd)* Did you want to . . .?

AUTOMATED VOICE Hi, this is an important message regarding your Payment Protection Insurance . . .

ANDY *slams the phone down.*

ANDY Oh piss off.

LIZ Let me guess, another PPI. Persistent Pain in the Intestine, I call them. Right, I'm off, I've got a hot date with a Fray Bentos steak and ale pie.

ANDY*'s phone rings again.*

ANDY Hello, CSL?

LIZ *(whispering)* Night night.

LIZ *departs and* ANDY *waves. He listens. Silence. Soft breathing on the other end of the phone.*

ANDY Hello?

CHLOE Is Victoria there?

ANDY Sorry, no, Victoria's not here tonight.

CHLOE Oh.

ANDY Was there something you wanted to talk about?

CHLOE What's your name?

ANDY I . . . I'm afraid we're not advised to give out our personal details.

CHLOE Victoria did.

ANDY Well, she's . . . no longer a volunteer here. But I am.

CHLOE OK.

CHLOE *sighs deeply. Sadly.* ANDY *thaws a little.*

ANDY You can tell me your name if you'd like.

CHLOE Chloe.

ANDY Hi, Chloe. I'm . . . here for you.

CHLOE Will you talk to me?

ANDY Of course.

Silence.

CHLOE What . . . do you want to talk about?

ANDY *seems frustrated.*

ANDY Well . . . I'm just here to listen so – you tell me.

CHLOE Well, I hate my life, I hate my mum, I hate my stepdad – especially hate my stepdad. I haven't done anything with my life . . .

ANDY How old are you, Chloe?

CHLOE Sixteen.

ANDY Well, there you are, you're still very young. You've got your whole life ahead of you.

CHLOE Ha! Yeah.

CHLOE *starts to moan. It goes on for some time.* ANDY *looks concerned.*

CHLOE *(cont'd)* Oohhhh!

ANDY Chloe . . .

CHLOE Ahhhhhhhh!

ANDY Listen, Chloe, I don't want to be rude, but if you're doing what I think you're doing, I'm going to have to ask you to stop, because . . .

CHLOE What? I've got stomach cramps.

ANDY OK, fine. It's just that we're not allowed to . . .

CHLOE I've taken some tablets.

ANDY Sorry?

CHLOE I've taken tablets.

ANDY Have you? OK . . . er, how many?

ANDY *scribbles a note on his pad.*

CHLOE Dunno . . . 30, 40?

ANDY Right.

CHLOE I just wanted someone to talk to before I go.

ANDY *is distressed. He looks left and right, but there doesn't seem to be anyone else around.* ANDY *tries to see into* GEORGE*'s office, but* GEORGE *is at his desk doing paperwork.*

ANDY Well, I can do that, Chloe, and I'm certainly going to keep talking to you, but if you had a mobile you could also dial 999 . . .

CHLOE No . . .

ANDY And ask for an ambulance.

CHLOE No, please don't do that.

ANDY I'm not going to do that, Chloe, I promise. We'll just talk.

CHLOE Thank you. It's hot.

ANDY Yeah, our windows are painted shut here, so we can't get any air in.

CHLOE That's a shame.

Silence.

ANDY Chloe? Are you all right?

CHLOE *(getting fainter)* Hmm. Will you sing to me?

ANDY Yeah, I'm not very good, but I'll give it a go. What do you want to hear?

CHLOE Well, I like 'American Pie', but I think it might be a bit long. Do you know 'Shine'?

ANDY Take That?

CHLOE Yeah.

ANDY I think I know some of it. *(Sings softly)* 'You, you're such a big star to me / You're everything I want to be / But you're stuck in a hole / And I want you to get out / I don't know what there is to see / But I know it's time for you to leave / We're all just pushing along / Trying to figure it out, out, out . . .' I don't really know the rest. How was that? Chloe?

Silence from the other end.

ANDY *(cont'd)* My name's Andy by the way.

After a long beat, ANDY *hangs up. He sits, staring forward. Numb. He looks at the photo of his sister. After a beat the phone rings again. He picks up the call.*

ANDY *(cont'd)* Hello, CSL.

A feeble voice speaks.

IVY I'm sorry to bother you, but I just couldn't sleep, you see. Picasso died last week and the house seems so empty without him. He was my cat, you see, and he meant the world to me. Hello?

ANDY Yes. I'm sorry to hear that.

IVY It's not just me; Binky misses him, and Percy – they were from the same litter. I just miss his little paws padding about. He had such a lovely miaow. They all have very different personalities, you know.

ANDY Hmmm.

IVY And Picasso was such a softy, really. Although he did have his moments. He would often bring me little parcels from the garden, a mouse or a shrew, and he would demand that I pick him up, but you're not supposed to encourage them. Anyway, I'm devastated to be honest. I just don't see how I can go on day to day. There's such a hole without him. It's like a terrible ache . . .

ANDY Oh well, it's a just a cat.

IVY I beg your pardon?

ANDY It's just a cat. It sounds like you've got other ones, have you?

IVY Yes – but nothing will replace Picasso.

ANDY Well, another cat would.

IVY I want your name . . .

ANDY *slams the phone down and leaves the booth.*

INT. CSL OFFICE. DAY.

The camera is on ANDY*'s empty chair in booth number 9. We hear* LIZ *gossiping from the opposite booth.* GEORGE *is in his office (CAM 2).*

LIZ I'd put them all in the green ones, but lose the headdresses, yeah. You don't want to go all *Big Fat Gypsy Wedding*, do you? And how much are they? Do Primark not do them?

GEORGE *emerges from his office and approaches.*

LIZ *(cont'd)* Hang on a sec . . .

LIZ *takes on a more professional demeanour, as if the call is 'legit'.*

LIZ *(cont'd)* I see . . . yeah.

GEORGE *walks into frame, in front of the chair in booth number 9. We see his bottom half.*

GEORGE Liz . . .

LIZ Just a minute, George.

GEORGE Terminate that call, please.

LIZ I'm with a client.

GEORGE No, you're not. Terminate the call.

LIZ I'm sorry, caller, my supervisor is instructing me to terminate this call, would you wait just one second?

LIZ *puts the caller on hold.*

LIZ *(cont'd)* What?

GEORGE You're not allowed personal calls – how many times do I have to tell you?

LIZ She called the helpline.

GEORGE Yes, to talk about bridesmaids' dresses.

LIZ She's very upset about it! It's a big decision.

GEORGE It is COMPLETELY against the rules to clog up the lines with personal calls and prevent . . .

LIZ Piss off, George, I'm working. Some of us are here to help people. Hello, sorry about that, you were saying . . .

GEORGE Put that phone down.

LIZ No, I'd go for white shoes . . .

GEORGE *stands there for a beat, then heads back to his office, but then changes his mind and marches back in again.*

LIZ *(cont'd)* They can wear their own at the reception, can't they? Yeah . . .

Suddenly GEORGE *runs back in and tries to grab the phone from* LIZ*'s hand.*

LIZ *(cont'd)* What are you doing!?

GEORGE Put that fucking phone down!

GEORGE *grabs the receiver from* LIZ*'s hand and slams it back down, then marches away.* LIZ *is aghast.*

LIZ What!? Are you for real? Did you all see that? It was an assault.

GEORGE *slams his office door.*

LIZ *(cont'd)* Psycho!

INT. CSL OFFICE. DAY.

GEORGE *is in his office.* ANDY *is back at his booth. He seems subdued.* LIZ *is next to him, prattling on.*

LIZ Anyway he's been reported, but they won't do anything, it's bad for the image. They don't want anyone knowing the volunteers are more fucked up than the people ringing in. How are you anyway?

ANDY Yeah, I'm all right, I was just a bit shaken. It was so weird, I actually heard someone die.

LIZ Well, you didn't, you were singing Take That, but I know what you mean.

JOANNE *can be seen coming down the stairs on CAM 4.*

ANDY You just feel so helpless. But I suppose you've got to do what Joanne said and pull the shutters down.

LIZ She would say that. She's got so much ice up her fanny I call her Jayne Torvill.

ANDY It's a coping mechanism.

LIZ Mechanisms are for robots, and that's what she is. I've never once seen her use that tampon machine in the ladies, you know.

JOANNE *passes by. She's carrying a take-out drink.*

JOANNE Hi, Andy, Hi, Liz.

LIZ Hi, chuck.

JOANNE How are you feeling?

ANDY A lot better, thanks.

JOANNE Good. Put it behind you, it wasn't your fault. I got you one of those drinks you like – I hope it's the right one.

JOANNE *hands* ANDY *an apple juice, similar to the cup of pee.*

ANDY Thanks.

JOANNE *goes to sit in her booth.* LIZ *watches her go.*

LIZ See? Complete bitch. 'Put it behind you!' She doesn't care less. The people who ring here want a friend, they want to be told what to do. Doing nothing makes it worse! Like, I had a man on this morning whose mother put her head in the gas oven because her cat had died. Imagine that.

ANDY What?

ANDY *is traumatised.*

LIZ He was absolutely inconsolable, sobbing his heart out, poor thing. I was able to talk to him like a mate, I told him about when my mother died. In George's world I wouldn't have been able to do that, would I?

ANDY What was the cat's name?

LIZ Eh?

ANDY The woman who killed herself. What was the cat's name?

LIZ Picasso. Why?

ANDY No reason. Excuse me.

ANDY *gets up and leaves.* LIZ *watches him go, intrigued. We follow his progress on the wide shot (CAM 3) as he approaches* GEORGE*'s office. He knocks on the door and* GEORGE *bids him in.*

In GEORGE*'s office (CAM 2) we see* ANDY *sit down and talk to* GEORGE*. He seems upset. He starts to cry, his head in his hands.* GEORGE *moves round to comfort him.*

JOANNE *has seen* ANDY *with* GEORGE*. She comes over to* LIZ*.*

JOANNE Is Andy all right?

LIZ I don't know, Joanne, I don't get involved.

LIZ's phone rings and she wheels back to answer it.

LIZ *(cont'd)* Hello, Comfort Support Line?

INT. CSL OFFICE. DAY.

GEORGE *is in his office with new recruit* MICHAEL. LIZ *is not in,* JOANNE *is at her booth.* ANDY *is on the phone.*

KEITH I saw her on Tuesday – no, Wednesday – no, Tuesday, Tuesday, Tuesday, and she came up to me, yeah, she actually came up to me and said 'hiya'. But it wasn't like 'hiya' like 'hiya', it was more like 'HI-ya', like 'HI-YA'. It wasn't like 'h'ya', not 'h'ya', like 'hiya!' 'Hiya!' Not like 'hiya', like 'hiya', it was more 'Hiya!'

ANDY Good. And what did you say?

KEITH I didn't say anything, I spat on her.

KEITH *hangs up.* ANDY *replaces the receiver.* GEORGE *approaches.*

GEORGE Andy, everything all right?

ANDY Yeah, yeah.

GEORGE Just to say, what we talked about yesterday is totally fine, there won't be any repercussions.

ANDY Thanks, George.

GEORGE This is a pressure-cooker environment and we've all snapped at certain points, so you mustn't dwell on it. Speaking of which, I've got to go and talk to the trustees about recent events involving me and Liz, so I wondered if you'd do me a favour and take Michael through his induction. Michael?

An overweight young man, MICHAEL, *shuffles forward.*

GEORGE *(cont'd)* This is Andy, and he's going to sit in on your first call.

MICHAEL Pleased to meet you.

ANDY Hi.

GEORGE Michael's transferred from our Wood Green office, so he knows the basics. Shouldn't be too long.

GEORGE *leaves as* MICHAEL *settles into a chair next to* ANDY. GEORGE *heads out of the office and up the stairs (CAM 4).*

ANDY Are you all right there? Can you squeeze in?

MICHAEL I think so.

ANDY If you need to use the loo, I'd go now before you get settled in – you don't want to get caught short.

MICHAEL I'm all right, thanks.

ANDY It can be quite harrowing . . .

MARTIN Yeah, especially if it's a number two . . .

ANDY No, no – I mean, some of the phone calls.

MICHAEL Right, yeah. But we don't say nothing, do we?

ANDY Well, not nothing, but it is important not to get too involved. You can't let your own emotions get in the way.

The phone rings. MICHAEL *looks to* ANDY, *who puts on the headphones.* MICHAEL *answers.*

MICHAEL Hello, Comfort and Support Line?

Silence.

MICHAEL *(cont'd)* Do you want to talk?

CHLOE I think so. What's your name?

MICHAEL Michael. Do you want to tell me your name? You don't have to.

CHLOE It's Chloe.

ANDY*'s eyes widen: is this the same girl?*

MICHAEL Hi, Chloe. What's on your mind today?

CHLOE Oh, just . . . I hate my life. I hate my mum, I hate my stepdad . . . especially hate my stepdad.

ANDY *suddenly pulls off the headphones and stands up.* MICHAEL *is startled.*

MICHAEL Erm, just a second, Chloe . . . *(Up, to* ANDY*)* Did I do it wrong?

ANDY No, no – keep going.

MICHAEL Sorry. Er, how long have you felt like this?

CHLOE Too long now. I don't . . . I don't want to carry on.

MICHAEL Well, it's never too late to change your life around.

CHLOE Ha, it might be. I've taken some tablets.

MICHAEL What? You've taken some tablets? How many, Chloe?

MICHAEL *looks up to* ANDY.

CHLOE . . . 30, 40?

MICHAEL OK, well, the thing to do is stay calm . . .

ANDY *reaches in and snatches the receiver from* MICHAEL.

ANDY Now you listen to me, you fucking little bitch.

CHLOE Andy?

ANDY I don't know what sick, twisted thrills you get from ringing these helplines but it stops now, do you hear me? Now!

CHLOE But I've taken some tablets.

ANDY Good!

CHLOE Andy?

ANDY Do you have any idea what you've done, the damage you've caused?

CHLOE What, what are you talking about? I just wanted you to sing me a song.

ANDY Fuck off!

ANDY *slams the phone down furiously.* MICHAEL *sits for a moment in stunned silence.*

MICHAEL Well, that's not how we do it in Wood Green.

JOANNE *stands up from her booth and looks across.*

JOANNE Everything all right, Andy?

ANDY Fine.

INT. CSL OFFICE. DAY.

GEORGE *stands in front of booth number 9 addressing the other volunteers, who stand around the office. These include* ANDY, LIZ, JOANNE *and* MICHAEL.

GEORGE As you know I'm not one for speeches, I'm more of a listener. I don't like saying goodbye either, especially after so many years. We've had our ups and downs in this office. I like to think I was always fair. But we can't ignore the powers that be, and the recommendations that they've made. So it's with great sadness that we have to see Liz go – I don't know if you want to say a few words, Liz?

The volunteers clap LIZ. *She addresses them.*

LIZ As you know I don't want to go, but I've been, shall we say, 'politely encouraged' to move on. I'll miss some of you – you know who you are. And I'll miss helping people. Because that's all I ever did. And if that's not what you're meant to do here then I'm sorry. Anyway, I bought a bottle of cava – have a little drink on me. Cheers, everybody.

Everybody claps, some cheers. GEORGE *quietens them down.*

GEORGE But let's not forget why we're here. There are lots of people out there that need us tonight. So . . . just be sensible, please. Don't go mad.

LIZ *goes over to* ANDY, *who is sitting in his booth. She hands him a scrap of paper.*

LIZ I know you won't, but if you ever want to ring me, this is my number.

ANDY Thanks, Liz. I'll have to give you mine.

LIZ That's all right. I know where you are.

LIZ *wanders off to pour everyone a drink.*

INT. CSL OFFICE. NIGHT 7.

An hour later. ANDY *is talking to a couple of the volunteers, so his booth is empty.* GEORGE *is in his office (CAM 2). Most of the others have returned to their booths.*

We hear LIZ *answer the phone in her booth.*

LIZ Hello, Comfort Support Line, how can I help you? . . . Andy? Yeah, I'll put you through.

The phone in ANDY*'s booth flashes with a red light.* LIZ *calls over to* ANDY.

LIZ *(cont'd)* Andy! It's for you.

ANDY *comes across to booth 9.* LIZ *goes back to her desk and picks up her phone.* ANDY *sits and picks up his.*

ANDY Hello?

CHLOE I've taken some tablets.

ANDY What do you want, Chloe?

CHLOE I just wanted to say sorry. I didn't mean to upset you . . .

ANDY You haven't upset me. I feel sorry for you. You need help.

CHLOE That's why I'm ringing a helpline.

ANDY No, you just want attention and I'm not giving it to you.

ANDY *hangs up. He sits for a moment, then the phone rings again.* ANDY *hesitates. After a few rings he picks up.*

ANDY *(cont'd)* Look, you ring this number again and I will track you down and shut your stupid whining mouth up for good.

ASIAN MAN Is this the Comfort Support Line?

ANDY Yes, how can I help you?

ASIAN MAN I'll . . . leave it for now, thank you.

The caller hangs up, as does ANDY. *A beat, then the phone rings again.* ANDY *snatches up the receiver but doesn't say anything.*

CHLOE *(singing)* 'You, you're such a big star to me . . .'

ANDY Stop it.

CHLOE 'You're everything I want to be . . .'

ANDY Stop it, Chloe.

CHLOE 'But you're stuck in a hole . . .'

Silence.

ANDY Right, I'm going to put you on to my colleague Liz . . .

CHLOE *(snapping)* No! I won't speak to anyone else, I only want to speak to you.

ANDY *(trying to be reasonable)* Listen, Chloe. I need you to understand something. Because of your actions an old lady died. Now that's very serious, the police could get involved. Do you see? Someone took their own life directly because of what you did.

CHLOE I don't think so, Andy. I think that's because of what you did.

ANDY What?

CHLOE You said 'it's just a cat', didn't you? Told her to get another one. Maybe *I* should talk to the police. Tell them what actually happened . . .

ANDY *is stunned.*

ANDY Who told you that?

CHLOE Are you having a party? I might come along. I know where you are.

ANDY *hangs up quickly. He looks around, frightened.*

INT. CSL OFFICE. NIGHT 7.

ANDY *sits at his booth. He looks haunted, lost in his own thoughts. His is the only booth with a light on; the rest of the office is in dark shadow.*

The phone starts to ring. ANDY *stares at it. He can't bring himself to answer. After several rings the phone stops.*

Silence.

ANDY *makes a decision and leaves his booth. We track him on the other cameras crossing the office, entering* GEORGE*'s office and turning on the light.* ANDY *seems to be searching* GEORGE*'s desk.*

We see a HOODED FIGURE *making their way down the stairs in CAM 4.*

In the wide shot of the office (CAM 3) we see a door open. A HOODED FIGURE *enters. The* HOODED FIGURE *crosses through the office like a ghostly spectre. All is silent.*

In GEORGE*'s office we see* ANDY *peep out and spot the* HOODED FIGURE*. We see* ANDY *sit at* GEORGE*'s desk and pick up the phone. After a beat, the phone in booth 9 rings.*

The HOODED FIGURE *crosses to booth 9 and picks up the phone, without revealing their face.*

HOODED FIGURE CSL?

ANDY Hello, Chloe.

HOODED FIGURE Sorry?

ANDY What are you doing here?

HOODED FIGURE I forgot my bag. Is that you, Andy?

The HOODED FIGURE *sits in* ANDY*'s chair and we see that it is* JOANNE.

ANDY Yeah. I'm over here in George's office.

JOANNE *looks round to the office.*

JOANNE Why?

ANDY Chloe knew about the cat lady committing suicide, she knew we were having a party tonight, it had to be someone in the office, and then you turn up.

JOANNE Yeah, to get my bag. Who's Chloe?

ANDY It's all right, Joanne, I've got the time-codes. I'm going to find the footage of you calling me and then I'm ringing the police.

JOANNE Andy, I don't know what you're . . .

ANDY *hangs up. In* GEORGE*'s office we see* ANDY *typing on* GEORGE*'s laptop.*

In booth 9 JOANNE *gets up and crosses to* GEORGE*'s office. We see her question* ANDY*, then he motions towards the laptop, which they both look at.*

The main image, which hitherto has been on booth 9 throughout, suddenly changes.

INT. CSL OFFICE. NIGHT 3.

JOANNE *sits in her booth, with an older time-code.*

DISTRESSED MAN It's just if I lose the farm then that's it, it's all gone.

JOANNE I see.

The image fast-forwards to later in the call.

DISTRESSED MAN . . . she won't do it, I know she won't. It's not even worth . . . Oh God, I don't know. If I tell her brother then that's out of the bag . . .

JOANNE *listens.*

INT. CSL OFFICE. NIGHT 7.

In GEORGE*'s office we see* JOANNE *point to something and* ANDY *press some more buttons.*

INT. CSL OFFICE. NIGHT 3.

Suddenly the main image changes to LIZ *at her booth with the same time-code and date.*

ANDY Oh piss off.

LIZ Let me guess, another PPI. Persistent Pain in the Intestine, I call them. Right, I'm off, I've got a hot date with a Fray Bentos steak and ale pie.

ANDY*'s phone rings again.*

ANDY Hello, CSL?

LIZ *(whispering)* Night night.

LIZ *departs and* ANDY *waves. He goes back to his phone.*

INT. CSL OFFICE. NIGHT 7.

In GEORGE*'s office we see* ANDY *and* JOANNE *discuss something and point again to the computer. The main image changes again.*

INT. CSL OFFICE. NIGHT 3.

GEORGE *sits at his desk doing some paperwork. His Bluetooth earpiece is flashing.*

ANDY *(V.O.)* Well . . . I'm just here to listen so – you tell me.

GEORGE Well, I hate my life, I hate my mum, I hate my stepdad – especially hate my stepdad. I haven't done anything with my life . . .

ANDY *(V.O.)* How old are you, Chloe?

GEORGE Sixteen.

ANDY *(V.O.)* Well, there you are, you're still very young. You've got your whole life ahead of you.

GEORGE Ha! Yeah.

The image fast-forwards.

ANDY *(V.O.)* Chloe? Are you all right?

GEORGE *(getting fainter)* Hmm. Will you sing to me?

ANDY *(V.O.)* Yeah, I'm not very good, but I'll give it a go. What do you want to hear?

GEORGE Well, I like 'American Pie', but I think it might be a bit long. Do you know 'Shine'?

ANDY Take That?

GEORGE Yeah.

ANDY I think I know some of it. *(Sings softly)* 'You, you're such a big star to me / You're everything I want to be . . .'

GEORGE *sits and listens to* ANDY *singing for a while. He smiles to himself. The image is paused.*

INT. CSL OFFICE. NIGHT 7.

In GEORGE*'s office* ANDY *and* JOANNE *look at each other in shock. As they have been watching this clip, we see* GEORGE *walk down the stairs towards the office in CAM 4 and appear in the wide of the office on CAM 3. He spots* JOANNE *and* ANDY *in his office and leaves. They don't see him. He appears back on the stairs (CAM 4). He is agitated and suddenly starts kicking a bin furiously. He picks it up and throws it against the wall. He then takes out his mobile and walks out of the shot.*

INT. CSL OFFICE. DAY.

ANDY *sits at his booth.* JOANNE *arrives with* GLEN*, who is a new volunteer.*

JOANNE Andy, this is Glen, he's replacing Liz.

ANDY Hi.

ANDY *shakes* GLEN*'s hand.*

JOANNE If you get yourself sat in there, I'll do your induction in a minute.

GLEN *sits in* LIZ*'s old booth with his back to us.* JOANNE *pulls up a chair to talk to* ANDY *privately.*

JOANNE *(cont'd)* Is he not in yet?

ANDY No.

JOANNE What do you think we should do?

ANDY I'm going to phone the police.

JOANNE Really?

ANDY You saw those clips. They go back years. This is more than nuisance phone calls. He's insane.

JOANNE I spoke to Victoria last night. Told her it was all him. She couldn't believe it. She's still on medication.

ANDY Exactly. He's got to be stopped.

JOANNE OK.

JOANNE *walks back to her booth. On her way she says to* GLEN*:*

JOANNE *(cont'd)* Won't be a minute.

ANDY*'s phone rings.*

ANDY Hello, Comfort Support Line, can I help you.

GEORGE *(as* CHLOE*)* Hello, Andy. It's me.

ANDY Hello.

GEORGE *(as* CHLOE*)* I don't think I'm going to be able to speak to you for a while.

ANDY No, I don't think you are.

GEORGE *(as* CHLOE*)* I just wanted to say thank you for listening.

Twenty-seven years I've listened to other people's problems. I just wanted someone to listen to me.

ANDY Hmm. Well, the police can listen to you, because I'm calling them. Goodbye, George.

GEORGE *(as* CHLOE*)* I have done one last naughty thing.

ANDY What's that?

GEORGE *(as* CHLOE*)* You know the lady who killed herself because her cat died?

ANDY Yes?

GEORGE *(as* CHLOE*)* I told her son where you worked.

GLEN *has stood up behind* ANDY

GLEN Andy?

ANDY Yeah?

ANDY *half turns, but* GLEN *has already pulled out a small gun and shot him in the head. Blood covers the camera lens.*

THE END

Episode 5

NANA'S PARTY

CAST LIST

PARAMEDIC – Christopher Whitlow

ANGELA – Claire Skinner

KATIE- Eve Gordon

JIM – Steve Pemberton

MAGGIE – Elsie Kelly

CAROL – Lorraine Ashbourne

PAT – Reece Shearsmith

EXT. SUBURBAN STREET. DAY.

An emergency response vehicle quickly turns into a suburban street with blue lights flashing.

PARAMEDIC *(V.O.)* Yeah, I'm just pulling in now. What number was it?

The vehicle pulls up outside a smart mock-Tudor house. The PARAMEDIC *gets out of the vehicle, speaking all the while on a headset. He walks round to fetch his kit from the boot.*

PARAMEDIC *(cont'd)* Right, who called it in? . . . Yeah . . . Oh God, doesn't sound too good, does it? Hope I'm not too late.

The PARAMEDIC *bangs on the door, and as the door opens we move off so we don't see who has answered.*

PARAMEDIC *(cont'd)* Hello there, through here, is it?

We move onto the wheelie bin at the side of the driveway, and see it marked with a large, neat number '9'.

TITLE: 'Nana's Party'.

EXT. JIM AND ANGELA'S HOUSE. DAY.

An establisher of a house, number 9 in a row of identical houses in a smart suburban street.

CAPTION: *'Earlier that day . . .'*

INT. HALLWAY. DAY.

ANGELA *is vacuuming the stairs with a small Dustbuster. She is in her late forties and nicely dressed but looks slightly pinched and fretful. She calls up the stairs.*

ANGELA Jim, have you sorted the music out like I asked you? Something appropriate this time, not the soundtrack to *The Mission*. I want it to feel like a party, not an advert for British Airways. Jim? Useless . . .

INT. LIVING ROOM. DAY.

ANGELA *moves through into the open-plan kitchen/living room.* ANGELA*'s teenage daughter* KATIE *is sitting on the sofa doing her homework. An open book and an empty glass are on the coffee table in front of her.*

ANGELA Oh my God, Katie, what have you been doing?

KATIE What?

ANGELA All this mess. It looks like a bomb site.

KATIE It's just a book.

ANGELA *looks down at the rug.*

ANGELA And you've knocked all those tassels over – are you trying to drive me mad? I've just tidied up in here.

KATIE It is tidy, I'm just doing my homework.

ANGELA Well, you'll have to do it upstairs. I can't have it looking like Vietnam, you know it's your nana's party today.

KATIE *wearily starts to put her things together.*

ANGELA *(cont'd)* Where's your father, is he upstairs?

KATIE Dunno. What time are they coming?

ANGELA Any minute. If he's in the deckhouse watching his *Countdown* videos I'll kill him. Have you signed your nana's card?

ANGELA *takes the birthday card to* KATIE *with a pen.*

KATIE No, I made her one with loads of glue and glitter.

ANGELA What? Oh, Katie, that's not funny. Are you trying to give me a stroke? Seventy-nine. I just wish it was the 80th, then we could have it all done.

KATIE That's nice!

ANGELA You know what I mean. It's a lot of work.

ANGELA *crosses over to the large dining table, which is laden with a spread of M&S party food on clingfilmed china plates. In the centre of the table is a large tiered birthday cake on a silver tray.* ANGELA *starts to put birthday candles into the candle-holders on the cake.*

ANGELA *(cont'd)* Just go and see if he's in the deckhouse, will you, Katie?

KATIE You mean the shed?

ANGELA And bring me in some of those sausage rolls from the freezer. I don't want to be caught short.

KATIE *exits.* ANGELA *surveys her table.*

ANGELA *(cont'd)* Right, let me think . . . plates, napkins, crisps for Carol . . .

ANGELA *picks up the cake and is shocked to find* JIM*'s head under it, smiling.*

JIM Boo!

ANGELA Aaarrghh!

ANGELA *screams and almost drops the cake.* JIM *laughs.*

JIM Heh-heh! That got you, didn't it!

ANGELA What the bloody hell are you doing? You'd better not have put a hole in that table!

JIM No, the middle leaf slides out.

JIM *climbs out from under the table. There is a hole in the table cloth where his head was.*

JIM *(cont'd)* So what do you think?

ANGELA About what?

JIM I'm going to be under there when Pat arrives with your mother. You ask him to move the cake and he'll get the shock of his life!

ANGELA Why?

JIM Oh come on, Angela, you know what he's like. You were furious when he put clingfilm over the downstairs toilet. And what about the time he put wallpaper paste in the birdbath?

ANGELA Oh, don't – I still see that one-legged tit.

JIM Exactly. He needs a taste of his own medicine.

ANGELA But not on my mother's birthday. Do it in your own time!

JIM He thinks I haven't got a sense of humour. He's unable to engage with me on an intellectual level so he has to resort to puerile practical jokes.

ANGELA You've just cut a hole in my second-best table cloth. I think the joke's on me!

JIM What time are they arriving?

ANGELA Any minute now. Can you straighten those tassels, please, they're literally driving me mad.

JIM *bends down to straighten the tassels on the rug.*

ANGELA *(cont'd)* I'm not happy about this, Jim. Pat's got enough on his plate without you turning into Justin Bieber!

JIM Who?

ANGELA You know! The little man with the beard that played tricks on people.

JIM Jeremy Beadle?

ANGELA Whoever it was. Pat's got the Carol situation to think about.

JIM Oh, what's happening with all that? Is it still bad?

ANGELA Worse, according to Pat. It's white wine in a coffee mug at nine-thirty in the morning apparently. Mind you, if I was married to Pat I think I'd be driven to drink.

JIM Now it's important that you don't light the candles, Ange. The exterior is all sugar-paste icing, but it's just cardboard underneath. I don't want to end up as Joan of Arc.

ANGELA Don't tell me, I'm not getting involved.

JIM *grabs* ANGELA *by the waist.*

JIM Come on, Ange, you're always saying I'm boring and I've got no sense of humour. Knock, knock.

ANGELA What, are they here?

JIM No, it's the start of a joke. Knock, knock.

ANGELA Who's there?

JIM Carol.

ANGELA My sister Carol?

JIM No, 'Carol who?'

ANGELA I don't know.

JIM You say, 'Carol who?'

ANGELA Carol who?

JIM Carol singers.

ANGELA *stares for a moment, confused.*

ANGELA Oh that's terrible, Jim. Pat's right.

JIM Traitor!

He laughs and they cuddle each other. KATIE *comes back in from the garden with the frozen sausage rolls.*

KATIE Oh, do you have to? I'm going to my room.

A car beeps outside.

ANGELA Oh God, they're here! I've got one Marigold inside out . . . what am I supposed to do again?

JIM *clambers under the table.*

JIM Just get Pat to pick up the cake.

ANGELA *starts to put the fake cake on* JIM*'s head.*

JIM *(cont'd) (from in the cake)* And don't let him plug his mobile phone in. All he ever wants to do is steal our electricity . . .

ANGELA *goes through to the front door.*

INT. HALLWAY. DAY.

We see the silhouettes of MAGGIE *and* CAROL *though the glass panels in the door.* ANGELA *opens the door and her mother,* MAGGIE*, steps in.* MAGGIE *is 79 and wears a nice party dress.*

ANGELA Hello! Happy birthday, Mum. Come in.

MAGGIE I need to spend a penny first, is it this one?

ANGELA Yeah, and you've no need to lock it this time . . .

MAGGIE *enters the toilet and we hear the door being locked from the inside.*

ANGELA *(cont'd)* We'll never get her out now. Hiya, Carol.

CAROL, *50, enters looking ill at ease in her best Primark clothes. She carries a big pink helium balloon, which reads 'Happy Birthday'.*

CAROL Hiya, love.

ANGELA That's nice.

CAROL Catalogue. Don't tell Pat.

PAT *(V.O.)* I heard that. Pardon?

PAT *enters wearing a full-head werewolf mask and carrying a cooler bag.*

ANGELA Hiya, Pat.

PAT I used to be a werewolf but I'm all right nooooowwwww!

ANGELA Can I give you a hand with anything?

PAT No, I've only got the one bag: have you met my wife Carol?

CAROL Take that mask off, you daft sod.

PAT You take yours off first!

PAT *takes off his mask, revealing a short, fat, jolly red-faced man in his late forties.* ANGELA *hangs up the coats.*

ANGELA Go through . . .

INT. LIVING ROOM. DAY.

CAROL *and* PAT *go through to the living room.*

CAROL Oh, you've got it lovely, Ange. *(Whispers)* Take your shoes off.

PAT Why?

CAROL You remember last time when you shuffled all that muck in, she went mad.

PAT It's their own fault. Who has a white carpet now, except for Elton John?

ANGELA *enters.*

ANGELA Right, what can I get you to drink?

A tense look between PAT *and* CAROL.

PAT She'll have a tea, won't you?

CAROL I can answer for myself! Yeah, I'll have a tea.

ANGELA You brought your own, Pat?

PAT Yes, I'll pop them in the fridge if I may?

PAT *goes over to the fridge and puts his cans of mild inside from the cooler bag.*

PAT *then reaches in and pulls out a tray of ice cubes. He makes sure no one is looking, then empties the ice cubes into the ice bucket with a grin.*

PAT *(cont'd)* Where's Jimbo?

ANGELA Oh, he's about somewhere. He's probably in the deckhouse.

PAT *Countdown* omnibus?

ANGELA Who knows? *(Raising her voice for* JIM*'s benefit)* We're just waiting for my mother to come back from the loo and then we'll do the cake, all right?

CAROL Oh, let her get settled first. Is Katie not here?

ANGELA She's in her room, studying. We hardly see her any more since we got her the tablet.

CAROL Oh, did you hear that, Pat? They've got Katie a tablet.

PAT A bit young to be on the Pill, isn't she?

ANGELA No, it's a computer device . . .

CAROL He knows what it is.

MAGGIE *enters.*

MAGGIE Right – it's not flushed, I can't make it flush.

ANGELA You push it, Mum, I showed you before.

MAGGIE I did push it, nothing happened.

CAROL I'll do it.

CAROL *goes out.*

PAT Here, take this.

PAT *presents her with a potato masher.*

MAGGIE Ew, don't be horrible! At least you didn't put that tinfoil over it again.

PAT Clingfilm.

MAGGIE Did your pedestal mat come out all right, Angela?

ANGELA We disposed of it, it's fine.

INT. DOWNSTAIRS TOILET. DAY.

CAROL *locks the door and looks at herself in the mirror for a long time. Suddenly she opens her handbag and takes out a large bottle of Ambre Solaire suncream. She flips up the lid and squirts some of the liquid into her mouth.*

INT. LIVING ROOM. DAY.

ANGELA *is in the kitchen area filling the kettle.*

ANGELA So are you still on that diet, Pat?

PAT Oh yes, it's a seafood diet. If I see food, I eat it!

ANGELA Well, there's plenty of salady things anyway.

MAGGIE Oh Angela, read this card he got for me, it's a scream.

MAGGIE *fishes out a birthday card from her handbag.*

PAT Do you mind if I just plug my phone in for an hour, Ange? It's running a bit low.

ANGELA Of course.

We sense JIM*'s annoyance from beneath the cake.* PAT *bends down by the table, looking for the socket.*

PAT Down here, is it . . .?

ANGELA No! No, give it to me, Pat, I'll do it up here.

PAT *hands over his phone and charger and* ANGELA *plugs it in in the kitchen.* MAGGIE *reads from the birthday card.*

MAGGIE 'Forget about the past, you can't change it. Forget about the future, you can't predict it. Forget about the present, I didn't get you one.' Isn't that a scream?

PAT Courtesy of Mr H. Allmark.

MAGGIE Did you hear it, Angela? 'Forget about the past, you can't change it . . .'

ANGELA Yes, Mum, it's . . . very funny. Well, shall we move this cake and make some room then? Pat, could you . . .?

MAGGIE Wait a minute, I want to take a picture of the spread. I promised I'd show your cousin Ann. Where's the camera . . . Pat, have you seen my camera . . .?

PAT It's in the car, Maggie – back in two shakes.

PAT *exits as* CAROL *comes in.*

ANGELA Don't be long!

CAROL You used too much paper, Mum. It's gone now.

MAGGIE Thanks, Carol, love. Here, come and look at our Angela's spread. She's done a prawn ring.

CAROL *casts her eye over the table.* ANGELA *bristles slightly.*

CAROL Oh, you can get them quite cheap now, can't you?

ANGELA *(haughtily)* It's all Marks actually. Apart from the ham, which I got from the local butcher's . . .

ANGELA *has pronounced it 'batcher's' in her faux posh Northern way and* CAROL *seizes on this immediately.*

CAROL From the what?

ANGELA From the butcher's.

CAROL The batcher's? What's a batcher?

MAGGIE Leave her alone! I like her talking posh.

ANGELA It's not posh, Mother, it's proper.

CAROL Oh, we're not 'proper', Mum.

MAGGIE I wanted both my girls to talk nice, that's why I sent you to electrocution lessons. You should say 'batcher', Carol. That's how you get on in life.

CAROL So what are we having for afters, sammer padding?

ANGELA Kettle's boiled.

ANGELA *goes to make the teas.* MAGGIE *stares hard at* CAROL *and nods towards* ANGELA.

CAROL I'll give you a hand.

CAROL *joins* ANGELA *in the kitchen.* MAGGIE *surveys the spread. She calls over to the girls.*

MAGGIE Marks is dear though, isn't it, Angela! They sell carrots, peeled.

MAGGIE *is looking at the cake. She lets an old-lady trump slip out, right in front of the cake.*

MAGGIE *(cont'd)* Get down!

PAT *enters with the camera.*

PAT Here we go, Maggie May. Ready for your close-up?

MAGGIE Oh yeah, go on. Get the spread in . . .

PAT OK . . . ooph, that meat's off.

MAGGIE No, it's fresh from the batcher's.

CAROL *comes over with the teas.*

CAROL Wait a minute, Mum, let me get the candles lit.

ANGELA No!

CAROL Eh?

ANGELA Don't do it yet. Wait for Jim, he'll want to see it . . .

CAROL *starts to light them anyway.*

CAROL Oh, he won't be bothered. You can always light them again.

PAT I think there's a special setting on here for candles . . .

PAT *fiddles with the camera.*

MAGGIE Come on then, everyone bunch in. I want both daughters. Three generations. Oh, where's your Katie?

ANGELA She's doing her homework – just take it, Pat . . .

CAROL They bought her a tablet.

MAGGIE A what?

CAROL A computer. She's 14.

MAGGIE Oh Angela, they don't need computers at 14!

ANGELA *notices that the candles are burning down rapidly.*

ANGELA They do if they want to get into St Catherine's. Come on, Pat!

PAT Here we go then . . . say 'Cheesy Wotsits!'

MAGGIE Cheesy Wotsits!

KATIE *(V.O.)* Hi, Nana, happy birthday!

KATIE *has appeared from upstairs.*

MAGGIE Oh Katie, you're here! Come and get in this, then I've got all my girls.

KATIE Hi, Auntie Carol, hi, Uncle Pat!

CAROL Hiya, darling.

PAT Bloody hell, who's this? You've shot up, haven't you? Proper little madam.

The candles are burning lower.

ANGELA Come on then, let's do this picture.

MAGGIE Three generations!

CAROL Come on then, one, two, three . . .

MAGGIE Oh wait!

ANGELA What?

MAGGIE I didn't show Katie the card.

CAROL Show her after, Mum.

MAGGIE No, I want to show her now. Listen to this, Katie: 'Forget about the past, you can't change it . . .

ANGELA Let's just . . .

MAGGIE 'Forget about the future, you can't predict it . . .

ANGELA Mother, you can do that in a minute . . .

MAGGIE 'Forget about the present, I didn't get you one.'

CAROL It's tickled you that, hasn't it, Mum?

MAGGIE It has. I don't know where he gets them from.

PAT Mr H. Allmark.

PAT *winks at* KATIE.

KATIE It's funny, Nana.

ANGELA Right, come on, Mother, blow your candles out, make your wish.

MAGGIE Hang on, I have to think what I want.

ANGELA *can see the candles are burnt to the very bottom and can bear it no longer. She leans in and blows out the candles.*

CAROL Hey!

KATIE Mum! It's Nana's cake!

MAGGIE She took my wish!

ANGELA Pat, will you move the cake now, please?

PAT No, battery's run out. I'll nip and get the charger from the car – you don't mind, do you, Ange?

ANGELA No, you can put it in next to your mobile.

PAT *exits.*

PAT Thanking you.

KATIE Well, I've got to do my homework now, Nana, so . . .

CAROL I'll just nip to the loo then. Where's my bag?

CAROL *grabs her bag and heads off to the toilet.*

MAGGIE Show me this tablet, Katie – what is it, a computer? I have 23 tablets a day!

MAGGIE *follows* KATIE *out and up the stairs, leaving* ANGELA *at the dining table. She lifts up the birthday cake to check* JIM *is all right. He is stony-faced.*

JIM Well, that went well, didn't it?

INT. KATIE'S ROOM. DAY.

KATIE *sits on her bed and* MAGGIE *sits at the desk holding an iPad/tablet.*

MAGGIE Is this all of it? It's thin. Would you not be better off with a typewriter – you can get electrical ones now if you want to be up to date.

KATIE It's all touchscreen, Nana, look, you just move things with your finger.

KATIE *demonstrates.* MAGGIE *is delighted.*

MAGGIE Oooh, look at that! Is it magnetic? You know, I bought your mum one of these – you had to drag iron filings onto a man's face and make little beards and funny hair. Can yours do that?

KATIE Don't know.

MAGGIE Hers did. There's nothing new.

KATIE You can play games on it as well, Nana, look . . .

MAGGIE Ooh . . . lovely colours!

KATIE *demonstrates the game to* MAGGIE. CAROL *enters. She's now slightly pissed.*

CAROL Hello, is this the Princess Palace? Ah, you've taken them all down! You used to have all the princesses, didn't you? Snow White, Cinderella, the Chinese one, what was she called, not Chinkerbell . . .?

KATIE Auntie Carol, you can't say that.

CAROL Yeah, I know, because she wasn't a proper princess, she was a fairy, I've always thought it. They try and bundle them all together, it's a rip-off. So – party in your room, is it?

KATIE No, I've got to get on with my homework.

CAROL Oh, there's time for work, Katie. It's your nana's birthday!

MAGGIE *(playing the game)* I'm building a path on my island – I don't know why!

CAROL You know, your problem is, you're like your dad. You're too much in your head.

CAROL *pokes* KATIE *in the forehead.*

CAROL *(cont'd)* There's a whole world out there, Katie. Just have fun. Because it goes by so fast. Will you let me do your nails, please?

KATIE I've just got to finish my maths . . .

CAROL I'll tell you maths . . . shall I? One takes away from one, and you're left with nothing. Do you think I'd make a good mum, Katie? Be honest.

KATIE Yeah.

CAROL Correct.

CAROL *sighs. A long, sad sigh.*

CAROL *(cont'd)* I'm just going to the toilet.

CAROL *staggers up and takes her large bottle of suncream from her bag.*

CAROL *(cont'd)* Have I shown you this? This is my block.

She reads from the bottle.

CAROL *(cont'd)* 'Apply liberally for 24-hour protection.'

CAROL *laughs snortingly.*

CAROL *(cont'd)* You won't get that. I do. Just have fun.

She shakes her head sadly and leaves. KATIE *is bemused.*

MAGGIE Now, how do I get back to 'Main Menu', Katie? I want to attack that village . . .

INT. LIVING ROOM. DAY.

JIM *is now out from under the table and is furtively looking up the stairs.*

ANGELA I think just leave it now, Jim. It didn't work, it's too late . . .

JIM It's not too late. *You* get under there and *I'll* get him to move the cake.

ANGELA I'm not doing it!

JIM Come on, he'll be back in a minute.

ANGELA Oh Jim, is it worth it?

JIM Yes! It's just a laugh, OK? Now get under the table.

ANGELA Well, make it quick then, I've got 24 sausage rolls to warm through . . .

INT. DOWNSTAIRS TOILET. DAY.

PAT *is surreptitiously opening up a bar of novelty soap. He places it by the sink in the downstairs toilet and chuckles to himself.*

INT. LIVING ROOM. DAY.

JIM *is straightening the tablecloth on the dining table.* PAT *appears.*

PAT Ah, here he is, the man himself! How are you, Jimbo?

JIM I'm all right, thanks, Pat. Angela's just nipped out to get some more . . . candles.

PAT I didn't see her, she didn't come past me.

JIM No, she went out the back and . . . through the gardens. It's slightly quicker.

PAT How is Angela? I thought she looked a bit tired. You know, a little bit puffy-eyed and pale?

JIM She's all right. You know what she's like, she's always got some project on the go.

PAT Yes. I wish Carol was like that.

JIM How is she these days?

PAT Oh fine, fine. We just need to get her a little job. She's ready now.

JIM Good. Do you want to give me a hand moving this cake? I just want to make some room.

PAT Righty-o. Oh, before I forget, I've got that *Countdown* video you lent me.

PAT *takes a video cassette from his coat pocket.*

JIM Oh, don't worry about it.

PAT No, no, I'm sure you'll want it back. Quite a decent episode, I thought. A lot happens.

JIM I can't remember to be honest . . .

PAT Well, there are three scenarios. The first one involves a blonde lady taking, shall we say, two from the top and one in the bottom.

JIM Pat! Let me get you a drink.

JIM *ushers* PAT *towards the fridge, away from the dining table.*

JIM *(cont'd)* You must be thirsty after that drive. Have they still got the roadworks up at Long Croft?

JIM *opens the fridge and gets a beer for* PAT.

PAT No, they've moved on to Ash Lane now. They have temporary traffic lights, but unless you're hitting the school run it's not too bad.

JIM So did you forgo the pleasures of the A352?

PAT Yes, I tend to take that cut-through on Meadowbank now, it's always quieter.

JIM Oh good, good. So, about this cake . . .

JIM *moves back towards the dining table.* PAT *picks up the video cassette from the kitchen top where* JIM *left it.*

PAT Don't be leaving this lying about, Jim. Wouldn't want Katie putting it on by accident.

JIM Yes, I'll take it back to the shed . . .

PAT You see, I'm like you, Jim: I can't watch hard-core pornography on a computer. Give me an old-fashioned video cassette any day of the week.

JIM Oh, well – good for you.

PAT I particularly enjoyed this week's Dictionary Corner. Might be returning to have another go at that one, if you don't mind!

JIM I don't know what you mean.

JIM *takes a look at the cake.*

PAT *Charlie's Anals*. Starring Farrah Forced-It, Katy Jacked-Off and Jaclyn Clit. Where do they come up with these names, I ask you!

JIM Indeed.

CAROL *emerges, clutching her suncream bottle and looking the worse for wear.*

CAROL Oh God, what are you two talking about? Is he boring you, Jim?

JIM No, no, we were just discussing . . . an episode of *Countdown*.

CAROL Oh weary! Let's get some music on, get some life in this house! Where's our Angela?

CAROL *staggers over to the hi-fi system and presses play. Ennio Morricone's* The Mission *blares out.*

JIM Oh, she went to the shop for candles.

PAT *picks up the suncream bottle, which* CAROL *put down by the hi-fi.*

PAT Bit cold outside for suncream, isn't it, Carol?

PAT *sniffs the bottle and knows she's been drinking.*

PAT *(cont'd)* How about a nice refreshing glass of Adam's Ale?

CAROL Oh piss off and leave me alone, you fat pig.

PAT As you wish.

PAT *sadly makes his way to the kitchen area.*

CAROL What the hell is this terrible music?

JIM It's Ennio Morricone, Carol. *The Mission*.

CAROL Oh. My favourite position.

CAROL *gives* JIM *a knowing look, then sashays over to the dining table to nibble at a bread stick.*

CAROL *(cont'd)* Your Katie's got a nice room, hasn't she?

JIM Yes, she picked it all out herself. She knows her own taste.

CAROL She's got a better bedroom than me. That's ironical, isn't it? Who sang that – 'it's ironical'?

JIM I . . . I don't know.

CAROL She's got a lovely big bed. Maybe we could christen it one afternoon. That'd be nice, wouldn't it?

PAT *comes over with a glass of water.*

PAT Here we go, my angel. Have a few sips on that.

CAROL Come on, Jim, let's dance.

JIM No! No. I think perhaps I'd better put the sausage rolls in the oven.

CAROL Yeah, I wish you would.

JIM *goes to the kitchen to switch on the oven.*

PAT Come on, Carol . . .

CAROL Drop dead.

CAROL *takes the water from* PAT *and throws it in his face.* PAT *slowly walks away, exchanging a weak smile with* JIM.

PAT Just go and . . . fetch a towel.

PAT *heads up the stairs.* CAROL *starts to dance by herself, swaying to the ethereal music.*

CAROL I wanna tell them, Jim.

JIM What?

CAROL I wanna tell Pat and whatsit . . . Angela.

JIM Oh Carol, shush – why are you saying all this?

CAROL Because you made promises to me, over the years.

JIM Years, what are you . . .?

CAROL I want them told today. It's humiliating for me to have to come here and see all she's got. Why are you still with her, Jim? You told me you can't stand the sight of her.

JIM That's not true, Ange . . .

CAROL I want this to be my house; I want this spread to be my spread. I want you to put your sausage rolls into my oven.

JIM Carol, stop it!

CAROL I waited for you. You promised me a baby, Jim.

JIM Stop it!

JIM *turns off the music.*

JIM *(cont'd) (calling up the stairs)* Katie, do you want to know what your sister's name was going to be?

JIM *shouts to* ANGELA*'s head in the box.*

JIM *(cont'd)* Don't listen to her, she's drunk!

CAROL I love you.

MAGGIE *appears with* KATIE, *still brandishing the tablet.*

MAGGIE Oooh, you'll have to get me one of these for my 80th. Hello, Jim, love, are you all right?

JIM Yes. Happy birthday, Maggie.

CAROL Here she is! Katie, dance with me. We'll show 'em!

CAROL *plays more music and forces* KATIE *to dance.*

MAGGIE Where's our Angela? I want to show her I've built a settlement.

JIM She'll be back soon, she's just running an errand.

MAGGIE It's got pigs and everything. I think I'll have a drink now, Jim. Can I have a gin and tonic, please?

JIM Right, do you want ice?

MAGGIE Yes, but don't be putting willies in it.

JIM What?

MAGGIE Pat has these ice cubes at his house in the shape of willies. You fill the tray with water, put it in the freezer and out come 24 little ice willies. It is comical. Isn't it, Carol? I'm telling Jim about Pat's willies.

CAROL I wouldn't know. I've not seen it in years. He keeps it hid. I'll have a jim and tonic if you're making one, Gin. Do you want one, Katie?

KATIE No – I've got to finish my maths.

CAROL Oh Katie – live! Live while you're still young. Don't let it pass you by.

JIM *has handed* MAGGIE *her gin and tonic.*

JIM Carol – I think you should go and have a lie-down.

CAROL Oh, your dad's trying to get me into bed, Katie, what do you think about that?

JIM Right, that's enough.

JIM *tries to walk her out into the garden.*

CAROL Don't touch me, I'm bonding with Katie. If I'm going to be her stepmum . . .

KATIE What?

KATIE *stops the music.*

JIM Oh for God's sake, Carol. Shut your mouth!

PAT *has entered and seen* JIM *shouting at* CAROL.

PAT Don't talk to her like that, Jim.

CAROL *starts to sob.*

PAT *(cont'd)* Carol, love . . . come here.

CAROL *(to* JIM*)* No. He's ruined my make-up now, I don't know why I bothered!

CAROL *runs out, sobbing.*

JIM I don't know what got into her.

PAT It's all right, Jim. It's all under control.

JIM She just started ranting and raving . . .

PAT Jim. I know. All right? I know.

PAT *looks at* JIM *knowingly.* JIM *doesn't know what to say.*

KATIE *(becoming upset)* Know what? What's he talking about? Where's Mum?

JIM Erm – she's just . . .

MAGGIE Right, everybody, I'm making my wish!

MAGGIE *stands over the cake with a big knife, about to cut into it.*

JIM No!

MAGGIE I want a tablet!

She shoves the knife forcefully into the cake. Jim dashes forward to the cake.

JIM Angela!

ANGELA *(V.O.)* What?

We see ANGELA *stood in the doorway with a shopping bag.*

ANGELA *(cont'd)* I nip out for five minutes and all hell breaks loose.

JIM Oh, thank God.

MAGGIE *looks at the hollow cake.*

MAGGIE There's nothing in this cake!

KATIE *rushes over to* ANGELA *and hugs her.*

ANGELA *(whispering)* I'm sorry for spoiling the trick, Jim, I couldn't stay under there any longer – my knees were killing me.

JIM No, it's all right, it was a stupid idea . . .

ANGELA I went and got my mum a proper cake. I nipped out when you and Pat were in the kitchen.

JIM Good, good . . . so you missed all the drama then?

ANGELA Why, what's happened?

JIM Oh, nothing. Just your sister acting up again.

KATIE *looks at* JIM *suspiciously. She looks across at* PAT*, who is ashen-faced and looks devastated. He looks at* KATIE *with tears in his eyes.*

KATIE *(to* ANGELA*)* Mum, I really need to speak to you.

ANGELA What's going on?

MAGGIE *starts to choke.* ANGELA *looks round.*

ANGELA *(cont'd)* Mum?

KATIE She's choking!

ANGELA Mother! *(To* JIM*)* What have you given her?

JIM Gin and tonic.

PAT It's the ice!

ANGELA If she's choking on one of your willies . . .

PAT *rushes over to the ice bucket.*

PAT No, it's spiders, I put spiders in them, look!

PAT *lifts the plastic spiders from the ice bucket.*

ANGELA You bloody idiot! Call an ambulance!

JIM *pulls* MAGGIE *out of the chair to begin giving her the Heimlich manoeuvre.*

JIM Come on, Maggie . . .

PAT Where's my phone?

PAT *rushes over to grab his phone, which is still plugged into the wall socket.*

CAROL *enters. Her face and hands are now black from the novelty soap.*

CAROL Patrick! What have you done with this bloody soap?

PAT *reaches for his phone and with his wet hands he gets a massive electric shock. There is a big spark and he flies back into the room.*

CAROL *screams and rushes over to him. There is a banging on the door.*

ANGELA That'll be the ambulance, let them in, Katie.

KATIE *runs out to the front door.*

KATIE We didn't call an ambulance . . .

CAROL *is caring for* PAT*, who is dazed but alive.*

CAROL Pat, are you all right? Don't leave me, don't you leave me . . .

We hear KATIE *open the door to the* PARAMEDIC.

PARAMEDIC *(V.O.)* Hello there, through here, is it?

The PARAMEDIC *enters the room with* KATIE.

PARAMEDIC *(cont'd)* Right, which one of you is Maggie?

ANGELA Here . . .

The PARAMEDIC *approaches* MAGGIE *and puts down his kit bag.*

PARAMEDIC Stand back, everyone.

The PARAMEDIC *opens up the kit bag, revealing a boom-box CD player. He hits play and the song 'Bad Case of Loving You (Doctor, Doctor)' by Robert Palmer blasts out. The* PARAMEDIC *begins a dance routine and strips off his fluorescent tunic to reveal an oiled, muscled body beneath.*

JIM What the hell . . . ?

The PARAMEDIC *dances to a bemused family.*

ANGELA Pat, is this you?

PAT *nods.*

INT. LIVING ROOM. DAY.

MAGGIE *sits with a cup of tea.* JIM *is tidying in the kitchen. He seems preoccupied.*

MAGGIE Well, what a day. I don't know what you're going to do for my 80th.

JIM Yes, we'll have to see.

MAGGIE I'm going to keep this spider. My lucky charm. Where's our Angela got to?

JIM She's upstairs with Katie. I don't know what they're talking about.

JIM *casts a baleful look upstairs.*

MAGGIE Do you think Pat'll be all right?

JIM Yeah, he'll be fine. He's got Carol to look after him.

MAGGIE Yeah. Nice of him to have booked that lad for me – he said he wasn't going to get me a present. Ooh, that reminds me, I didn't read you his card, did I? Listen to this . . .

MAGGIE *takes out* PAT*'s card.*

MAGGIE *(cont'd)* 'Forget about the past, you can't change it. Forget about the future, you can't predict it . . .'

ANGELA *appears at the foot of the stairs, followed by* KATIE. ANGELA *has been crying; her mascara has run. She carries a small case. She stares, angry and heartbroken.*

MAGGIE *(cont'd)* . . . 'Forget about the present – I didn't get you one.' Isn't that a scream?

JIM *and* ANGELA *stare at each other over the desolate remains of their marriage.*

THE END

Episode 6

SEANCE TIME

CAST LIST

TERRY – Reece Shearsmith

TINA – Sophie McShera

ANNE – Alison Steadman

CLIVE – Dan Starkey

GEMMA – Cariad Lloyd

AMANDA – Alice Lowe

PETE – Steve Pemberton

WILLIAM – Caden Ellis Wall

EXT. FOGGY STREET. DAY.

A London street on a foggy day. On a row of imposing Victorian terraces, we find a large black door with a Gothic '9' on it.

TITLE: *'Seance Time'.*

INT. PARLOUR. DAY.

A large Victorian parlour lit by gaslight. Gloomy and oppressive. A large mirror hangs over the fireplace. A circular table is placed in the centre of the room, covered with a yellowing lace cloth. All is set for a seance, the usual paraphernalia is scattered on the table: a bell, maraca, tambourine. In the quiet of the room, the tambourine shifts slightly on the table and jangles, then all is still again.

TINA, *a nervous woman in her thirties, is led into the room by a middle-aged man, Hives (*TERRY*).*

TERRY This way, please. Thank you for being prompt. Madam Talbot doesn't enjoy latecomers.

TINA Thanks. Sorry.

TERRY Let me take your coat. Would you care for a glass of water?

TINA No, I'm fine, thank you.

TERRY What is it you do, if I may ask?

TINA I work in a phone shop.

TERRY Ah – from one line of communication to another. May I ask, have you ever made contact before?

TINA At the phone shop?

TERRY No, no. Through mediumship.

TINA Oh – sorry, I'm a bit nervous. No, my sister recommended Miss – Madam Talbot, but I've never been to anything like this before.

TERRY Please take a seat here, and may I request that if you do have a mobile telephone, you switch it off now. I will tell Madam Talbot you are ready.

TERRY *exits with* TINA*'s coat.* TINA *sits in her seat nervously. She takes out her mobile and switches it off. She looks around the room.* TINA *lifts the* *lid on a small music box on the table. Tinkling music begins to play. The gas lights on the wall flicker, the flames getting larger for a second.* TINA *looks frightened and closes the lid.*

The door slowly opens with a dramatic creak and TERRY *re-enters. He carries a lit candle and dims the gas lamps on the walls.*

TERRY *(cont'd)* Tina – please may you stand.

TINA Yes. Sorry.

TINA *hastily gets to her feet.*

TERRY May I present . . . Madam Talbot.

*A very old lady, dressed all in black, glides into the room. This is Madam Talbot (*ANNE*). We cannot see her face behind a black lace veil, but she cradles a swaddled baby in her gloved hands. She takes her seat at the table.* TERRY *places the candle in the middle of the table.*

TERRY *(cont'd)* You may be seated.

TINA *sits back down.* TERRY *takes a seat.* ANNE *speaks in a high-pitched voice. Innocent and child-like. Very creepy.*

ANNE Why have you come here, my child?

TINA My sister saw you after she lost her husband. I haven't actually lost anyone recently, but I . . .

ANNE I understand. The curious are often drawn here for a glimpse of Summerland.

TINA What's Summerland?

TERRY Good question: it means the Astral plane.

ANNE Let us see who may be waiting for you there. Hives . . . Mary is sleeping now.

TERRY *stands up and gently takes the baby from* ANNE. TINA *notices that it is in fact a Victorian doll, with one eye missing and a cracked porcelain face.*

TERRY *then goes over to an old gramophone. He moves a horrible wet-looking teddy bear lying on the pile of records. He picks up the top one and places it on the record player.*

He starts it up. The old hymn 'Bringing in the Sheaves' starts playing quietly in the background.

TERRY *returns to his seat.*

TERRY All is ready.

ANNE *dramatically lifts up her veil.* TINA *gasps. She is indeed very old. Wispy hair, with sightless cataract-covered eyes.*

ANNE Let us link hands.

ANNE, TINA *and* TERRY *link hands around the table.*

TINA Sorry – sweaty palms.

During TERRY*'s speech,* ANNE *begins to breathe deeply, her head lolls and she judders and moans.*

TERRY Now let us bow our heads in meditation and prayer. If there are indeed any Astrals here tonight, we ask you humbly to let yourselves be known to us.

Suddenly the tambourine flies off the table. TINA *lets out a yelp of fear.*

TERRY *(cont'd)* Do not break the circle, Tina. The circle is our protection.

ANNE *suddenly speaks in a deep voice, unlike her own.*

ANNE Who calls?

TERRY Please indulge us here on this earthly plane – may we ask your name?

ANNE *opens her mouth and a curl of smoke seems to drip out and snake into the centre of the room. She croaks horribly as this happens.* TINA *is terrified and shuts her eyes.*

TINA Oh God. I don't like it.

TERRY Keep looking, Tina. What is your name? Is anyone amongst us here known to you?

ANNE Tinaaaaaaaa!

The candle flares up in a large flame.

TINA Argh, shit!

TERRY Talk to it, Tina! Ask it who it is!

TINA I don't want to!

TERRY You must!

TINA Who are you?

The gramophone record jumps and scratches, repeating as it sticks. The baby in the cot starts crying inexplicably and the cot starts rocking on its own.

ANNE I am in pain, Tina! Help me!

TINA What do you want me to do . . .?

ANNE I will come to you . . .

TINA I don't like it . . . I don't like it . . .

ANNE I am here.

TINA No . . .

CLIVE *(as demon)* Tina . . .

TINA *looks over her shoulder to see the terrifying face of a blue demon dwarf (*CLIVE*). The small figure is dressed in a monk's cowl, and has straggly hair, long black nails and rows of sharp teeth. The demon's face and hands are mottled blue, like it has risen from the grave.*

An unearthly wind rushes through the room, blowing the curtains and generally turning the parlour into something out of The Exorcist. TINA *screams and jumps from her chair.*

TERRY Don't break the circle!

TINA *backs away towards the cot, only to spot the mewling Victorian doll lumbering up and trying to get out of the cot. She screams again.*

ANNE *slumps forward, gibbering and moaning.* CLIVE *malevolently advances toward* TINA, *his body hunched and bent.*

TERRY *(cont'd)* Tina – you have to stop it!

TINA I can't!

TERRY You have to!

TINA I don't know how!

TERRY There's only one way!

TINA How?!

TERRY By smiling at the camera and saying, 'Hi, I'm on *Scaredy Cam*!'

Suddenly the lights in the room snap on. The advancing CLIVE *gives a big thumbs up, and* ANNE *smiles.*

A black-clad PUPPETEER *emerges from the cot, waving the doll on his hand.* TINA *is stunned.*

TINA What?

TERRY *removes his fake moustache and glasses and* TINA *recognises him straight away.*

TINA *(cont'd)* Oh my God, it's you!

TERRY That's right – look through there . . .

TERRY *points at the mirror above the fireplace, which we now see is a two-way mirror. A* CAMERAMAN *can be seen operating a camera with a red light on the front.*

TERRY *(cont'd)* Give us a wave . . .

INT. KITCHEN DINING ROOM. DAY.

We see TINA *and* TERRY *on the monitor behind the scenes, which is set up in a normal-looking kitchen.*

TERRY *(on monitor)* . . . and say, 'Hi, I'm on Scaredy Cam!'

TINA *(on monitor)* I used to be such a massive fan, I can't believe . . .

TERRY *(on monitor)* Just say it.

TINA *(on monitor)* Hi, my name's Tina and I'm on *Scaredy Cam*!

The show's producer, GEMMA, *is watching, timing the segments with a stopwatch. A bored make-up girl,* AMANDA, *files her nails nearby.* GEMMA *presses a button to address the 'studio'.*

GEMMA All right, we've got that, Terry, thanks.

GEMMA *addresses her unseen assistant on cans.*

GEMMA *(cont'd)* John, did you hear we had a 'shit' at 10:05? Can we get away with that, do you think . . . ? A 'shit' for two 'bloodies'? Seems fair enough . . .

INT. PARLOUR. DAY.

A PROPS PERSON *starts to re-set the room.* GEMMA *speaks to* TERRY *through the speaker.*

GEMMA *(V.O.)* Terry, while you're there, can we get you to do the link into part two, please?

TERRY Yep – can I get a cold Diet Coke?

GEMMA *(V.O.)* Sure.

CLIVE Yeah, I'd like a Diet Coke as well, please, Gemma.

No response to CLIVE. TINA *approaches* TERRY.

TINA So am I actually going to be on the telly?

TERRY You'll be part of a montage. We do it a few times – get the best reactions.

TINA Brilliant. 'Cause I thought they'd cancelled it . . .

TERRY They did, but it's back now.

TINA On ITV?

TERRY No. *(To* GEMMA*)* I'm ready.

GEMMA *(V.O.)* Yeah – we're rolling.

TERRY *(on screen)* So join us after the break when we'll be counting down our Top 10 Terrors . . .

INT. KITCHEN DINING ROOM. DAY.

We see TERRY *recording his piece to camera on one of the monitors.* GEMMA *watches it.*

TERRY *(on monitor)* . . . and we reveal which prank you voted as our funniest ever fright. Don't you dare go away.

TERRY *finishes his bit to camera, then berates the* PROPS MAN.

TERRY *(cont'd) (on monitor)* Could you not move about whilst I'm recording. Really distracting. And there was a bear on the records, can someone shift it . . .

AMANDA I'll need to do checks on Anne before we go again. And the little . . . what's his name?

GEMMA Er, I'm not sure.

GEMMA *and* AMANDA *get up to go through to the set. We follow them through the secret door into the parlour.*

INT. PARLOUR. DAY.

TERRY *is looking at his mobile with* TINA *chattering away to him.*

TINA My favourite one was with you as the gorilla, and there was a little boy . . .

TERRY Yeah, I know, I was there, I did it. Gemma, could you . . .?

GEMMA *rushes over to rescue* TERRY.

GEMMA Yes, sorry. Tina, do you want to come through here with me? I'll just get you to sign the release forms . . .

TINA *and* GEMMA *head out to the kitchen.*

CLIVE Can I get a water, please, Gemma? I'm parched.

GEMMA *(exiting)* Sure.

ANNE *addresses* TERRY.

ANNE Terry, darling, could you leave me more of a gap before coming in with the 'Let us bow our heads in meditation and prayer' bit? I wanted to get into the heavy-breathing, trancy stuff, and I felt it all got a bit trampled over.

TERRY Yes, Anne, no problem.

ANNE It's just a beat, but I think it's more dramatic, don't you?

TERRY *exits, muttering.*

TERRY *(to himself)* It's a hidden-camera show, not the fucking National Theatre.

ANNE And could someone fetch me a footstool, please? My ankles are swelling.

AMANDA *is checking* CLIVE, *applying blue make-up.*

AMANDA How's the blue holding up? Could you try not sweating quite so much?

CLIVE It's very hot in there. I don't know why I have to be blue anyway.

AMANDA *(disinterested)* Just in the script, wasn't it? Blue Demon Dwarf. How are the nails?

CLIVE Lost one. Said I would, didn't I? Always happens.

CLIVE *shows that one of his black nails is missing.*

AMANDA Well, we'll have to find it, they're specially made. So do you play a lot of demons?

CLIVE No, why do you say that? A part's a part, isn't it? Doesn't matter if you're Dick Wittington's cat in Darlington for three months or Hamlet.

AMANDA Have you played Hamlet?

CLIVE No. Love to.

ANNE Amanda, sweetie, I need these contacts out before we go again. I can't have red eyes, I'm on stage tonight.

AMANDA Yes, sorry, Anne. I'll just go and fetch my solution. *(To* CLIVE*)* Keep pressing on that.

AMANDA *rushes away from* CLIVE, *who holds his new nail on.* CLIVE *decides to make small talk.* ANNE*'s not interested.*

CLIVE So, are you treading the boards at the moment, Anne?

ANNE Yes.

CLIVE Any good?

ANNE Not really, director's useless.

CLIVE Oh. What's wrong?

ANNE He's a drunk, darling, shits the bed.

CLIVE Right. We had a tricky director on *Wittington*, actually . . .

INT. KITCHEN DINING ROOM. DAY.

TERRY *sits at the monitor. He can see* ANNE *and* CLIVE *through the mirror.* ANNE *looks trapped by the boring* CLIVE. GEMMA *is filling in a form.*

TERRY Gemma, can you put the warm prop back in its box, please? It's pissing Anne off and I'll be getting calls from her agent again.

GEMMA Sure, one second . . .

TERRY I don't know why we keep booking dwarves, they're always a pain in the arse.

GEMMA I don't think he is a dwarf, is he?

TERRY Course he is, look at him! How did that last one look? Was it all right?

GEMMA Good, it was . . . funny.

TERRY Funny?

GEMMA And scary.

TERRY The girl was a bit dead-eyed, wasn't she? I've seen roadkill with better reactions.

GEMMA *moves to reveal* TINA *lurking behind.*

TINA Sorry, would it be possible to get your autograph?

TERRY Course! No problem. What's your name again?

TINA Tina.

TERRY *signs a piece of paper for* TINA.

GEMMA So, Terry, with this Top 10 thing, do you still want the scarecrow at number one?

TERRY Yes, please. There you go.

TERRY *hands* TINA *the autograph.*

GEMMA Because I've been looking online and people seem to love the gorilla one . . .

TINA Yeah, that's my favourite, with the little boy. It was so funny.

TERRY No, I don't want that one in the Top 10.

TINA When he wet himself!

TERRY Yeah, well, it was live so we couldn't do anything about that.

GEMMA Because I was thinking we could try and track the boy down and get him back on . . .

TERRY No! It's a public vote, so just stick to the ones I chose, OK? I'll get my own Diet Coke then, shall I?

TERRY *wanders off.*

TINA He comes over much nicer on the telly.

GEMMA *raises her eyebrows and smiles knowingly.*

GEMMA It's all done in the edit.

INT. PARLOUR. DAY.

AMANDA *has helped* ANNE *get her contacts out.*

ANNE Thank you, sweetie. And could I have a tissue, please? I need to blow my nose. I don't know why but wearing contacts always makes me snotty.

CLIVE I have that when I eat a curry!

AMANDA *hands* ANNE *a tissue and she blows her nose.* GEMMA *approaches.*

GEMMA Anne, could we step you off for a minute, the FX team need to look at your ectoplasm pipe.

AMANDA There's an offer you can't refuse!

ANNE No. I just need five minutes without being fiddled with. I've got a performance of *Hedda Gabler* tonight and I'm not doing it looking like Christopher Lee.

AMANDA *pulls a chair out from the table.*

AMANDA Did you say you wanted a chair, Anne?

ANNE No thank you, I'm not an invalid.

GEMMA *addresses* CLIVE, *opening up a trunk in the corner of the room.*

GEMMA Right, could we get you back in position, please, erm . . . Mr Demon.

CLIVE Could I get some water first? It's so hot in there.

ANNE It's stifling, Gemma, we need aircon units. I said this last week. You wouldn't have cattle in this heat.

AMANDA It is warm.

ANNE I'm serious. You would not be allowed to have cattle in heat like this. But actors – it's fine . . .

GEMMA Amanda, could you get some water for the artists, please? *(To* CLIVE*)* So can we get you . . .?

AMANDA *wanders off.* TERRY *comes in, passing* CLIVE.

CLIVE Oh Terry, can I ask you something?

TERRY *rolls his eyes.*

TERRY Yes.

CLIVE In the original script I got sent it said the character was 'Spirit of Little Boy'.

TERRY Yes, we changed it.

CLIVE Can I ask why?

TERRY Because 'Blue Demon Dwarf' is scarier.

CLIVE But will it be in the credits as 'dwarf'? Because obviously . . .

TERRY What?

CLIVE I'm not a dwarf.

TERRY Right.

CLIVE Did you think I was?

TERRY No, course not.

CLIVE Because I never would have taken the part if I knew it was going to be all scary dwarf acting.

TERRY Right. So what kind of acting do you normally do?

CLIVE A variety, you know. Like last year I did a short film about this guy in a park who meets a really gorgeous girl with a dog, but the dog keeps looking at me and it turns out . . .

TERRY One second – I do want to hear this – Gemma!

TERRY *approaches* GEMMA *and whispers to her.*

TERRY *(cont'd)* Just tell me I need to go and put my moustache back on, I don't want to get trapped with him, I can't bear it.

GEMMA *(loud voice)* Terry, you need to go and put your moustache on.

TERRY OK, will do.

TERRY *mimes his apologies to* CLIVE *and heads for the door. As he departs he sees a puddle of water in the corner of the room.*

TERRY *(cont'd)* And can someone mop that water up, please! That's how accidents happen.

TERRY *leaves.* GEMMA *is ushering* CLIVE *towards the trunk.*

GEMMA Our next victim has arrived, he's a bit early. We really need to get you back in your hutch, I'm afraid.

CLIVE Hutch? I'm not a gerbil!

CLIVE *reluctantly gets back into the trunk and* GEMMA *closes the door.* GEMMA *checks on the* PUPPETEER, *who is resetting his position.*

GEMMA Carl, all good?

The black-clad PUPPETEER *nods.* AMANDA *enters with the water.*

AMANDA Who wanted water?

CLIVE *(V.O.)* Me.

ANNE Yes, please.

ANNE *takes a water.*

GEMMA Oh yes, we need a mop, Terry said . . .

GEMMA *looks in the corner, but there is no puddle.*

GEMMA *(cont'd)* Oh, never mind. And can we get Anne's contacts back in, soon as possible please . . .?

ANNE *starts to make her way out of the room with* AMANDA *in tow.*

ANNE There's too much fiddling on this. I was in and out of a coma for a BBC thing; it could have been a nightmare, but it wasn't because the prop boys were fantastic.

GEMMA Can we reset the lights?

The lights dim as GEMMA *is the last to leave. The mirror becomes a mirror again. Silence in the room.*

CLIVE *(V.O.)* Did my water come?

Everything is still for a moment. Suddenly the door bursts open and GEMMA *runs to the cot. The Victorian doll is raised up by the* PUPPETEER *for her to grab. She runs out with it.*

INT. KITCHEN DINING ROOM. DAY.

GEMMA *runs back to the monitor. We see the parlour empty and primed.*

GEMMA OK, roll cameras, and good luck studio.

INT. PARLOUR. DAY.

PETE, *a big man in his forties, is led into the room by* TERRY. PETE *looks at his own feet.*

TERRY This way, please. Thank you for being prompt. Madam Talbot doesn't enjoy latecomers.

PETE I'm really sorry – I think I've stood in some dog shit.

TERRY *is thrown.*

TERRY Oh . . .

PETE I have, look. Have you got a tissue or summink?

TERRY Er . . .

PETE It's everywhere. Fucking hell . . .

TERRY Please – take off your shoe.

PETE Sorry about this.

PETE *takes off his shoe and hands it to* TERRY.

PETE *(cont'd)* Meant to be lucky, isn't it? Or is that just if a bird shits on you?

TERRY It's just birds, I think, yes.

PETE Mate of mine was going out with this bird, and she wanted him to lie under a glass coffee table . . .

TERRY I'll just take this outside. I won't be a moment.

TERRY *leaves with the offending shoe.* PETE *walks around the room. He looks at the things on the table. He picks up the tambourine and can see it is attached to some fishing line.*

INT. KITCHEN DINING ROOM. DAY.

GEMMA *and* AMANDA *watch on the monitor as* PETE *holds the tambourine by the fishing line.* PETE *pulls the line from the tambourine.*

GEMMA What's he doing?

AMANDA He's pulled it off.

GEMMA Oh God, we can't use any of this . . .

Suddenly PETE *yelps as he has stood on something sharp.*

PETE Shit! What the fuck . . .?

GEMMA *is despairing of the language.*

INT. PARLOUR. DAY.

PETE *sits in one of the chairs and looks at his stockinged foot. He pulls out one of* CLIVE*'s black talons.*

PETE *is looking at it as* TERRY *returns.*

TERRY There.

PETE This just stuck in my foot.

TERRY What is it?

PETE Dunno – looks like a black nail.

TERRY I'm so sorry. It may be one of Madam Talbot's. I do apologise. May I ask, have you ever made contact before?

PETE No, mate. I don't really know what I'm doing here to be honest. My mates put me up to it. I ain't that bothered, truth be told.

TERRY Great. Well, please take a seat here, and may I request that if you do have a mobile telephone, you switch it off now. I will tell Madam Talbot you are ready.

PETE All right, fella.

TERRY *leaves the room.* PETE *gets out his mobile. Instead of turning it off, he rings a number.*

PETE *(cont'd)* Martin. It's me. I'm at that ghost woman's house and it better not be a fucking wind-up. Ring me back and don't take me for a prick, yeah. I've got better things to do.

INT. KITCHEN DINING ROOM. DAY.

GEMMA *watches on in despair at all* PETE*'s swearing.*

GEMMA We're going to have to bleep all this. Cue gas lights.

INT. PARLOUR. DAY.

As PETE *looks down at his phone the gas lights grow bright as they did before, but* PETE *misses it.* TERRY *re-enters the room with his candle.*

TERRY Peter – please may you stand. May I present Mad–

Just then PETE*'s phone rings and he answers it.* ANNE *is half in the room.*

PETE Hang on . . . All right, mate, that was quick, I just left you a message. Yeah . . .

TERRY Madam Talbot.

ANNE *enters the room carrying the baby as before, and veiled in black.* TERRY *dims the lights.* PETE *sees* ANNE *for the first time.*

PETE Oh fucking hell, here we go, she's here. Talk to you later, Mart . . . Yeah, cheers buddy.

PETE *puts his phone away. He looks amused at* ANNE*, who has taken her seat at the table.*

PETE *(cont'd)* All right!

TERRY *places the candle in the middle of the table.*

TERRY You may be seated.

ANNE Hives . . . Mary is sleeping now.

TERRY *stands up and gently takes the baby from* ANNE. PETE *laughs at* ANNE*'s high-pitched voice.*

PETE Sorry – I didn't mean to laugh.

ANNE Why have you come here, my child?

PETE Good question. My mate Martin said I should. He said you're like Derren Brown. He likes shit like that.

TERRY *goes to put the doll in the cot and moves to the records. He sees that the wet teddy bear is back on top of them again. He shoots an annoyed look to the two-way mirror, then he removes the teddy, putting it on the floor.* TERRY *puts on the record and 'Bringing in the Sheaves' starts playing quietly in the background.*

ANNE The curious are often drawn here to glimpse Summerland.

PETE I'm not curious.

TERRY *returns to his seat.*

TERRY Good question: it means the Astral Plane.

PETE What?

TERRY *realises he has responded to a question* PETE *never asked. He moves on.*

TERRY All is ready!

ANNE *dramatically lifts up her veil. She has only managed to get one cataract back in.*

PETE What's wrong with her eyes?

TERRY *regards* ANNE.

TERRY Madame Talbot suffers from cataracts. But she's only managed to get one done.

ANNE Let us link hands.

ANNE, PETE *and* TERRY *link hands around the table.*

PETE You're having a laugh, ain't you . . .?

ANNE *begins to breathe deeply.*

TERRY Now let us bow our heads . . . sorry.

TERRY *realises he has jumped in over* ANNE*'s breathing again and he was going to leave a gap. She throws* TERRY *an annoyed look. He lets her do some groans before continuing. Within her juddering, she sort of gives him a nod to carry on.*

TERRY *(cont'd)* Now let us bow our heads in meditation and prayer. If there are indeed any Astrals here today, we ask you humbly to give us a sign.

TERRY *regards the tambourine, which lies motionless on the table.*

TERRY *(cont'd)* Anything? OK, erm . . .

INT. KITCHEN DINING ROOM. DAY.

GEMMA *is panicking. She speaks into her headset.*

GEMMA Shit! Cue Clive!

INT. PARLOUR. DAY.

TERRY *carries on.*

TERRY Is anyone amongst us here known to you?

ANNE Tiinnnnnaaaaa!

TERRY No.

ANNE Peeeettttteeer!

The candle flares up in a large flame.

PETE Whoa!

The gramophone record jumps and scratches, repeating as it sticks. The baby in the cot starts crying inexplicably and the cot starts rocking on its own.

TERRY Talk to it, Peter! Ask it what it wants?

PETE What do you want?

ANNE *(as little boy* WILLIAM*)* Mummy . . .

TERRY What?

PETE I didn't say anything.

ANNE *(as little boy* WILLIAM*)* Where's Mummy . . .?

TERRY Anne?

CLIVE *has appeared behind* PETE.

CLIVE Peeeteeerrrr . . .

PETE Aaargghh!

SMACK! PETE *spins round and delivers an almighty punch right in* CLIVE*'s face.* CLIVE *falls back onto the floor, where he lies still.* ANNE *and* TERRY *are shocked.*

ANNE Er, what has happened, Hives? For I am blind, you see, and can only sense . . .

TERRY All right, drop it, Anne. What are you doing, you moron?

GEMMA *bursts into the room.*

GEMMA Peter! It's a prank . . .! It's a prank!

PETE What?!

GEMMA You're being filmed for *Scaredy Cam*!

PETE What's *Scaredy Cam*?

TERRY Fuck off! It's a hidden-camera show! Where do you find these people, Gemma? And someone tell Pepe and his Friends we've stopped.

GEMMA *looks around and sees the rather pathetic mewling Victorian doll peeping out over the top of the cot.*

GEMMA Carl . . .

TERRY *examines* CLIVE. *He is bleeding.*

PETE I'm sorry, I'm so sorry . . .

PETE *slumps down into one of the chairs.* AMANDA *runs in with tissues.*

AMANDA Is he all right?

ANNE He's bleeding.

AMANDA Not on the wig, I hope, it's a hire.

GEMMA *is trying to revive* CLIVE.

GEMMA Are you OK . . . what *is* his name?

ANNE I didn't ever hear it.

AMANDA I want to say Tom for some reason . . . or am I thinking of Tom Thumb?

GEMMA It's just 'Blue Demon Dwarf' on the call sheet.

TERRY Who cares what his name is, just get him up!

AMANDA I'll phone an ambulance.

AMANDA *takes out her phone and dials.*

ANNE I told you there should have been a unit nurse, I said on day one.

TERRY Only because you wanted a Lemsip!

ANNE Excuse me, eight shows a week and a telly in the daytime? You'd be wanting medication.

PETE I'm sorry, mate, I thought he was a monster.

GEMMA He's an actor.

ANNE Broadly speaking.

PETE I didn't mean to hurt him, I just panicked.

AMANDA *(on the phone)* Yes – we've got a . . . little person, he's been involved in an accident . . . No, not a child, he's of . . . a short . . .

TERRY For God's sake, you can say 'dwarf'.

CLIVE *manages to murmur . . .*

CLIVE I'm not a dwarf . . .

GEMMA He's come to . . . can you hear me?

AMANDA *(on the phone)* Well, he *is* blue at the moment. But he might not be underneath . . .

TERRY Would you take that outside, please, Amanda?

AMANDA *leaves the room on the phone.*

ANNE Nobody bite my head off – but do you think I might be permitted to take my slap off and go? I can't do three hours of Ibsen on an empty stomach, and I did spy a YO! Sushi on the corner . . .

TERRY Oh shut up will you, Anne?

ANNE I beg your pardon?

TERRY I said shut up, I'm trying to think!

ANNE No one has ever talked to me like that before, and I've done *Shoestring*.

GEMMA Oh my God, he's stopped breathing!

GEMMA *leans in and performs mouth to mouth.*

TERRY Brilliant. This show got cancelled last time because a little boy pissed his pants on live TV. We got 97 complaints and I ended up doing bingo adverts. Well, I'm not going back there, Gemma, do you understand me?

He looks round to see GEMMA *looking up at him. Her face is blue where she's tried mouth to mouth.*

GEMMA He's dead.

PETE Oh God . . .

GEMMA We'd better ring the police.

TERRY Fuck's sake.

ANNE 'Good night, sweet prince: / And flights of angels sing thee to thy rest!' I'm not too old for Gertrude, am I?

TERRY *storms out.*

INT. KITCHEN DINING ROOM. DAY.

TERRY *enters and sees* AMANDA.

AMANDA The ambulance is on its way.

TERRY He's dead. He died.

AMANDA Aw! Can I just pop in and grab his teeth then? They cost a fortune.

TERRY *crosses to the monitors.*

TERRY I wouldn't touch him if I were you. The police will want to talk to us all.

AMANDA Why? I haven't done anything. I've just been sitting on my make-up box the whole time.

TERRY Yep.

TERRY *acknowledges this is all* AMANDA *usually does.*

TERRY *(cont'd)* Go and wait in the green room. They'll be here soon enough. Why is it always me?

AMANDA I will need that wig, it needs to go back into storage.

AMANDA *gets up and leaves.* TERRY *rewinds the footage on the monitor and plays back the punch.*

TERRY Fucking shame. It's really funny.

ANNE *comes in.*

ANNE Where's Amanda – I need this contact out. I look like Columbo.

TERRY She's in the green room.

ANNE Oh, I'll de-rig myself then, shall I? All hands to the pump. It's like doing a profit-share.

ANNE *roots around on the make-up table and starts wiping her face.* GEMMA *and* PETE *come in.* PETE *looks distraught.*

GEMMA Police are on their way.

TERRY I hope you didn't mention me.

GEMMA I did – but they'd never heard of you.

PETE What do you think will happen?

TERRY Probably cancel the series, again. Stop any repeats. My contract won't be renewed and I'll be blacklisted from the channel.

PETE No, I mean, what will happen to me?

TERRY I don't know. You'll probably end up as a clip on YouTube. Three million hits that pissing boy got and I never saw a penny of it.

PETE Sorry for spoiling your programme.

GEMMA That's all right. You were swearing too much anyway.

TERRY And that was *before* you murdered a dwarf – or . . . whatever he was.

PETE I didn't murder him!

TERRY No, of course you didn't, if anything it was his fault.

GEMMA Whose fault?

TERRY Little . . . what's-his-name. He missed his cue.

TERRY *turns to* ANNE.

TERRY *(cont'd)* And what were you saying anyway? 'Where's Mummy?' – what was that all about?

ANNE I don't remember, I must have dried. Same thing happened to me in *A Taste of Honey* at the Exchange. I suddenly went into a recipe for banana bread – audience never clocked. Right, I'm going to get changed before the police get here. Did you know I was very nearly Marple? They said I wasn't sweet enough. Fuckers.

ANNE *leaves.*

TERRY *(to* PETE*)* Look, it was an accident. You can't predict these things, OK?

PETE Thanks. Can I get my shoe back?

GEMMA Sure, it's in the corridor.

PETE Sorry.

TERRY Don't worry, you'll be fine.

PETE *leaves.*

TERRY *(cont'd)* Can we do a background check on him, see if he's got any history of mental illness?

GEMMA What do you mean?

TERRY Well, then this isn't our fault, is it? We can pin it all on him.

GEMMA Terry, that's the last thing on my mind at the moment.

TERRY Oh sorry, I'm just trying to save the programme. Don't you want a career?

GEMMA Not if it means treating people like shit.

TERRY You're in the wrong job then.

GEMMA Yes, maybe I am.

GEMMA *starts to leave.*

GEMMA *(cont'd)* Good luck with your bingo adverts.

TERRY Yeah, well, Les Dennis is doing them now, so . . .

But she's gone.

TERRY *sits down at the monitor and opens up his Diet Coke. He glances at the monitor and is surprised to see* CLIVE *standing in the far corner of the room with his face to the wall.*

TERRY *(cont'd)* Thank Christ.

TERRY *decides to go in.*

INT. PARLOUR. DAY.

TERRY *comes into the parlour. It is eerily quiet.* TERRY *slowly approaches the figure of* CLIVE, *still facing into the wall.*

TERRY Hello? Are you . . . all right?

No response.

TERRY *(cont'd)* You had us all worried there for a minute. Sorry, I don't know your name . . .

CLIVE Spirit of Little Boy.

TERRY No, we changed that, remember?

CLIVE I'm sad.

TERRY Yes, I'm sorry about that. At least you're all right now.

CLIVE I didn't like it.

TERRY No, but we're going to do everything in our power to make sure that guy gets prosecuted.

CLIVE I didn't like it when you were the gorilla. I was scared.

TERRY Gorilla?

TERRY *notices a stream of urine trickling along the floor from the figure's legs. It comes towards him.*

CLIVE They all laughed at me. It was easy to jump in the river.

TERRY What?

CLIVE Mummy didn't see . . . it was cold in the water. Tom-Tom didn't like it.

CLIVE*'s arm drops down and we see he is holding the wet teddy.* TERRY *is distraught.*

TERRY I . . . I'm sorry, I didn't know . . . it was just a stupid bit of telly, I didn't think . . .

Something dawns on TERRY. *His fear drops away and he looks around.*

TERRY *(cont'd)* Oh, hang on! Oh, very funny. Yeah, well done. Very elaborate, guys. You nearly had me. Hello!!

TERRY *waves at the camera through the mirror.*

INT. KITCHEN DINING ROOM. DAY.

On the monitor we see TERRY *waving at the camera, but he is alone. There is no figure of* CLIVE *in the corner.*

INT. PARLOUR. DAY.

TERRY *approaches* CLIVE *in the corner.*

TERRY I've got to hand it to you, mister. You're a much better actor than I thought.

TERRY *goes over and puts his hand on* CLIVE*'s shoulder.* CLIVE *drops to the floor. We see his blue face.*

WILLIAM *(V.O.)* Where's Mummy?

TERRY *turns to see the crouched figure of* WILLIAM *peering through the bars of the cot. The boy's face is deadly pale and his eyes and mouth black. It is a quick glimpse, but it fills* TERRY *with dread and fear.*

INT. KITCHEN DINING ROOM. DAY.

GEMMA *re-enters with a* POLICEMAN.

GEMMA Terry, the police are here . . . oh, he must be in the other room.

She leads him towards the parlour.

INT. PARLOUR. DAY.

GEMMA *enters the parlour with the* POLICEMAN *in tow.* CLIVE*'s body is on the floor.* TERRY *stands over him.*

GEMMA Terry? What's happened?

TERRY *slowly turns round. He is clutching* WILLIAM*'s teddy. He has wet himself, a dark patch filling his crotch. He looks like a broken man, haunted and downbeat.*

TERRY I'm on *Scaredy-Cam* . . .

THE END

SERIES
3

Foreword

> — The sentence has a surface reading, which makes perfect sense in and of itself, but when you break it down to its component parts it reveals a whole new meaning, hiding in plain sight.
>
> 'The Riddle of the Sphinx'

When asked about our writing process there are generally two lines of enquiry: where do you get your ideas from, and how do you spend your writing day? To answer the second question first, we usually like to be in the same room, working on the same script. We meet between 9 and 10 a.m. and the last to arrive has to bring the coffees. We won't always know which of us will be the last to arrive, resulting in four large lattes to get through, but more often than not the system works well.

After a good 30 minutes of preamble chat, we will crack open the laptop and begin to type, pausing for long breaks to discuss whether Findus sounds better than Fray Bentos ('The Devil of Christmas') or Ilkley is funnier than Otley ('The Bill'). We frequent the same restaurant for lunch, scanning the same menu and choosing the same dishes, before downing a couple of cappuccinos and resuming work from 2 until 5.30 p.m.

There is always a discussion phase at the start of every series, and indeed at the start of every episode, where we spend two or three days just talking through various ideas. The hope is that one of these will force its way to the forefront of our minds so we can start to develop it, but there are long silences while we mull over possibilities and secretly hope that the other is having a brainwave. During one such lull over lunch, we became aware of a politely heated conversation coming from a neighbouring table. Three pensioners, a man and two ladies, are arguing over who should pay the bill. 'Put it away, Margaret, it's my turn to treat you.' We silently catch each other's eye and know that we have something to start writing about in the afternoon.

Inspiration can come from anywhere, often when you least expect it. Walking to the office and spotting a lone shoe on the pavement, idly wondering who it could belong to and the circumstances of it ending up there. Like the argument about the bill, it seems universal and packed with narrative possibility. During a non-writing phase, the shoe would have been barely acknowledged, but when the receptors are open and greedily hunting for stories, it is suddenly imbued with comic and dramatic potential.

Other times, an idea must be laboriously forced from the brain like the last bit of toothpaste in the tube. Wanting to base an episode around the legend of the Krampus, we started to write about a family trapped in a spooky Austrian chalet. The dialogue felt stilted and the whole thing had an unsatisfying whiff of *Scooby-Doo* about it. On the verge of abandoning the premise, we had a brainwave: turn it into a pastiche of a 1970s *Thriller* episode. A desire to write about the multiple recipients of organ donation was enlivened by writing it as a *giallo*-esque Agatha Christie.

We were obviously over-inspired during the writing of this third series as two of the episodes came in substantially over 29 minutes once we had shot them. You will read a whole different ending to 'Diddle Diddle Dumpling', one we had to cut in the edit but which now seems less satisfying than the more cryptic denouement we ended up with. 'The Riddle of the Sphinx' was given a 31-minute running time by the bosses at BBC Two and we still had to lose chunks of dialogue, and you may enjoy spotting the extra lines in these pages.

So where do the ideas come from? That remains a mystery to writers everywhere. If you go looking for the lone shoe on the pavement, you will almost never find it. The trick is to keep your eyes, ears and mind open and to follow your instincts.

Episode 1

THE DEVIL OF CHRISTMAS

CAST LIST

KLAUS – Reece Shearsmith

CELIA – Rula Lenska

KATHY – Jessica Raine

JULIAN – Steve Pemberton

TOBY – George Bedford

DENNIS FULCHER – Derek Jacobi

INTERVIEWER – Cavan Clerkin

YOUNG DENNIS – Naz Osmanoglu

INT. TV STUDIO. DAY.

We see a countdown clock with the title 'The Devil of Christmas' written on white masking tape.

TECHNICIAN *(V.O.)* VTR 7226, 'The Devil of Christmas', part one, take one.

The hand counts down to zero, followed by a beep.

EXT. ALPINE VILLAGE (STOCK FOOTAGE). NIGHT.

Old stock footage of an alpine village nestled among snow-capped mountains. The footage should come from the 1970s and is on grainy film. The scene is accompanied by a scary synth score, with crashing chords and electric guitar.

The title 'The Devil of Christmas' crashes onto screen, followed by the legend 'A Film by Dennis Fulcher'.

The stock footage cuts to a shot of a large, isolated log cabin in the snow.

INT. LOG CABIN, LIVING AREA. NIGHT.

The door opens and an elderly Austrian man, KLAUS, *enters, followed by the Devonshire family. Dad* JULIAN, *Mum* KATHY, *son* TOBY *and mother-in-law* CELIA.

KLAUS Please, *komm*. Is warm inside. I have already made a fire for you.

There is a Gothic wooden '9' on the door, and we may also notice a framed picture of a devil on the wall.

The episode is filmed in 1979. It is typical of the Tales of the Unexpected/ Thriller/Beasts *episodes with harsh studio lighting shot on video with motion blur, 4:3 aspect ratio, obtrusive camera moves and shaky production values.*

KLAUS *and* JULIAN *are carrying suitcases. They must be empty and light as a feather. A flurry of polystyrene snow is thrown in by an unseen stagehand, while another waggles some dingle to suggest a cold, wintry night.*

KLAUS *carries the cases inside.*

CELIA Oh, that's better. Close the door, Toby dear, or we'll all catch our deaths.

TOBY *closes the door and the wind sound effect stops.*

KATHY What a gloomy thought: 'Catch our deaths.'

JULIAN Yes, Mummy, we're here for a two-week holiday, let's keep things jolly, eh!

CELIA I wouldn't worry about that, dear, it's just a saying. Though it is rather dim.

KLAUS *is on the other side of the room.*

The log cabin is unusually large (to allow for the dolly) and decorated in a traditional Alpine 1970s style. Cheaply. And everything looks brand new and placed by the art department.

KLAUS Here, let me.

KLAUS *switches on a small lamp. Suddenly the set is brightly illuminated. On a dimmer switch. A beat after the lamp is turned on.*

JULIAN, KATHY *and* CELIA *look round the cabin.*

JULIAN Looks bigger than it did in the brochure.

CELIA I'd rather that than the other way round. Remember that awful hotel we stayed at in Greece?

JULIAN Oh, it wasn't so bad. I rather liked it. Though as I recall the local tipple was fairly wretched!

CELIA Do you remember it, Kathy?

KATHY No, I wasn't married to Julian then. It must have been when Elizabeth was still alive.

JULIAN *shoots* CELIA *a look, then crosses to* KATHY. *He cradles her stomach from behind.*

JULIAN How are you feeling, darling? That pilot gave us one hell of a bumpy landing.

KATHY Fine, I'm fine.

JULIAN *rubs* KATHY*'s tummy.*

JULIAN Well, no skiing for you, not in your condition. We'll have the slopes to ourselves, won't we, Toby?

TOBY I'm not sure I want to ski. Boring.

KATHY Toby! Your father's gone to a lot of trouble to book this holiday, you really oughtn't to be so ungrateful.

CELIA *steps forward. She looks down to find her mark before speaking.*

CELIA You spoil him, Kathy, all these treats and indulgences. You've made him too used to getting his own way. There, I've said it.

JULIAN Mummy, let's not argue, we've only just arrived!

KLAUS *appears with a tray of wine glasses. The 'wine' is diluted Ribena, too pale and clear.*

KLAUS Here, some refreshments for you. This is a traditional Austrian drink.

CELIA Good, I'm parched.

CELIA *takes a sip.*

CELIA *(cont'd)* Mmm, lovely.

JULIAN *takes a glass, then addresses* KATHY.

JULIAN Sorry, no wine for you, darling.

KATHY It's fine, I'm not thirsty anyway.

JULIAN We need rest and plenty of it. Doctor's orders, remember?

KATHY *throws her arms around* JULIAN. *She shadows his face from the light.*

KATHY I will, I'll have plenty of rest and do nothing at all!

CELIA *pipes up from nearby.*

CELIA *(to herself)* Nothing new there then.

KATHY It's perfect. Absolutely perfect.

JULIAN And you're not too angry I invited Mummy?

KATHY It's your money, darling, I can't tell you how to spend it.

TOBY *has wandered over to the fireplace.*

TOBY *(V.O.)* Urgh!

KATHY What is it, Toby?

TOBY Horrible picture.

KATHY *and* JULIAN *join* TOBY *to look at the framed picture above the fireplace. It is a painting of a devilish black-furred figure with horns, cloven hooves and a long red tongue, carrying a screaming child on its back in a hessian sack.*

JULIAN Good grief! 'The Devil of Christmas'. What's this all about then, Klaus?

KLAUS Ah, Krampus. This is a local legend. As you know, the sixth of December is St Nicholas Day . . .

The sound level dips low and we can hear the voice of DENNIS FULCHER *begin his commentary.* DENNIS *is an old-school film director in his seventies.*

DENNIS Oh, I just want to point out a continuity error – can we whizz it back . . .?

INTERVIEWER OK. And could you just introduce yourself so people know who you are?

DENNIS Yes, I'm Dennis Fulcher and I'm the director.

Suddenly the image starts to rewind. We spool back through to the beginning of the scene when the characters enter the chalet.

DENNIS It's just occurred to me now, seeing the Krampus picture, but . . . if you look by the front door as they all troop in . . . there it is again, see it?

We notice the framed Krampus picture is by the door.

INTERVIEWER Oh yes!

DENNIS Now what happened was, we started filming and we noticed up in the gallery that the painting had been set in the wrong place by the bloody art department. Luckily it was a long scene, so I sent a stagehand down to move it.

KLAUS *switches on the lights. When we cut back to* JULIAN, *the painting has disappeared from its spot by the door.*

DENNIS See, it's gone.

INTERVIEWER I never noticed.

DENNIS No, people don't. Meanwhile it's being re-hung in its proper position above the fireplace. The little boy was a bit distracted by it, look, but otherwise I think we got away with it.

There is a shot of TOBY *looking towards the unseen stagehand during the scene.*

DENNIS *(cont'd)* The whole pregnancy thing was my idea. I just felt it would tee up the ending if you sensed there was something *inside* Kathy – made it more . . . poignant, in a way.

Over a shot of CELIA. *She looks down.*

DENNIS Nancy, there, looking for her mark. Her eyes were going by this stage, bless her.

INTERVIEWER Nancy . . .?

DENNIS Nancy Mason. Dead now, of course.

We watch the repeated scene for a few beats with the sound low. KLAUS *brings the tray of drinks over.*

DENNIS Look at that, three glasses of watered-down Ribena. Terrible. I very nearly didn't do this film, but there was so little work around, I felt I couldn't say no. The week before I'd had a meeting about *Worzel Gummidge* but Pertwee had his favourites, I knew that from *Who.*

INTERVIEWER And this was all filmed in one day?

DENNIS Yes, one day, three cameras. Unless someone bumps into the furniture, you would just carry on. They film *Doctors* in much the same way.

TOBY *crosses to look at the painting, now above the fireplace.*

DENNIS *(cont'd)* And there's the picture again, look, hung in the right place this time.

We watch for a while longer, almost back where we left off by the fireplace. We see KLAUS *come over.*

DENNIS Ralph Cosgrove, lovely actor. Always thought he had a Prospero in him, but I don't think he ever pursued it.

The sound fades up on the episode again.

KLAUS ... St Nicholas gives out treats to the good boys and girls, but those who have behaved badly are dealt with by the Krampus.

TOBY He looks mean.

The camera pushes in on the Krampus painting.

KLAUS Cloven-hooved, with two horns and a long serpent's tongue, he is both human and beast. In the clutch of the Krampus, even the most unruly child will promise to turn from his wicked ways.

JULIAN We had a nanny like that.

CELIA Oh Julian, don't exaggerate.

KATHY *is seemingly spellbound by the picture.*

KATHY So he is the dark side of Santa Claus? A sort of Jekyll and Hyde?

KLAUS The Krampus walks the streets for three nights. If you hear the cowbell you will know he is close by. On the first night, if you have been bad, you will find a switch in your shoe.

TOBY Like a light switch?

JULIAN No, darling, a switch is a rod or a twig used for whipping horses.

CELIA Or naughty children.

KLAUS It is a warning to mend your manners. On the second night, if you are still bad, Krampus will leave his mark upon you. You will wake up with scratches where he has visited you in the night. And on the third night, my God, if you are still not mended, he will come for you.

DENNIS Goes on a bit, this speech.

KLAUS You will be shackled with chains, stuffed into his sack and hurled down into the flames of Hell.

JULIAN Typical Friday night in Berkhamsted, eh darling?

KATHY *isn't listening. She stares at the picture.*

KATHY His eyes ... something about his eyes. Like he knows something. Everything.

The wood in the fire makes a loud pop and sparks flare up. It makes the group jump. They laugh in relief – the moment broken.

JULIAN I think we'll stick with good old Santa Claus if it's all the same to you, Klaus. Now come on, let's go and unpack.

JULIAN, CELIA, TOBY *and* KLAUS *all leave the room.* KATHY *stays looking at the picture of Krampus. She looks concerned.*

As the camera moves in, a boom shadow crosses her face.

JULIAN *(V.O.) (cont'd)* Come on, darling.

INT. TOBY'S BEDROOM. NIGHT.

TOBY *is in bed saying his prayers.* KATHY *is watching him.*

TOBY Now I lay me down to sleep, / I pray the Lord my soul to keep, / If I shall die before I wake, / I pray the Lord my soul to take. Amen.

KATHY Good boy, Toby. Sleep well.

KATHY *turns off the bedside lamp. The room remains just as bright. If not brighter.*

TOBY But I'm not tired.

KATHY Try and rest. You need your energy for all that skiing tomorrow.

KATHY *opens the door to leave the room. She is shocked to see* TOBY*'s boots neatly left outside his room in the hallway.*

KATHY *(cont'd)* Toby? What's this?

TOBY What?

KATHY Your boots. What are they doing out here?

TOBY I left them out. For Krampus.

KATHY What?

TOBY Klaus said if you have been a good boy, St Nicholas will come and leave coins and sweets in your shoes. Or presents in your sack.

DENNIS Not the best actor in the world. But very hard to find a good child, given the subject matter of the film.

TOBY *(cont'd)* But if you've been naughty, the Krampus will leave a twig to beat you with. I wanted to check. If I've been good or bad.

KATHY Oh darling. That's just a story. Krampus isn't real.

KATHY *goes to close the door.*

TOBY And Santa?

KATHY Go to sleep.

KATHY *smiles and closes the door.*

INT. CORRIDOR. NIGHT.

KATHY *picks up the shoes, but then decides she is being silly and puts them back on the floor.*

She walks down the corridor. Behind her she suddenly hears a creak (or was it a low moan?) and swings round – frightened. She peers into the darkness at the end of the corridor.

Is there someone there in the shadows? Suddenly the door she has stopped beside opens. KATHY *jumps in alarm.* JULIAN *is standing in the bathroom in his shorty seventies dressing gown.*

KATHY Oh!!

JULIAN Everything all right, darling? You look like you've seen a ghost!

KATHY It's nothing. All these myths and legends. I don't like that man coming in, scaring Toby like that.

JULIAN I'd say it's not Toby he's scared. You're shaking like a leaf. Come to bed.

KATHY All right, I will.

JULIAN *kisses* KATHY, *then goes to bed whistling a Christmas carol as* KATHY *enters the bathroom.*

INT. BATHROOM. NIGHT.

A cheap bathroom set, minimally furnished with an unplumbed suite.

KATHY *closes the door. A beat. Anxiously she opens the bathroom cabinet and takes out a bottle of pills. She looks at them, considering whether to take one. She makes up her mind and instead tips them down the sink.*

KATHY *replaces the empty pot in the cabinet.*

As she closes the cabinet door, we catch a flash of the boom arm in the mirror.

INT. LOG CABIN, LIVING AREA. DAY.

Close on TOBY*'s boots, which are placed on the table. Sticking out from one of them is a switch of birch twigs, like a miniature witch's broom.*

The camera pulls out to see CELIA *and* JULIAN *looking at the boots.*

They stare for slightly too long before beginning their dialogue.

JULIAN Don't look at me, I didn't put it there.

CELIA Well somebody did and Toby hasn't stopped crying all morning.

JULIAN Where is he now?

CELIA Klaus took Kathy and him down to the village for a hot chocolate.

JULIAN Oh, well, that ought to cheer him up. Just a bunch of old twigs anyhow.

JULIAN *takes the switch out of the shoe and examines it. We may be aware of some backstage noise, plates being readied for the next scene.*

JULIAN *(cont'd)* Maybe it was one of the locals – trying to scare the gullible tourists and keep us entertained.

CELIA Yes, maybe. Or perhaps . . .

JULIAN Perhaps what?

CELIA Oh, nothing.

JULIAN No, come on – spit it out.

CELIA Perhaps Kathy put them there herself.

JULIAN Why on earth would she do that?

CELIA Oh Julian, you know what I think. Toby reminds Kathy of your first wife and she resents him for it.

JULIAN Don't be ridiculous.

CELIA It's true.

CELIA *steps forward, flicks down her eyes for her mark, but she's overshot it and blocks the camera's view of* JULIAN.

CELIA *(cont'd)* It wouldn't surprise me if she put those sticks in there just to frighten the poor boy. I think she's unstable.

JULIAN Mother – Kathy is not unstable. I know she can never replace Elizabeth, but Toby needs a mother.

CELIA I don't trust her. Disappearing for days on end . . .

JULIAN *slowly leans out, aware that he's been blocked.*

CELIA *(cont'd)* . . . she should be looking after you! That's what a wife is there for, you know. For richer, for poorer, in sickness and in health. And if she doesn't want to fulfil her duties then . . . well, perhaps you should move on.

DENNIS *(over the ensuing dialogue)* Nancy's overshot her mark again, look. She wouldn't wear glasses, said they were wrong for the character. But Brian saved the day.

JULIAN I've no intention of divorcing Kathy, Mummy. I love her and she loves me, and if you don't like that you can get the next plane home to Berkhamsted.

CELIA Fine. But Klaus said these sticks were a warning.

JULIAN Rubbish. And you know what we do with rubbish?

JULIAN *throws the switch on the fire, where it lands at the back of the grate.*

We cut to a close-up of the switch in the flames, but it has now been placed too perfectly by the art department in the centre of the fire. It begins to burn away, the sound effect of the roaring fire not quite matching the few insipid flames the SFX guys were able to conjure up on the day.

INT. LOG CABIN, LIVING ROOM. DAY.

Close on the empty table.

FLOOR MANAGER *(V.O.)* Ralph, could we just see the plate in for a moment . . .

KLAUS *holds the plate of food in to check its position.*

FLOOR MANAGER *(V.O.)* That's great, thank you. Quiet on the floor, please, a lot of noise in that last take. And in five, four, three . . .

After two beats, the plate is again placed into shot and the scene begins.

KATHY, JULIAN, TOBY *and* CELIA *are sitting round the dining table.*

TOBY And then Klaus showed us how they train the reindeer, and then we went on a husky ride through the snow.

CELIA It sounds like you've had a very busy day.

TOBY Can I have a husky, father?

JULIAN Ha ha, I doubt it.

TOBY Pleeeeease!

KATHY Don't pester your father, Toby. Off you go to bed now. I'll be up in a moment.

TOBY Goodnight.

TOBY *leaves, walks precisely three paces, then turns and delivers his line to* KLAUS.

TOBY *(cont'd)* Thank you, Klaus. I had a lovely day.

KLAUS *stops serving the food.*

KLAUS You are welcome, Master Toby. *Schlaf gut.* See you in the morning. Don't forget your sack . . .

KLAUS *holds up a sack and* TOBY *runs over to take it, then places it under the Christmas tree.*

KLAUS *(cont'd)* Today is the sixth of December. The Feast of St Nicholas.

TOBY *runs up the stairs.* JULIAN *smiles at* KATHY. *The image freezes as the tape is paused.*

DENNIS Just a word here about eating scenes. Any actor will tell you it's an absolute nightmare. You end up with cold food for take after take and half a stone heavier in the process. So you'll notice here, no one eats a thing.

The picture un-pauses and the action continues.

JULIAN Well, he seems to have brightened up.

KATHY Yes, Klaus was very good with him, weren't you, Klaus? Kept him busy.

KLAUS *Ja*, he is a very good boy.

CELIA Well, not according to Krampus.

JULIAN Don't start on about that, Mummy.

KATHY No, no, it's fine. I've worked out what happened.

CELIA Pray, tell?

KATHY Darling, do you remember that time just after we'd moved into the new house? You heard a noise downstairs, we went down to investigate and found Toby in front of an open fridge, drinking milk from the bottle and eating an onion as if 'twere an apple.

JULIAN Yes – that was just sleepwalking. The doctors said he was unsettled because of the move.

KATHY Exactly. And that's what happened last night. Klaus put those silly stories into his head – sorry, Klaus – and . . . and he put the switch there himself, into his own boot.

CELIA Sleepwalking? What a terribly convenient explanation.

KATHY It is what happened, I'm sure of it.

JULIAN All right darling. Don't upset yourself. You know what the doctor said – we must have peace and calm.

KATHY But he's been happy today. Like he didn't have a care in the world. That's right, isn't it, Klaus?

KLAUS Master Toby has been a good boy. The Krampus will not return.

JULIAN Here, here! This food is delicious by the way. Any chance of seconds!

They all laugh, but CELIA *is unconvinced.*

EXT. ALPINE VILLAGE. NIGHT.

Stock footage of an alpine village at night. It's probably the exact same footage as was used at the beginning of the film.

INT. LOG CABIN, LIVING AREA. NIGHT.

The room is empty. The Christmas tree fairy lights are twinkling and there is light from the dying fire, but otherwise it is quite dark in the room.

The camera creeps towards the ominous framed picture of Krampus on the wall. A hint of camera shadow as it creeps a little too close.

Suddenly we hear a creak. We see that the front door handle is slowly turning, and the door begins to open . . .

INT. TOBY'S BEDROOM. NIGHT.

TOBY *is asleep in his bed. We hear from downstairs a cowbell chime and the dragging of chains.*

TOBY *wakes and sits up. He rubs his eyes, then gets up to investigate.* TOBY *leaves his room.*

INT. CORRIDOR. NIGHT.

TOBY *emerges from his bedroom and looks down the dark landing. On the floor is a trail of sweets. He walks down the corridor, picking them up as he goes.*

INT. LOG CABIN, LIVING AREA. NIGHT.

TOBY *is slowly coming down the stairs that lead into the living room. The front door is open and banging in the wind. Snow is blowing in.* TOBY *gets to the bottom of the stairs and goes to close the door.*

TOBY *looks back into the room and sees cloven hoofprints left in the snow, leading into the house.*

TOBY *hears an ominous low groan from somewhere in the room. He looks into a dark corner and sees what appears to be a devil standing there, with horns on his head and a tail.*

TOBY *is petrified and puts the room light on. We see that the 'devil' is just a coat on a hanger; the horns are on the wall as alpine decoration, and the tail is a scarf hanging down.*

TOBY *is relieved. He turns off the light and the coat and hanger resume looking like a scary figure.* TOBY *is about to go back upstairs when he sees his sack under the Christmas tree. It is now full. He looks at the label with his name 'TOBY' written on it, smiles and goes back up to bed.*

We stay on the sack and as TOBY *is going up the stairs, we see something shift inside.*

DENNIS I've forgotten how scary this sequence was actually.

INT. CORRIDOR. NIGHT.

TOBY *walks back down the corridor. He chews one of the sweets and goes back into his room.*

INT. TOBY'S BEDROOM. NIGHT.

TOBY *enters his room and is surprised to see* CELIA *standing there waiting for him. She wears a nightgown and has her grey hair plaited down one side.*

The plait is in fact too long for the amount of hair she normally has, but it looks good.

CELIA Toby, where have you been!? You scared me.

TOBY I couldn't sleep. I heard a noise.

CELIA Get back to bed at once.

TOBY I've been a good boy, Granny, I know I have. St Nicholas has left me some presents.

CELIA Get back to bed at once. Get to sleep.

DENNIS Mini-fluff there.

CELIA Creeping around in the middle of the night!

TOBY Sorry, Granny.

TOBY *gets into bed,* CELIA *leaves the room.*

INT. CORRIDOR. NIGHT.

CELIA *walks back down the corridor and goes into her bedroom.*

In the foreground we see a black silhouette loom into view, as if reaching the top of the stairs. It has horns and shuffles forward . . .

INT. BATHROOM. DAY.

It is the next morning. JULIAN *is having a shower. We are in the shower with him. He is wet and covered in soap.*

We hear KATHY *scream.* JULIAN *hurriedly switches off the water and steps out of the shower, soaking wet.*

INT. TOBY'S BEDROOM. DAY.

KATHY *is sitting on* TOBY*'s bed; she cradles him, crying.* JULIAN *enters, hair perfectly combed and fully made up, wearing a short bathrobe.*

JULIAN What is it? What's wrong?

KATHY Look!

KATHY *opens* TOBY*'s pyjama top to reveal three scratches across his chest.*

JULIAN Good God. What happened, Toby?

TOBY I don't know – I woke up this morning and they were there. I thought I'd been good.

JULIAN We can't put this down to sleepwalking.

KATHY No, it's Krampus! It's the second night and he's left his mark. Exactly as Klaus said he would, just as in the legend.

JULIAN Kathy, calm down. You mustn't get excited.

KATHY It's all coming true. And if what Klaus says is right, then tomorrow night he'll take Toby away! Oh please don't let him!

JULIAN That's enough!!

JULIAN *slaps the hysterical* KATHY. *He is nowhere near her face.*

JULIAN *(cont'd)* Can't you see you're scaring the boy? Toby, get dressed, we're leaving.

FLOOR MANAGER *(V.O.)* Brian, Dennis is asking for the last line again, but even angrier, please.

JULIAN OK. 'Can't you see you're scaring the boy? Toby, get dressed, WE'RE LEAVING!'

FLOOR MANAGER *(V.O.)* Great, we've bought that, thank you.

INT. LOG CABIN, LIVING AREA – DAY

JULIAN *stands, holding the telephone.*

JULIAN Only two seats left? All right – let me call you back.

JULIAN *hangs up and turns to* KATHY.

JULIAN *(cont'd)* Well, looks like we're not going anywhere.

KATHY But we've got to do something. Toby's in danger.

JULIAN There's nothing we can do . . .

CELIA *(V.O.)* I'll take him.

We see CELIA *is now standing with them in the living room. She is dressed and ready to go. A big furry hat on her head. Vaguely ridiculous.*

CELIA *(cont'd)* I've already packed my case. Perhaps it will be for the best to get Toby away from . . .

KATHY What? Say it! From me! You think I did this, don't you?

JULIAN She didn't say that, Kathy.

KATHY No, but she thinks it!

JULIAN You've been under a lot of strain recently . . .

CELIA And so have you, Julian! This holiday wasn't just about Kathy, remember?

JULIAN *(to* KATHY*)* Could it be possible that you accidentally made those marks on the boy as you were getting him undressed? Not deliberately, but . . .

KATHY Why would I? Why would I hurt my own son?

CELIA He's not your son! Book those tickets, Julian, I'll see you both in a week's time.

CELIA *sweeps up the stairs, leaving* KATHY *and* JULIAN. *She is forced to stop at the top as she has run out of stairs.*

DENNIS She ran out of stairs . . .

INT. LOG CABIN, LIVING AREA. DAY.

Two (empty) cases are placed down by KLAUS.

DENNIS . . . and this always annoys me. Empty suitcases. Light as a feather.

Pull out to reveal that CELIA *and* TOBY *have their coats on and are ready to leave.* KATHY *and* JULIAN *stand nearby.*

KLAUS Here, this is everything, I think. We must leave soon, there is a storm on the way.

JULIAN Then you should go now. We don't want you missing that flight. Goodbye, Toby, look after Granny for me.

TOBY I will. I'm going to miss you though.

KATHY Don't worry, darling, we'll see you in a couple of days.

TOBY No, I meant I'll miss Klaus.

KATHY *looks hurt.* TOBY *runs to hug* KLAUS.

KLAUS Ho-ho, and I will miss you, Master Toby. But you will be back, I'm sure . . .

The scene of the family saying goodbye continues, but the volume dips and we hear DENNIS*'s commentary for a while.*

KLAUS *(cont'd)* We have a saying in these parts: 'All journeys have secret destinations of which the traveller is unaware.'

DENNIS This was all a bit of padding, really, before we go into the final act. I think it still holds up as an intriguing little tale.

JULIAN And we have a saying too, Klaus, 'Home is where the heart is.' We've enjoyed our little sojourn, but it's time to get Toby home, isn't it, young man?

DENNIS People often get obsessed with guessing the twist in these types of films, but of course that was never what it was all about. In actual fact, the story is quite irrelevant.

TOBY It's not fair, I want to stay!

KLAUS *picks up the cases and the group all walk very slowly towards the door in a straight line, all facing the camera.*

DENNIS Now you'll see here they're all in a line . . .

KATHY Now you will remember to telephone us as soon as you get back, won't you?

DENNIS . . . that's because I had to send the other two cameras off to get into position for the next scene.

INTERVIEWER Why's that?

DENNIS We were running out of time and I was trying to get ahead.

CELIA Yes, yes, I'll take good care of him. I have brought up children of my own, you know.

JULIAN All right, Mummy, don't start.

CELIA Take care, Julian. Kathy. Klaus, I'm ready now.

The scene finishes with KLAUS, CELIA *and* TOBY *leaving.* JULIAN *hugs* KATHY.

INT. MASTER BEDROOM. NIGHT.

KATHY *sits at the dressing table combing her hair in her nightdress.* JULIAN *enters in his pyjamas. He looks out of the window and there is a flash of lightning and a rumble of thunder.*

DENNIS I knew we were losing Brian at six o'clock – he had a voiceover for Findus or something – so I told them both to get a lick on.

JULIAN Looks like Klaus was right, there is a storm on the way.

KATHY I do hope the pilot knows what he's doing.

JULIAN *does seem to be hurrying through his dialogue.*

JULIAN Oh, I'm sure they'll be fine, besides Toby likes a bit of turbulence; he says it's like being on a ride at the fairground.

KATHY But what if . . . ?

JULIAN *(quickly)* Yes, what is it? Say what's on your mind, darling?

KATHY Well, I was just thinking . . .

DENNIS Penny was being deliberately slow here; I think she was onto him – about the advert.

KATHY We've sent Toby and your mother away with this man Klaus, and we don't know the first thing about him.

JULIAN Of course we do, he's the caretaker, he runs this place – how else would he have the keys?

KATHY He could have . . . I don't know . . . rented the place himself from the real owners and pretended to be the caretaker.

JULIAN Why on earth would he do that? It makes no sense. Now come on, it's been a long day. Get into bed and I'll turn off the light.

A rumble of thunder outside.

KATHY Brush my hair for me, Julian. You know I've never liked thunder.

JULIAN Of course.

JULIAN *crosses and starts to brush her hair.*

KATHY I'm being silly, I know. Toby and your mother will be fine, won't they? I just got carried away by that silly Krampus story.

JULIAN That's right, darling. I told you before, there's no such–

JULIAN*'s eyes widen. Another rumble of thunder (the exact same sound effect).*

We see that JULIAN *has spotted some scratches on* KATHY*'s back.*

KATHY Julian, what is it?

JULIAN Nothing.

KATHY There is something, I can tell.

KATHY *turns to look at her back in the mirror. She sees the scratches.*

JULIAN Your back. It's covered in scratches.

KATHY It's the Krampus. He's coming for me!

JULIAN That's impossible.

KATHY My shoes, the wardrobe!

JULIAN *strides to the wardrobe, flings open the doors and we crash zoom in on* KATHY*'s boots. In one of them is a switch of birch twigs.*

JULIAN No!

KATHY I told you, it's all true.

JULIAN But it makes no sense, the Krampus only comes for children, the legend says so.

KATHY Julian . . .

KATHY *stands up and places her hands on her stomach.*

KATHY *(cont'd)* I'm pregnant.

JULIAN *is aghast. Suddenly there is a loud crash from downstairs and the sound of tinkling glass.*

JULIAN Wait there.

JULIAN *strides to the door.*

INT. CORRIDOR. NIGHT.

JULIAN *walks down the corridor. He hears a bang from* TOBY*'s room, which he enters.*

INT. TOBY'S ROOM. NIGHT.

JULIAN *enters* TOBY*'s room and sees that a large branch has blown through the window in the storm. He crosses and pushes the branch out and closes the curtains.*

KATHY *appears in the doorway.*

JULIAN It was just a branch, the storm must have blown it in. You get to bed. I'm going to check all the doors are locked. Real or not, Krampus isn't getting in here tonight.

JULIAN *exits, squeezing past* KATHY *in the doorway.*

INT. MASTER BEDROOM. NIGHT.

Close on JULIAN *in bed. We hear the conspicuous ticking of a clock. The ticking suddenly stops and* JULIAN *opens his eyes.*

JULIAN Kathy?

JULIAN *turns to reveal that* KATHY *is no longer in the bed with him. He gets out of bed and puts on his robe and slippers before exiting the room.*

INT. CORRIDOR. NIGHT.

JULIAN *walks down the corridor.*

JULIAN Kathy, where are you?

JULIAN *opens another door and looks inside, then continues down the corridor.*

INT. LOG CABIN, LIVING AREA. NIGHT.

JULIAN *comes down the stairs into the living room.* KATHY *is standing by the fireplace, looking at the painting of the Krampus. She is in her nightwear. She looks like she's mesmerised by it.*

JULIAN Darling? Everything all right?

KATHY *doesn't respond.*

JULIAN *(cont'd)* Come back to bed, you'll catch your death.

KATHY There's that expression again: 'Catch your death.'

JULIAN Is something wrong?

KATHY Yes. I understand now. You said the Krampus only comes for children. And I'm pregnant.

JULIAN Yes?

KATHY But that's not all, is it? He only comes for the bad children.

JULIAN What are you getting at?

KATHY There's something I haven't told you. Something about this child . . .

KATHY *cradles her stomach. Suddenly the phone rings very loudly, making* JULIAN *jump. He crosses and answers it.*

JULIAN Hello? Hello, Mummy. So you're home safe then? Toby all right? Good, thanks for letting me know. Yes, yes, we're fine. Goodnight, Mummy.

KATHY *has been pacing the room, biting her thumb. She stands in the corner of the room, with the shadow of the coat hangers behind her.*

JULIAN *(cont'd)* Well, you were saying?

KATHY I've been bad, Julian. This baby . . . it's not yours.

JULIAN What?

Lightning strikes and briefly illuminates the room. We see the dark corner behind KATHY. *But this time, instead of the coat and hangers, we see the terrifying form of the* KRAMPUS.

It is a leering devil, covered in black fur, with horns, a tail and claw-like talons.

JULIAN *is terrified.*

JULIAN *(cont'd)* Kathy, behind you!

Before KATHY *can react, the* KRAMPUS *jumps forward and grabs hold of her, covering her mouth and waist with its claws.*

KATHY *tries to scream. The* KRAMPUS *lifts* KATHY *and starts to drag her away.*

JULIAN *grabs a poker from the fireplace.*

JULIAN *(cont'd)* Let go of her, you fiend!

JULIAN *raises the poker, but immediately clutches his chest, having suffered a massive heart attack. He drops the poker.*

The KRAMPUS *is dragging* KATHY *away. She screams.*

JULIAN *falls to his knees, helpless to do anything for his wife. He gurgles and gasps for air.*

The KRAMPUS *has* KATHY *by the front door.*

JULIAN *falls to the floor. He tries to crawl forward but is losing strength with every second. His face is a mask of terror and panic. His breathing is laboured. His dying breaths.*

Close on JULIAN*'s twisted face. A pair of bare feet walk into shot.* JULIAN *looks up.*

KATHY *is standing above him. She crouches to address her husband.*

JULIAN *(cont'd)* Pills . . . my pills . . .

KATHY These pills?

KATHY *holds up the pill bottle from the bathroom.*

KATHY *(cont'd)* I'm sorry, I threw them away. Goodbye, darling.

The KRAMPUS *steps forward and pulls off his mask. We see that it is actually* KLAUS. *But now he doesn't have an Austrian accent.*

KLAUS Don't worry, I'll look after her now. Merry Christmas.

We see JULIAN *die.*

DENNIS And there's your ending. Well, not quite.

KATHY *turns and kisses* KLAUS.

FLOOR MANAGER *(V.O.)* Right, we've got ten minutes to get the final scene – cameras round to the bedroom, please. Dennis is coming down to the floor.

The cameras wheel round to the bedroom set. KATHY *crosses to the bedroom and gets into the bed. She is handed a bottle of fake champagne by the* STAGEHAND.

INTERVIEWER What does that mean? Come down to the floor?

DENNIS The studio floor. I needed to be there for the ending. Such a rush now. Always the way with filming. It's *Gandhi* in the morning, *Hollyoaks* in the afternoon.

FLOOR MANAGER *(V.O.)* Thanks, Penny, in five, four, three . . .

KATHY *is sitting up in bed wearing her nightdress. She pops open the bottle of champagne and pours two glasses.*

There is no pop. It is barely coloured water.

We can hear the sound of a shower running in the bathroom next door. KATHY *calls through.*

KATHY I've poured you a glass of champagne. I know I shouldn't drink, what with me being pregnant with your baby, but a little glass won't do any harm, will it? Besides, you deserve a treat, spending all that time in character. Fancy having to spend a whole day with that little brat Toby, I don't know how you bore it.

KLAUS *comes in, still wearing the Krampus suit but no mask.*

KATHY *(cont'd)* Oh, I thought you were having a shower. Couldn't keep your hands off me, eh?

KLAUS *takes* KATHY*'s hand and chains it to one of the bedposts.*

KATHY *(cont'd)* What's this? Kinky. I wondered what those chains were for.

KLAUS *moves to the other side and chains her other hand up.* KATHY *muses.*

KATHY *(cont'd)* I'll call the police in the morning. It's perfect, really. Julian had been under a lot of stress, the doctors suggested this holiday, but his medication ran out and I found him lying dead at the bottom of the stairs. We should have the insurance money in time for New Year. I can't wait to see Celia's face. Oh, she'll suspect something, but where's the proof? Like I said, it's perfect. Ow, darling, that hurts.

KLAUS *stands at the foot of the bed.*

KATHY *(cont'd)* Well, what are you waiting for? Aren't you going to ravish me, Simon?

KLAUS *(Simon) has a strange look in his eyes.*

KLAUS Simon? I don't know anyone called Simon. I'm . . . Krampus . . .

Close on KATHY*'s distressed face.*

KATHY No . . . No! Arghhh . . .

KATHY *screams.*

DENNIS *(V.O.)* And cut!

KATHY *stops screaming.*

DENNIS *(V.O.) (cont'd)* Great, thanks Ralph, if we could step you off.

KLAUS *disappears. We stay on* KATHY*, chained to the bed, in a wide shot.*

KATHY Oh, are you done, darling? Aaah, well, I'll see you at the screening if they have one, yes?

But KLAUS *has disappeared. Two* STAGEHANDS *enter the frame and start to open up a large plastic sheet.*

DENNIS *(V.O.)* All right, keep rolling, we're setting up for scene 18B.

They quickly and very matter-of-factly lift KATHY*'s legs and pull the plastic sheet under her body onto the mattress and pillows.*

KATHY Oh, what . . .? Is this a new scene, Dennis?

DENNIS *(V.O.)* Quick as you can, please.

KATHY I don't think I got this, did we get pink pages?

CAMERAMAN *(V.O.)* Just changing camera position.

The camera swings to the side and we see off the set. We see a BALD FAT MAN*, bare-chested, putting on the Krampus mask and gloves.*

KATHY *(V.O.)* Dennis? Can someone tell me what's going on, please?

The camera is repositioned. KATHY *is still chained to the bed. One of the* STAGEHANDS *starts to tie a gag round* KATHY*'s mouth and she becomes visibly distressed.*

The sound dips and we hear DENNIS*'s commentary.*

DENNIS Always a strange moment. When you see them realise what's going on. You see there's no acting here, that's genuine fear. I don't think I want to watch the ending.

DENNIS *(V.O.)* All right, when you're ready, Max. Action!

KATHY *squirms in terror. The bare-chested* MAX *marches in, wearing the Krampus mask and gloves. He carries a large machete. He holds* KATHY *down and raises the knife.*

The picture cuts off abruptly to the colour bars. A beep.

DENNIS Well, that's it. Can't believe it's surfaced again after all these years. In its defence, it was one of the better ones, but . . . if only I'd got *Gummidge*. Never mind.

INTERVIEWER Police interview with Dennis Fulcher terminated at 16:05.

A long, harsh beep; the screen crackles.

THE END

Episode 2

THE BILL

CAST LIST

ARCHIE – Reece Shearsmith

ANYA – Ellie White

MALCOLM – Steve Pemberton

KEVIN – Jason Watkins

CRAIG – Philip Glenister

TIM – Callum Coates

EXT. NO. 9 RESTAURANT. NIGHT.

A smart bistro on a Northern high street. The name of the restaurant is simply 'No. 9', which is on the sign outside.

TITLE: *'The Bill'.*

INT. NO. 9 RESTAURANT. NIGHT.

It is approaching 11 p.m. and the bistro is getting ready to close. Only three tables are occupied, two by couples and one by a group of men.

The waitress, ANYA, *a pretty Eastern European, is clearing the coffee mugs and saying goodnight to one of the couples, who get up and leave.*

As ANYA *passes the corner table, one of the men,* ARCHIE, *leans out to ask:*

ARCHIE Excuse me, can we have the bill, please?

ANYA Of course.

ANYA *smiles and disappears into the kitchen.*

The men's table has the detritus of desserts, coffees and whiskies. Round the table sit CRAIG *(a younger, successful Southerner);* MALCOLM *(a loud-mouthed braggart);* KEVIN *(quieter, clever, but a bit miserly);* ARCHIE *(fun, but quick-tempered).*

MALCOLM *is holding court, telling a story to* CRAIG.

MALCOLM Anyway we were at Lingfield, '89, was it?

KEVIN No! It was after Diana died.

MALCOLM What? What's she got to do with it?

KEVIN I just remember.

MALCOLM All right well, '99, whenever, and the Professor here . . .

MALCOLM *points to* KEVIN.

MALCOLM *(cont'd)* . . . had worked out that if we put this accumulator on seven races, we could have made – what was it?

ARCHIE Half a million.

KEVIN It wasn't half a million, it was 469 thousand.

ARCHIE All right, fucking hell, we're not to the nearest quid, are we?

MALCOLM Anyway, we all had to pick a horse and put a tenner each in the diddlum.

CRAIG In the what?

MALCOLM The diddlum.

CRAIG *laughs.*

CRAIG What's a diddlum?

MALCOLM The diddlum, it's a whatsit, where you all chip in!

ARCHIE It's a diddlum, have you never heard of a diddlum?

CRAIG *(laughing)* No.

ARCHIE It's where you pay in a bit each week . . .

KEVIN It's a savings scheme.

CRAIG It must be a Northern thing. 'Put tha money in't diddlum and buy some whippets and barm cakes . . .' Sorry, go on.

MALCOLM Anyway, we'd all put in our diddlum money and picked a horse each and Archie chose – what was it . . . Hoof Hearted?

ARCHIE Hoof Hearted, three to one, second favourite.

MALCOLM Prof chose some fancy writer thing, what was it, Outrageous . . .

KEVIN Outrageous Fortune.

MALCOLM That's it, after the Bette Midler film.

KEVIN Shakespeare.

MALCOLM And I had Mashie Niblick at forty to one.

CRAIG Clever boy, you went for an outsider.

MALCOLM Yeah, to push the winnings up. Anyway, I gave the diddlum to Archie.

ARCHIE He didn't.

MALCOLM I did!

ARCHIE He says he did, but he was found . . .

MALCOLM No, let me finish . . .

ARCHIE He was found in the hospitality area . . .

MALCOLM Rubbish!

ARCHIE With two dolly birds and a full English breakfast.

KEVIN Slightly the worse for wear.

MALCOLM Well, I was upset that Diana had died.

ARCHIE And he'd spent the whole lot.

CRAIG No!

ARCHIE Yep.

CRAIG You diddled the diddlum?

KEVIN He did indeed.

CRAIG Malcom! And don't tell me – all three horses came in.

ARCHIE Yeah. Half a million down the drain.

KEVIN Well, 469 thousa–

MALCOLM Yeah, well, it's only money, isn't it, Craig? I've made it up to you since, haven't I?

ANYA *approaches with the bill.*

ANYA Here you go, gentlemen, hope you enjoy your meal?

ARCHIE It was lovely, thanks.

CRAIG *takes the saucer with the bill on it.*

CRAIG Excuse me, darling, could we get some mints?

ANYA Please?

CRAIG A few mints from the bowl near the till? Just to cleanse the palate.

ANYA Oh no, the kitchen boy will cleanse the plates.

CRAIG No, no, the palate. I mean the mints, little . . . sucky-sucky.

ANYA Oh, sorry, I get you some. It is my first day!

ANYA *departs.* CRAIG *looks after her.*

MALCOLM Well, she's not getting a tip.

CRAIG I wouldn't mind giving her my tip.

ARCHIE What are you doing asking for piss-mints?

CRAIG Eh?

ARCHIE The piss-mints by the till?

CRAIG Why are they piss-mints?

MALCOLM Cause people come out the bogs, don't wash their hands and reach in for a mint on the way past.

CRAIG No! People aren't animals.

KEVIN They are actually. They did a test.

ARCHIE Exactly. They tested a bowl and found 15 different types of piss.

CRAIG What do you mean, 'types'? There's not different 'types' of piss.

MALCOLM There are, like fine wines.

CRAIG Jesus Christ, I can't wait to get back to Chiswick.

ARCHIE Oh yeah, because London piss is like sparkling water, isn't it? You could just drink it straight back down again.

CRAIG Pretty much, yeah.

ARCHIE Well, I'm just telling you, mints in Northern restaurants are all drenched in piss.

KEVIN And faecal matter.

ANYA *arrives with the mints on the bill saucer.*

ANYA There you go, sorry about that. I gave you big handful.

CRAIG Thanks.

CRAIG *gingerly pulls the bill from under the mints.*

CRAIG *(cont'd)* I'll . . . take them back for the kids.

ANYA *leaves.*

MALCOLM How many kids do you have, Craig?

CRAIG Two. It's half-term so they've come up with the au pair. I told them it was like a safari but with poor people.

ARCHIE *laughs.* CRAIG *looks at the bill.*

KEVIN *has sorted his money out already, to the nearest penny. He has a small pocket-purse.*

KEVIN Well, there's my contribution, including 10 per cent service charge.

MALCOLM Ten! You tight bastard, give her 15 like a normal human being.

KEVIN Ten is industry standard.

MALCOLM What industry? She's slopping plates around for a room full of fat pigs. Give it here, I'm going to get this.

CRAIG No, Malcolm!

ARCHIE No way, that's not right . . .

MALCOLM Shut up, I am, it's on me.

ARCHIE No, you got it last time, let me get this one.

ARCHIE *reaches for the bill but* MALCOLM *holds it away.*

MALCOLM Get off, I'm paying it. How much is it?

MALCOLM *looks at the bill.*

MALCOLM *(cont'd)* Jesus Christ, go on then.

MALCOLM *pretends to hand the bill over but snatches it back.*

MALCOLM *(cont'd)* I'm joking, I don't mind, honestly.

ARCHIE No, I'm not having that. I invited Craig along and I was going to pay for him anyway, so . . .

MALCOLM It doesn't matter!

ARCHIE It does, you're messing it all up, it's not fair.

CRAIG Guys, guys, listen – I'd like to get it.

CRAIG *snatches the bill from* MALCOLM*'s hands.*

MALCOLM/ARCHIE No!

CRAIG Yes! I'm off back to civilisation soon and I know you Northerners are very poor, with your Christmas Clubs and your diddle-dums . . .

ARCHIE Diddlums!

CRAIG . . . so I'd like to treat you all, please, no arguments.

KEVIN Well, that's very kind of you, Craig, thank you.

MALCOLM Bloody hell, Kevin, that was quick! You thanked him before he'd even offered.

ARCHIE He doesn't miss a trick, does he!

KEVIN No, I offered to pay my way.

KEVIN *gestures to his pile of change.*

ARCHIE Yeah, like the time you offered me petrol money for that league game in Otley!

KEVIN That was based on mileage as the crow flies divided by the four us . . .

ARCHIE Two pounds.

KEVIN It was mathematically sound.

MALCOLM Yeah, all in coppers.

They all laugh, except for KEVIN.

ANYA *approaches with the card machine.*

ANYA Right, shall I split you four ways?

CRAIG No, though I'd like to split you four ways . . .

MALCOLM No, I'm getting this, Craig . . .

MALCOLM *snatches the bill back off* CRAIG.

MALCOLM *(cont'd)* It's been lovely to meet you, you played very well tonight and the pair of you beat Kevin and me fair and square, so *victoribus spolia* – to the victor, the spoils.

CRAIG Oh well, I won't argue with you, Malc—

ARCHIE No, I'm sorry, Malcolm, but that is bullshit.

MALCOLM Eh?

ARCHIE We've never played that before, loser pays.

KEVIN *(terrified)* It would be a rather dangerous precedent to set.

MALCOLM It's not a precedent. I would like to pay for your meal. Put it on this, please . . .

MALCOLM *hands a card to* ANYA, *but* ARCHIE *stops him.*

ARCHIE No, put it on this, please, I insist. You get the next one.

KEVIN Thank you, Archie, that's very kind of you.

KEVIN *scoops his cash into his little purse.*

ANYA *takes the card and places it into the machine.*

CRAIG *(to* ARCHIE*)* Bloody hell, I didn't think badminton was this competitive.

ARCHIE It's not competitive. It's just that Malcolm is over-generous at times, aren't you, Malc? This is my treat, everybody.

MALCOLM *is brooding.* ANYA *is examining the machine.*

ANYA Sorry, is run out of paper, I'll be back.

ANYA *leaves.* CRAIG *laughs.*

CRAIG 'I'll be back!' *Terminator.*

MALCOLM Very clever, Archie, very clever trick. I can see what you're doing.

ARCHIE What do you mean?

MALCOLM Letting me get the next one, which is – ooh, let me think – wives and girlfriends night at Browns.

ARCHIE So?

MALCOLM So it'll be double the price, won't it? Even more if your Susie puts it away like she did at the Christmas do. All those Mojitos . . .

CRAIG Oh, I like the sound of Susie. Has she got a sister?

ARCHIE You shouldn't bring Susie into it, Malcolm. That's wrong.

A tense moment.

MALCOLM Anyway it's fine, you just get this little starter and I'll pay for the proper grown-up meal next time. Well done.

ARCHIE Fine, I'll pay for the next one as well if you're keeping track.

MALCOLM Eh, no one's keeping track.

ARCHIE Well, you clearly are if you're thinking one ahead like that. It hadn't even occurred to me what the next one was!

KEVIN Why don't you split it then?

MALCOLM *and* ARCHIE *turn to look at* KEVIN.

MALCOLM Eh?

KEVIN Why don't you split it two ways? Then nobody loses face.

ARCHIE Who's losing face? I'm not losing face.

MALCOLM Why only two ways anyway, why not three?

KEVIN Well fine, if Craig wants to . . .

MALCOLM I meant with you! Jesus, what a blue-cock.

CRAIG What's a blue-cock?

MALCOLM A tight-fisted wanker.

CRAIG Ha ha, good one, I'm having that.

ARCHIE He had double glazing put in so the kids couldn't hear the ice cream van.

KEVIN *pulls the money from his little purse.*

KEVIN Fine, I'm happy to pay my way, I've already demonstrated that . . .

MALCOLM Oh, put your little purse away, Ebenezer, we don't need your shrapnel.

KEVIN *(testily)* Do you want me to pay or not?

ARCHIE Yeah, three ways, so we can treat Craig.

CRAIG It really isn't necessary.

KEVIN Fine, but I don't drink and I didn't have a starter, so . . .

ARCHIE So what? You're contributing to the evening, to the company provided, not just what's in your belly.

ANYA *comes back with the machine.*

ANYA Right, so, Mr Simkins?

ARCHIE Yes.

CRAIG No, no, honestly, guys, I've got this.

CRAIG *proffers his card.*

MALCOLM Put it away.

ARCHIE No . . .

KEVIN I'll pay.

This stuns the table into silence. MALCOLM *and* ARCHIE *turn to look at* KEVIN. KEVIN *swallows hard.*

KEVIN I'd like to pay the whole bill, please.

CRAIG Kevin, that's so generous of you. Are you sure?

KEVIN Yes. Perhaps you can all put in for the tip.

ANYA *crosses to* KEVIN. KEVIN *hands over his credit card.*

KEVIN *(cont'd)* Can you put it on this, please?

ANYA *places* KEVIN*'s card in the credit card reader.*

MALCOLM Wonders never cease.

KEVIN Oh, and I have these vouchers for 50 per cent off.

ARCHIE What?

MALCOLM Whoa, whoa, whoa – 50 per cent off?

KEVIN Yes, they're from a coupon website.

ARCHIE And you were just going to sit there and let me pay for it?

KEVIN I was saving them for another time.

ARCHIE What other time, you never go out!

MALCOLM No, I'm sorry, Kevin, if you're paying for dinner, you're paying for dinner. None of this coupon shit.

ANYA They're out of date anyway, sorry.

CRAIG, MALCOLM *and* ARCHIE *laugh.*

ARCHIE Ha ha ha, like your condoms, Kevin! Use by January 2000!

MALCOLM Get your pound notes out, with Isaac Newton on the back!

KEVIN *(to* ANYA*)* Sorry about that . . . I just . . .

KEVIN *starts to root in his purse.* ANYA *is embarrassed for him.*

ANYA I come back in a minute. Can I offer you guys to be shot or something?

CRAIG Sorry?

KEVIN She means a free drink.

ARCHIE Oh, that's made his eyes light up, look!

CRAIG Do you have any Limoncello?

ANYA Please?

CRAIG Limoncello?

ANYA I will look, I'll be back.

ANYA *leaves.*

MALCOLM You wait, she'll come back with a lemon and a cello.

CRAIG Look, guys, I don't want to cause any bad feeling, let me pay, please.

MALCOLM/ARCHIE No!

ARCHIE Kevin's paying.

MALCOLM Kevin, leave it, I'll get it.

ARCHIE You're not getting it, I've told you.

CRAIG Honestly, it's no skin off my nose.

ARCHIE Yeah, we all know you're really rich, Craig.

CRAIG What's that got to do with anything?

MALCOLM I don't care if he's Bill Gates; he played at our club, I'm club sec, I'm paying for his meal.

ARCHIE And there it is in a nutshell, Craig. You've been bought, kerching.

MALCOLM Oh, not this again.

ARCHIE Yes, I'm afraid so, Malcolm. This again. How many votes was it? Tell him.

MALCOLM I don't remember.

ARCHIE Seventeen to five and he's club secretary. I'd been there seven years before him.

KEVIN Don't dredge up old graves, Archie, it's unseemly. There was no funny business.

ARCHIE *(to* KEVIN*)* Who did you vote for then?

MALCOLM You don't have to tell him, Kevin.

KEVIN It was anonymous.

ARCHIE You were seen, Kevin – a Garfunkel's lunch every day for a fortnight.

KEVIN That's not true.

MALCOLM What, were you spying on us? Bloody hell, if you're that desperate, put your name up next time, I won't stand again.

ARCHIE Don't worry, I will!

MALCOLM If that's all you've got to worry about then I'm very happy for you, Archie, you must have a very nice life.

ARCHIE Oh piss off, Malcolm.

CRAIG Guys, guys, don't! It's just a couple of hundred quid, it's literally nothing.

ARCHIE Oh, nothing is it, Mr Monopoly?

CRAIG Archie, what's got into you?

MALCOLM Besides, the club would never have allowed somebody with a criminal record to be club secretary.

ARCHIE No one cares about that, that was just me utilising a clause in a mortgage contract . . .

MALCOLM Also known as 'fraud'.

ARCHIE You're the fraud, pal, you bought every single one of those votes.

MALCOLM Because I treated Kevin to a foot-long from Subway?

ARCHIE Yes. And this is what he's doing now, Craig, just be aware.

MALCOLM Bullcrap.

ARCHIE He's putting you in his pocket in case he needs you at a later date.

MALCOLM I'm offering to buy everyone's meal!

ARCHIE Yes, because you're a selfish prick.

CRAIG He isn't, Archie, calm down, he isn't. Because *I* am paying for this meal and that is the absolute end of the matter.

ANYA *approaches with the Limoncellos on a tray.*

ANYA Here we go, four Limoncello for you. And have you decide yet who pay the bill?

CRAIG Yes! Put it all on this, please.

CRAIG *fishes out his card from his wallet.*

CRAIG *(cont'd)* And put on 25 per cent for yourself.

Raised eyebrows between KEVIN *and* MALCOLM.

CRAIG *hands round the drinks as* ANYA *punches the numbers into the card machine.*

CRAIG *(cont'd)* Right, gentlemen, I would like to thank you all for your company tonight, for a good game of badminton, and if any of you find yourselves in the Chiswick area, please don't hesitate to not ring me. Cheers.

The others raise their glasses and cheers with each other, ARCHIE *and* MALCOLM *slightly reluctantly. They all down their shots. There is an awkward pause.* KEVIN *breaks the ice.*

KEVIN I don't envy you going back to London, Craig. All those pickpockets.

CRAIG Yeah, it's not what it was, Kevin. I'd be happy to move on to be honest with you. I do crave a bit of excitement. When I was climbing in Canada last year . . .

ANYA *leans in to speak to* CRAIG.

ANYA Excuse me, sir, but your card is not welcome.

CRAIG What?

ANYA It is reject. Bad. Do you have perhaps other card?

CRAIG Not on me, no. I don't understand it, there's at least 250 in that account.

MALCOLM *turns to* KEVIN *and mouths 'thousand'.* KEVIN*'s eyes widen.*

ARCHIE Well, that settles it, let me pay.

CRAIG No, no, no, hang on, I've got an Amex at the hotel, I can get the au pair to give me the number, one sec . . .

CRAIG *dials a number on his phone.*

ANYA Oh, I'm not sure . . .

ARCHIE Craig, there's no need . . .

CRAIG *shushes* ARCHIE.

CRAIG Anoushka, it's me, can you go to my room, please . . . yes, very nice thanks. Can you go into my room, to the bedside cabinet . . . open the second drawer down, no, no, not the top one, do NOT open the top one, the second . . . yes, and in there you'll find my Amex card, yes, the gold one, now I need the long number and the four digits on the front. No, the digits . . . tell you what, can you bring me the card . . .

The others all shake their heads and mime 'No, no.'

CRAIG *(cont'd)* They'll be fine, they'll be fine, they're asleep, aren't they? Just leave quietly . . . Well, if you're that worried unplug everything!

MALCOLM Craig, no . . . No!

MALCOLM *takes* CRAIG*'s phone and speaks into it.*

MALCOLM *(cont'd)* Don't worry, Babooshka, you don't have to come, it's fine.

MALCOLM *hangs up.*

MALCOLM *(cont'd)* I appreciate what you're doing, but it's daft putting your kids' lives in danger when I've got a good card right here.

KEVIN Or we can split it.

MALCOLM No, I'm getting it.

ARCHIE All right, fine. *(To* ANYA*)* Will you give us a second, please, love?

ANYA Of course.

ANYA *disappears.*

ARCHIE This is not the way I wanted to do this, but I've got something to tell you.

KEVIN You've got a voucher?

ARCHIE No, I haven't got a voucher, I've got . . . a brain tumour.

MALCOLM You're joking.

ARCHIE No, I'm not, Malcolm. I wish I was. It's inoperable – and I've got three months at best, I'm afraid.

KEVIN Archie – I'm so sorry.

ARCHIE Thanks, Kevin. And that is why I wanted to pay for this meal. I'm sorry, Malcolm, I should have told you sooner.

MALCOLM Excuse me.

MALCOLM *jumps up and walks off.*

A beat.

CRAIG Listen, Archie – there was someone in my office recently with a similar problem and we took them out to Switzerland . . .

KEVIN To Dignitas?

CRAIG No, no – to one of the top surgeons out there. And he had the best treatment possible.

KEVIN Did he survive?

CRAIG No. But he had a private room, 52-inch plasma and all the channels.

ARCHIE Thanks, Craig, but I've talked it over with Susie and we just want to make it as normal as possible for the kids' sake. So, if you would do me the honour, the very great honour of allowing me to get this bill – probably for the last time . . .

KEVIN Don't say that . . .

ARCHIE Just in case, Kevin. It really would mean the world to me.

CRAIG Of course. Thanks, Archie.

CRAIG *reaches out and grips* ARCHIE*'s hand.* KEVIN *joins in.*

KEVIN If you want, we can pay the tip.

ARCHIE No, it's fine, Kevin. I'll pay all of it. It's just nice to spend what time I've got left amongst friends.

MALCOLM *comes marching back from the toilet brandishing his phone.*

MALCOLM You lying fucking monster!

ARCHIE Eh?

MALCOLM I've just texted Susie. She doesn't know anything about a tumour – he's lying. He's a liar!

KEVIN Is this true, Archie?

ARCHIE I haven't told her yet – I wanted you to know first . . .

CRAIG But you said you talked it over . . .

MALCOLM I can't believe you'd pretend to be dying just so you can pay for a tapas meal.

ARCHIE Well, I can't believe you'd ring up to check! Texting a dying man's wife to check out his story.

MALCOLM You're not dying though, are you!

KEVIN I can't take much more of this.

MALCOLM How dare you. How dare you try and swindle your way into paying for this meal.

ARCHIE You've driven me to it, Malcolm. You're a control freak! Why can't I have a pat on the back – 'Good old Archie!' for a change. Swooping in and claiming every act of generosity . . .

CRAIG You're both unbelievable. The pair of you. Ridiculous behaviour. All this strutting around, point scoring – it's pathetic.

ARCHIE You're the one who was happy for his kids to be burnt to death just so he could flash his gold card.

CRAIG What?

MALCOLM Right – give me that bill.

MALCOLM *goes to grab the bill from the table.* ARCHIE *grabs his arm and they scuffle.* KEVIN *jumps up to try and stop the fight.* CRAIG *joins in, trying to wrestle the bill free from* MALCOLM *and* ARCHIE.

MALCOLM *(cont'd)* I'm paying this bill!

ARCHIE You're not!

KEVIN Let go of him!

CRAIG Give it to me!

ANYA *(V.O.)* STOP THIS NOW!

The shout from ANYA *stops the men in their tracks.*

ANYA Stop it! Or I call the police.

CRAIG Sorry.

ANYA There is no one else here now. I need to close the restaurant. The manager say this meal can be at the home.

KEVIN She means on the house.

ANYA Yes. Please, let me take the bill and we all go home.

They all consider this utterly reasonable solution.

MALCOLM No. We're going to settle this once and for all. It's not about the bill. It's gone beyond that now.

KEVIN Look – shall we just split it four ways? I'm happy to put in for the drink. Even though I never had any.

MALCOLM Miss, would you bring us the sharpest knife you have in your kitchen, please?

ANYA No. The matter is closed. There is no bill.

ARCHIE There's always a bill. Someone has to pay.

MALCOLM *walks off to the kitchen.*

CRAIG Look – whatever you're thinking about doing, I would probably advise against it. There must be an alternative.

KEVIN What *is* he doing, Archie?

ARCHIE I know.

MALCOLM *returns with a long thin knife from the kitchen. He also carries a chopping board. He clears a space on the table and sits down. The others stand around, watching expectantly.*

MALCOLM Stab Scotch, also known as Pin Finger, Nerve . . .

ARCHIE Or Five Finger Fillet.

MALCOLM Archie and I have played this since school. We used a compass then.

ARCHIE Or the sharp end of a 2B pencil.

MALCOLM The rules are very simple. You pass the knife between every finger and back again five times. Fastest time wins and the winner pays the bill. Agreed, Archie?

ARCHIE If you wish, yes.

MALCOLM Kevin, could you time this, please?

KEVIN Malcolm, wait. Think what you're doing. We've got the county semis coming up in Doncaster. We can't have you butchering yourself like this . . .

MALCOLM I'll be all right. I know what I'm doing.

MALCOLM *puts his hand on the chopping board and sets the knife to one side of his thumb.*

CRAIG I'm not sure I want to go through with this . . .

ARCHIE You don't have to. This is between me and Malcolm now.

MALCOLM Tell me when.

KEVIN *looks at his watch. He waits ages.*

KEVIN Sorry – I'm just waiting for it to get to the top.

CRAIG Oh look – I'll do it on my phone.

CRAIG *gets his iPhone out and sets the stopwatch.*

ANYA I cannot allow this.

MALCOLM Don't watch then.

CRAIG Shhhhhhhh. Three, two, one, go!

MALCOLM *begins stabbing back and forth between his fingers. It is horrible to watch. The others watch with bated breath.* MALCOLM *completes the challenge.*

MALCOLM Done!

CRAIG *stops the clock.*

CRAIG Twenty-three seconds.

MALCOLM Good. Not bad.

MALCOLM *gets up and shakes his hands out.*

ARCHIE Well done.

ARCHIE *takes the seat at the table. He picks up the knife.*

KEVIN This isn't fair. He might have double vision because of his tumour . . .

CRAIG He hasn't got a tumour, remember?

KEVIN Oh yeah. Carry on.

ARCHIE*'s hand is trembling holding the knife.*

MALCOLM I'm happy to pay the bill now – and we'll all go home.

ARCHIE No thank you, Malcolm. I'm fine. When you're ready, Craig . . .

CRAIG *gets ready with the stopwatch.*

CRAIG Three, two, one – go!

ARCHIE *starts stabbing between his fingers. He is cautious to start with. Slower than* MALCOLM.

ARCHIE How long?

CRAIG Fifteen seconds.

ARCHIE *starts to speed up. As he does he begins to nick his fingers – they are bleeding but he carries on.*

CRAIG *(cont'd)* Stop!

KEVIN Stop now, Archie! You're bleeding!

ANYA Make him stop!

CRAIG *tries to grab the knife from* ARCHIE *and pulls his arm backwards from the table. In the struggle* ARCHIE*'s arm swings backwards over* CRAIG*'s shoulder, passing right in front of* ANYA.

CRAIG Get off!!

ARCHIE *appears shocked – so* CRAIG *turns to see what he is looking at.* ANYA *is standing there looking slightly dazed. Her head tips backwards and blood seeps from a cut right across her neck. She drops to the floor, gurgling. Everyone just stares, not knowing what to do. Finally* MALCOLM *checks the body.*

KEVIN *turns to* CRAIG.

KEVIN What did you do that for?

CRAIG I didn't do anything.

ARCHIE It wasn't his fault. It was an accident.

MALCOLM Get me some napkins . . .

KEVIN *grabs a handful of pink cloth napkins and tries to staunch the flow of blood.*

KEVIN What do we do? Shall I call an ambulance? Police . . .? What?

CRAIG I don't know. Is she alive?

MALCOLM Only just. Her windpipe's been severed.

ARCHIE Give me that knife.

ARCHIE *takes the knife from a bemused* CRAIG. *He wipes it down.*

KEVIN Archie, what shall I do? Shall I phone the police?

ARCHIE Give me your phone.

ARCHIE *walks to the back of the room.*

KEVIN I haven't got much credit left – but it's fine. Use it . . .

MALCOLM *gets up with blood on his shirt.*

MALCOLM She's dead.

CRAIG Oh God, no.

MALCOLM Look – we've got to get our story straight. It was Archie that did it. You were trying to stop him.

CRAIG I *was* trying to stop him.

MALCOLM Yeah, and that's what we'll say.

KEVIN Do we mention the stab cock?

MALCOLM What?

KEVIN The game – the fillet o' finger?

MALCOLM No, it's irrelevant. We'll just say we were arguing over the bill and all of a sudden he grabbed a knife. He's got cuts on his hand anyway . . .

ARCHIE *comes back and gives* KEVIN *his phone.*

ARCHIE Right – it's been sorted. We all need to disappear and this will be dealt with.

CRAIG What do you mean?

ARCHIE The less you know the better. Don't let your wives or girlfriends see you. Get rid of your clothes, get clean, have showers. Clean your showers.

CRAIG You sound like you do this on a weekly basis.

ARCHIE You don't spend time in prison without making contacts. People who watch your back.

MALCOLM What – while they're bumming you?

ARCHIE Fine. I'll cancel it then. We'll phone the police instead.

CRAIG I can't be here, guys. This was just meant to be a tapas meal with the badminton people. I'm going home tomorrow!

KEVIN But what about the girl? Surely she'll be missed?

ARCHIE You heard what she said. She's only just moved here. She's probably illegal anyway. It's a risk we'll have to take.

KEVIN Malcolm?

MALCOLM OK, do it.

MALCOLM *picks up his bag as if to go.*

ARCHIE Right, well, before we go, we need to sort out the money.

MALCOLM Oh, you can pay it, Archie, I'm not bothered now.

ARCHIE No, I mean for this. The clean-up. It's not a free service, you know. I've not got a couple of coupons.

CRAIG How much does he want?

ARCHIE Two hundred . . .

KEVIN That's actually very reasonable.

KEVIN *gets out his purse.* MALCOLM *clarifies.*

MALCOLM Thousand.

KEVIN I haven't got that.

ARCHIE It's all right – we'll split it four ways.

MALCOLM What, 50 grand each?

ARCHIE Yeah.

KEVIN I'm assuming there's no tip.

CRAIG I can get it wired first thing in the morning.

ARCHIE It has to be cash. And he wants it tonight.

MALCOLM That's just unrealistic. It's half-eleven.

KEVIN Now I didn't actually touch the knife so technically I think I probably owe less . . .

ARCHIE Oh, here we go!

KEVIN No, no – I'm just saying my involvement amounts to considerably less . . .

MALCOLM Look, how are we supposed to have that kind of money?

CRAIG *gets his phone out and starts ringing.*

CRAIG I have. Anoushka – it's me again. I need you to go back into my room and go into the right-hand wardrobe, NOT the left, do not go in the left – in there you'll find a grey safe. I want you to open it. The number is . . .

CRAIG *accidentally steps on the dead hand of* **ANYA**.

ANYA Ouch!

Everybody freezes.

CRAIG *looks at* **ANYA**, *who is biting her tongue but in pain.* **CRAIG** *looks up at the group.*

MALCOLM Oh, she's still alive!

ARCHIE But we'll still need the money to clean everything up, won't we . . .?

KEVIN *interrupts, suddenly much more assertive than he has been up to now.*

KEVIN Forget it, it's over. She's blown it.

ANYA *now speaks in a Lancashire accent.*

ANYA He stood on my hand. Don't blame me.

MALCOLM So close. We'd have had him if you'd kept your mouth shut.

CRAIG Anoushka, I'll call you back.

CRAIG *hangs up and looks round at the others.*

CRAIG *(cont'd)* What's going on?

KEVIN I would have thought that was obvious.

ARCHIE Do you really have 200 grand in your right-hand-side wardrobe?

ANYA Never mind that – I want to know what's in the left-hand side?

CRAIG Archie – what is this?

ARCHIE It's a wash-out. I told you it was too elaborate.

KEVIN It was going fine. It's just geography – he stood on her hand.

MALCOLM And she's going way over the top with that accent, it's barely believable now. 'Can I offer you guys to be shot?'

ANYA Piss off, Gerry, you couldn't do it. And you were the one who mentioned Susie. No names, remember?

KEVIN All right, that's enough! Go and clean yourself up.

ANYA *departs.* **KEVIN** *stares at* **CRAIG**.

KEVIN *(cont'd)* I'm afraid I'm going to have to ask for your phone.

CRAIG What? Why?

ARCHIE *picks up the knife from the table.*

ARCHIE We can't have you ringing the police, can we?

CRAIG You just tried to rob me of £200,000.

MALCOLM You got a free meal out of it.

CRAIG So it's all been a scam? *(To* ARCHIE*)* I thought we were friends?

ARCHIE Think of it as a holiday bromance. And you are very rich.

KEVIN Hand it over.

CRAIG Sorry, no. I'm not going to do that.

KEVIN Well then – we've got a bit of a problem, haven't we.

ARCHIE *toys with the bloody knife.* CRAIG *is surrounded.*

INT. RESTAURANT. NIGHT.

We drift over a few empty tables, listening to a familiar voice holding court. We see MALCOLM *with* ANYA *sat next to him;* KEVIN *and* ARCHIE *are either side of a new face –* TIM*, their latest victim. He smiles enthusiastically at* MALCOLM*'s story.*

MALCOLM So Jack had chosen a horse at three to one, what was it called . . .?

ARCHIE Hoof Hearted.

MALCOLM Hoof Hearted, and I'd gone for the favourite, Mashie Niblick.

ARCHIE Excuse me, can we have the bill, please?

ARCHIE *gestures to the waiter, who turns to reveal that he is in fact* CRAIG.

CRAIG Certainly, sir. Won't be a second.

CRAIG *looks round at* KEVIN*, who gives him a little nod.*

THE END

Episode 3

THE RIDDLE OF THE SPHINX

CAST LIST

NINA – Alexandra Roach

SQUIRES – Steve Pemberton

TYLER – Reece Shearsmith

EXT. CAMBRIDGE UNIVERSITY. NIGHT.

The quad of one of Cambridge University's elite colleges. The moon picks out a FIGURE *scurrying across the lawn in the dead of night.*

INT. CORRIDOR. NIGHT.

The FIGURE *stealthily tiptoes down the corridor and stops in front of one of the doors. They slide a hand along the top of the cubby hole next to the door before finding a key.*

We stay on the cubby hole, which indicates that the room is number 9.

TITLE: 'The Riddle of the Sphinx'.

INT. PROF. SQUIRES' ROOM. NIGHT.

A room in darkness. There are lots of academic books lined up on shelves, a large blackboard used for lectures and seats laid out for private seminars. In one corner is a table with tea- and coffee-making facilities. The curtains are closed.

The room is quite cluttered and messy, with papers and reference books scattered across the desk. Many old newspapers are piled up in one corner of the room. There is a covered easel near the blackboard.

Slowly the door creaks open and the FIGURE *enters carrying a torch. The beam searches the room, picking out various items of academia. The torch beam finds a trophy cabinet with several small silver cups and rosettes inside.*

On top there is a photograph of a donnish-looking man, PROFESSOR SQUIRES, *in front of a large filled-in crossword puzzle. He is proudly holding one of the cups with his wife Monica by his side. A shabby bearded man stands beside him applauding glumly.*

The FIGURE *then moves across to the easel and removes the cover, revealing a large, over-sized 15-squared crossword grid.*

Suddenly the room's main light comes on. The FIGURE *at the easel is revealed to be a youngish girl,* NINA, *who is wearing a short dress and a leather jacket. She screams.*

NINA Aarghh!

PROFESSOR NIGEL SQUIRES *stands in the doorway, having just switched on the light. He is wearing pyjamas and a dressing gown. He holds a walking stick in one hand and a pistol in the other.*

SQUIRES What's going on? Who are you?

NINA Oh, for God's sake! Oh, you scared the living crap out of me, Jesus!

NINA *clutches her chest.* SQUIRES *is concerned.*

SQUIRES Are you all right?

NINA Yeah, I just need to sit down for a second. Shit.

NINA *sits.*

SQUIRES I'm sorry, I didn't mean to startle you . . .

NINA That's all right. You haven't got a towel, have you?

SQUIRES Yes.

SQUIRES *fetches a towel from the kitchen area and* NINA *dries her hair.*

NINA Thanks. It's wetter than a nun's cucumber out there. Could you put the gun down, please?

SQUIRES Of course. It's not loaded, it was just a prop from a student production of *The Seagull* . . .

SQUIRES *puts the gun down.*

SQUIRES *(cont'd)* Can I ask what you're doing in my rooms? I presume you didn't break in for a towel.

NINA I didn't break in – well, not technically. My boyfriend says professors always keep a key on top of their glory hole, so I just sort of let myself in. It was a stupid thing to do, I'm so sorry.

SQUIRES And you are . . .?

NINA Nina. Nina . . . Noonah.

SQUIRES Nina Noonah.

NINA Yes. Well, not really, obviously, but I don't want to get in any trouble. You won't ring the police, will you? I'm such an idiot, I never should have come . . .

NINA *becomes upset.*

SQUIRES It's all right, Miss Noonah, my bark is worse than my bite. Just tell me why you are here. Is it rag week?

NINA No! I'm not due for another fortnight, not that it's any of your business. The thing is, Simon, my boyfriend, is a student at King's College. He's properly clever, with a bike and a scarf and all the Harry Potter shit, and he's sort of obsessed with doing the crossword. Not the quick one, with a picture of Vanessa Feltz in the middle like you get in *Chat* magazine, I mean the cryptic.

SQUIRES I see.

NINA And I try and help him sometimes and I look at the clues and I feel like such a div because I can't make head nor tail of them – they may as well be written in Chinese.

SQUIRES In Mandarin, yes – and you are a student also?

NINA God, no, I work at Greggs. I'm more – whatsit? – emotionally intelligent.

SQUIRES Sadly that won't help with the cryptic.

NINA Tell me about it! Anyway, Simon reckons that you're the Spinx or something – you set the crossword in the student paper?

SQUIRES That's correct. Crossword setters traditionally use a pseudonym – a made-up name . . .

NINA Like Nina Noonah!

SQUIRES Yes, and I am known as Sphinx. It's not exactly a secret, especially here on campus.

NINA Anyway, I thought if I could see the answers to this week's crossword then I could sit with Simon and I'd be like, 'Oh, 18 down, isn't that "parachute"?' and he'd be like, 'Yeah, wow, you're so clever,' and . . . it was only meant to be a joke. I'm so sorry.

SQUIRES No, I quite understand. We all crave approbation on some level. What does your boyfriend study, Miss Noonah?

NINA Architecture.

SQUIRES Ah, architecture. Well, I teach.

NINA Yeah, I know. I didn't think you were a student! Simon said you teach classics – is that like *Gone with the Wind* and *Pretty Woman* and stuff?

SQUIRES I teach wild creature without hospital building.

NINA Sorry?

SQUIRES *writes the sentence up on the board.*

SQUIRES I teach wild creature without hospital building. Twelve letters.

NINA Oh, it's a clue.

SQUIRES Yes. Not a very good one, I admit, as you put me on the spot. So. A cryptic clue always offers up two means of solution. The beginning or the end of the sentence is the *definition* of the word, much as you might get in a standard vanilla crossword.

And the rest of the clue is the *wordplay*, if you like, which is a kind of riddle.

NINA Yeah, like on *Catchphrase*!

SQUIRES In a manner of speaking. So here we have a 12-letter word meaning 'I teach' or 'building'. Now, in the middle we have the word 'wild', which is what we refer to as an 'anagram indicator'. It suggests that the letters can be jumbled up and rearranged, so anything such as 'upset', 'excited', 'insane' . . .

NINA 'Mashed up'!

SQUIRES Yes, if you like . . .

NINA 'Wankered'.

SQUIRES That . . . type of thing – it tells us to mix up the letters. So if we take the words 'I', 'teach' and 'creature' and make them 'wild' we might come up with the solution.

NINA OK . . . but that's too many letters.

SQUIRES Very good! We're two letters over, so we look here, 'without hospital'. What could hospital be?

NINA H?

SQUIRES Yes, but we need two letters. If you were to have an accident, if I'd shot you here in the dark . . .

NINA With an empty gun? Good luck.

SQUIRES But if I had, then you'd head straight for . . . which department?

NINA A&E?

SQUIRES Excellent, so if we remove A and E from 'creature' – i.e. 'creature without hospital' – and mix it up with 'I teach' . . .

SQUIRES *hurriedly writes all this up on the board.*

SQUIRES *(cont'd)* Then we find an anagram of 12 letters meaning 'building' . . .

NINA Sorry, what?

SQUIRES Which is . . . 'architecture'! 'I teach, wild, creature without hospital . . .' You see? Not so hard, was it?

NINA Er, if you say so.

SQUIRES The sentence has a surface reading, which makes perfect sense in and of itself, but when you break it down to its component parts it reveals a whole new meaning, hiding in plain sight, as it were.

NINA Right. So is that in this week's crossword?

SQUIRES No, no, I haven't parsed it properly – I buried the anagram indicator in the fodder – it was merely an illustration.

NINA Like Pictionary? Can you draw it?

SQUIRES No, I was . . . I was showing off. Trying to give you some insight. I'm sorry.

NINA Cool. Oh well, thanks anyway, Professor. Sorry I woke you.

SQUIRES It's Nigel.

NINA Nina.

They shake hands. NINA *heads for the door.* SQUIRES *is reluctant to see her leave.*

SQUIRES If you like I can show you the clues to tomorrow's crossword? See if any of them make sense?

NINA You'd teach me?

SQUIRES Yes.

NINA 'I teach wild creature'?

SQUIRES It's not quite *Pygmalion*, but I can give you some pointers. Here . . .

SQUIRES *opens the drawer and pulls out a sheet of crossword clues. He points to the blank crossword on the easel.*

SQUIRES *(cont'd)* The answers all go in this grid. Have a look at one across and I'll make us some tea.

SQUIRES *hands over the clues and goes to prepare two cups of tea in the corner.*

NINA 'To wound and wander destitute.' Four, three, three. Is it another nanagram?

SQUIRES Possibly . . . look for a verb or an adjective which suggests movement.

NINA 'Wander'?

SQUIRES Bingo!

NINA *writes 'TO WOUND AND' on the board. She looks at it for a while, trying to make an anagram.*

NINA So how many of these have you done?

SQUIRES Crosswords? Four or five hundred.

NINA Wow. You must have a very devious mind.

SQUIRES It has been said. The Sphinx was a mythical creature of Greek legend, a woman's head on a lion's body. She guarded the gates of the ancient city of Thebes and any traveller wishing to pass through had to solve her riddle. If they failed the test she would kill them by means of asphyxiation and then eat the remains.

NINA No pressure then.

SQUIRES She was devious and deadly, perfect for a cryptic crossword setter.

NINA 'Down and out'. Meaning 'destitute'.

NINA *writes in one across on the grid.*

SQUIRES Excellent. 'By Jove, she's got it!' Have some refreshment.

SQUIRES *brings over the tea tray.* NINA *crosses to look at the trophy cabinet.*

NINA So is that what all the cups are for?

SQUIRES Sorry?

NINA In the cabinet.

SQUIRES Ah yes. The Cambridge Cruciverbalist Club, the C.C.C. Much like the K.K.K. only slightly less benevolent. We have bi-monthly meetings if you or your boyfriend were interested?

NINA *picks up the framed photo of* SQUIRES *winning the cup.*

NINA Is this your wife?

SQUIRES Yes, Monica.

NINA Does she do the crossword?

SQUIRES She did – she died last year.

NINA Oh, I'm sorry. Did you have kids?

SQUIRES No, no. 'There is no more sombre enemy of good art than the pram in the hall.'

NINA You've certainly won a lot.

NINA *replaces the photo and joins* SQUIRES *at the table.*

NINA *(cont'd)* It's not exactly the boat race though, is it?

SQUIRES How do you mean?

NINA You can't beat somebody at a crossword, can you?

SQUIRES Oh, competitive solving is quite combative, believe me. Blood has been spilt, metaphorically of course. What's black and white and red all over? The Cambridge Crossword Competition.

NINA Or a nun chewing a razor blade.

SQUIRES Or a penguin with sunburn.

NINA Oh, I've got one! It's quite rude though.

SQUIRES I teach Catullus, dear, I'm hardly a prude.

NINA What's long and hard and full of semen? A submarine.

SQUIRES Ah, very good. And what's pink and hard in the mornings?

NINA A cock?

SQUIRES The *Financial Times* crossword.

SQUIRES *smiles but looks uncomfortable at where the conversation has led.*

SQUIRES *(cont'd)* Have a look at two down.

NINA 'This cover sounds like a 50 Cent song.' Does that mean a cover version?

SQUIRES 'Sounds like' indicates a homophone. Do you know what a homophone is?

NINA No idea. Is it an app for gays, like Grindr?

SQUIRES No, it's two words which are spelled differently but sound the same. Like 'their' and 'there'.

NINA *(confused)* Where?

SQUIRES What do you call a fish with no eyes?

NINA Oh, you're confusing me now!

SQUIRES Fsh. You see? That's a homophone-based joke, 'eyes' and the letter 'I' – it's cryptic.

NINA Which bit's the joke?

SQUIRES Think of a word meaning 'cover', which *sounds* like a type of song. Beginning with W.

NINA 'Wrap'!

SQUIRES Correct. That's two in two minutes! You'll be challenging for the cup before long.

SQUIRES *gets up and writes in 'WRAP' for two down.*

SQUIRES *(cont'd)* And one down, 'Indian national product of French-Italian agreement', is simply 'of' in French . . .

SQUIRES *writes in 'DE'.*

SQUIRES *(cont'd)* Followed by an Italian form of agreement . . .

SQUIRES *writes in 'SI'.*

SQUIRES *(cont'd)* To make 'DESI', meaning a person from India.

NINA I'm sorry but how the f— . . . fsh is *anyone* supposed to get that? Why do you have to use such difficult words?

SQUIRES Every word is chosen for its letters, Nina. The creation of a crossword is a very precise art and it's the setter's job to confound and bamboozle. For example, have a look at 18 across . . .

NINA *reads the clue as* SQUIRES *chalks it up.*

NINA 'Tory leader on board for English flower.' So it's a five-letter word for a Tory leader.

SQUIRES Or?

NINA An English flower. Daisy!

SQUIRES No.

NINA Poppy!

SQUIRES Don't guess, Nina, dear. Deduct.

SQUIRES *hands* NINA *the chalk and she approaches the blackboard.*

SQUIRES *(cont'd)* And don't take anything for granted. What could Tory leader be?

NINA Boris?

SQUIRES No, look at the word . . .

NINA T!

SQUIRES Yes, the leader of Tory is T. Put T onto a four-letter word for 'board' . . .

NINA Plank!

SQUIRES Four letters.

NINA Wood! Twood.

SQUIRES Board has more than one meaning, remember . . .

NINA Fed up?

SQUIRES No . . .

NINA Erm . . . cardboard? Snowboard . . .

SQUIRES The kind of board that you pay.

NINA Exam board?

SQUIRES No, rent. You pay to 'board' somewhere. So Tory leader 'T' on 'rent' gives us?

NINA 'TRENT'. That's not a flower.

SQUIRES Who said it was a flower?

NINA You did.

SQUIRES No, you said flower, but what I actually wrote was 'flow-er'. Something that flows – in this case an English river called the Trent.

NINA Oh my goodness, that's so clever.

NINA *writes 'TRENT' on the crossword grid.*

NINA *(cont'd)* I knew you were devious!

NINA *sits and has some tea. She watches as* SQUIRES *sips from his tea. They smile.*

NINA It's very satisfying, isn't it?

SQUIRES It is. So your boyfriend is reading architecture at King's, is that correct?

NINA Yeah. There's a joke about erections, but I can't quite . . .

SQUIRES Is he studying under Pugh or Fairbrother?

NINA Er, the first one.

SQUIRES And how's he getting on with old Pugh?

NINA Oh, he likes him.

SQUIRES Gladys Pugh.

NINA He likes her.

SQUIRES You do realise that Pugh and Fairbrother are characters from the comedy series *Hi-de-Hi!*

NINA I haven't seen it.

SQUIRES Well, lucky you. So, Simon, if that's his real name, isn't a student at all. He's a 'muggle', just like you. Why did you lie?

NINA I didn't think you'd take me seriously otherwise.

SQUIRES Does he work in Greggs also?

NINA He's a bookkeeper.

SQUIRES Ah, the only word in the English language with three consecutive doubles: double O, double K, double E. You must be very proud.

NINA Don't patronise me, Professor Squires. I only want to learn.

SQUIRES Of course.

SQUIRES *gets up and approaches the board. He writes up the next clue.*

SQUIRES *(cont'd)* Nine across: 'Degas evacuated and bathed before putting big picture in bog.'

NINA Oh for fuck's sake . . .

SQUIRES *writes up 'DEGAS'.*

SQUIRES Patience, Nina, dear. 'Degas evacuated' – if you evacuate something then you clear it out, so we lose the middle letters to get 'DS' – with me? 'Bathed' is another word for 'swam', so 'bathed before' means we put 'SWAM' in front of 'DS'. Then 'putting big picture in', we need to insert a word for 'big picture', a grand scheme, a . . .

NINA Plan.

SQUIRES Plan, precisely, so we put 'PLAN' between 'SWAM' and 'DS' to get 'SWAMPLANDS' meaning 'bog'. Yes?

NINA Er . . .

SQUIRES Yes?

NINA Shouldn't it be 'bogs'?

SQUIRES No, not necessarily.

SQUIRES *coughs.*

NINA Cos you said it has to be precise.

SQUIRES It is precise, not a word wasted.

NINA Otherwise it would be cheating, wouldn't it?

SQUIRES I never cheat. Never!

SQUIRES *coughs some more.* NINA *passes him his cup.*

NINA Sorry, I didn't . . . here, have something to drink.

SQUIRES *sits and empties his tea.*

NINA *(cont'd)* Let's have a bash at three down, that should be easy. 'A disturbed setter concealed tiny amount? Why it's enough to take one's breath away.' Hmm, well, the crossword 'setter' is you, Mr Sphinx – have you concealed a tiny amount? Maybe.

SQUIRES *looks on, red-faced and wheezing now, seemingly unable to breathe.* NINA *writes the letters into the grid as she speaks.*

NINA *(cont'd)* So it's 'A' followed by an anagram of 'SPHINX'; 'tiny amount' is 'IOTA' – also the ninth letter of the Greek alphabet, as I'm sure you know, Professor Squires – and 'Why' is a homophone for the letter 'Y' . . .

NINA *adds the letter 'Y' to the other letters.*

NINA *(cont'd)* Meaning 'to take one's breath away'.

NINA *writes the word 'ASPHYXIATION' into three down.*

She has subtly changed her character, dropping the dim-girl act.

NINA *(cont'd)* Rather prescient, don't you think? I spotted it as soon as I saw the clues. Some fairly easy ones this week, I thought, a little bit 'vanilla' for the King of the Cambridge Cruciverbalists . . .

NINA *fills in some of the other clues on the grid.* SQUIRES *is breathing sporadically now, seemingly paralysed in his chair.*

NINA *(cont'd)* 'Dickens character undertakes to be a cabinet maker.' That's obviously 'SOWERBERRY' from *Oliver Twist*. You'll be needing his services pretty soon. 'Some smart-aleck, no wit allegedly.' 'KNOW IT ALL'.

We see the letters inside 'smart alecK NO WIT ALLegedly'.

NINA *(cont'd)* But you don't know it all, do you, Prof? You didn't know, for example, that I study marine biology. 'What's the *porpoise* of that?' you might ask. Well, for one, I was able to get hold of some tetrodotoxin from the liver of a puffer fish. Highly toxic, as all the best sushi chefs know, and if consumed in, say, a cup of tea, will lead to the gradual paralysis of the internal organs, starting with the diaphragm. Resulting in respiratory failure and death by three down. The asphyxiation of the Sphinx.

NINA *fills in some more of the crossword as she speaks.* SQUIRES *can only look on, immobile.*

NINA *(cont'd)* Simon was my brother. He got to the final of the crossword competition six years ago, the first non-student ever to do so. And he won. He beat you fair and square. But you challenged him on the word 'AUTEUR' – do you remember? Said the first 'U' looked more like a 'V'. And the committee found in your favour – the Old Boys network looking after their own – so Simon was disqualified. And do you know what he did? Do you, you pathetic old man? He hung himself.

NINA *is now looking directly at* SQUIRES, *who stares at her for a moment before breaking into normal speech.*

SQUIRES I'm afraid that's incorrect, Miss Noonah. Pictures can be 'hung', people are 'hanged'. 'He hanged himself' would be the correct conjugation, for which, of course, you have my deepest sympathy.

NINA *is in a state of shock.* SQUIRES *gets up from his chair.*

NINA What . . .? No, what the fuck? You're supposed to be dead!

SQUIRES On the contrary, I'm very much alive. It's you who are dead.

NINA *is confused.*

SQUIRES *(cont'd)* Will you permit me?

SQUIRES *takes the pen from* NINA.

SQUIRES *(cont'd)* Twenty-two down: 'What is a frankfurter's number one bun? Don't start!' Well, if we don't start 'one' or 'bun' we get 'NEUN', which is a number if you come from Frankfurt. And 23 down: 'The Origins of a Species popularised savage serpents'. 'Origins' meaning the first letters of . . .

SQUIRES *writes them into the grid. 'ASPS'*

SQUIRES *(cont'd)* 'A Species Popularised Savage', giving us the serpents.

NINA So?

SQUIRES There it is, hiding in plain sight.

SQUIRES *circles the unchecked letters on a diagonal through the crossword, revealing the hidden message 'I SWAPPED CUPS'.*

SQUIRES *(cont'd)* I swapped cups. Very prescient, as you say, but the individual's urge for self-preservation is a strong one.

NINA *launches herself at* SQUIRES, *but she is weakening and he can quite easily hold her off.*

NINA You bastard!

SQUIRES Please. No unnecessary violence.

NINA *dashes over to the waste-paper bin and kneels by it, sticking her fingers down her throat and gagging.*

SQUIRES *(cont'd)* I shouldn't bother, the toxin is already swimming around in your bloodstream by now, as well you know. Now who's pathetic?

SQUIRES *crosses to the telephone and dials a number.*

SQUIRES *(cont'd) (into phone)* It's me. Yes, she is, I think your services will be required.

SQUIRES *hangs up.*

SQUIRES *(cont'd)* That was Dr Tyler, your personal tutor and confidante. He's on his way over with the antidote right now.

NINA *(slurring)* He told you?

SQUIRES Yes.

NINA He wouldn't do that.

SQUIRES I'm afraid he felt it was his duty. A brilliant student halfway through a Masters degree in marine biology but driven by a dark desire for revenge. You needed his expertise to extract the poison from the *poisson* and he came straight to tell me – we go back a long way, Tyler and I. There is indeed an Old Boys network here, but it's more often used for good than bad.

NINA *starts to get up but stumbles.*

SQUIRES *(cont'd)* Here, let me help you . . .

SQUIRES *helps a weakening* NINA *into the chair. Her face and body are numb and she is slurring badly now.*

NINA Why dinnou cawa pleece?

SQUIRES Sorry, what's that?

NINA Why dinn ou caw tha pleece?

SQUIRES Well, why call the police when we could have a little fun with the crossword? These sorts of challenges are what keep one's mind active. I remember your brother, of course . . .

SQUIRES *goes to look at the framed photograph.* SIMON *is the shabby man glumly applauding.*

SQUIRES *(cont'd)* A brilliant mind, but very sloppy handwriting. There's no room for imprecise character formation, the rules are quite clear on that.

NINA Yw che-ed.

SQUIRES He reminded me of myself when I was young. Full of vim and energy, couldn't get the words down quick enough. He wanted to study medicine, I believe? Certainly had a doctor's handwriting. What a waste . . .

SQUIRES *replaces the photograph and looks at his watch.*

SQUIRES *(cont'd)* Well, while we're waiting, let's have a crack at five down: 'Knocked back beer and wine, then put on one French undergarment.' Any thoughts? Well, 'knocked back' is telling us to put something in reverse, in this instance a type of beer – 'PILS' – and a type of wine – 'RED'. And if we 'put on one French', which is 'UN', then we get an undergarment. See? 'UN-DER-SLIP'. Do young girls still wear underslips, I wonder?

NINA *is now paralysed in the chair, only her eyes can show the fear she is feeling.*

SQUIRES *(cont'd)* I always found it quite sexy to have an extra layer to tackle. Made the game rather more interesting.

SQUIRES *moves closer to* NINA. *He puts his face right in hers.*

SQUIRES *(cont'd)* Pretty little thing, aren't you?

SQUIRES *sinisterly kisses* NINA *lightly on the lips.*

SQUIRES *(cont'd)* If only I were 20 years younger.

SQUIRES *heaves himself up.*

SQUIRES *(cont'd)* Now, if you'll excuse me, nature calls.

SQUIRES *exits the room, hobbling on his stick.*

After a few seconds, the door slowly opens and DOCTOR JACOB TYLER *enters. He is a meek-looking man in a polo neck and glasses. He carries a briefcase.*

TYLER *sees* NINA *on the chair. He crosses to her slowly and lifts her head.*

TYLER Charlotte? Charlotte, are you still with us? You hang on in there, OK? Won't be long now.

TYLER *spots the crossword on the easel.*

TYLER *(cont'd)* Ooh, crossword. 'I hear American poet solved the riddle of the pseudo hotel patron.' What? It's a cryptic, I suppose. 'I hear American poet solved the riddle of the pseudo hotel patron . . .'

SQUIRES *enters from the other door.*

SQUIRES 'American poet' is Edgar Guest, Mr E. Guest. A riddle solved is a mystery guessed, and a pseudo hotel patron is a . . .

TYLER 'MYSTERY GUEST'. Very clever.

TYLER *writes the answer in.*

SQUIRES Where have you been? You said you'd be waiting outside.

TYLER I had to go via my office, pick up some things.

SQUIRES It's a bit bloody dangerous leaving me alone with a young girl in that condition. It was all I could do not to slip her one.

TYLER Oh no, I don't think that would be appropriate.

SQUIRES I'm a red-blooded mammal, Tyler, not like those bloody dolphins you spend half your time with. She's still breathing, I take it?

TYLER Yes, the body can survive up to six hours in this state. She can still see and hear and feel everything, she just can't move. It's horrible.

SQUIRES Yes, well, let's not feel too sorry for her. That's what she wanted to do to me, remember?

TYLER You wouldn't have lasted half as long if you'd drunk it. Well, you are getting on.

SQUIRES Brain's still sharp though. I don't mind so much losing the corporeal as long as the cerebral remains intact. Go on then, give her the bloody vaccine and let's send her on her way. *(To* NINA*)* And please remember, Nina Noonah, or whatever your name is, attempted murder is a very serious crime. You're lucky I haven't contacted the authorities. *(To* TYLER*)* Go on then.

TYLER Sorry?

SQUIRES Give her the antidote.

TYLER Oh, there is no antidote.

SQUIRES What?

TYLER For tetrodotoxin poisoning. She needs her stomach pumped, some aggressive airway management and an intravenous drip as soon as possible or she'll be dead within half an hour.

SQUIRES But you said four or five hours?

TYLER Only with hospital treatment.

SQUIRES Shit. Right, well, let's do it then.

TYLER No. There's something I want you to do first.

TYLER *puts his briefcase on the desk and opens it.*

TYLER *(cont'd)* Is that going in this week's *Varsity*?

SQUIRES What?

TYLER The crossword.

SQUIRES Yes, but – what are you doing? What's all this about?

TYLER *has removed a small frying pan and a set of very sharp knives from his case.*

TYLER I want you to eat her. Not all of her, of course, just a sliver. Just enough that you can say you devoured your victim.

SQUIRES *is horrified.* TYLER *remains calm. He crosses to the kitchen corner and turns on one of the hotplates, then adds a little oil to the frying pan.*

SQUIRES Jacob, what . . .? Have you lost your mind?

TYLER When the Sphinx posed her riddle to the Thebans, she strangled and ate anyone who failed to answer correctly. That's right, isn't it? I haven't misremembered it?

SQUIRES Yes.

TYLER What was the riddle again?

SQUIRES *swallows hard.*

SQUIRES I won't do this, Jacob.

TYLER 'What creature walks on four legs in the morning, two legs at noon and three in the evening?' It's like something from a Christmas cracker rather than a Greek tragedy, isn't it? And it was Oedipus that gave the correct answer: man. He crawls as a baby, then walks on two legs before needing a stick in his old age. A bit like you, Nigel.

TYLER *holds up a sharp scalpel-like knife.*

TYLER *(cont'd)* So, do you prefer leg or breast?

SQUIRES Right, that's it, I'm calling the police . . .

SQUIRES *picks up the telephone.*

TYLER And tell them what, exactly? That you're the victim of a student prank? In 25 minutes you'll have a dead girl in your rooms in the middle of the night. You'd found out who she was, she'd threatened you, so you killed her.

SQUIRES No, I'll tell the truth, say it was an accident.

TYLER Then how do you explain this?

TYLER *points to the crossword.*

TYLER *(cont'd)* You compiled this crossword two days ago. It proves pre-meditation. The 'know it all' received a 'mystery guest' and before long there's an 'asphyxiation' . . . What's seven down? 'Catch a train before poisonous bite'? Well, a 'catch' usually stands for 'fish', I know that much. 'A train before' – that could be 'puffer'. So, yeah, 'PUFFER FISH' – you've even concealed the murder weapon. I knew you wouldn't be able to resist.

TYLER *writes 'PUFFER FISH' on the crossword.*

SQUIRES That was just a bit of fun. I was trying to teach the girl . . .

TYLER You're publishing this in the student paper for everyone to see – classic psychopathic behaviour. Tomorrow morning it'll be in every cubby hole in Cambridge and on the inside back page . . . is your confession.

SQUIRES *looks at the crossword, seeming now to damn him.*

TYLER *(cont'd)* And when a 'down and out' finds the girl 'wrapped' in her 'underslip' floating in the 'swamplands' . . . well, the police won't have to look very far for the culprit, will they?

SQUIRES That isn't what happened!

TYLER No, but it could be. Little drive out to the Fens, acquaint our brilliant student with some of the marine life she loves so much.

NINA*'s eyes flicker with fear.*

TYLER *(cont'd)* You see, you're not in charge of this situation. You can't fit it all neatly into a 15-squared grid; this is messy and illogical and out of control. This is my revenge, Nigel. So sit down while I prepare your food.

SQUIRES She's your student, for God's sake!

TYLER *shrugs.*

TYLER Plenty more fish in the sea.

SQUIRES *is utterly shaken. He slumps into his chair.*

TYLER *approaches and rolls* NINA *over onto her side.*

TYLER I think I'll take a bit off the rump.

We stay on NINA*'s face as* TYLER *cuts a small strip of flesh from her buttock, but we don't see it happen.*

TYLER *carries it over to the frying pan and drops it in. It sizzles, like bacon.*

TYLER *(cont'd)* Why don't you tell 'Nina' the story. I bet she'd like to hear it – keep her mind active as her body seizes up.

NINA*'s tear-streaked eyes look out helplessly from her frozen face.* SQUIRES *meets her gaze and reluctantly begins.*

SQUIRES Jacob and I were students here, almost 30 years ago. We roomed together for a while, and then he met Monica, a physicist from Keele.

TYLER *(cooking, matter-of-factly)* They were madly in love . . .

SQUIRES They were madly in love, they married, they even had two children – twins. But Monica and I . . . we began an affair. We used to do the *Observer* crossword together every week in the library and it started from there. *(To* TYLER*)* I didn't mean for it to end the way it did!

TYLER *lifts the cooked flesh out of the pan and onto a plate.*

TYLER I was about to begin my doctorate, which probably would have led to a teaching post and a room of my own, very much like this one. Instead, I divorced my wife and took my babies away to bring them up by myself in the Brecon Beacons.

TYLER *lays the plate in front of* SQUIRES.

TYLER *(cont'd)* Here, the chef recommends this dish medium rare.

I haven't seasoned it – I didn't want to take away from the natural flavour.

SQUIRES Jacob, this is . . . this is preposterous!

TYLER Eat it. Or I let the girl die, and you rot in prison.

SQUIRES *slowly takes up his knife and fork. His hands are shaking.*

TYLER *(cont'd)* It tastes like chicken apparently, but then doesn't everything?

SQUIRES *slowly lifts a piece of the cooked meat to his lips.* NINA *looks on impassively.* SQUIRES *forces himself to put the fork into his mouth. He chews, trying to suppress his gag reflex.*

TYLER *(cont'd)* And so the mighty Sphinx consumes the flesh of his conquest.

TYLER *turns to look at the large crossword grid.*

TYLER *(cont'd)* I always hated cryptic crosswords. Why can't people just say what they mean instead of trying to trick you all the time? How is a flower suddenly a river? How is a sewer a seamstress or a number an anaesthetist? It's bullshit. So when my son started getting into them I wasn't happy. He became obsessed with entering this stupid Cambridge Crossword Competition. Maybe he thought he could re-earn his mother's love by beating her new husband, I don't know.

SQUIRES What . . . Simon was . . . your son?

TYLER He entered himself in the competition under a pseudonym – you knew him as Rex. After *Oedipus Rex*, the play by Sophocles. But you cheated him out of his victory.

SQUIRES But . . . that means . . .

SQUIRES *looks across at* NINA. *She is weeping now, but her face remains immobile.*

TYLER Charlotte and I, we hatched a revenge plan, didn't we? We said we'd bring down that cheating Professor Squires if it was the last thing we did. And it may well be, at least for her.

SQUIRES She's your daughter.

TYLER Mmm. Crazy, isn't it, what the unhinged mind is capable of?

SQUIRES But . . . she came here tonight to kill me, to poison me . . .

TYLER That was the plan.

SQUIRES So, why did you tell me about it? Just so I'd write the crossword?

TYLER Pretty much, yes. I needed leverage.

SQUIRES You . . . you sacrificed your own daughter just to get at me?

TYLER That's the thing, see. When Simon died there was an autopsy and quite a thorough investigation and . . . it seems they're not my kids. They're yours.

SQUIRES *is horrified.*

TYLER *(cont'd)* I always suspected that affair had started before you said it did.

SQUIRES Oh God . . .

SQUIRES *rushes over to* NINA *and takes her head in his hands.*

TYLER So there I was. I'd given everything up – my wife, my home, my job, my entire life . . . all for a lie. So I'm sure you understand, Nigel, why I had to seek my revenge.

SQUIRES Please, help me get her to a hospital . . .

TYLER Oh, I think we're past that now. Just enjoy the time you have left together.

TYLER *checks his watch.*

TYLER *(cont'd)* Anyway, I'd better get back to the cinema – I bought a ticket to the midnight screening at the Arts. I was never here, you see.

SQUIRES *cradles* NINA *in his arms.* TYLER *takes a single bullet from his pocket and lays it on the table.*

TYLER *(cont'd)* There's a little present for you there, Nigel. You know what Anton said: never show a gun in Act One if you're not going to fire it by Act Five. Otherwise people feel cheated.

SQUIRES *sobs.* NINA *is probably dead by now.*

TYLER *stops on his way out and looks at the crossword.*

TYLER *(cont'd)* Isn't your middle name Hector by the way?

SQUIRES Yes.

TYLER How funny . . .

TYLER *circles something on the crossword but we can't read it yet. He leaves.*

SQUIRES *hauls himself up and staggers to the table. He picks up the bullet and goes over to find the gun, leaving us to push in slowly on the crossword.*

TYLER *has circled another hidden message in the grid using unchecked letters in a horizontal line: 'R.I.P.N.H.S.'*

BANG!

A spatter of blood on the crossword. Black and white and red all over.

THE END

Episode 4

EMPTY ORCHESTRA

CAST LIST

GREG – Reece Shearsmith

CONNIE – Tamzin Outhwaite

FRAN – Sarah Hadland

ROGER – Steve Pemberton

JANET – Emily Howlett

DUANE – Javone Prince

CHANTEL – Rebekah Hinds

EXT. KARAOKE CLUB. NIGHT.

Establisher of a karaoke bar in London's West End.

INT. KARAOKE CLUB, CORRIDOR. NIGHT.

GREG *walks down the corridor. He is wearing a large inflatable sumo wrestler outfit. The dull thud of music from adjoining rooms.*

GREG *locates the correct door and enters. We see an illuminated '9' above the door. The light comes on, indicating that the room is in use.*

TITLE: *'Empty Orchestra'.*

INT. KARAOKE BOOTH. NIGHT.

The karaoke room is moodily lit and the walls are partially padded for soundproofing. One of the walls has a large mural.

There is banquette seating around the room, a couple of fixed tables and a large flat-screen for displaying the song lyrics. A separate smaller screen acts as a menu for choosing songs.

GREG *selects a song from the menu, and the Human League's 'Don't You Want Me' starts to play. The sound is rich and full, not tinny.* GREG *picks up a microphone and tests it.*

GREG Hello, hello . . .

The mic is not switched on. GREG *turns it on and his voice is amplified.*

GREG *(cont'd)* Hello. Testing one, two, three . . .

He adjusts the settings to get the correct amount of reverb.

GREG *(cont'd)* 'You were working as a waitress in a cocktail bar / When I met you / I picked you out, I shook you up and turned you around / Turned you into someone new . . .'

GREG *tries the different light settings using a switch by the door. He switches from normal to UV, to glitterball and back to moody.*

GREG *(cont'd)* 'Now five years later on you've got the world at your feet / Success has been so easy for you . . .'

There is a knocking at the door. GREG *opens the door to reveal* CONNIE.

CONNIE *enters, carrying three drinks. She is dressed as Amy Winehouse, with a figure-hugging dress and large beehive.*

She has to duck down as she enters. GREG *carries on singing. The dialogue is very much in the background, sound-wise.*

CONNIE Shit! Nearly snapped my hair off.

GREG 'But don't forget it's me who put you where you are now / And I can put you back down too.'

CONNIE *places the drinks down and takes a big gulp.*

GREG *(cont'd)* 'Don't, don't you want me?'

CONNIE Not dressed like that.

CONNIE *hands* GREG *a drink.*

GREG 'You know I can't believe it when I hear that you won't see me / Don't, don't you want me?'

CONNIE *slides her hand down to* GREG*'s crotch.*

GREG *(cont'd)* Don't! 'You know I don't believe you when you say that you don't need me / It's much too late to find . . .'

CONNIE *kisses* GREG *passionately.*

The lyrics on the screen behind them read 'You'd better change it back or we will both be sorry . . .'

Suddenly the door opens and they spring apart.

FRAN *enters, dressed as schoolgirl Britney Spears. She's carrying a bag of party paraphernalia.*

FRAN Whoooo! 'Don't you want me, baby?' Eh, it's nice, isn't it? Well done, Greg.

FRAN *crosses to kiss* GREG *on the cheek, then goes to put the presents down.*

CONNIE *indicates to* GREG *that he should wipe the lipstick from his face. He continues to sing.* FRAN *sings along.*

GREG/FRAN 'Don't you want me, baby? Don't you want me? Oh!'

CONNIE *has taken up the second microphone.*

CONNIE 'I was working as a waitress in a cocktail bar . . .'

FRAN *has pulled a banner from her bag.*

FRAN *(to* GREG*)* Help me put this up, babe.

CONNIE 'That much is true / But even then I knew I'd find a much better place / Either with or without you. The five years we have had have been such good times / I still love you . . .'

GREG *and* FRAN *stand on the banquette to put up a home-made banner, which reads 'CONGRATULATIONS!' As* CONNIE *sings, she and* GREG *exchange glances.*

CONNIE *looks like she means it.* GREG *looks guilty.* FRAN *sings along blithely unaware.*

CONNIE *(cont'd) (knowingly)* 'But now I think it's time I lived my life on my own / I guess it's just what I must do.'

GREG *jumps down and snatches up the other microphone. His end of the banner falls and the letters drop off the string.*

GREG 'Don't! Don't you want me?'

FRAN Greg! Bloody hell!

FRAN *is peeved. She starts to thread the letters back onto the string.* GREG *sings meaningfully.*

GREG 'You know I can't believe it when I hear that you won't see me / Don't, don't you want me? / You know I don't believe you when you say that you don't need me . . . / It's much too late to find / When you think you've changed your mind / You'd better change it back or we will both be sorry.'

The door opens again and in walk JANET *and* ROGER. JANET *is a young secretary. She is deaf and is dressed as Boy George.*

She is accompanied by ROGER, *the stressed-out boss. He is dressed in a suit and tie. He winces as he enters.*

ROGER Oh God.

FRAN *cheers.*

ROGER *(cont'd)* Hi, everyone. Sorry I'm late.

FRAN No, it's fine! Come in.

JANET *and* ROGER *edge into the room.*

GREG/CONNIE/FRAN 'Don't you want me, baby? Don't you want me? Oh! / Don't you want me, baby? Don't you want me? Oh!'

FRAN Have you not got a costume?

ROGER *produces a flashing red nose and places it onto his own. The effect is tragic rather than fun.*

ROGER *removes his jacket and an envelope drops out.* GREG *goes to pick it up. He sees a list of names on the back with some of them crossed out. His own name has a question mark next to it.*

GREG Is this yours, Roger?

ROGER *quickly snatches the envelope back again and* GREG *resumes the song.*

GREG/CONNIE 'Don't you want me, baby? Don't you want me? Oh! / Don't you want me, baby? Don't you want me? Oh!'

FRAN Do you like it, Rog?

ROGER Yes. I thought it'd be a bit bigger.

FRAN That's what I keep saying to Greg!

CONNIE It's not the size of the boat, Fran, it's the motion of the ocean.

The women cackle. GREG *eyes* ROGER *nervously.* JANET *turns down her hearing aids.*

GREG 'Don't you want me, baby? Don't you want me? Oh! / Don't you want me, baby? Don't you want me? Oh!'

The track comes to an end. Everyone claps.

CONNIE Whoo! Cheers, everyone.

CONNIE *raises her glass. She hands a drink to* ROGER.

CONNIE *(cont'd)* There you go, Roger. And Fran put that up for you.

CONNIE *nods to the banner, which has had its letters put back on in the wrong order.*

ROGER *(reading)* Cuntgrotalaions.

FRAN Eh? *(To* GREG*)* That was your bloody fault. It's meant to say 'Congratulations'.

ROGER Yes, I worked that out.

JANET *Countdown* conundrum.

CONNIE What's that, Janet?

JANET It's like a *Countdown* conundrum.

CONNIE Never seen it.

FRAN Anyway, to Roger! Hope you remember us all now you're heading to the sixth floor!

CONNIE Yeah, to Roger!

They all 'cheers' their drinks.

GREG They're not planning any more lay-offs, are they, Rog?

ROGER Greg, you know I can't divulge . . .

CONNIE Hey, no shop-talk, remember! This is a night of *fun*! Who's next?

FRAN Greg, will you put me down?

GREG Thought you'd never ask.

FRAN For a song, I mean. What's he like?

CONNIE *(loaded)* Don't get him to choose, you'd be waiting forever.

GREG I have chosen, Connie.

FRAN Which one?

The introduction to 'Saturday Night' by Whigfield begins. GREG *looks from* CONNIE *to* FRAN.

GREG 'Dee, dee, na, na, na.'

FRAN Whoooo!

FRAN *screams and grabs the microphone.* ROGER *sighs and closes his eyes wearily.*

ROGER It's not going to be one song after another, is it?

CONNIE You not drinking, Janet?

JANET Duane's getting me one.

CONNIE Is he? Mind he doesn't slip you a roofie!

JANET *is confused. She mimes to* GREG *in sign language: 'Roof?' He signs back: 'A drug.'*

CONNIE *starts the 'Saturday Night' dance with* FRAN*: it's a sort of line-dance with hand moves, claps and turns.*

FRAN Come on, Jan!

FRAN *pulls up a reluctant* JANET *to join the dance.*

FRAN *(cont'd)* 'Saturday night, I feel the air is getting hot / Like you, baby / I'll make you mine, you know I'll take you to the top / I'll drive you crazy . . .'

CONNIE On your feet, Roger!

ROGER No, no, I've got a bit of a headache . . .

CONNIE *pulls* ROGER *into the line.*

ROGER *(cont'd)* I don't know it!

CONNIE You'll pick it up.

GREG *hurries into the line next to* ROGER.

FRAN 'Saturday night, dance, I like the way you move / Pretty baby / It's party time and not one minute we can lose / Be my baby / Da, ba, da, dan, dee, dee, dee, da nee, na, na, na / Be my baby / Da, ba, da, dan, dee, dee, dee, da nee, na, na, na / Pretty baby.'

FRAN *leads* JANET, CONNIE, ROGER *and* GREG *in the dance.*

ROGER *is a beat behind and can't quite get into the rhythm.* JANET *knows the dance but is very shy.* CONNIE *takes the opportunity to do some sexy dancing for* GREG. FRAN *is loving it.*

GREG *tries to talk to* ROGER.

GREG I know you've been waiting on that Butler contract, Roger, and I should have it on your desk by Monday . . .

ROGER *(confused)* What?

Suddenly the door opens and in walks DUANE, *dressed as Michael Jackson. He carries some bottles of beer.*

The dancers are all in a line, facing away from him. DUANE *watches as they dance, until they turn and come face to face with him.* GREG, FRAN *and* CONNIE *cheer.* JANET *smiles.*

FRAN 'Saturday night, I feel the air is getting hot . . .'

CONNIE Where've you been?

FRAN '. . . like you baby.'

DUANE Had to see a man about a dog, innit.

DUANE *hands beers to* JANET, ROGER *and* GREG.

FRAN 'I'll make you mine, you know I'll take you to the top . . .'

JANET Thanks.

FRAN 'I'll drive you crazy.'

DUANE *(to* GREG*)* Cheese and Rice, what have you come as, bruv? Blobby Williams?

FRAN 'Saturday night, dance, I like the way you move / Pretty baby . . .'

GREG They told me it was Gangnam Style.

FRAN 'It's party time and not one minute we can lose / Be my baby.'

During the dance break, DUANE *grabs the mic.*

DUANE All right, peeps, listen up, it's party time! And that means Duane's Famous Pill Roulette!

DUANE *holds up a small velvet bag from his bumbag. He shakes it.*

CONNIE Yeay!

DUANE Inside there's one Ecstasy, one Viagra, one ketamine, one paracetamol, one laxative and one orange Tic Tac.

ROGER Could I please have the paracetamol?

DUANE Sorry Mr C., it's pot luck, I'm afraid.

ROGER *puts his hand in the bag. He pulls out an unseen pill, throws it in his mouth and downs his beer.*

DUANE *(cont'd)* That's the way to do it, straight down the hatch.

ROGER *slumps down heavily.* JANET *looks concerned.* DUANE *shakes the bag and offers it to* FRAN.

FRAN I hope I don't get the ketamine again, it gave me really hard poos.

CONNIE Are you sure it wasn't the Viagra?

FRAN *takes a random pill and downs it.* DUANE *offers the bag to* JANET. *She hesitates.*

DUANE You don't have to, it's fine.

JANET *decides that she will take one after all, to impress* DUANE. *She smiles at* DUANE *and he smiles back.* JANET *swallows her pill.*

CONNIE *watches this, unimpressed. She is next in line, and quickly takes a pill and swallows, then carries on dancing.*

FRAN 'Saturday, Saturday, Saturday night, Saturday night.'

DUANE *offers the bag to* GREG. *He puts his hand in.*

DUANE *takes the last pill for himself and chases it down with his beer. He puts his bumbag on the table and joins the dance.*

ROGER *takes the envelope from his jacket pocket again. He looks at the list of names. He looks up at the group dancing.* **GREG** *eyes him nervously.*

ROGER *crosses out a couple of names and puts a circle round one (we don't see whose).* **GREG** *watches him.*

FRAN *(cont'd)* 'Saturday, Saturday, Saturday night, Saturday night . . .'

DUANE You all right, mate?

GREG *(to* **DUANE***)* Yeah! I'm just shitting myself I got the laxative.

DUANE Well, I'm not changing your nappy.

FRAN 'Saturday, Saturday, Saturday night, Saturday night . . . Saturday, Saturday, Saturday night, Saturday night . . .'

ROGER *shoves the envelope back in his pocket, downs the rest of his drink, then springs up from his seat.*

ROGER Right, we need more drinks.

ROGER *barges out of the room, knocking his jacket onto the floor.* **JANET** *hangs it on the back of the door.*

CONNIE Jesus, he blows hot and cold.

DUANE And which way do you blow?

CONNIE Not yours!

DUANE *smiles, then moon walks back to look at the menu screen.*

FRAN 'Saturday, Saturday, Saturday night, Saturday night. Saturday, Saturday . . .' Bit limited these lyrics, aren't they? '. . . Saturday night . . .'

DUANE *looks across at* **JANET**. *He mimes, 'Are you going to sing?'*

JANET *shakes her head coyly. She mimes, 'Are you?'* **DUANE** *nods: 'Oh yes.'*

CONNIE *clocks this.*

FRAN *(cont'd)* 'Saturday, Saturday, Saturday night, Saturday night . . .' Oh thank God for that.

The song comes to an end. A round of applause for **FRAN**.

FRAN I smell like a meat pie. Who's next? Connie?

CONNIE Not me, I'm tone deaf. No offence, Janet.

JANET *hasn't caught this.*

JANET Sorry? Did you say something?

CONNIE No.

JANET *joins* **DUANE** *to look at the list of songs.*

CONNIE *(cont'd) (to* **FRAN***)* Have you seen this? She's all over him like clingfilm on a buffet.

FRAN She's just letting her hair down.

CONNIE I know she's disabled and everything, but I can't stand her.

FRAN Why?

CONNIE She knows everyone feels sorry for her and she uses it. How do you think she got that PA job?

FRAN I was surprised it wasn't you, Connie.

CONNIE No, I'm not saying that, but it's interesting, isn't it? I bet she's not being laid off any time soon.

GREG *steps in.*

GREG Who's being laid off? What have you heard?

FRAN Nothing! It's a private conversation, we're just having a bit of craic.

CONNIE Yeah, don't go poking your nose into other people's craics, Greg.

CONNIE *looks at* **GREG** *knowingly.*

The intro to 'Wham Rap!' by Wham! begins.

DUANE OK, let's do this. Let's learn to rap like a white man. You ready?

CONNIE/FRAN Yeay!

DUANE 'You got soul on the dole / You're gonna have a good time down on the line / You got soul on the dole / You're gonna have a good time down on the line / I said get get get on down / I said get get get on down / I said get get get on down / I said get get get on down / Hey, everybody take a look at me / I've got street credibility . . .'

CONNIE No, you haven't!

DUANE 'I may not have a job but I have a good time / With the boys that I meet down on the line / I said D. H. S. S. / Man, the rhythm that they're givin' is the very best / I said b-one b-two / Make the claim on your name's all you have to do . . .'

GREG *is speaking to* **JANET** *using sign language. We see the captions for what they're saying.*

JANET I honestly don't think he's made a decision.

GREG But someone's getting sacked, aren't they?

JANET I don't know. I've heard rumours.

GREG Based on sales? Because I know I haven't done as well as some other people this year . . .

GREG *looks across at* **DUANE**.

JANET I don't know, Greg, honestly.

DUANE 'Well, folks can be a drag / If work ain't your bag / And when you let them know / You're more dead than alive / In a nine to five / Then they say you'd got to go and . . .'

CONNIE/FRAN '. . . get yourself a job!'

DUANE 'Or get out of this house.'

CONNIE/FRAN 'Get yourself a job!'

DUANE 'Are you a man or a mouse? / A finger in each ear / You pretend not to hear / Gotta get some space / Get out of this place.'

CONNIE *sees* DUANE*'s bumbag on the table. She surreptitiously leans down and takes out his phone.*

FRAN What you doing?

CONNIE *shushes her. She types a text message using* DUANE*'s phone.* FRAN *reads it and is shocked. She puts her hand over her mouth.* CONNIE *smiles and replaces the phone.*

DUANE 'Wham! Bam! I am a man / Job or no job / You can't tell me that I'm not / Do you enjoy what you do? / If not just stop / Don't stay there and rot.'

GREG *watches* DUANE*, deep in thought. He turns to look at* ROGER*'s jacket on the back of the door. He can see the envelope poking out of the pocket.*

DUANE *(cont'd)* 'On the streets / In the cars / On the underground / If you listen real hard / You can hear the sound / Of a million people / Switching off for work / Well listen, Mr Average / You're a jerk.'

ROGER *re-enters the room. He is carrying a tray of small shot glasses.* GREG *holds the door open for him.*

GREG Let me get that for you!

ROGER *goes and sits in a corner with the tray.*

FRAN Oooh, shots! Thanks, Rog.

ROGER *takes a shot and downs it. He takes another shot and downs it.* CONNIE *and* FRAN *exchange glances. He isn't going to offer anyone else a drink.*

DUANE 'Not me – you can't hold me down / Not me – I'm gonna fool around / Gonna have some fun / Look out for number one / You can dig your grave / I'm staying young / Wham! Bam! I am a man / Job or no job / You can't tell me that I'm not / Do you enjoy what you do? / If not just stop / Don't stay there and rot.' Come on, Greg . . .

DUANE *thrusts the microphone in* GREG*'s face.*

GREG What . . .? Oh . . . 'If you're a pub man or a club man / Maybe a jet-black guy with a hip hi-fi / A white cool cat with a trilby hat / Maybe leather and studs . . .' It's too fast!

DUANE *sings the rest.*

DUANE All right, Greg, it's not a competition! 'Make the most of everyday / Don't let hard times stand in your way / Give a wham, give a bam / But don't give a damn / Cause the benefit gang are gonna pay / Now I reach up high and touch your soul / The boys from Wham! will help you reach that goal / It's gonna break your mama's heart!'

CONNIE/FRAN 'So sad!'

DUANE 'It's gonna break your daddy's heart!'

CONNIE/FRAN 'Too bad!'

DUANE 'But you'll throw the dice and take my advice / Because I know that you're smart.'

JANET *goes across to* **ROGER**, *concerned, but he bats her away and downs another shot. She goes to sit back down.*

JANET *looks at her phone to see a text message has arrived from* **DUANE**. *She looks up at* **DUANE** *and he smiles at her as he sings.*

JANET *opens up the text and reads it: 'I hope you know how much I like you. Do you like me? Sing a song for me tonight and I'll know. Duane xxx'*

JANET *is secretly thrilled and can't hide her excitement.*

CONNIE *and* **FRAN** *watch her.* **CONNIE** *smirks.* **GREG** *slumps down beside them.* **FRAN** *tries to put her arm around him but he moves away.* **CONNIE** *gives* **GREG** *a knowing smile and a wink.*

DUANE *(cont'd)* 'Can you dig this thing? (Yeah!) / Are you gonna get down? (Yeah!) / Say wham! Wham! / Say bam! Bam! / Wham! Bam! I am a man / Job or no job / You can't tell me that I'm not / Do you enjoy what you do? / If not just stop / Don't stay there and rot / Wham! Bam! I am a man / Job or no job / You can't tell me that I'm not / Do you enjoy what you do? / If not just stop / Don't stay there and rot . . .'

The song comes to an end. **DUANE** *bows as the others clap and cheer.*

DUANE *(cont'd)* Thank you! Right, who's next?

JANET *looks like she is going to sing. She nervously half-stands, but then* **ROGER** *suddenly lurches up and grabs the microphone from* **DUANE***'s hand.*

ROGER Me. It's my party, and I want some rock.

JANET *sits back down again.* ROGER *punches a song into the menu screen.*

JANET I . . .

DUANE I'll get some more beers.

DUANE *exits.*

GREG *sits nervously scratching his wrist.* CONNIE *joins him.*

CONNIE What you doing?

GREG It's my eczema, it flares up when I'm stressed.

CONNIE Oh great, so I'm shagging the Singing Detective. So, have you made your choice?

GREG Yeah, I can't decide between 'The Birdie Song' and 'Wind Beneath My Wings'.

CONNIE You know what I mean! Between me and Fran.

JANET *is looking at them from a distance. She looks away guiltily.*

GREG Connie, I can't get into that at the moment. The future's precarious enough.

CONNIE What do you mean?

FRAN *joins them, referring to* ROGER, *who is starting his song. The intro to 'Since You've Been Gone' by Rainbow.*

FRAN What's got into him?

CONNIE Dunno. Maybe he took the E.

GREG He has to sack one of us.

CONNIE What? How do you know?

GREG I just do.

FRAN Do you know who it is?

GREG No, but I think we can find out.

GREG *looks over at* ROGER*'s jacket hanging on the back of the door.*

ROGER 'I get the same old dreams, same time every night / Fall to the ground and I wake up / So I get out of bed, put on my shoes, and in my head / Thoughts fly back to the break-up / These four walls are closing in / Look at the fix you've put me in / Since you been gone, since you been gone / I'm outta my head, can't take it . . .'

JANET *watches. She checks her text again and smiles to herself.*

ROGER *(cont'd)* 'Could I be wrong? / But since you been gone / You cast the spell, so break it / Ohh, whoa, ohh / Since you been gone . . .'

CONNIE *is dancing in front of* ROGER *as he sings.*

ROGER *(cont'd)* 'So in the night I stand beneath the back-street light / I read the words that you sent to me . . .'

CONNIE *looks across at* GREG, *who is making his way crab-like to the door in time to the music.*

ROGER *(cont'd)* 'I can take the afternoon / The night-time comes around too soon / You can't know what you mean to me . . .'

We see that FRAN *is crouching behind* GREG*'s large sumo outfit and sidling along with him, out of sight.*

JANET *watches this, frowning.* FRAN *makes a 'shush' sign to* JANET.

ROGER *(cont'd)* 'Your poison letter, your telegram / Just goes to show you don't give a damn . . .'

CONNIE *watches as* GREG *and* FRAN *make their way towards the door.*

ROGER *(cont'd)* 'Since you been gone, since you been gone / I'm outta my head, can't take it . . .'

GREG *stands in front of the door.* FRAN *is behind him. She is reaching for the jacket when the door suddenly opens and in walks* DUANE, *sending* FRAN *toppling over.*

ROGER *(cont'd)* 'Could I be wrong? / But since you been gone / You cast the spell, so break it / Ohh, whoa, ohh / Since you been gone . . .'

DUANE *crosses over towards* CONNIE. *He passes* JANET, *who looks up at him expectantly.*

CONNIE *is looking over at* GREG, *who is helping up* FRAN.

DUANE Ay-ay. Tripod alert.

DUANE *nods towards* ROGER. *We see that he is singing with a large erection in his trousers.*

CONNIE At least we know who had the Viagra.

DUANE There was no Viagra – they were all just Tic Tacs!

CONNIE What?

DUANE Oh, just because I'm black I'm a drug dealer, is that it?

CONNIE I thought I was starting to feel a buzz.

DUANE Yeah, sugar rush.

JANET *looks across at* DUANE, *who is dancing with* CONNIE. CONNIE *dances provocatively with* DUANE. JANET*'s confused and upset.*

ROGER 'If you will come back / Baby, you know you'll never do wrong . . .'

GREG *turns to see that* ROGER*'s jacket has fallen to the floor. He picks it up and looks round to make sure he's not being watched, then searches the pockets to find the envelope.*

ROGER *(cont'd)* 'Since you been gone, since you been gone / I'm outta my head, can't take it / Could I be wrong? / But since you been gone / You cast the spell, so break it / Whoa, ohh, ohh, ohh . . .'

GREG *pulls the envelope out and sees a list of names, mainly crossed out bar* FRAN*'s, which is circled. He hurriedly opens the envelope and pulls out the letter inside.* FRAN *joins him.*

FRAN What is it?

GREG *is frowning at the letter. Behind him we hear* ROGER.

ROGER Had a good look, have you?

GREG Sorry, Rog, it was just on the floor . . .

ROGER Fuck it, I don't care. It's divorce papers. Mary's leaving me, everyone. I thought I was happily married until four o'clock on Friday. Turns out I'm not.

CONNIE Oh Roger, I'm so sorry . . .

ROGER We had tickets for Neil Sedaka in June. Royal Albert Hall. Private box . . .

He lurches towards CONNIE*; she hugs him.*

CONNIE Aaah . . . oh! Steady on, Roger, you're stabbing me a little bit.

CONNIE *tries to move away from* ROGER*'s powerful erection.* JANET *has lost the thread of the conversation.*

JANET What's happened?

CONNIE Leave it, Janet.

JANET Are you all right, Roger?

CONNIE Don't make him repeat it, for God's sake, you can see he's upset. Have some sensitivity for once in your life.

The backing track has ended. GREG *is replacing the envelope in* ROGER*'s pocket.*

FRAN So we still don't know who he's going to sack?

GREG No, no, it was just divorce papers.

GREG *smiles at* FRAN *and looks across at* CONNIE. ROGER *is sitting down, finishing off his shots.*

DUANE *approaches* FRAN.

DUANE Put another song on.

FRAN *moves to the menu screen.*

DUANE *(cont'd)* Come on, guys, we've paid for the hour, let's not get all bummed out.

The intro to 'I Know Him So Well' by Elaine Paige and Barbara Dickson comes on.

DUANE *(cont'd)* It's not all bad, is it, Roger? You've still got your promotion, right? Fresh start and all that. New horizons . . .

ROGER I suppose so.

DUANE Yeah. That's the spirit. Anyway, it's not over yet, is it? You haven't signed the papers. Who knows, you might be able to talk her round!

FRAN *starts to sing.*

FRAN 'Nothing is so good it lasts eternally . . .'

DUANE *(sarcastically)* Oh brilliant! Well done, Fran.

FRAN *(to* ROGER*)* 'Perfect situations must go wrong . . .'

A look between GREG *and* CONNIE.

FRAN *(cont'd)* 'But this has never yet prevented me / Wanting far too much / For far too long . . .'

FRAN *approaches* GREG *and takes his hand.* CONNIE *watches, annoyed.*

FRAN *(cont'd)* 'Looking back I could have played it differently / Won a few more moments / Who can tell . . .'

ROGER *downs another drink.* GREG *dances with* FRAN.

JANET *looks towards* DUANE. *He notices her looking and gives a polite smile back.*

FRAN *(cont'd)* 'But it took time to understand the man / Now at least I know / I know him well . . .'

CONNIE *has picked up the other microphone.*

FRAN *(cont'd)* 'Wasn't it good?'

CONNIE 'Oh so good!'

FRAN 'Wasn't he fine?'

CONNIE 'Oh so fine!'

FRAN 'Isn't it madness . . .'

CONNIE/FRAN 'He can't be mine.'

ROGER *is lost in his own thoughts. He takes out his wallet and looks at a photo of himself and his wife Mary.*

FRAN 'But in the end / He needs a little bit more than me / More security . . .'

CONNIE 'He needs his fantasy and freedom.'

FRAN 'I know him so well!'

FRAN *starts to slow-dance with* GREG. CONNIE *watches them sadly.*

CONNIE 'No one in your life is with you constantly / No one is completely on your side / And though I'd move my world to be with him / Still the gap between us is too wide . . .'

GREG *goes to get his drink. As he passes* CONNIE *he whispers to her.*

GREG I know who's getting sacked.

CONNIE 'Looking back I could have played it differently . . .' *(To* GREG, *mouthing)* Who? 'Won a few more moments who can tell?' *(To* GREG*)* Me?

GREG *shakes his head and returns to* FRAN.

CONNIE *(cont'd)* 'But I was ever so much younger then / Now at least I know / I know him well . . .'

GREG *points to* FRAN *behind her back.* CONNIE *smiles.*

FRAN 'Wasn't it good?'

CONNIE *(beaming)* 'Oh so good!'

FRAN 'Wasn't he fine?'

CONNIE 'Oh so fine!'

CONNIE/FRAN 'Isn't it madness / He won't be mine!'

JANET *plucks up the courage to approach* DUANE. *He's a little shocked but too polite to refuse, so they also start to slow-dance.*

CONNIE/FRAN *(cont'd)* 'Didn't I know / How it would go? / If I knew from the start / Why am I falling apart?'

GREG *is between* CONNIE *and* FRAN. *He smiles at* CONNIE.

ROGER *gets up and crosses to get his divorce papers from his pocket. He sits down and signs them quickly.*

FRAN 'Wasn't it good? Wasn't he fine?'

CONNIE 'Isn't it madness . . .'

CONNIE/FRAN 'He won't be mine!'

FRAN 'But in the end / He needs a little bit more than me / More security . . .'

CONNIE 'He needs his fantasy and freedom . . .'

FRAN 'I know him so well.'

JANET *looks up at* DUANE. *He smiles.*

CONNIE 'It took time to understand him . . .'

CONNIE/FRAN 'I know him so well.'

JANET *leans in and impulsively kisses* DUANE, *half on the lips.* DUANE *is a little taken aback but just puts it down to the drink. He smiles.*

The song finishes, clapping all round. JANET *goes to the menu screen.*

ROGER Fran, can I have a word?

FRAN *joins* ROGER *in a corner of the room.* CONNIE *and* GREG *watch them.*

CONNIE He's not going to tell her now, is he?

GREG Dunno, he might do. He's pissed enough.

CONNIE Ah, poor Fran. Still, means we won't have her beady eyes on us at work every day.

GREG It's such a relief. I thought it was going to be me.

In the corner, ROGER *is talking to* FRAN. *She looks shell-shocked. She is shaking her head in disbelief.*

CONNIE Maybe you should give her her notice as well. Give her a fresh start. It's what she deserves.

GREG Yeah. Yeah, I think you're right.

GREG *surreptitiously squeezes* CONNIE*'s hand.* JANET *is the only one who spots this.* CONNIE *notices* JANET *staring.*

CONNIE *(to* JANET*)* Can I help you?

JANET *looks back down to the menu screen. In the corner,* ROGER *is holding* FRAN*'s hand.*

ROGER Are you OK?

FRAN Yeah, it's just . . . so out of the blue.

ROGER I know and I apologise for that, but circumstances got out of my control.

FRAN And I can't change your mind?

ROGER I'm afraid not. But you've got Greg, and he'll help you through it.

FRAN *smiles and looks across at* GREG. *He smiles back.*

Suddenly JANET *can be heard on the microphone.*

JANET *(V.O.)* I'd like to sing a song.

All eyes turn in surprise to JANET, *standing in front of the screen holding the microphone.*

JANET *(cont'd)* This is a request from someone very special. They know who they are. And in answer to your question, yes, I do. Very much.

CONNIE *and* FRAN *exchange glances.* CONNIE *is smirking.* DUANE *looks at* GREG *and* ROGER, *nonplussed.*

The intro to Yazoo's 'Only You' begins.

JANET *(cont'd)* 'Looking from a window above / It's like a story of love / Can you hear me?'

CONNIE No.

JANET 'Came back only yesterday / I'm moving farther away / Want you near me . . .'

CONNIE *is struggling not to laugh.* FRAN *looks ashamed.* DUANE *is watching supportively.*

JANET *dares to meet* DUANE*'s eye and sings to him. He is confused.*

JANET *(cont'd)* 'All I needed was the love you gave / All I needed for another day / And all I ever knew / Only you . . .'

FRAN *takes* **GREG** *'s hand.*

GREG Are you OK?

FRAN Yeah. I need to talk to you.

ROGER *drinks melancholically.*

JANET 'Sometimes when I think of her name / When it's only a game / And I need you / Listen to the words that you say / It's getting harder to stay / When I see you . . .'

FRAN *moves across to* **DUANE** *and whispers in his ear. He looks confused, then pissed off.* **JANET** *watches this as she sings.*

DUANE *reaches into his bag and pulls out his phone to check a text. He looks annoyed with* **CONNIE**, *who acts defensive.*

JANET *(cont'd)* 'All I needed was the love you gave / All I needed for another day / And all I ever knew / Only you . . .'

DUANE *gets up and crosses to the menu screen. He stops the backing track.*

JANET *(cont'd)* Duane, what . . .?

DUANE I'm really sorry, Janet, but I didn't send you that text. Connie did.

CONNIE Yeah, as a joke!

JANET I don't understand . . .

GREG *signs, 'It was a joke.'* **JANET** *looks deeply hurt.*

DUANE That was a shitty thing to do, Connie.

GREG All right, Duane, don't make it worse.

DUANE How could it be worse? Look, Janet, I do like you, we have a laugh, but not in that . . .

JANET It's OK, it's fine . . . I'm not . . .

CONNIE *(mock-innocent)* I just thought you'd make a lovely couple, that's all.

DUANE Oh fuck off.

ROGER *has taken up the microphone.*

ROGER All right, everyone, can I just have a word before things get too heated. Are you all right, Janet?

JANET *nods but is mortified.* **DUANE** *goes to comfort her, but* **JANET** *shrugs him off and sits down.*

ROGER *(cont'd)* That wasn't nice, Connie, but we're out of office hours so I'm going to draw a line under it.

CONNIE Oh yeah, we all know she's got you wrapped round her little finger.

ROGER Enough! Now I know there's been a lot of rumours flying around recently about voluntary redundancies. And it's true, I was charged with the unhappy task of letting one of you good people go. I fought with management tooth and nail over it, until they promoted me, and now I am management, so . . . I've no choice. Someone has to go, to balance the books, and the person I've decided is leaving the company is . . . me.

Shocked reactions.

ROGER *(cont'd)* With Mary gone, I'm going to start over. I've a brother in Florida I don't see much of, so I'm heading out there. And that means I'll need a replacement. And the person I'm going to recommend to the board . . . is Fran.

CONNIE *and* GREG *exchange looks.* FRAN *smiles at* GREG *and squeezes his hand.*

ROGER *(cont'd)* I couldn't think of anyone better to take the team forward. I know you and Greg are hoping to tie the knot and I hope this will help to send you on your way.

FRAN Thanks, Roger.

GREG Congratulations, babe. That's just . . . incredible.

GREG *hugs* FRAN. CONNIE *is furious.*

FRAN Can we start looking for a bigger flat now, please?!

GREG Yeah, definitely.

ROGER, DUANE *and* CONNIE *clap.* GREG *can't meet* CONNIE*'s eye.*

DUANE Well done, Fran.

FRAN Thanks.

CONNIE Yeah. Cuntgrotalaions.

CONNIE *hugs* FRAN. *She looks at* GREG *over* FRAN*'s shoulder.*

CONNIE *(cont'd)* We need to have a chat about who's going to be your new PA, don't we?

Suddenly the door bursts open and a group of a dozen or so identically dressed women stream into the room. They are a HEN PARTY *and already well oiled. One of them heads straight for the menu screen. The maid of honour,* CHANTEL, *speaks.*

CHANTEL Excuse me, we've booked this room, sorry.

DUANE I don't think so, darling, we've got it till half past.

CHANTEL Well, it's nearly half past now – we don't mind you joining in, do we, girls?

The HENS *whoop and cheer.*

ROGER Well, I'm not sure we've quite . . .

ROGER *is swallowed up in a sea of* HENS.

David Guetta's 'Titanium' starts on the system. CONNIE *approaches* GREG.

CONNIE So you're buying a bigger flat, are you?

GREG No, course not! I had to say something though, didn't I, or she'd have been suspicious. Just let the dust settle, then I'll tell her. Promise.

CONNIE *sees* FRAN *talking to* ROGER *and gives* GREG *a quick kiss on the lips.*

CONNIE I'm never letting you go.

JANET *sees this.* CHANTEL *sings.*

CHANTEL 'You shout it out / But I can't hear a word you say / I'm talking loud, not saying much . . .'

ROGER *is dancing with a pretty* HEN PARTY GIRL, *who pours him a drink from a bottle.* FRAN *approaches.*

FRAN I think you're in there, Roger.

ROGER No! She's half my age.

CHANTEL 'I'm criticised but all your bullets ricochet / You shoot me down, but I get up . . .'

FRAN So? Women like a silver fox. Go for it.

ROGER Maybe I will. I wonder if she likes Neil Sedaka . . .

CHANTEL 'I'm bulletproof, nothing to lose / Fire away, fire away . . .'

CONNIE *approaches* JANET, *who is standing by herself.*

CONNIE Are you still here? I thought you'd have slunk off by now. Will you sing us another song? You've got such a nice voice.

JANET *signs, 'Piss off.'*

CONNIE *(cont'd)* What's that?

JANET Why don't you ask Greg?

CONNIE Don't worry, I will. Oh and by the way, I've already had a chat to Fran about her new PA and guess what? She wants someone with skills, someone who can hear.

JANET I've got skills, Connie. I can lip-read.

JANET *goes off to speak to* FRAN. CONNIE *watches as* JANET *whispers in* FRAN*'s ear.*

CHANTEL 'Ricochet, you take your aim / Fire away, fire away / You shoot me down but I won't fall / I am titanium / You shoot me down but I won't fall / I am titanium . . .'

FRAN *looks horrified by what she's hearing. She stares at* CONNIE *across the room.* GREG *approaches* CONNIE.

GREG What's going on?

As the music swells, the lights turn to UV light and everyone's clothes and make-up are luminescent.

CONNIE*'s lipstick gives off a very distinctive glow, and this same lipstick colour is revealed on* GREG*'s face.*

FRAN *sees the final evidence she needed.* JANET *is defiant. The* HENS *dance around as* FRAN *marches up to* GREG.

GREG *(cont'd)* All right, babe . . .

FRAN *pulls the plug on* GREG*'s inflatable costume and he starts to deflate.*

FRAN You're fired. Both of you.

FRAN *goes over to* CHANTEL *and defiantly joins in with her singing.*

FRAN/CHANTEL 'I'm bulletproof, nothing to lose / Fire away, fire away / Ricochet, you take your aim / Fire away, fire away / You shoot me down but I won't fall / I am titanium / You shoot me down but I won't fall / I am titanium!'

ROGER *is dancing with the* HENS. *The whole room is jumping.*

CONNIE *and* GREG *are mortified. She tries to wipe the lipstick from his face.*

JANET *is approached by* DUANE. *He whispers something. She laughs. They start to dance. They kiss.*

THE END

Episode 5

DIDDLE DIDDLE DUMPLING

CAST LIST

DAVID – Reece Shearsmith

LOUISE – Keeley Hawes

SALLY – Rosa Strudwick

CHRIS – Steve Pemberton

DJ – Danny Baker

TED – Mathew Baynton

EXT. LEAFY STREET. DAY.

A middle-aged man, DAVID, *is jogging down the street towards his house. He is listening to the 'Spring' suite from* The Four Seasons *by Vivaldi.*

DAVID *slows down by a tree and looks down at the pavement. Sitting at the foot of the tree is a single black slip-on shoe. It looks too new to have been thrown out as rubbish, and there is nothing else around it.*

DAVID *looks around the area but nobody else is visible.* DAVID *jogs past, then turns around and goes back to the shoe. He picks it up and places it on a garden wall so it is more visible. He then jogs on to his house.*

EXT. DAVID'S HOUSE. DAY.

DAVID *runs up to his house, lets himself in and closes the door, revealing a number . . . 22.*

EXT. LEAFY STREET. DAY.

We push in towards the black shoe on the wall, eventually going inside the shoe where we see that it is a size 9.

TITLE: *'Diddle Diddle Dumpling'.*

INT. KITCHEN-DINER. DAY.

A child's drawing of a tree with a few leaves, a sheep, some bluebells. At the bottom of the picture, in childish handwriting, the word 'Spring'.

DAVID *comes into the large kitchen-diner of his pleasant family home, still in his jogging gear. He goes to get some water from the fridge.*

DAVID*'s wife* LOUISE *is eating toast and looking through the cupboards. She wears a smart business suit.*

LOUISE Hi.

DAVID Hi.

LOUISE You haven't thrown those jam jars away, have you? I was collecting them for the Spring Fair.

DAVID No, they're under the sink.

LOUISE You've got to put stuff in them for raffle prizes.

DAVID What's wrong with the jam? That's a good prize.

LOUISE Not according to the PSA. There's a list of approved items – it's on the fridge.

DAVID Like what, iPhones?

LOUISE Yeah, probably. Oh, and remember Sally's got a play-date with Gertrude.

DAVID Gertrude? Isn't that the cow from *The Magic Roundabout*?

LOUISE No, that was Ermintrude.

DAVID Ridiculous.

LOUISE You said you wanted her to have more friends.

DAVID Yeah, but I'd rather they weren't Shakespeare characters, Greek goddesses or French wines.

LOUISE Fine. I'll tell Sauvignon's mother we're cancelling, shall I?

DAVID You are joking?

LOUISE Maybe. How was your run?

DAVID Yeah, fine. Weird though . . .

LOUISE Why, what?

DAVID Just coming in now, there was a shoe on the pavement.

LOUISE *starts to get her bag ready.* **DAVID** *leans against the kitchen counter, seemingly deep in thought.*

LOUISE A shoe?

DAVID Yeah, just one single black shoe. Looks like it's been placed. It's not old, it's like a brand-new shoe.

LOUISE Right. You haven't seen my keys, have you?

DAVID I put it up on the wall, anyway, see if someone claims it. It's really odd. What's the story behind it?

LOUISE *finds her keys.*

LOUISE OK, I'm going. Make sure she brushes her teeth, and if you get the chance, try and sneak a look in Gertrude's book bag.

DAVID Why?

LOUISE Just to see what she's reading.

DAVID Seriously?

LOUISE I don't want Sally falling behind.

DAVID She's seven. She should be reading 'Janet and . . . Whatsit Have Two Mummies' or whatever they read these days.

LOUISE *crosses and shouts up the stairs.*

LOUISE Bye, Sally, see you later!

LOUISE *heads out of the front door.*

LOUISE *(V.O.) (cont'd)* See you tonight.

DAVID Yeah, OK. See if that shoe's still there when you go by . . .

The front door slams. DAVID *looks concerned. Vivaldi's 'Spring' strikes up again.*

INT. LIVING ROOM. DAY.

DAVID *is dusting in the living room. He is polishing a framed family photo, though we do not dwell on it. He stops, something nagging at the back of his mind. He crosses to the window and looks out.*

EXT. DAY.

We see the shoe still on the wall. Beyond it we see DAVID *looking at it through his window.*

INT. KITCHEN-DINER. NIGHT.

The music continues as background. DAVID *is preparing the evening meal as* LOUISE *enters with her bag and coat on.*

LOUISE Hi, sorry I'm late, I had a conference call with Bombay and it took ages to get everyone on the same line.

DAVID Better than watching 50 episodes of *Fifi and the Flowertots.*

LOUISE Ah. Is she still up?

DAVID No, she tried to stay awake but she fell asleep with the book in her hand, bless her.

LOUISE Oh God, I feel bad now.

LOUISE *goes to put her bag on the table. The black shoe is sitting in the middle of the table.*

LOUISE *(cont'd)* What's this?

DAVID Oh, it's that shoe I was telling you about.

LOUISE What shoe?

DAVID That shoe from this morning, I told you it was outside the house.

LOUISE So what's it doing in here?

DAVID I thought I'd bring it in.

LOUISE And put it on the table? You don't know where it's been, it could have dog shit all over it!

DAVID It's brand new, that's the whole point.

LOUISE Well, if it's new don't put it on the table then, it's bad luck.

LOUISE *takes the shoe off the table.*

DAVID All right, I just didn't want anyone stealing it.

LOUISE So *you* stole it?

DAVID It just felt wrong leaving it outside, that's all. Give it to the school for the Spring Fair if you're that bothered. Put toys or Tiffany earrings in it.

LOUISE *puts the shoe down on the floor.* DAVID *brings the food over.*

DAVID *(cont'd)* Here. This was nicer two hours ago . . .

LOUISE Sorry.

LOUISE *starts to eat her meal. She broaches a new subject, trying to be light.*

LOUISE *(cont'd)* Oh, I spoke to Chris Hutchinson today.

DAVID Oh yeah.

LOUISE They're taking over that empty shop next to Planet Organic. He said they were looking for new reps.

DAVID Right.

LOUISE That's not a million miles away from what you were doing at Fraser's, is it?

DAVID Yeah, it sounds good, I'll drop him a line. Oh, I managed to sneak a look into Gertrude's book bag by the way.

LOUISE Oh? And what's she reading?

DAVID *Anna Karenina.*

LOUISE *laughs.*

DAVID *(cont'd)* And it was in Russian.

LOUISE I wouldn't be surprised. I was talking to her mother the other day – she's the really mean-faced one with bad breath . . .

LOUISE *continues to talk but* DAVID *isn't really listening.* DAVID *looks down under the table and kicks the shoe out from under it. He looks at* LOUISE *and nods, then back at the shoe. He smiles.*

INT. LIVING ROOM. DAY.

SALLY, *a cute seven-year-old, has put a doll in the shoe and is pushing it around the carpet – like a car.* DAVID *comes in and sees what she is doing.*

DAVID What are you doing? You mustn't do that! Give it here.

He grabs the shoe from SALLY *and throws out the doll from inside it.*

SALLY I was giving Suzie a ride.

DAVID This is not your property, Sally!

SALLY Whose is it then?

DAVID Well, we don't know, do we? That's what Daddy is trying to find out. Go to your room. You can play in there.

DAVID *gives* SALLY *the doll and goes to leave the room. The door slams and* LOUISE *comes in.*

LOUISE *(V.O.)* David?

LOUISE *enters the living room brandishing a leaflet.*

LOUISE *(cont'd)* What's this?

DAVID We've got to speak to Sally about respecting other people's things.

LOUISE I found this tied to all the lamp posts down the street.

DAVID Yeah, I did 20 of them but the printer ran out of ink.

LOUISE *(reading)* 'Found – one black man's shoe.'

DAVID Yeah, I wasn't sure about that. Because it could sound like we're saying the shoe belongs to a black man, which it might do, we don't know, but – do you think we should change it?

LOUISE You've put our phone number on it!

DAVID Well – how else are they going to get in contact?

LOUISE I don't want them to get in contact! I just don't like the idea of our number being displayed up and down the street.

DAVID So what?

LOUISE People could ring us now and find out if we're in or not. Burglars.

DAVID You're making too much out of this.

LOUISE You haven't even put a picture on. It's just a drawing.

DAVID I'm not going to give away all the details, am I? Or else anyone could claim it. They'll have to describe it to me when they get in touch.

LOUISE David – it's a single tramp's shoe you found in the street. Just give it to Oxfam.

DAVID They won't have it. They wouldn't take those *Angelina Ballerina* videos. Nothing wrong with them.

LOUISE *(losing it)* They were videos! Nobody has video players any more!

DAVID The library does.

LOUISE *takes a deep breath.*

LOUISE Is this something to do with . . .?

DAVID What?

LOUISE *shakes off the idea. She doesn't want to escalate the argument.*

LOUISE Did you print your CV off for Chris Hutchinson?

DAVID No.

LOUISE David!

DAVID It ran out of ink, I told you!!

LOUISE You've got to get your priorities straight . . .

The phone begins to ring. They both look at it.

DAVID I'll get it. No, you get it. Ask them exactly whereabouts they lost it. Don't mention the size!

LOUISE *answers the phone.*

LOUISE Hello? Oh hi, Mum. Yeah, I'm good, thanks. Oh, did you? Who did you go with?

DAVID *(whispering)* Hurry up! People could be trying to get through!

LOUISE *is annoyed and leaves the room to carry on talking.*

LOUISE Yes, she's fine. It's the school fair on Friday so we're doing stuff for that . . .

Vivaldi's 'Summer' suite from The Four Seasons *begins.* DAVID *picks up the leaflet and looks at it. 'Found, one black man's shoe. Latimer Road. Please call 0207 946 0168 for details.'*

DAVID *compares his drawing of the shoe to the real shoe. It's a pretty good match.*

DAVID *crosses to the window and looks outside.*

INT. LIVING ROOM. DAY.

A child's drawing of a tree in full bloom, sun in the sky, two children playing wearing sunglasses and eating ice cream. The word 'Summer' written at the bottom.

The music continues. DAVID *still looks out of the window, but he's now dressed differently – more summery, in polo shirt and shorts.*

LOUISE *and* SALLY *are opening* SALLY*'s birthday presents.* SALLY *gets a new doll and is delighted.* LOUISE *looks across at* DAVID, *who is preoccupied at the window.*

LOUISE Daddy, come and see what Sally's got.

DAVID *turns and forces a smile.*

DAVID Ooh, that looks nice. What's her name?

DAVID *crosses to join* SALLY *and* LOUISE. *The single black shoe is on the windowsill.*

INT. KITCHEN-DINER. EVENING.

DAVID *and* LOUISE *are having a meal with their guest,* CHRIS HUTCHINSON. *He is holding court about his business ventures.* DAVID *is in the kitchen area pouring drinks.*

CHRIS You take on a refurb like that, you're always going to be looking at some time overspend, but we've not done too badly. And the footfall from Planet Organic will be really good for us. All those yummy mummies and their yoga mats.

LOUISE Don't! I should go, but I haven't got time.

CHRIS No, you don't need that, you look smashing.

DAVID *brings the drinks over. There are already drinks on the table.*

DAVID Here we go . . . oh, you've already got drinks?

CHRIS Yeah, you just poured them out.

DAVID Oh, I don't know what I'm doing – trying to get you pissed!

CHRIS No, I'm not complaining! Anyway, let's get down to business. What do you think?

DAVID About what?

CHRIS Louise said you might be ready to jump back on the gravy train? Bit of part-time work.

DAVID Yeah, no, it sounds good, but I am a bit busy at the moment.

CHRIS Oh – other irons in the fire, eh?

DAVID Well, I've just got a bit of a project on the go . . .

LOUISE No, you haven't.

DAVID Yes, I have! The shoe.

LOUISE David.

DAVID What?

LOUISE Not now.

CHRIS What's this?

DAVID Well, about three weeks ago . . .

LOUISE More like three months ago.

DAVID Well, all right, whenever it was – a few weeks ago I found a shoe outside the house. Not like a thrown-away, discarded one – this was black, slip on, good-quality leather, hardly a mark on it.

CHRIS And you're trying to find a retail outlet for them? You see them as a new range?

DAVID No, no. I just . . . found a shoe.

LOUISE Someone lost a single shoe.

DAVID Well, no, we don't know – that's the point. We don't know what happened, do we? Could be an accident, someone has fallen over, the shoe's come off. Could be an older gentlemen – with Alzheimer's, say – goes for a wander, doesn't know where he left it. Could be kids dressing up – took the dad's shoe out of the house, maybe Penny for the Guy . . .

LOUISE In April?

CHRIS *is puzzled – trying to make sense of the story.*

CHRIS Right. So . . . it's a bit of a mystery.

DAVID Exactly.

DAVID *jumps up.*

DAVID *(cont'd)* Do you want to see it?

CHRIS Yes, if you like.

LOUISE Don't David!

DAVID *looks for the shoe in a drawer. It isn't there.*

DAVID I'm just showing Chris – he's intrigued. Have you moved it, Louise? It was in here. Where is it?

LOUISE It's gone, David.

DAVID I know it's gone. I can see it's gone. Where is it?

LOUISE I threw it away.

DAVID *looks at* LOUISE. *Takes this in.*

DAVID You fucking what?

LOUISE I got rid of it. I put it in the bin. It was too much, you were getting obsessed with it.

DAVID I'm not obsessed!

LOUISE Of course you are! *(To* CHRIS*)* He's created a website, he's been badgering the police for CCTV footage . . .

DAVID It's public-spirited. *(To* CHRIS*)* You know Mike Evans, don't you?

LOUISE It's insane! Look at you, you can't go two minutes without banging on about some stupid bloody shoe you found!

DAVID Course I can!

LOUISE You can't!

DAVID All right then, time me. Go on, Chris, two minutes, time me.

CHRIS There's no need . . .

DAVID No, she thinks I'm insane . . .

LOUISE I never said that, I said *it's* insane . . .

DAVID Well, let's see, shall we? See who's making an absolute mountain out of a molehill.

LOUISE *(to* CHRIS*)* Do it. I want you to see.

CHRIS OK. Two minutes.

CHRIS *looks at his watch.* DAVID *sits back down. Tense silence.*

DAVID You going away this summer, Chris, or . . .?

CHRIS Er, I might just go and see my mum in Hastings. Got to be around for the shop.

DAVID *nods.* LOUISE *sips her wine. Time passes.*

DAVID How long?

CHRIS Three or four days.

DAVID No, I mean how long . . .?

DAVID *nods to* CHRIS*'s watch.*

CHRIS Oh, er . . . 30 seconds.

DAVID *is struggling. Time is passing slowly.*

DAVID *(to* LOUISE*)* This is very cruel, what you're doing.

LOUISE I don't mean it to be. I just want to help you, David.

Seconds tick by in uncomfortable silence. The tension builds. Finally DAVID *can take it no more. He jumps up from the table.*

DAVID Which bin is it in?

LOUISE That was barely a minute.

DAVID TELL ME!

LOUISE The green one.

DAVID *marches out of the room to go and look in the bins outside.*

LOUISE *(cont'd)* Sorry about this, Chris.

CHRIS It's OK, Lou. No problem.

LOUISE You know he's . . . not been well . . .

CHRIS It's fine. I understand. But you've been through a lot too, you know.

CHRIS *puts his hand on* LOUISE*'s hand. They share a moment. She takes her hand away.*

LOUISE Sorry, I can't.

DAVID *returns with the shoe.*

DAVID Here we go, Chris. Sorry about that, panic over.

He plonks the shoe down in the middle of the table. DAVID *sits back down.*

DAVID *(cont'd)* Now then. If you saw that in the street, you wouldn't think someone had thrown it, would you? You'd think it had been lost.

CHRIS Yes, I see what you mean.

CHRIS *goes to pick it up.*

DAVID Careful.

CHRIS *picks it up carefully and takes a closer look.*

CHRIS So you're trying to find the rightful owner. Like *Cinderella*.

DAVID Exactly! We need to do a proclamation throughout the land! Get the media involved! Have celebrities talking about it! We need it trending on Twitter – hashtag the-lost-shoe!

LOUISE *gets up and walks out.* DAVID *turns to* CHRIS.

DAVID *(cont'd)* You know what I mean though, don't you, Chris? I'm not going mad. A pair of shoes deserve to be together. They have to be. That's how they belong.

CHRIS *nods.*

CHRIS I understand. I'll have a word with Laurence who does my PR, see what we can do.

DAVID Thank you! Finally someone gets it . . .

DAVID *smiles and tucks into his food.* CHRIS *regards him pityingly.*

INT. KITCHEN-DINER. NIGHT.

DAVID *is listening intently to an interview on his portable radio. The tone is light-hearted, but* DAVID *listens gravely to every word.*

DJ *(V.O.)* And so you've offered a reward, is that right?

DAVID *(V.O.)* Yeah – I thought there'd be some incentive there for people to come forward – you know, with any information . . .

DJ *(V.O.)* So if you've got any old shoes lying around in the garden, bring them round to David's place – it might be your lucky day!

DAVID *(V.O.)* Well, no. No, the reward would be specifically for the pairing of the shoe in question. I don't want time-wasters.

DJ *(V.O.)* I could have done with you this morning when I was sorting out my sock drawer. We've had an email from Jacqueline in Barnet, simply asking, 'Why not give that money to a homeless shelter? Why concentrate on this one shoe?'

DAVID *(V.O.)* Because, Jacqueline, someone somewhere is missing a shoe and if I can bring that person and that shoe together then I will have achieved . . . that.

DJ *(V.O.)* OK. But let's say, for a second, I'm the person that lost that shoe, I go back to look for it, but it's not there because you've got it in your house. Then what?

DAVID *(V.O.)* Well, as I say – and all this is on the website . . .

DAVID *turns off the radio angrily.*

DAVID Stupid question.

The phone rings. DAVID *snatches it up.*

DAVID *(cont'd)* Yes? Really? Can I take your name, please?

He gets a pad and jots down the details.

DAVID *(cont'd)* OK. And – first question, what size is the shoe, please? . . . OK, and where did you lose it? . . . Right, and what colour are the laces? . . . Well, that's funny because there are no laces, so fuck you, cunt.

DAVID *slams the phone down.* DAVID *turns and notices* SALLY *standing in the doorway.*

DAVID *(cont'd)* Sally – you all right? What are you doing out of bed?

SALLY Can't sleep.

DAVID Do you want a drink of water?

SALLY nods. DAVID gets her a drink.

SALLY Are you all right, Daddy?

DAVID What do you mean, 'Are you all right?' Course I'm all right. I'm just busy doing my work.

SALLY Do you have to do it?

DAVID Well, yes, it's important to me.

SALLY Why?

DAVID Because . . . it's like if you were reading a really good story, and all of a sudden all the words slipped off the page and fell on the floor in a jumble. You really want to get to the end, but you can't now because you've got to sort out all the bits and pieces. That's what it's like for Daddy sometimes. In Daddy's head. It takes me time to . . . put the pieces together.

SALLY Like a jigsaw?

DAVID Yes, but imagine a jigsaw with no picture. How would you know where to begin? I just have to try one piece at a time. Takes me a bit longer.

SALLY Is that why you don't read me stories any more?

DAVID I do read you stories. What about *The Very Hungry Caterpillar*?

SALLY That's for babies.

DAVID Oh sorry, let's go and read *Hamlet* then, shall we? Find out where Gertrude got her name from.

SALLY We could read *Cinderella*.

DAVID Oh yes, that's a good one.

DAVID *scoops up* SALLY *and goes towards the door.*

DAVID *(cont'd)* Once upon a time there was a beautiful princess who lived with her nasty stepmother and her two horrible stepsisters . . .

DAVID *walks out of the room carrying* SALLY.

We see the shoe placed on a cushion on the sofa.

INT. LIVING ROOM. DAY.

The Four Seasons, *'Summer', plays as* DAVID *comes into the house from a run.*

DAVID *goes and gets a drink of water. He checks the phone for messages. None. He opens up his laptop and goes to his website. He looks at the viewer counter. It says 42 views. 'Be the first to post' glares the barren message board.*

The doorbell rings. DAVID *leaves the room to answer it. We stay in the room and hear* DAVID *open the door.*

TED *(V.O.)* Hi – I've come about the shoe.

DAVID *(V.O.)* Sorry?

TED *(V.O.)* The missing shoe. I think it's mine.

DAVID *(V.O.)* Oh right. Well – you'd better come in.

DAVID *re-enters followed by* TED, *an ordinary-looking bloke carrying a plastic bag.*

DAVID *(cont'd)* Come through.

TED Thanks.

DAVID Do you want to take a seat?

TED No, you're all right, thanks.

DAVID Right. So, can I ask how you heard about us?

TED My daughter heard you on the radio, whenever that was.

DAVID Oh right. You live locally?

TED No, I live in Norfolk, but we were here for a wedding. My shoes were in the bottom of my suit bag. One of them must have fallen out. We were parked just by that tree outside.

DAVID Right. Whose wedding was it?

TED I don't think you'd know them. What's that got to do with anything?

DAVID Nothing. I'm just trying to get a full picture. OK, I just have to ask a couple of questions, I'm sure you understand.

TED *(warily)* OK . . .

DAVID *gets his pad and pen.*

DAVID What size was the shoe you claim you lost?

TED Nine.

DAVID Correct. Good start.

Next, DAVID *presents* TED *with four photocopied pictures of four different shoe treads.*

DAVID *(cont'd)* Next, I'm going to show you some photographs and I want you to tell me which one is the correct tread: A, B, C or D.

TED *looks carefully as* DAVID *presents each picture one at a time.* TED *considers.*

TED Can I see B again?

DAVID *shows him B again.*

TED *(cont'd)* OK. I think it's C.

DAVID *is inscrutable. He makes a note.*

DAVID 'C'. Next – what colour were the laces?

TED It didn't have laces, it was a slip-on. I've got the other one here if you need proof . . .

TED *pulls out a matching shoe from a carrier bag.* DAVID *puts on his glasses and examines carefully.*

TED *watches* DAVID, *a little disturbed.*

DAVID Mmm. Looks the same. Similar tread. And it just fell out of a suit carrier, you say?

TED Yeah. Can't have been zipped up properly.

DAVID Right, well. Seems plausible. It looks like we've got a match. Well done.

TED Can I have it then?

DAVID What, you want to take it now?

TED Well, that's why I've come.

DAVID Erm – right, well. Do you want a drink or anything, to celebrate?

TED No thanks. I'd better get off. My car's on a meter.

DAVID OK.

DAVID *goes to a cupboard, takes out a box, and from inside the box he produces the shoe. It is wrapped in cloth. He unwraps it carefully.*

DAVID *(cont'd)* Here he is. I've looked after him. I won't make you try it on, that would be weird, wouldn't it!

TED Yes.

DAVID *is reluctant to part with it.*

DAVID Sorry, can I just have a minute, please? I'm finding this really hard.

TED *is bemused by* DAVID*'s behaviour but doesn't want to appear ungrateful.*

TED Sure. Can I use your loo then?

DAVID Yes – it's just by the front door.

TED *leaves to go to the toilet.*

DAVID *holds the shoe close to himself. He is very emotional. He holds it to his face and smells it.*

DAVID *carefully places the two shoes side by side. He lets out an exhausted but relieved sigh. He smiles.*

DAVID *hears the toilet flush and quickly puts both shoes in the bag.* TED *comes back in.*

TED All right?

DAVID Yeah. There you go. They're both in there. That's that done now. Mission accomplished.

He hands the bag over to TED.

DAVID *(cont'd)* Oh, I need to get you some money for the reward . . .

TED No, don't worry about that. I'm not bothered. I just wanted the shoe. Thanks very much.

DAVID No, thank you. And, erm, you know where we are now, so . . .

But TED *has already gone. The door slams shut. The 'Autumn' suite from* The Four Seasons *begins.* DAVID *is alone and desolate.*

INT. KITCHEN-DINER. DAY.

A child's drawing of a tree with a few brown and falling leaves. A bonfire burns and a pumpkin stares out menacingly. The word 'Autumn' written at the bottom.

We see that SALLY *is putting the finishing touches to her autumn picture.* LOUISE *is helping her.*

LOUISE That's right, and 'autumn' has a silent 'n' on the end, like 'column' or 'hymn'.

SALLY Who?

LOUISE No, a hymn that you sing. In church.

SALLY Like a funeral?

LOUISE Yes, or a wedding or a harvest festival . . .

SALLY Gertrude says she doesn't believe in God. Or Jesus or Santa or the Tooth Fairy.

LOUISE Well, that's just silly. You can't not believe in things just because you can't see them. Gertrude's mummy doesn't believe in oral hygiene, but we know it exists, don't we?

The front door slams. DAVID *enters wearing a shirt and tie and holding a briefcase.*

DAVID Hello! How are my girls!?

SALLY Daddy!

SALLY *runs over and gives him a cuddle.*

DAVID Wow . . . what's this? You've made an autumn picture? There's a bonfire, and leaves falling, and there's Mummy . . .

SALLY It's a pumpkin!

DAVID Oh yes, silly me!

LOUISE Cheeky! Go and put it in your book bag, darling. You can take it in tomorrow.

SALLY *goes out with the picture.* DAVID *gives* LOUISE *a kiss.*

LOUISE *(cont'd)* How was today?

DAVID Good. We got those new tiles in from Italy. Chris says there might be a trip out there in a couple of months.

LOUISE Very nice. Can wives come?

DAVID We'll have to see, won't we.

LOUISE How's Chris's new girlfriend?

DAVID Oh, she's very 'hands on', I don't think the other staff like her. They all call her Yoko Ono.

LOUISE That's mean!

SALLY *comes back in.*

SALLY Daddy – can I show you my assembly? I've got lines.

DAVID Oh, yes please – go on!

SALLY We're doing nursery rhymes.

LOUISE No, not now, Sally. Let Daddy get a cup of tea first, he's just come in.

DAVID No, I don't mind. Come on, Sal. I'll be the audience.

DAVID *sits down and watches* SALLY. LOUISE *looks slightly nervous.*

SALLY Well – I'm here, and Annabel's here, and Christian's here, and he says, 'Diddle diddle dumpling, my son John', and Annabel says, 'Went to bed with his trousers on'.

LOUISE *looks at* DAVID. *He has a fixed smile on his face.*

SALLY *(cont'd)* And then I say, 'One shoe off and one shoe on', and we all say, 'Diddle diddle dumpling, my son John'.

There is a silence at the end of this. LOUISE *doesn't know how* DAVID *will react. Suddenly* DAVID *starts clapping loudly.*

DAVID More! More! Encore! Well done!

SALLY *gives* DAVID *a big hug.* LOUISE *looks relieved.* DAVID *smiles, but he's dead behind the eyes.*

Vivaldi's 'Autumn' suite plays.

EXT. DAY.

LOUISE *is coming down the street towards her house when she spots something on the ground by the tree. It makes her stop dead in her tracks.*

Lying by the tree, in exactly the same spot, is the single black shoe. She looks frightened.

INT. LIVING ROOM. DAY.

DAVID *is in the living room. The room is a tip – the curtains closed and lamps on. Pieces of paper and receipts are strewn all over the floor, along with lots of old family photographs.*

DAVID *is poring over everything carefully.* LOUISE *comes in. She's holding the shoe.*

LOUISE David. What have you been doing?

DAVID Mmm. I could ask you that, Louise. Couldn't I?

LOUISE What do you mean? What was this doing outside?

DAVID What do you think? It's back where it belongs.

LOUISE What are you talking about? The owner came and got it. You said it was all sorted weeks ago.

DAVID *holds up a photo. It is a group shot of* LOUISE *looking younger amongst a group of friends. He points at one of the men.*

DAVID Who's that?

LOUISE *peers at the photo.*

LOUISE Er, I dunno, looks like people from college.

DAVID Your college?

LOUISE Yes. What is this?

DAVID I was doing a photobook for your birthday. I thought it'd be a nice surprise. So I got all your old pictures out and I found him. Your friend. What's his name?

LOUISE Ted.

DAVID Oh, it's Ted, is it? When did you last see Ted?

LOUISE I can't remember. It's been a while.

DAVID Right. Because I saw Ted six weeks ago when he came and pretended that he owned the shoe.

LOUISE I don't know what you're talking about.

DAVID Well, this'll really confuse you then. Because after I found the picture I got your VAT file out and went through your receipts and I found this . . .

DAVID *picks out a receipt and hands it to* LOUISE.

DAVID *(cont'd)* From Stead and Simpson, black slip-ons, size 9 . . .

LOUISE David . . .

DAVID Dated two days before Ted came to see me. How do you explain that?

LOUISE OK, look, he did it as a favour. I was trying to help you.

DAVID By lying to me? Giving me false hope?

LOUISE Oh God, David, please listen to yourself. I just wanted an end to it. What does it matter who took the fucking stupid shoe?

DAVID It's not about the shoe, is it! It was never about the shoe!

LOUISE I know it isn't, but . . . it's not healthy, David. For any of us.

LOUISE *takes a breath and gathers herself.*

LOUISE *(cont'd)* It's been six years.

DAVID Oh sorry, is that my time limit? Should I be over it now?

LOUISE I'm not saying that, but . . . we still have Sally, and we have to live our lives, for her sake. She doesn't even remember she had a brother.

DAVID Not brother, twin! Two halves, Louise, and one of them's gone.

LOUISE I know that! I was there when we buried him, remember? And I understand now what you were trying to do, but . . . we can't do that, David. Joseph is dead. He died.

DAVID *snatches the shoe from* **LOUISE** *and looks down at it sadly.*

DAVID They should be together.

LOUISE *notices that* **DAVID***'s cuff is stained with blood. She looks at her own hands and sees blood smears on them.*

LOUISE Where did you get that shoe from?

DAVID I went to see Ted.

LOUISE In Norfolk?

DAVID Yes, in Norfolk. He didn't want to give me it. He said something about me being unreasonable.

LOUISE What did you do? David? What did you do?

DAVID I can't remember.

LOUISE *takes out her phone and dials a number, walking out of the room.*

LOUISE Oh God . . .

DAVID *cradles the shoe. A blue flashing light appears at the window.*

'Winter' from The Four Seasons *begins to play.*

INT. KITCHEN-DINER. DAY.

A child's drawing of a bare tree. White, desolate. 'Winter'.

It is three months later. **LOUISE** *is in the kitchen preparing food for* **SALLY** *and her precocious friend* **GERTRUDE**. *They sip on drinks.*

LOUISE There we go. Do you want ketchup, Gertrude?

GERTRUDE No, it's very bad for you, it's full of E-numbers. Do you have any passata?

LOUISE Erm . . . no, I don't think so. We don't like passata, do we, Sally?

SALLY We've never had it.

LOUISE We have, you little liar! Now, do you want some carrots?

GERTRUDE Are they organic?

LOUISE *(lying)* Yes . . . yes, they are.

GERTRUDE All right then.

LOUISE You'll have to scrape the mud off with your knife!

SALLY My mummy says organic is a waste of money.

LOUISE No, I didn't!

We hear the front door open.

LOUISE *(cont'd)* Hi, darling, we're through here.

CHRIS *appears, carrying his briefcase.*

CHRIS Hi.

LOUISE This is Sally's friend Gertrude.

CHRIS Oh, hello, Gertrude. I've heard all about you.

GERTRUDE You're not Sally's daddy.

CHRIS No, I'm Chris, I'm a good friend of Sally's mummy.

SALLY They snog.

LOUISE Sally!

GERTRUDE My mummy told me that your daddy's in prison.

CHRIS Well, it's not prison, it's a place where people who aren't feeling very well go to have a bit of a rest.

GERTRUDE A mental health facility?

CHRIS Erm . . . yes, basically. Sorry, have I just walked into *The Midwich Cuckoos*?

GERTRUDE Pardon?

LOUISE Go and play upstairs, girls, I'll call you when it's ready.

GERTRUDE *and* SALLY *leave.*

CHRIS Bloody hell, you weren't kidding, were you?

LOUISE How was your lunch?

CHRIS Fine, they've made Mike superintendent now, so it's good to have friends in high places.

LOUISE Yeah, he can help you with that restraining order for Yoko Ono.

CHRIS Don't, poor girl.

LOUISE *dishes out the food.*

CHRIS *(cont'd)* Mike was asking about David. He thinks he'll probably be released in a couple of months if he sticks to his medication.

LOUISE I'm not going to tell Ted, he's barely off his crutches.

CHRIS I'm sure the lawyers will deal with all that. So David has no memory of it? Of what he did to Ted?

LOUISE Apparently not.

CHRIS Do you believe him?

LOUISE Oh yeah, he's had blackouts before.

CHRIS Since Joe died?

LOUISE Yes, all the time. That's why he used to go running in the mornings; he said it helped to clear his head. Why are you bringing all this up now?

CHRIS Mike gave me this . . . it's from last summer.

CHRIS *produces a DVD in a clear plastic case.*

CHRIS *(cont'd)* You might want to have a look.

SALLY *shouts from upstairs.*

SALLY *(V.O.)* Mummy, will you tell Gertrude? She says I'm racist because none of my dolls are lesbians.

CHRIS I'll go. I'm thinking of a brick wall . . .

CHRIS *leaves.* LOUISE *waits a moment, staring at the DVD. Eventually she puts it into her laptop and presses play.*

EXT. LEAFY STREET. DAY.

CCTV footage shows DAVID *emerge from his house in his running gear. He carries a black shoe in his hand. He places the shoe carefully at the foot of a tree outside his house.*

DAVID *runs off up the street.*

INT. KITCHEN-DINER. DAY.

LOUISE *stares at the footage. She starts to cry. She goes through to the living room . . .*

INT. LIVING ROOM. DAY.

LOUISE *picks up the framed photograph that* DAVID *was dusting earlier on.*

We see a smiling DAVID *in happier times, the proud father of two young twin babies.* LOUISE *looks down at his shoes.*

Black slip-ons. Size 9 . . .

THE END

Episode 6

PRIVATE VIEW

CAST LIST

NEIL – Peter Kay

CARRIE – Morgana Robinson

BEA – Montserrat Lombard

MAURICE – Reece Shearsmith

JEAN – Fiona Shaw

KENNETH – Steve Pemberton

PATRICIA – Felicity Kendal

ELLIOT QUINN – Johnny Flynn

REPORTER – Muriel Gray

INT. BASEMENT GALLERY, CHAIR ROOM. NIGHT.

The action takes place in a basement art gallery. 'nine' is a contemporary space in an old building, with vaulted ceilings and exposed brickwork.

The chair room is dark and creepy, with the sound of crows cawing and a low repeating drone being piped in.

Spot-lit in the centre of the room is a nasty-looking wooden torture chair, but with a large fluffy cushion on it. Two sharp knives stick out of the cushion.

NEIL *enters, stuffing his face from a plate piled high with canapés.*

NEIL Hello? Is anyone in here?

NEIL *is large and wears a blue nurse's tunic with his anorak over the top and a lanyard round his neck.*

NEIL *inspects the chair as he eats. He reads the sign by the side of the chair.*

NEIL *(cont'd)* 'Make yourself comfortable'. I'm guessing that's supposed to be funny.

NEIL *hears the door behind him close. He turns to see a* DARK FIGURE *silhouetted against the light.*

NEIL *(cont'd)* Oh, hello, I'm just having a quick nosy round now because I've got to work tonight. I'm Neil . . .

NEIL *wipes his sticky fingers and offers up his lanyard.*

NEIL *(cont'd)* I've been booked as a chaperone. I don't know good art from a good fart, but this seems a bit spooky-juju to me.

The DARK FIGURE *approaches slowly.*

NEIL *(cont'd)* I'm assisting one of the guests when they arrive. I don't suppose it's you, is it? They're supposed to be visually impaired, though that might be a good thing. Have you seen the state of this . . .?

The FIGURE *moves closer and closer as* NEIL *speaks. Suddenly a pair of gloved hands reach out and push* NEIL *backwards and he falls into the chair. He cries out but quickly succumbs.*

From behind the chair we see NEIL*'s arms flop down by his sides. The silhouetted* FIGURE *departs as we drift down to see blood begin to drip from the seat of the chair.*

INT. LIFT AREA. NIGHT.

We watch as the illuminated numbers by a lift descend until they reach 'B' for Basement.

The doors ping open to reveal CARRIE. *She dresses quite glam, fake tan, hair extensions, etc.*

CARRIE *comes out of the lift, checks her invite and walks towards the main gallery. She passes a neon sign on the brick wall spelling out the word 'nine'.*

TITLE: *'Private View'.*

INT. MAIN ROOM. NIGHT.

In the main room there is a tall plinth bearing a plain white plaster cast of a human head. There are other plinths around it with dramatic uplights, a bit like Stonehenge.

On one wall is a large fractured mirror, on another is an installation featuring a collage of shop dummy pieces. On the opposite wall is the title of the exhibition: 'FRAGMENTS by Elliot Quinn'.

There is a table covered in a white cloth and glasses of champagne. The waitress, BEA, *stands by it with a tray of drinks. She has dyed black hair and looks like a goth who has been made to look presentable. She has a nose ring, tattoos on her chest and a sarcastic attitude. She also has scar tissue on her neck.*

CARRIE *walks over to* BEA.

CARRIE Excuse me, is this the private view for 'Fragments' by Elliot Quinn?

BEA I'm not sure, if only there was a way of finding out.

CARRIE *spots the large words printed on the wall behind* BEA.

CARRIE Oh my God, it says it right there, doesn't it! What am I like?

BEA Would you like a glass of champagne, madam?

CARRIE I'll just have the one 'cos I've got another opening to go to after this.

CARRIE *takes a glass from* BEA*'s tray, then looks around.*

CARRIE *(cont'd)* I'm never usually the first to arrive!

BEA You're not. Someone else has already gone through.

CARRIE Is it another celeb? 'Cos I might know them.

BEA *Another* celeb? The implication being . . .?

BEA *looks at* CARRIE *questioningly.* CARRIE *smiles, thinking she's been recognised.*

CARRIE Yes, it's me. Carrie from *BB8*. Will there be any photographers coming, do you know?

BEA No idea.

CARRIE I don't mind – although I once got papped at the *Narnia* premiere and I had a massive sweat patch under my arm. I thought, OMG, that's going straight in *Heat* magazine; Circle of Shame. *(Disappointed)* They didn't use it though.

CARRIE *necks her champagne, puts down the empty glass and takes another full one from the tray.*

BEA That is a shame.

INT. LIFT AREA. NIGHT.

The lift doors ping once again and the doors open to reveal MAURICE, *a lecturer in art history. He wears tweeds and spectacles, and is pompous and somewhat lecherous.*

INT. MAIN ROOM. NIGHT.

MAURICE *approaches* BEA *with his invitation.* CARRIE *is exploring the other exhibits.*

MAURICE Good evening. Maurice Wickham. You don't need to see my 'stiffie', do you?

BEA I certainly don't.

MAURICE *reaches for a glass of champagne from the tray.*

MAURICE I'll help myself to one of these, shall I?

BEA I've only got two hands.

MAURICE Two of everything by the look of it.

BEA Don't bother, Grandad, I'm out of here in three hours.

MAURICE Well, at least you're keen. Are you an art lover?

BEA Nope.

MAURICE And yet you have . . .

MAURICE *looks down at* BEA*'s cleavage.*

BEA Tits?

MAURICE Tattoos. Body art is still art, after all.

BEA Yeah, and it's not for sale, so you can keep your little red dot away from me.

MAURICE Thanks for the drink.

MAURICE *wanders off to look at the art.*

From the lift area we hear laughter from JEAN, *a dinner lady who has never been to a gallery before in her life. She wears her smartest coat and is baffled at the very idea of a 'private view'.*

She is accompanied by KENNETH, *a council official, with a lanyard round his neck. He is looking at his phone.*

JEAN *approaches* BEA. *She refers to* KENNETH.

JEAN Oh my God, that's classic, that is absolutely classic! Eh, you'll never guess what his name is.

BEA Rumpelstiltskin?

JEAN No, tell her.

KENNETH *has joined them.*

KENNETH Kenneth Williams.

JEAN Kenneth Williams! And he's never seen any of the *Carry Ons*!

BEA Really?

KENNETH Yeah, I don't watch comedy, I've got no interest in it, really.

JEAN We're not together by the way, we just bumped into each other in the lift, didn't we?

KENNETH Hmm. There's no signal down here, is there?

BEA No, because we're in a basement.

KENNETH No, it's because the arsehole contractors can't be bothered putting a signal booster into the Cat-4 webbing – pisses me off.

KENNETH *stalks off, fiddling with his phone.*

BEA Well, he's a laugh a minute.

JEAN Now, people aren't going to be jumping out at me, are they? I've never been to anything like this before.

BEA No, it's just a gallery, you wander round and look at things.

JEAN I don't have to buy one, do I?

BEA I don't think so.

JEAN Good. My husband'd kill me. I bought two ice creams at *Lion King*. Eight pound! Think how much bread you can get for that.

BEA Hmmm.

On the other side of the room, CARRIE *has been joined by* MAURICE *at one of the exhibits. It is a collage of pieces of shop dummies arranged on the wall, like* Guernica.

The pair of them stand and contemplate it in silence.

CARRIE Is there a set amount of time you're meant to look at each thing before you move on?

MAURICE Not necessarily. Depends on the piece and what it says to you. For example, what this one is saying to me is, 'Gas Explosion at Debenhams.'

CARRIE Right. And you know all this because you teach art in a collage?

MAURICE No. I teach art in a college, but one of the disciplines *in* art is *collage*. The assemblage of disparate elements, which together create a new whole.

CARRIE That's like me with my chillies – I chuck everything in, I'm known for it. When I did *BB8* I put bananas in and on *BBBOTS* they were all, 'What is she like?'

MAURICE Sorry, you've lost me. What's BB8?

CARRIE *Big Brother 8*? I was one of the contestants. It was the year when Trevor and Viveca had the row about the rice cakes and then had sex in the secret bunker.

MAURICE I didn't see it, I'm afraid.

CARRIE Oh you should, it was a classic year. I got down to the last six.

JEAN *wanders by and looks at the dummies.*

JEAN Has this been done . . . on purpose?

MAURICE I'm afraid so.

JEAN Ridiculous. I'd be mad if I found that.

We hear a woman's voice calling for assistance.

PATRICIA *(V.O.)* Hello? Is someone there?

INT. LIFT AREA. NIGHT.

PATRICIA, *a smartly dressed blind woman, is standing by the lifts with her fold-up white stick. She speaks forcefully and snappily.*

PATRICIA Can I have some assistance, please? I'm partially sighted. Yes?

She holds out her hand expectantly. **BEA** *approaches* **PATRICIA**.

BEA Are you all right, do you need a hand?

PATRICIA They said someone would be here to meet me, is that you?

BEA No, but there is a man here – I'll take you to him.

BEA *takes* **PATRICIA**'*s arm.*

PATRICIA Er, are *you* blind?

BEA What?

PATRICIA Are you blind? I take your arm, you do not take mine.

BEA *(under her breath)* Jesus, £8 an hour, is it worth it?

PATRICIA *takes* **BEA**'*s arm.*

PATRICIA I'd like a drink first if it's not too much trouble.

BEA Of course.

BEA *takes* PATRICIA *towards the drinks table.*

INT. MAIN ROOM. NIGHT.

JEAN *spots* BEA *leading* PATRICIA *into the room and goes over to* KENNETH, *who is looking at one of the empty plinths.*

JEAN Eh, Kenneth, I've seen it all now. Look over there.

KENNETH *looks towards* PATRICIA.

KENNETH Unbelievable.

JEAN I'm not being funny, but what's she going to get out of it?!

KENNETH Perhaps she's going to feel her way round. Galleries do that now, you know, touch tours. And don't get me started on ramps.

JEAN Well, she'll have no trouble smelling 'em, they are crap.

Suddenly we hear the voice of the artist, ELLIOT QUINN, *speaking to the room.*

ELLIOT *(V.O.)* Hello everybody. I'm over here.

Everyone looks around but can't figure out where the voice is coming from.

ELLIOT *(V.O.)* Up here. Can you see me now?

MAURICE *spots that a projection of* ELLIOT*'s face has begun speaking from the head on the main plinth. He walks towards it and others begin to gather round to watch.*

ELLIOT *(V.O.)* Yes, that's right. Welcome. Welcome to my exhibition. I'm Elliot Quinn and three years ago I died. Don't be alarmed, I knew it was going to happen, and it really made me think about my life and my work and how I wanted to be remembered.

We pan across the gathered guests as they look up at the hologram.

ELLIOT *(V.O.)* So I set about creating this installation. 'Fragments' is an immersive work that seeks to answer those big, important questions: 'Who are we?' 'How did we come to be here?' and 'If all the world's a stage, then where does the audience sit?'

JEAN *(whispering)* He's left a gap there for us to laugh, but no one did.

ELLIOT *(V.O.)* All of you have been hand-picked to attend this evening – it's a very exclusive private view. I hope by the end you know why. Enjoy.

The face flickers and disappears from the white head.

JEAN Now that was clever, I liked that.

CARRIE They've got one of them in Madam Tussauds except it's Simon Cowell.

KENNETH So Elliot Quinn is dead?

BEA That's what he said.

KENNETH I wanted to meet him. We've got space for a mural at that pocket park in Goole Street and I was hoping to get a freebie. Sorry, I work for the council – Kenneth Williams.

CARRIE Oh my God! I've heard of you. Are you famous?

JEAN Ooh, matron!

KENNETH Yes, yes. I've heard it all before. 'Stop messing about!' 'Frying tonight!' No, I'm not that Kenneth Williams, I'm not famous. I'm Mr Dull Boring Ordinary Health-and-Safety Nobody.

CARRIE Oh. But I bet underneath it all, if people get to know you, you're a really interesting character.

KENNETH No. No, I'm not.

CARRIE *has hit a brick wall.*

CARRIE I'll just get a top-up.

CARRIE *immediately loses interest in* KENNETH *and wanders off. He gets a cigarette out.*

BEA Sorry, sir – you're not allowed to smoke down here.

KENNETH It's battery! Under UK law I'm permitted to use it in any public space that hasn't been fitted with a vape alarm.

JEAN Oh, I had one of them, but it kept going off in Argos.

PATRICIA Excuse me, I seem to have been parked over here – I was promised a drink at some point, I presumed they meant the same evening.

BEA Yes, I won't be a sec.

BEA *heads off.* JEAN *puts her drink into* PATRICIA*'s hand.*

JEAN Here, you can have mine, I'm not enjoying it. Creases me up, champagne. It really burns.

PATRICIA Thank you.

MAURICE Why have we all been 'hand-picked', do you think? None of us know each other, it would appear we have very little in common . . .

KENNETH I hadn't heard of this Elliot Quinn until I got the invite. I don't know anything about art.

JEAN My next-door neighbour does have a Citroën Picasso . . .

PATRICIA The name rings a bell. Has he ever brought out a book?

JEAN My neighbour?

PATRICIA Elliot Quinn. I'm in publishing, perhaps that's the connection.

MAURICE Judging by the first few pieces, maybe it's some sort of endurance test.

PATRICIA Are you an artist yourself?

MAURICE I dabble from time to time. I teach art history.

PATRICIA Ah, those who can, do; those who can't, teach.

MAURICE Absolutely. And those who can't teach, teach PE. See you at the other end.

MAURICE *leaves.* JEAN *turns to* PATRICIA, *who looks a bit stranded.*

JEAN Right, shall me and you chum up? I had a great-aunt who was blind, so I know what I'm doing.

PATRICIA I'm not blind – I'm visually impaired.

JEAN *whispers to* KENNETH.

JEAN Judging by your make-up, it's the same thing.

PATRICIA I beg your pardon?

JEAN No, it looks good. I'm a big fan of clowns. Come on.

JEAN *bustles* PATRICIA *off round the gallery.* BEA *returns with the drinks tray, looking for* PATRICIA.

BEA Oh – she's gone.

KENNETH I'm going to have a look round. See if I can spot any fire hazards.

BEA Sounds like fun.

KENNETH There's nothing funny about being trapped in a fire, miss.

BEA I know there isn't.

KENNETH *notices the scar tissue on* BEA*'s neck.*

KENNETH Right, well, I'll just . . .

BEA Carry on?

KENNETH Yeah.

KENNETH *heads out of the room.*

INT. CORRIDOR. NIGHT.

CARRIE *wanders down the corridor, sipping her champagne. She hears a low drone and the cawing of crows. She follows the sound into the chair room.*

INT. CHAIR ROOM. NIGHT.

CARRIE *enters the room.* NEIL *is still slumped in the chair, head down on his chest. A large pool of blood circles the chair, and the ceiling lights reflect in it.* NEIL *looks like he is part of the installation. The sound of crows and the low drone add to the creepy atmosphere.*

CARRIE *approaches and inspects the piece. She is a little disturbed by it. She moves closer to inspect the body.*

MAURICE *(V.O.)* Creepy.

CARRIE *jumps. She turns to see* MAURICE *in the doorway.*

CARRIE Oh my God, you made me jump!

MAURICE *walks into the room.*

MAURICE A little bit derivative of Ron Mueck, but I like the idea of a blood mirror, like Wilson's oil at the Saatchi.

CARRIE It's horrible. What's it called? He's got a thing round his neck . . .

CARRIE *leans in to try and have a look at* NEIL*'s lanyard.*

MAURICE I wouldn't touch the exhibit if I were you . . .

CARRIE *pulls the lanyard, and the body falls with it.* NEIL *falls forward heavily, revealing the two large knives that were attached to the back of the chair. They are covered in blood.* CARRIE *screams.*

MAURICE *(cont'd)* Good God!

MAURICE *comes forward and joins* CARRIE. *She grabs hold of him.*

CARRIE He's been stabbed!

MAURICE All right, calm down. This could be part of the installation.

MAURICE *nudges* NEIL*'s body with his foot.*

MAURICE *(cont'd)* Come on, old chap, get up, you've got to re-set for the next lot coming in.

CARRIE Stop kicking him, he's dead! He's a big fat dead man!

KENNETH *comes running in.*

KENNETH Jesus Christ, what's happened here?

CARRIE He was just sitting there . . . I thought it was a dummy. I can't be here. I cannot be here I'm meant to be at Edwina Currie's perfume launch by nine o'clock.

MAURICE I think they'll want to interview you.

CARRIE I know, for *Grazia*.

MAURICE I meant the police.

CARRIE I didn't do anything!

JEAN *enters with* PATRICIA *on her arm.*

JEAN Oh, this must be a good one, Pat, they're all gathered round it.

PATRICIA It's Patricia. And why do I smell blood?

KENNETH There's been an incident. Has anyone seen any cones? I need to ring-fence this entire area.

PATRICIA Why, what's happened?

JEAN *has stepped forward to look at the body on the floor.*

MAURICE We don't know, but it does seem like foul play. Someone's been stabbed in the back – nothing new in the art world, of course.

PATRICIA Who's been stabbed?

CARRIE *reads from the lanyard.*

CARRIE Neil Francis. He's a male nurse.

JEAN We have a dinner lady at school who's a man. He's a gay, we all love him. He has a different colour shirt everyday.

KENNETH Right, well, there's no signal down here, not even for a triple nine. We'll have to go upstairs.

MAURICE I'll wait here. Make sure nobody touches anything.

KENNETH Good call.

KENNETH *leads the way out, helping* CARRIE. JEAN *offers her arm for* PATRICIA.

JEAN Come on, Pat, I don't want you going anywhere near that blood. Not with those cream stilettos. Are they from Matalan?

PATRICIA *and* JEAN *leave.* MAURICE *looks at the dead body of* NEIL.

MAURICE Physician, heal thyself.

INT. MAIN ROOM. NIGHT.

KENNETH *crosses towards the lift.* CARRIE *goes to get another glass of champagne.*

KENNETH You wait here, I'll call the authorities.

CARRIE All right, but no photographers. Well maybe one or two – if I get picture approval.

INT. LIFT AREA. NIGHT.

KENNETH *crosses to the lift and presses the button. No response. He looks up at the numbers, but they are not illuminated.*

KENNETH You're joking . . . Come on . . . *(Calling through)* That's the trouble with these Andersons: if they get called by multiple users the pull system freezes.

KENNETH *keeps pressing the buttons.*

INT. MAIN ROOM. NIGHT.

CARRIE *looks over her shoulder but is more intent on pouring herself another drink. She's getting pissed now.*

CARRIE Oh right . . . whatever.

PATRICIA *and* JEAN *appear and join her.*

KENNETH *(V.O.)* Could someone give me a hand, please? I'll need to prise the door.

JEAN *(calling through)* I'll do it. *(To* PATRICIA*)* I'm letting go of your arm now, Patricia, but you're all right, you're with . . . what's your name, love?

CARRIE Carrie.

JEAN Did you get that, Pat? Carrie, like the film.

PATRICIA Yes, I'm not deaf.

JEAN *(to* CARRIE*)* She's impartially sighted, but she doesn't have a blue badge. Won't be a sec.

JEAN *leaves.*

PATRICIA Didn't your boob pop out in the jacuzzi?

CARRIE Sorry?

PATRICIA *Big Brother 8.*

CARRIE Yes! Did you . . .?

PATRICIA See it? Yes. It was just after my op. I had 20/20 vision for a year before it failed again.

CARRIE Oh, well, it's lucky my boob managed to fall into that . . . little chink.

PATRICIA Yes, one of the last things I ever saw. What an honour.

INT. LIFT AREA. NIGHT.

KENNETH *and* JEAN *are trying to prise open the doors.*

KENNETH Right, I'm going to try and pull these apart. See if you can get your fingers in the crack.

JEAN Oooh, Kenneth, that was a proper *Carry On* line!

KENNETH This is serious! I'm trying to get us out of here, OK?

JEAN Sorry, I'm in shock, I think. I go a bit daft.

KENNETH *strains to pull the doors a tiny amount.*

KENNETH Here . . . use my phone, see if you can put it in for me . . .

JEAN 'Infamy! Infamy! They've all got it in–' Sorry.

INT. MAIN ROOM. NIGHT.

PATRICIA *is chatting with* CARRIE.

CARRIE So how many books have you actually written?

PATRICIA I've done one a year for the past 15 years.

CARRIE God, so that's like 12 books?

PATRICIA Something like that. The first few were pretty softcore, swooning nurses, 'the hardness in his breeches', that sort of thing. But after all that *50 Shades* nonsense I had to up my game. The scenarios became more and more outrageous, people having sex in extraordinary places . . .

CARRIE Like up the bum?

PATRICIA I was thinking more of locations, but yes, I have lowered myself once or twice.

CARRIE That's the best way to do it apparently. Doesn't hurt as much.

CARRIE *drinks more champagne.*

INT. LIFT AREA. NIGHT.

JEAN *and* KENNETH *are opening the doors.*

KENNETH That's it, I've got it . . . and pull!

They pull the doors apart. JEAN *looks inside and screams. Inside we see the body of* BEA, *the waitress.*

BEA *is dead, her lifeless eyes staring out. She is slumped against the inside of the lift with the telephone cable wrapped around her neck. The phone receiver has been shoved into her mouth.*

CARRIE *rushes in, shortly followed by* PATRICIA.

CARRIE Is that . . .? Oh my God, not another one.

PATRICIA What is it, what's happening?

JEAN It's that lovely young waitress, she's dead in the lift.

KENNETH This is too much of a coincidence.

PATRICIA Who was the last person to see her?

KENNETH I was – but I left her tidying up.

CARRIE *starts to jab the buttons of the lift.*

CARRIE We've got to get out, why isn't it working?!

KENNETH There must be a fire escape, let me think . . .

KENNETH *closes his eyes to concentrate.*

CARRIE We should go and tell Maurice. It's not safe down here.

PATRICIA How did she die?

JEAN I'm not *Murder, She Wrote*, but I'd say she's been strangulated, wouldn't you?

KENNETH All right, I think I know where it is. There should be a fire door that comes out onto the end of Duke Street. Wait here.

JEAN I'll go with you, love. I'd like to see the rest of the rooms anyway; I've not been round it all yet.

KENNETH Right, come on then. *(To* CARRIE, *of* PATRICIA*)* Keep an eye on her.

PATRICIA I will.

KENNETH *and* JEAN *run out.* CARRIE *takes another look at the deceased* BEA *and shudders.*

INT. CORRIDOR. NIGHT.

KENNETH *is striding purposefully through the gallery.* JEAN *trots behind.*

JEAN It's handy you knowing your way around these buildings, isn't it? I can barely find my way round Asda.

KENNETH Well, it's my job.

JEAN I'm a dinner lady at St Michael's. 'Chips or mash?' that's me. Twenty-five years. I love the kids though.

KENNETH I don't want kids. Too many hazards.

JEAN Yes, it is a worry. I barely managed to keep my own in one piece.

KENNETH No, I meant *the kids* are the hazards. Just look at *Charlie and the Chocolate Factory*.

Suddenly MAURICE *appears from one of the anterooms.*

MAURICE There you are. Police on their way?

KENNETH No, we couldn't get out.

JEAN The lift was blocked.

MAURICE For goodness' sake! Well, couldn't the girl ring the manager or something?

KENNETH She's dead.

MAURICE What?

MAURICE *looks concerned.*

INT. MAIN ROOM. NIGHT.

CARRIE *goes to top up her champagne from the bottle.* PATRICIA *sits nearby.*

PATRICIA There is something a little bit Agatha Christie about all this, isn't there? None of us know each other, we've all been invited here by someone we've never met, and now it would seem we're being picked off one by one.

CARRIE Oh don't, it's just *Big Brother* all over again. I hope I don't get booed when I leave.

PATRICIA If you leave.

CARRIE At least this time I made it to the final five.

CARRIE *suddenly freezes. She starts to have a seizure, unable to breathe, silently gasping for air.*

PATRICIA I once tried to write a murder mystery, but it's much harder than it seems. It's so easy to find yourself knee-deep in clichés. The problem with the genre nowadays is it's too much murder and not enough mystery.

CARRIE *falls down to the floor.*

INT. FIRE DOOR. NIGHT.

KENNETH *shakes the door, but it has been chained from the outside.* JEAN *and* MAURICE *watch on.*

MAURICE Someone's chained it from the outside.

KENNETH Illegal. I shall be reporting this.

JEAN How are we going to get out now? We're like fish in a basket.

MAURICE Barrel.

JEAN Oh yeah, I was thinking of scampi. Is anyone else hungry?

KENNETH We've got other things on our plate at the moment.

JEAN I haven't got a plate, that's what I'm saying – I thought there'd be nibbles.

MAURICE Look, we're in an art installation surrounded by wire and metal. There's got to be a pair of pliers or bolt-cutters lying around somewhere.

JEAN Do you know, I was in Homebase only this morning.

MAURICE *(expectantly)* Yes?

JEAN No, I was just doing a paint match. I can't decide between Elephant's Breath and Clown's Pocket.

MAURICE Clown's Pocket?

KENNETH Look, can I suggest we split up? It'll be quicker that way.

MAURICE Fine, let's meet back here in 15 minutes.

KENNETH *runs off down the corridor.* MAURICE *heads into one of the anterooms.*

JEAN *(to* MAURICE*)* Deep Cavern, not Clown's Pocket. They all sound ridiculous anyway . . .

JEAN *wanders off to search the rooms.*

INT. MAIN ROOM. NIGHT.

PATRICIA *is sitting as she was before.*

PATRICIA And then, of course, they all split up, which is the one thing you would never do in that situation. And before you know it, that's another one gone.

CARRIE *lies motionless on the floor.*

PATRICIA *(cont'd)* Are you still there, darling? Not bored you to death, have I? Hello?

PATRICIA *gets up and unfolds her white stick.*

PATRICIA *(cont'd)* Carrie? Are you all right?

PATRICIA *taps forward, but then hits the prone body of* CARRIE.

PATRICIA *(cont'd)* Oh dear God.

PATRICIA *bends to feel* CARRIE. *She stands again and unsteadily makes her way towards the exit.*

PATRICIA *(cont'd)* Help! Someone, please . . .

INT. CORRIDOR. NIGHT.

MAURICE *walks along and stops to listen. Was that someone shouting? He carries on walking.*

INT. CORRIDOR. NIGHT.

PATRICIA *is stumbling her way down a different corridor.*

PATRICIA We need help . . . anybody?

PATRICIA *stops. She listens. She thinks she can hear footsteps behind her.*

PATRICIA *(cont'd)* Is someone there?

The footsteps stop. PATRICIA *listens, then turns to walk forward and the footsteps begin again.*

Now scared for her life, PATRICIA *starts to hurry, feeling the walls as she goes. We hear the footsteps approaching.*

PATRICIA *turns a corner and comes across a door. She opens it and pops in quickly. We see that the door is the men's toilet.*

INT. MEN'S TOILETS. NIGHT.

PATRICIA *feels her way towards the cubicles and enters one of the stalls and locks the door. After a beat the door opens again and she emerges.*

PATRICIA No, I'm sorry, that stinks.

PATRICIA *feels her way to the last cubicle and enters.*

INT. TOILET CUBICLE. NIGHT.

PATRICIA *locks the door. She listens. The toilet door creaks open and we hear footsteps in the room.* PATRICIA *looks scared.*

INT. MEN'S TOILETS. NIGHT.

We see the toilet from the KILLER*'s POV. The* KILLER *moves towards the stalls and lowers to look for feet in the gaps under the doors. There are no feet visible.*

INT. TOILET CUBICLE. NIGHT.

PATRICIA *is now crouching on the toilet seat. She's trying not to make a sound. She hears footsteps.*

PATRICIA *surreptitiously reaches into her pocket and pulls out her phone.*

INT. MEN'S TOILET. NIGHT.

The KILLER *stands up and looks into the mirror. We see the* KILLER*'s reflection. It is* JEAN*! She turns to leave the toilets when she hears from the last cubicle:*

SIRI Let me check that for you. Here's what I found on the web for 'How do I use a stiletto as a weapon?'

JEAN *slowly turns her head towards the final cubicle.*

JEAN Is that you, Pat?

INT. MAIN ROOM. NIGHT.

KENNETH *hurries into the room and looks around. He spots the dead body of* CARRIE *on the floor.*

KENNETH Jesus Christ, not another one. It's worse than a public information film . . .

He spots something in her hand and picks it up. It is a bottle of pills. He reads the label and frowns. Suddenly he hears a scream from JEAN.

KENNETH *pockets the pills, looks around for a weapon, then pulls one of the dummy arms from the collage on the wall and exits.*

INT. CORRIDOR. NIGHT.

MAURICE *runs down the corridor and into the men's toilets. He's carrying some bolt-cutters.*

INT. MEN'S TOILETS. NIGHT.

MAURICE *enters to find* JEAN *cowering by the sinks.*

MAURICE What is it, what's happened?

JEAN *points to the cubicle.*

JEAN In there. It's horrible.

MAURICE Well, just flush it away.

JEAN It's Pat. She's dead.

MAURICE *goes to look in the cubicle. He sees* PATRICIA *slumped on the seat. Her glasses have been removed and so have her eyes. The empty sockets stare out.*

MAURICE Good God. What's happened to her eyes?

JEAN I don't know, I just found her like that.

KENNETH *comes in.*

KENNETH What's going on?

MAURICE You don't want to know.

JEAN It's Pat.

MAURICE Let's get out of here. I found these, look.

MAURICE *shows the bolt-cutters. He passes by* KENNETH, *who regards him suspiciously.*

MAURICE *leaves and* KENNETH *whispers to* JEAN:

KENNETH Whatever happens, stay close to me.

They follow MAURICE *out of the door.*

INT. CORRIDOR. NIGHT.

MAURICE, JEAN *and* KENNETH *have arrived at the fire door.* MAURICE *approaches the door with the bolt-cutters.*

MAURICE Right, this should do it.

KENNETH *holds up the dummy arm.*

KENNETH I was going to say do you want me to give you a hand, but . . .

JEAN And he says he doesn't like comedy!

KENNETH *pulls the bottle of pills from his pocket.*

KENNETH I found these, by the way. They've got your name on.

MAURICE *takes the pills.*

MAURICE Thanks, it's my heart medication.

JEAN Heart medication?

MAURICE Tacrolimus, it's an anti-rejection drug. I've had a heart transplant.

KENNETH When was this?

MAURICE Three years ago now, but I'm doing fine, touch wood.

KENNETH I had a lung transplant three years ago. Saved my life.

JEAN Pat had had her eyes done, she told me. Two new cornettos.

KENNETH That waitress had some kind of skin graft . . .

MAURICE *is still trying to cut the chain holding the doors together.*

MAURICE Let's get out of here first and we can ponder that later. I've nearly got it . . .

BOOM! MAURICE *has been banged on the head by* KENNETH *using the dummy arm.* MAURICE *falls to the ground, out cold.*

KENNETH *drops the arm and reaches for his cigarette.*

JEAN What are you doing? He has a heart condition!

KENNETH Those pills. I found them in Carrie's hand. She's dead as well.

JEAN Oh my goodness, we're dropping like flies.

JEAN *is taking a plastic bag from her coat pocket.* KENNETH *looks down at* MAURICE.

KENNETH For some reason that's the link. We've all had transplants. But why would he want to kill us all? What have we done wrong?

JEAN Well, I don't think you should be smoking, Kenneth, for a start.

JEAN *quickly pulls the plastic bag over* KENNETH*'s head and holds it tight.* KENNETH *struggles for breath and drops to his knees.*

INT. MAIN ROOM. NIGHT.

MAURICE *slowly comes round. He is now tied to a wheelchair in the middle of the main gallery's exhibit.*

MAURICE *has long pieces of red ribbon stretching out from his body to each of the plinths that surround him. The plinths are lit from below as before, but now on each one is a bell jar. In each jar is a different organ, harvested from the bodies of the guests:* NEIL*'s kidneys are in one; a large section of* BEA*'s skin (we recognise her tattoo on it) is pressed between two Perspex plates;* CARRIE*'s liver is in a third;* PATRICIA*'s eyes are sitting in a fourth and* KENNETH*'s freshly dissected lung is in the fifth.*

As MAURICE *takes in this horror, the projection of* ELLIOT QUINN *talking starts up on the plaster head again.*

ELLIOT 'All of you have been hand-picked to attend this evening – it is a very exclusive private view. I hope by the end you know why. Enjoy.'

The projection goes off and JEAN *appears from behind the main plinth with* ELLIOT*'s plaster head on it.*

JEAN That was my son. He died three years ago from a brain tumour. Nothing else wrong with him, apart from that. He decided to donate himself. Every organ. He told me to keep tabs on all the people that he 'helped' and gather them together. You were going to be the art: a living exhibition. A celebration, of him and how his life gave others a wonderful opportunity. But it didn't work out like that, did it?

MAURICE What do you mean?

JEAN You squandered him. He was wasted on all of you.

JEAN *goes over to the jars.*

JEAN *(cont'd)* This fat pig, Neil Francis – new kidneys, but he still gave himself diabetes by eating too much. That waitress burnt her skin off in a fire that she started in some pathetic attempt at attention-seeking. She gets a piece of my son and still she sullies his flesh with self-pitying tattoos.

MAURICE I don't understand.

JEAN This talentless non-entity drank like a fish on a reality television show, despite having my son's liver. Patricia spent every day squinting at her pornographic stories through the corneas of my son's eyes. And Kenneth Williams – still smoking, despite having the gift of Elliot's lung inside him.

MAURICE It was an e-cigarette.

JEAN Still. And then there's you, Maurice. You were lucky enough to get my son's heart.

MAURICE Yes, and I've looked after it. I exercise, I watch what I eat . . .

JEAN But it hasn't stopped you being a heartless critic, has it?

MAURICE That's a bit of a stretch – I'm a lecturer, not a critic.

JEAN It doesn't matter. You're undeserving, same as the others. You've looked after Elliot's heart well enough. But I'd like it back now, please.

JEAN *crosses to a side table, which is laid out with medical paraphernalia, scalpels, etc. She reaches for a syringe.*

MAURICE *struggles with his bonds. He tries to slip his hand from the rope tying him to the wheelchair. He almost succeeds, slowly working his wrist free.*

JEAN *prepares the syringe, seeing the first bit of fluid shoot from the needle. She turns to* MAURICE.

JEAN *(cont'd)* It's time to complete Elliot's masterpiece.

JEAN *approaches a terrified* MAURICE, *who is still struggling, his hand almost free.*

INT. MAIN ROOM. NIGHT.

Close on a heart in a display jar. We slowly pull out to reveal the complete art installation; the heart is now the centrepiece and the other organs are linked by red ribbon as before.

REPORTER *(V.O.)* It's been described by some as 'ghoulish' and 'in poor taste', but the installation behind me last night scooped the £40,000 Turner Prize, and has broken new box-office records here at the 'nine' gallery in East London.

We have now pulled out to reveal a REPORTER *standing in front of the art piece.*

REPORTER *(cont'd)* The artist behind this extraordinary sculpture, who has seemingly come from nowhere to take the art world by storm, joins me now.

We reveal that the REPORTER *is talking to* MAURICE.

REPORTER *(cont'd)* Maurice Wickham, congratulations.

MAURICE Thank you.

REPORTER So, talk us through the exhibition – you obviously put your heart into it?

MAURICE Well . . . not quite.

MAURICE *smiles.*

THE END

PERMISSIONS ACKNOWLEDGEMENTS

Sardines

'A Baby Sardine' reproduced with permission from Spike Milligan Productions LTD.

Cold Comfort

'Shine' Written by Gary Barlow, Stephen Robson, Mark Owen, Jason Orange and Howard Donald licensed courtesty of Domino Publishing Company Limited.

Empty Orchestra

'Don't You Want Me': Words & Music by John Callis, Philip Wright & Philip Oakey licensed courtesy of Domino Songs Limited. © Copyright 1981 BMG Rights Management (UK) Ltd., a BMG Company. All Rights Reserved. International Copyright Secured. Used by permission of Hal Leonard Europe Ltd.

'Saturday Night': Words & Music by Alfredo Pignagnoli & Davide Riva. Copyright © 1992 by BMG Rights Management Italy Srl / Energy Production Srl / SM Publishing (Italy) Srl / Star Srl / Kassner Associated Publishers LTD. Used by permission. All rights reserved.

IT 00D 94.002.01 © & (p) 1994 Energy Production Srl. All Rights Reserved. International Copyright Secured. Reproduced by kind permission of Hal Leonard Europe Srl - Italy for SM Publishing (Italy) Srl admin share (12,50%). BMG Rights Management (UK) Ltd., a BMG Company. All Rights Reserved. International Copyright Secured. Used by permission of Hal Leonard Europe Ltd.

'WHAM RAP! (ENJOY WHAT YOU DO)': Words and Music by ANDREW RIDGELEY and GEORGE MICHAEL. WHAM MUSIC LIMITED (GB 2) (PRS) and WARNER CHAPPELL MLM LIMITED (PRS). All rights administered by WC Music Corp.

'Since You've Been Gone': Words & Music by Russell Ballard. © Copyright 1988 Russell Ballard Ltd. BMG Rights Management (UK) Ltd., a BMG Company. All Rights Reserved. International Copyright Secured. Used by permission of Hal Leonard Europe Ltd.

'I Know Him So Well': Words & Music by Björn Ulvaeus, Benny Andersson & Tim Rice. © Copyright 1984 Three Knights Ltd. Universal Music Publishing Ltd. All Rights Reserved. International Copyright Secured. Used by permission of Hal Leonard Europe Ltd.

'Only You': Words & Music by Vincent Clarke. © Copyright 1997 Musical Moments Ltd SM Publishing (UK) Ltd. All Rights Reserved. International Copyright Secured. Used by permission of Hal Leonard Europe Ltd.

'Titanium': Words & Music by Sia Furler, David Guetta, Giorgio Tuinfort & Nick Van De Wall. Giorgio Tuinfort Hipgnosis Songs Fund Ltd. © Copyright 2011 Piano Songs/Afrojack Publishing/ EMI Music Publishing Ltd./What A Publishing Ltd./Hipgnosis Songs Fund Ltd. EMI Music Publishing Ltd./BMG Rights Management (US) LLC/Kobalt Music Publishing Ltd. All Rights Reserved. International Copyright Secured. Used by permission of Hal Leonard Europe Ltd.

9